LABOUR IN CRISIS

MANCHESTER
UNIVERSITY PRESS

Labour in crisis

THE SECOND LABOUR GOVERNMENT 1929–1931

Neil Riddell

Manchester University Press

MANCHESTER AND NEW YORK

distributed exclusively in the USA by St. Martin's Press

Published by Manchester University Press
Oxford Road, Manchester M13 9NR, UK
and Room 400, 175 Fifth Avenue, New York, NY 10010, USA
http://www.man.ac.uk/mup

Distributed exclusively in the USA by
St. Martin's Press, Inc., 175 Fifth Avenue, New York,
NY 10010, USA

Distributed exclusively in Canada by
UBC Press, University of British Columbia, 6344 Memorial Road,
Vancouver, BC, Canada V6T 1Z2

British Library Cataloguing-in-Publication Data
A catalogue record for this book is available from the British Library

Library of Congress Cataloging-in-Publication Data applied for

ISBN   0 7190 5084 7 *hardback*

First published 1999

06 05 04 03 02 01 00 99   10 9 8 7 6 5 4 3 2 1

Printed in Great Britain
by Bookcraft (Bath) Ltd, Midsomer Norton

To My Parents
Kenneth and Rosemary Riddell

The eyes of millions of Socialists all over the world are fixed upon the British Labour Party, which seems to possess a bigger chance of putting into effect an instalment of Socialism than any other Socialist party in existence. The Labour Party to-day is the one great hope of the democratic Socialism of the world. If it is defeated, or it transforms itself back into a Liberal party, international socialism will have lost its Battle of the Marne.

E. Wertheimer, *Portrait of the Labour Party* (London, 1929), pp. 211–12.

The miracle has happened. The faith has proved great enough and the mountains have been removed by the devoted and untiring services of a multitude of people in town and village, who, despite having to labour hard for a meagre livelihood, have yet laboured no less mightily for a cause. Truly it has been a wonderful quarter of a century, and now a future is before us which we must strive to make conspicuous both by its living faith and its great achievement.

Ramsay MacDonald, Labour Party leaflet on the twenty-fifth anniversary of the PLP, 12 February 1931.

What was tried, and found wanting ... in 1929–31, was not merely two years of a Labour Cabinet, but a decade of Labour politics.

R. H. Tawney, 'The Choice Before the Labour Party', *Political Quarterly* 3 (1932), p. 326.

CONTENTS

Contents

ACKNOWLEDGEMENTS

The journey from a Ph.D. research proposal to a published monograph is inevitably a long and winding one. On a number of occasions over the last eight years, I have had cause to doubt whether I would complete that journey. That I have done so, and survived not only largely intact, but hopefully a little wiser, owes much to the support and assistance from many quarters which I have received along the way. I wish to thank the University of Exeter for a two-year postgraduate bursary, which enabled me to get the project off the ground, and the British Academy for the award of a Major State Studentship, which gave me the opportunity to undertake the extensive travel necessary to do it justice. The staff at the many libraries and record offices which I visited have been most helpful; in particular, I would like to single out Nuffield College Library, Oxford; Westminster Diocesan Archives; the Modern Records Centre at Warwick University; and the South Wales Miners' Library in Swansea.

Crown-copyright material in the Public Record Office is reproduced by permission of the Controller of Her Majesty's Stationery Office.

I would like to thank the following for allowing me to reproduce copyright material of individuals: the Cardinal Archbishop of Westminster (Cardinal Bourne and Cardinal Hinsley); Patricia D. Citrine (Walter Citrine); H. J. D. Cole (G. D. H. Cole); Lady Cripps (Sir Stafford Cripps); British Library of Political and Economic Science (Hugh Dalton, Sidney Webb [Lord Passfield] and Beatrice Webb); Borthwick Institute, University of York (Major David Graham Pole); Ishbel Lochhead (Ramsay MacDonald); Nuffield College Library (Herbert Morrison); Lord Ponsonby (Lord Ponsonby); Robinson Library, University of Newcastle (Sir Charles Trevelyan).

I am grateful to the following organisations for allowing me to reproduce copyright material: the Amalgamated Society of Locomotive Engineers and Firemen; the Fabian Society; the Labour Party; the Trades Union Congress; the Transport and General Workers' Union; Birmingham Borough Labour Party; the Working Class Movement Library (Nelson and Colne Labour Party).

The following periodicals gave permission to use quotations: *Political Quarterly*, *New Statesman* and *The Tablet*. I am grateful also to the following for permission to quote from published works: Cambridge University Press (P. Williamson, *National Crisis and National Government*); David Higham Associates (D. Marquand, *The Progressive Dilemma*); Oxford University Press (R. I. McKibbin, *Evolution of the Labour Party* and N. Dennis and R. H. Halsey, *English Ethical Socialism*).

Finally, I am grateful to the following for allowing me to include in this book extensive extracts from my own published articles: Cambridge University Press ('"The Age of Cole"?') and Oxford University Press ('The Catholic Church and the Labour Party').

Barry Sheerman, MP, was kind enough to find the time to talk to me and to give me draft chapters of his jointly authored book on Harold Laski, and Tony Benn, MP, sent me copies of the Cabinet Minutes for the August 1931 crisis. My home town,

Acknowledgements

Worthing in Sussex, is not a place where one would expect to discover very much about the second Labour government or Labour politics in general. I learnt a great deal about local Labour parties, however, from an interview with Jack Barnes, a retired Worthing Labour activist; and the late, and greatly missed, John Hammond, of Worthing Labour Party, lent me numerous books from his extensive Labour history collection, as well as providing much valued encouragement and enthusiasm. It is a cause of much sadness to me that John did not live to see this book published.

The support of my parents, in both financial and moral terms, has been tremendous throughout, and it is to them that this book is dedicated. The debt which I owe to my Ph.D. supervisor, Dr Andrew Thorpe, is also immeasurable. His enthusiasm, willingness to discuss ideas, and general support, in both good times and bad, have been indispensable. The Department of History and Archaeology at Exeter has given constant encouragement, both when I was a postgraduate student and since I have become an Honorary Research Fellow of the department. In particular, I would like to thank Dr John Critchley, Dr Bruce Coleman and Dr Jonathan Barry. The Department of History at the University of Hull, where I spent a frenetic year as a temporary lecturer, and the History Team in the School of Humanities and Cultural Interpretation at the University of Plymouth, where I am currently employed, have also been most supportive. Mr John Major, Mr John Lepper, Dr David Starkey, Dr Kevin Jefferys, Dr G. H. Bennett and Dr Nick Smart are singled out for particular thanks. The external examiner of my Ph.D. thesis, Professor John Turner, has offered both valuable support and useful advice. Vanessa Graham, Carolyn Hand and Louise Edwards at Manchester University Press have been both helpful and patient beyond the cause of duty. The comments of an anonymous MUP reader were useful in the often difficult transition from Ph.D. dissertation to published monograph.

In addition, I am indebted to the students I have taught at the universities of Exeter, Hull and Plymouth. I have, in various ways, learnt as much from them as I hope that they have from me. My history teachers at Worthing Sixth Form College, Mr Chris Corin and Mr Alex Bristow, must also be thanked. Their exemplary 'A' Level teaching played a central role in my choosing to read history at university as an undergraduate. My late grandparents, Charles and Ethel Nicholls and Henry and Mae Riddell, were important, even if at a subconscious level only, in firing my interest in the inter-war years. Finally, I am grateful to the many friends, old and new, who have offered both their support and a much-needed distraction from the thrills of 1929–31: Mark Gant, Marion Gibson, Ken Gloag, Neil Gregor, Zoe Haroon, Margaret Harrington, Sally Holmes, Sarah Pearce, Jo Pennell, Simon Rippingale, Phil Semper, Kevin Stannard, Dominic Waggett, Stuart Walker, Bruce Williams and Steve Williams.

ABBREVIATIONS

ASLEF	Amalgamated Society of Locomotive Engineers and Firemen
ASW	Amalgamated Society of Woodworkers
BISAKTA	British Iron and Steel and Kindred Trades Association
BJL	Brynmor Jones Library, University of Hull
BLP	Borough Labour Party
BLPES	British Library of Political and Economic Science
BNL	British Newspaper Library, Colindale
CC	Consultative Committee (Labour Party)
CPGB	Communist Party of Great Britain
CSCA	Civil Service Clerical Association
DLP	Divisional Labour Party
EAC	Economic Advisory Council
GC	General Council (Trades Union Congress)
HC Debs.	*House of Commons Debates*
ILA	Independent Labour Association (Wolverhampton)
ILO	International Labour Organisation
ILP	Independent Labour Party
LPA	Labour Party Archive, National Museum of Labour History, Manchester
LSE	London School of Economics
MFGB	Miners' Federation of Great Britain
MRC	Modern Records Centre, University of Warwick
NASOHSPD	National Amalgamated Society of Operative House and Ship Painters and Decorators
NC	Nuffield College Library, Oxford
NEC	National Executive Committee (Labour Party)
NFRB	New Fabian Research Bureau
NJC	National Joint Council
NUGMW	National Union of General and Municipal Workers
NUR	National Union of Railwaymen
PLP	Parliamentary Labour Party
PRO	Public Record Office
RL	Robinson Library, University of Newcastle
SDF	Social Democratic Federation
SPD	Social Democratic Party (German)
SSIP	Society for Socialist Inquiry and Propaganda
SWCA	South Wales Coalfield Archive, University College, Swansea
SWML	South Wales Miners' Library, Swansea
TCLP	Trades Council and Labour Party
TGWU	Transport and General Workers' Union
TUC	Trades Union Congress
WEA	Workers' Educational Association

Introduction

The period 1929–31 was a pivotal one for inter-war British politics. The party system was transformed, with the uncertain three-party politics of the 1920s replaced by a decade of National Government dominance. Economic policy underwent a process of lasting change; the attempts of the 1920s to return to pre-1914 'normalcy' were now largely forsaken, with the gold standard abandoned as the basis of Britain's currency and growing support for protection ensuring that the long era of free trade would come to an end. There were significant developments also in the British Empire, with the creation of the British Commonwealth of self-governing Dominions and the beginnings of a move for limited self-government for India. For the British Labour movement these years were equally momentous, with the great expectations of the 1920s giving way to a decade of frustrating opposition.

The rise of the Labour Party after 1918 had been one of truly phenomenal proportions. After returning only 57 MPs in 1918, four years later the party won 142 seats to became the official opposition. In December 1923 this figure increased to 191, and Ramsay MacDonald, having returned to the party leadership in 1922, in 1924 became Prime Minister in Labour's first government. Whilst this minority administration lasted less than nine months and collapsed in the unfortunate circumstances of the 'Campbell Case', Labour had demonstrated that it could govern the country 'responsibly'. Despite losing forty seats at the 1924 election, the party increased its vote to 5.5 million. The General Strike of 1926 proved highly embarrassing for the parliamentary leadership, but the end of industrial militancy in its wake enabled MacDonald to consolidate his hold on the party. In the May 1929 election, Labour made a spectacular gain of 138 seats on its 1924 figure and, with 287 MPs, was once again in a position to form a minority government. The leadership's strategy

1

of 'gradualness' appeared to have been successful and, convinced of the inevitability of Labour's progress, the Labour movement was generally optimistic that the administration, despite its dependence once again on Liberal support, would be able to lay the foundations for a socialist society.

MacDonald chose a Cabinet broadly similar to that of 1924, and one that was designed to demonstrate the party's moderation (see Appendix 1). The financially orthodox Philip Snowden returned to the Exchequer and the moderate J. R. Clynes, former Chairman of the parliamentary party, was made Home Secretary. After much internal wrangling, Arthur Henderson, the Party Secretary, won his claim to the Foreign Office, and the final member of Labour's 'Big Five', J. H. Thomas, was forced to settle for the position of Lord Privy Seal with special responsibility for unemployment. Lord Sankey was brought in as Lord Chancellor, Arthur Greenwood (an under-secretary in 1924) became Minister of Health, A. V. Alexander became First Lord of the Admiralty, and William Graham was chosen to be President of the Board of Trade. Margaret Bondfield became Britain's first female Cabinet minister in the difficult position of Minister of Labour. George Lansbury was the token 'left-wing' figure in the minor position of First Commissioner of Works.

The government began well enough. The scope of the Widows and Old Age Pensions Act was extended and an Unemployment Insurance Act liberalised the procedure for the obtainment of benefit. Diplomatic relations with the USSR were restored in November 1929 and MacDonald's visit to the USA in October resulted in a Five Power Naval Conference in London the following January. Snowden secured much praise for his stubborn stand over Britain's share of reparations at the Hague conferences in August 1929 and January 1930. Henderson became a prominent figure at the League of Nations, particularly in connection with disarmament. Both Snowden and MacDonald were granted the Freedom of the City of London in December 1929, which represented a great mark of respectability. Such was the level of confidence that at the October 1929 Labour Conference, Herbert Morrison (Minister of Transport) was able to claim that Labour was 'the miracle of politics'.[1]

Before long, however, the government was running into trouble over its proposed domestic measures, in particular its plans for coal-mining, education and the repeal of the handicapping 1927 Trades Disputes Act. It also began to face growing problems abroad, particularly in India, where a campaign of civil disobedience was launched in March 1930, and in Palestine, where relations between Jewish settlers and native Arabs deteriorated throughout 1930. Far more damaging, however, was the alarming growth in unemployment, which by December 1930 had reached 2.5 million (see Appendix 3). This was due largely to the contraction of world trade following the Wall Street Crash of October 1929, but Labour had pledged itself at the election to solve Britain's structural unemployment (which stood at 1.1 million when it took office) and increasingly the fate of the government became intertwined with the performance of the British economy. In the face of this 'economic blizzard', as MacDonald described it, and possessing a strategy which believed that socialist reforms could be introduced piecemeal off the back of an expanding capitalism, the government had little to offer. By early 1930, criticism of Thomas began to increase. Limited public works, rationalisation of industry and increased ties with the Empire were clearly not able to deal with a problem of such magnitude. MacDonald was reluctant to remove Thomas, however, and even when he finally did so, in mid-1930, he failed to create any effective machinery for dealing with unemployment. The Economic Advisory Council, composed of 'economic experts' and created in February 1930, had no executive powers and its more radical proposals were blocked by Snowden, who was committed dogmatically to balanced budgets, free trade and to the gold standard.

This government inertia provoked a revolt within the party, led by Sir Oswald Mosley, the upper-class Chancellor of the Duchy of Lancaster. In early 1930 he produced his own 'Memorandum', which put forward an ambitious policy for combating unemployment on quasi-Keynesian lines, but he resigned in May after the proposals' inevitable rejection by the Cabinet, and went on to form the New Party in March 1931 in the misguided belief that a more radical party would attract a mass following. Meanwhile, unemployment increased to over 2.7 million by July 1931, which represented a tremendous burden on the Exchequer. Increasing calls were to be heard from the Treasury, the City and the opposition parties for cuts in social services to ensure that the budget was balanced for the coming year. The Holman Gregory Commission, set up to investigate the Unemployment Insurance Scheme, added weight to these arguments, producing an interim report in June 1931 which proposed higher contributions and reduced benefits. In the face of the united opposition of the trade union movement, the government was forced to declare that it would not adopt these recommendations. None the less, in the face of much Labour opposition, it did introduce an 'Anomalies Act' in June in order to correct 'abuses' in the system.

In February 1931 the government accepted a Liberal amendment setting up a committee to look into possible reductions in national expenditure, under the chairmanship of Sir George May. Snowden believed this would strengthen the case for the cuts. The publication, however, of the sensational May Report in July, calling for spending cuts of £96 million, created a run on sterling at a time of financial crisis in Europe. The Cabinet was forced to create an emergency economy committee of five to attempt to balance the budget, secure foreign loans for the short term and restore financial confidence. Having agreed tentatively upon a £56 million package of economies, however, the Cabinet split finally on 23 August over the issue of a cut in unemployment benefit. The bulk of the Cabinet now expected that a Conservative government would assume office but were astounded to discover on 24 August that MacDonald had agreed to the King's request that he should head a 'National Government' and was to take Snowden, Thomas and Sankey with him.[5]

MacDonald's initial intention was that the government should be of a strictly temporary nature. Under pressure from the Trades Union Congress (TUC), however, a Henderson-led Labour Party resolved to oppose the government and all of the proposed cuts and, in due course, to expel its erstwhile leaders. After the passing of the economy legislation, MacDonald now decided to fight an election as the head of the National Government. In this election of October 1931, a still bewildered Labour Party was to suffer the most catastrophic electoral defeat in its history when it was reduced to a rump of only forty-six seats.

The politics of the 1929–31 period have received extensive attention from historians. The bulk of the historiography has, for obvious reasons, focused on the 1931 political crisis. In the three decades after 1931, the views of the Labour Party itself were able to dominate. Labour and the working classes had been double victims in 1931, it was alleged: first at the hands of the capitalist establishment, in particular the banking community, who were held to have plotted the government's fall through 'the bankers' ramp'; and secondly as a result of the treachery of the party leaders, MacDonald, Snowden and Thomas, who had 'betrayed' the party in August 1931.[2] For Labour historians of the immediate post-1945 period, 1931 and the second Labour government were to be passed over as unfortunate, but temporary, setbacks on the road to 1945, when the party was finally to fulfil its destiny to become a party of majority government.[3] With the 1930s viewed as 'the Devil's decade' and the domestic and foreign policy record of the National Governments widely condemned, even non-Labourites were unprepared to defend MacDonald's actions in 1931.

Only in 1958, through the work of Reginald Bassett, did a countervailing view emerge. Bassett sought to debunk the conspiracy theories surrounding 1931 and to rehabilitate the reputation of MacDonald.[4] This process of reassessment was continued in subsequent decades, with the publication of biographies of leading inter-war politicians, most significantly David Marquand's study of MacDonald, which made full use of government archives and MacDonald's private papers to provide a more rounded account of MacDonald's motivations during the Labour government and the crisis.[5]

Robert Skidelsky's *Politicians and the Slump*, published in 1967, is the first and only single-volume study of the second Labour government. For Skidelsky, the government's collapse was to be understood not in the context of the 1931 crisis but in relation to its longer-term failure to deal with the economic problems facing it from 1929. The key struggle during 1929–31, he argued, was not between 'left' and 'right', or between 'socialism and capitalism', but between what he termed 'the economic radicals' and 'the economic conservatives'. The crux of Skidelsky's argument was that Labour's 'Utopian Socialism' had prevented it from adopting the radical solution on offer to deal with unemployment – the Keynesian programme of 'interventionist' capitalism, in the form of deficit financing and extensive public works.[6]

Although a powerful thesis, *Politicians and the Slump* was very much a product of its time and place. By the 1960s, Keynesian ideas had become the new orthodoxy and it seemed logical to suggest that they would have provided the solution to the economic problems of the 1920s and the 1930s, if only politicians had been sufficiently enlightened to adopt them. Few historians in the 1990s, however, would accept Skidelsky's central premises. First, it is not at all clear that Keynes and his sympathisers possessed a coherent economic package which Labour politicians could have adopted wholesale. Secondly, the weight of orthodox opinion in the civil service, amongst the financial institutions, business interests, and within the three main political parties should not be underestimated. Finally, it now seems unlikely that the proposals of 'the economic radicals' would have succeeded. R. I. McKibbin, in the most systematic dismantling of Skidelsky's thesis, argues that Keynesian-type approaches met with mixed results in other countries later in the 1930s, and that, since Britain's economic problems were structural, heavy reflation would have had few positive results and might have been detrimental.[7]

Two recent works have provided more balanced, and more nuanced, accounts of the 1931 crisis and of the political events of 1929–31 in general. Philip Williamson has examined the transformation of British politics and policy between 1926 and 1932 in reaction to the three component's of Britain's 'deep national crisis' as he defines it: economic recession, imperial difficulties and the problems of the party political system.[8] Andrew Thorpe, meanwhile, has produced a detailed study of the 1931 general election.[9] The central focus, however, of both Williamson and Thorpe is the 1931 political crisis, and the transition to the National Government which followed. As Skidelsky commented as long ago as 1967, then, the second Labour government continues to be treated by historians largely as a prelude to the events of August 1931.[10] As such, there remains ample scope for a new analysis of the second Labour government in its own right.

Eschewing the largely 'high politics' approach of much of the existing historiography, this study seeks to understand the second Labour government not primarily in relation to the 1931 political crisis, or to the economic debates of the period, but in the context of 'the wider Labour movement'.[11] This is taken here to mean the trade unions, the local Labour parties, the

Parliamentary Labour Party (PLP) and the party's intellectuals.[12] As such, the book is both a history of the second Labour government and a history of the Labour movement in the years 1929–31. Its central belief is that, by studying the government and the movement together, it will be possible to deepen understanding of them both. It will address a number of fundamental, and often overlapping, issues. First, the relationship between the movement and the government. What did each component expect from the government and what were their reactions to the disappointments which followed? Were any in a position to influence the Cabinet and, if so, what did they achieve? How substantial was the diversity of aspiration and the degree of tension within the movement itself and between movement and government? Finally, did the movement significantly determine the course of the second Labour government and, most importantly, the nature of the government's demise? Was the crisis of 1931, rather than being solely an incident of 'high politics', shaped by the expectations of, and the constraints imposed by, the wider Labour movement?

Secondly, this survey is used to raise the key question of who exercised power in the movement. Political historians have largely accepted the arguments of R. T. McKenzie (who drew on the work of Robert Michels) that, as a consequence of its acceptance of the conventions of the parliamentary system, it was inevitable that effective power in the Labour Party would be concentrated in the hands of the parliamentary leadership, particularly when the party was in office.[13] Was this the case, or did the experiences of the second Labour government demonstrate that the wider Labour movement exercised more power in the Labour Party of this period than is generally accepted? Equally significantly, how important was the Labour leadership in holding the movement together and to what extent did personalities play a significant role in the functioning of the party? And, to what degree were power structures modified in the wake of the fall of the government?

Thirdly, the failure of the government will be used to address the central issue of ideology. Was the government's failure linked to ideological weaknesses? What were the alternatives available to the government and who was articulating them? How was Labour policy worked out and could policy documents have been constructed more effectively? Was the party restrained by its 'Labourist' beliefs and how much ideological freedom of manoeuvre did the leadership possess? Finally, was the party able to draw ideological lessons from the government's defeat in 1931, or did the movement hold on to many of its old positions?

The book is divided into six chapters. Chapter 1 looks at the Labour movement of May 1929. It analyses each component in turn, assessing its position within the movement, its expectations for a future Labour government and its reactions to the 1929 general election. Chapters 2 to 5, beginning with the trade unions, followed by the local parties and the PLP, and ending with the socialist intellectuals, look at the movement and the government between June 1929 and July 1931. Finally, Chapter 6 is concerned with the role of the wider movement in the 1931 crisis, the reaction of each component to it and the manner in which their respective roles within the movement were affected in the longer term.

NOTES

1 Labour Party, *Annual Report 1929* (London, 1929), p. 150.

2 S. Webb (Lord Passfield), 'What Happened in 1931: A Record', *Political Quarterly* 3 (1932), 1–17 was to become the classic Labour conspiracy theory. See also Labour Party Archive, Manchester, Pamphlets and Leaflets, *Two Years of Labour Rule*, October 1931; H. Morrison, *An Autobiography: By Lord Morrison of Lambeth* (London, 1960), pp. 126–7; P. Snowden, *An Autobiography, Vol. 2: 1919–1934* (London, 1934), pp. 929–58; L. M. Weir, *The Tragedy of Ramsay MacDonald* (London, n.d., 1938).

3 See, for example, G. D. H. Cole, *A History of the Labour Party from 1914* (London, 1948) and F. Williams, *Fifty Years' March: The Rise of the Labour Party* (London, 1949). Many subsequent Labour historians accepted much of this reasoning. Even the 'new left', like R. Miliband in his *Parliamentary Socialism: A Study in the Politics of Labour* (London, 1961), whilst arguing that Labour failed because of its exaggerated respect for parliamentary institutions, claimed that primary responsibility lay not with the party as a whole, but with the Labour leadership for being too conservative. Both the 'new' and the 'old left', like M. Foot, *Aneurin Bevan: A Biography, Vol. 1: 1897–1945* (London, 1962), believed Labour would have been more successful if its leadership had been attuned to the 'instinctive' militancy of the rank-and-file.

4 R. Bassett, *Nineteen Thirty One: Political Crisis* (London, 1958).

5 D. Marquand, *Ramsay MacDonald* (London, 1977).

6 R. Skidelsky, *Politicians and the Slump: The Labour Government of 1929–1931* (London, 1967).

7 R. I. McKibbin, 'The Economic Policy of the Second Labour Government, 1929–1931', *Past and Present* 68 (1975), 95–123, reprinted in McKibbin, *The Ideologies of Class: Social Relations in Britain, 1880–1950* (Oxford, 1990).

8 P. Williamson, *National Crisis and National Government: British Politics, the Economy and Empire, 1926–1932* (Cambridge, 1992).

9 A. Thorpe, *The British General Election of 1931* (Oxford, 1991).

10 Skidelsky, *Politicians and the Slump* (London, 2nd edn, 1994), p. xi.

11 R. I. McKibbin's, *The Evolution of the Labour Party, 1910–1924* (Oxford, 1974) looks at Labour organisation 1910–24. B. Pimlott, *Labour and the Left in the 1930s* (Cambridge, 1977) and T. Buchanan, *The Spanish Civil War and the British Labour Movement* (Cambridge, 1992) have important things to say about the movement of the 1930s. In between there is a serious historiographical gap.

12 Some would question the use of the term 'intellectuals', but I would defend it in light of its acceptance by most political scientists and its common usage in the period itself.

13 R. T. McKenzie, *British Political Parties: The Distribution of Power Within the Conservative and Labour Parties* (London, 1955); R. Michels, *Political Parties: A Sociological Study of the Oligarchical Tendencies of Modern Democracy* (London, 1915).

1

The Labour movement in May 1929

The trade unions

It must not be forgotten that the Labour Party owes its very existence to the trade unions, which generously have provided strength, succour and stability.
D. E. McHenry, *The Labour Party in Transition, 1931–1938* (1938)[1]

In theory, the trade unions dominated the Labour Party in every aspect in the 1920s. In 1929 the TUC provided the party with 90 per cent of both its finance and its membership.[2] Through their control of many divisional Labour parties (DLPs) and the use of the block vote, the unions were able to dominate policy formulation. Throughout the 1920s the unions sponsored over one-third of Labour MPs, and union figures played a prominent part on the National Executive Committee (NEC) and within the Labour leadership.

Yet the unions did not possess total control of Labour policy, strategy and leadership. In part, this was because they did not desire it, for a number of reasons. First, they wished to retain independence in the industrial sphere. Too close an involvement with Labour could hamper this flexibility; even in the 1920s prominent trade unionists were still questioning the long-term viability of the Labour alliance.[3] Secondly, many unionists continued to distrust the apparatus of government and the manoeuvrings of party politics. The often hypothetical arguments and flowery speeches of Westminster could appear of dubious worth to trade unionists facing industrial tensions requiring immediate solutions. Thirdly, from 1920 genuine fear of the disruptive tactics of the Communist Party of Great Britain (CPGB), and its affiliates in the industrial wing, encouraged this disassociation from politics. Fourthly, only one-quarter of the workforce was unionised in 1929 and the TUC had therefore to devote a continuing proportion of its energies to preaching the benefits of unionism. Finally, and perhaps most importantly, the majority of union leaders wished to concentrate upon the central objective of trade unionism: the defence and improvement of working conditions. With the emergence of such enormous structures as the Transport and General Workers' Union (TGWU) and the National Union of General and Municipal Workers (NUGMW), the job of the union official became very much a full-time occupation, leaving little time for political participation.

Conversely, non-union members of the Labour Party did not desire union domination and, despite numerical inferiority, were able to enjoy a disproportionate influence on party policy. The PLP and the NEC were able to exercise discretion over the implementation of decisions passed by party conference. Non-union influence was increased by the decline in the proportion of union-sponsored MPs; in 1906, 23 of 30 Labour MPs (77 per cent) had union backing, in 1929, only 115 of 287 (40 per cent). In 1923 the General Secretary of the TUC, previously an MP, was barred from participating in parliamentary work and by 1935 there were only three general secretaries in Westminster, not one of whom came from a major union.[4] With the development of a larger PLP, union-backed MPs became more detached from their unions as they increasingly defined themselves as politicians first and foremost. Finally, and most importantly, the party leadership envisaged a subordinate role for the unions. Both MacDonald and Snowden were keen to play down the union link in their attempt to transform Labour into a national party of government, and Clynes, Thomas and Henderson, despite their union backgrounds, were all in basic agreement with this strategy. By 1929, such a strategy appeared to be reaping dividends. In the 1929 election the party would attract over twice as many votes as there were union members (8,370,417 compared to 3,673,144).

Hence, the relationship that emerged in the 1920s was one of separate spheres rather than full integration. Co-ordination was therefore essential if conflict was to be avoided. This need had been recognised most clearly by Arthur Henderson, the Party Secretary. Impressed by the structure of the German Social Democratic Party (SPD), Henderson after 1918 favoured the creation of joint institutions to ensure that the two spheres worked together as one movement. This led both to the creation of the General Council (GC) of the TUC, to replace the outmoded Parliamentary Committee, and, in 1921, to a number of joint departments, to be supervised by a National Joint Council (NJC) constituted from members of the GC and the NEC. Not everyone in the movement shared Henderson's monolithic ideal, however, and as early as the mid-1920s the joint machinery was beginning to break down. The experience of the first Labour government in 1924 was to convince the TUC that it should retreat from close involvement with Labour.

In 1924 the TUC had hoped for a government sympathetic to union interests. MacDonald and the bulk of the Cabinet, however, wished to demonstrate
that the government was not a union puppet and saw it as their national duty
to remain neutral during industrial stoppages. This difference in outlook
came closest to a serious confrontation when Ernest Bevin, General Secretary
of the TGWU, threatened a major transport strike, leading the government to
make preparations for the use of emergency powers. The majority of trade
unionists were bitterly disappointed by what they perceived as the timidity of
the MacDonald administration.[5] Some felt the answer was to change the leadership and Bevin was a prime mover in the attempt to remove MacDonald in
1925. More significantly, however, the TUC drew the conclusion that there
should be more emphasis on independent activity. Fred Bramley, TUC General
Secretary, felt that:

> Experience of the Labour Government when in office made it quite clear that the
> policy of the TUC General Council could not permanently remain in the present
> association with that of the Labour Party.... The Labour Party can not have it
> both ways. If when in office we are to be detached from the Labour movement,
> we cannot be treated as an integral part of that movement when Labour is out of
> office.[6]

In consequence, at the end of March 1926 the TUC withdrew from the joint
departments for research, press/publishing and international matters, and
only the Labour Library and telephone operator remained under combined
control. As for the NJC, its meetings became increasingly irregular and in
June 1929 it had not met for over eighteen months.[7]

The failure of the General Strike and the rearguard action against the
handicapping 1927 Trade Disputes Act, however, had a positive effect on relations. The GC now appeared to accept the limitations of industrial action and
to see the Labour Party as the best means of securing union political ends.
Superficially the prospects for a more united Labour movement looked bright.
A closer examination, however, reveals that the scope for conflict remained
disturbingly wide. The TUC was no more prepared than previously to be the
subordinate partner in the alliance. Rather, it continued to believe the unions
should pursue independent objectives. Equally, the GC held on to the belief
that unionism remained the best vehicle for working-class betterment in the
long term. Its more progressive members began to develop a new vision of its
future role independently of its Labour connections, to be articulated most
lucidly by the two figures who were to dominate union affairs for the next
decade: Bevin and Walter Citrine, General Secretary of the TUC from 1925.[8]

The partnership which developed between these two men was truly
remarkable, not least because their personal relations were far from harmonious.[9] They developed similar ideas in the 1920s of a future in which the trade

unions would become an essential component of the state and would participate in the formulation of industrial and social policy at the highest levels of government. Bevin's instinctive distrust of the political leadership had not been dispelled by the experience of the first Labour government. Although moderated by the failings of 1926, his outlook on union–party relations remained true to the statement he made in 1924, when he declared, 'we must not lose sight of the fact that governments may come and governments may go but the workers' fight for betterment of conditions must go on all the time'.[10]

Citrine believed that the TUC and the Labour Party were very different organisations and that the commitment of the membership of the former was far superior to that of the latter.[11] Aided by Walter Milne-Bailey at the TUC Research Department, Citrine was able to develop a new strategy for trade unionism. The TUC of the future would be highly centralised and would attempt to avoid conflict wherever possible through the use of conciliation and arbitration. It would also play a prominent role in the state, regardless of which party was in power. This had major implications for future union relations with a Labour government. Whilst he acknowledged that a favourable administration could do much for the working classes, Citrine was wary of the capacity for continuing tensions between the two halves of the movement. In 1929 he emphasised both that a Labour government would offer no miraculous cures and also the need for union independence. Labour had 'its own functions' and was 'a valuable asset' to the unions, but, stressed Citrine, 'The TUC, whether there is a Labour Government in office or not, will pursue its legislative function'.[12]

This new philosophy of trade unionism found practical expression in the shape of the famous Mond–Turner talks of 1928–29. The extent to which these discussions represented a commitment to corporatism has been the subject of much debate.[13] Without doubt, they were an important departure in employer/union relations and in union attitudes to the state and to the Labour Party. Not only do they imply a more moderate union movement but they also demonstrate a TUC keen to discuss issues of a wider scope than wages and conditions.[14] It is misleading, however, to suggest that they portray a TUC which was not keen to enter a partnership with a future Labour government on industrial issues.[15] In fact, the TUC envisaged a relationship in which a Labour government would involve them in government affairs to an unprecedented degree. The partnership which Bevin and Citrine envisaged was certainly one of equality and, arguably, a good deal more than that. They would judge a future Labour government, first and foremost, upon how well it served the interests of the unions. Arguably, both men desired already a Labour Party under the general control of the TUC. To that extent, it is possible to argue that the 'General Council's Party' of 1932 had long been envisaged by Citrine and Bevin.[16]

The perspective of the Labour leadership could scarcely have been more different. Both MacDonald and Snowden had a poor record of relations with the trade unions. Never themselves union members, they regarded the union link as an unfortunate burden to carry. MacDonald's often vague evolutionary socialism had little room within it for unionism; never sympathetic with workers' control or direct industrial action, he distrusted instinctively the union ethos. Snowden had never ascribed to the philosophy of unionism at all; essentially he retained the outlook of an early Independent Labour Party (ILP) thinker, seeing strikes as economically damaging and detrimental to industrial harmony. Always keen to emphasise that only one-quarter of the workforce was unionised in the late 1920s, and that the 'working class' was far from synonymous with the unions, Snowden perceived Labour's responsibilities in wider terms than its union connections. Despite the tensions it had created in 1924, both Snowden and MacDonald, together with the other members of Labour's 'Big Five', held to the view that close links between a Labour government and the unions would be detrimental to the 'responsible' image which they wished to promote. Clearly, then, the likelihood of a major clash of interests between a future Labour government and the trade union movement remained pronounced.

The 1929 election

Despite the continuing commitment to the primacy of trade unionism outlined above, the degree of optimism with which the unions approached the election in 1929 should not be underestimated. Faced with long-term unemployment, the damaging effects of the Trade Disputes Act and the structural problems of British industry, the unions recognised that scope for industrial action was limited. The prospect of a Labour government seemed a beacon of hope in an otherwise bleak environment. Even the ex-syndicalist, A. J. Cook, Secretary of the Miners' Federation of Great Britain (MFGB), looked to a Labour victory as the only hope for short-term improvement in the lives of both the miners and the working classes in general.[17] Cook's enthusiasm was enhanced by MacDonald's pre-election promises. MacDonald could not guarantee nationalisation of mining immediately but did commit a Labour government to a repeal of the Eight Hours Act of 1926, a raising of the school leaving age to fifteen, retirement at the age of sixty, the transference of unemployed miners to those areas where they could be used, and a suspension of outside recruitment to the coal industry.[18] Cook was delighted with these proposals and even consented to speak in support of MacDonald at Seaham Harbour.[19]

Trade unionists from all industries looked forward to the legislation a Labour government could introduce. The 1929 Labour manifesto promised to rescue the depressed trades through an extension of the market for British goods, and to deal 'immediately and practically' with the one million unemployed. Labour also promised a new factories Bill, the ratification of the Washington Hours Convention (an international Labour agreement for a maximum 48-hour week), amendment of the Workmen's Compensation Acts to extend cover for those involved in industrial accidents, and the repeal of the extremely unpopular Trade Disputes Act. In addition, Labour would appoint committees of inquiry to look into the textile and iron and steel trades with a view to their reorganisation.

Trade union journals portray a union movement working hard to rally members to Labour's cause. The editorial of *The Record* in September 1928 enthused that Labour's programme 'offer[ed] the greatest contribution ever made to end the economic evils under which the mass of the people suffer'.[20] *The Miner* described the forthcoming election as 'the most momentous ... of our time'.[21] During the election campaign, many prominent unionists spoke in support of Labour candidates.[22] The TUC's *Call to the Workers* fully endorsed the party programme, and emphasised that only Labour offered the possibility for the political implementation of union demands.

Reactions to the May 1929 result were enthusiastic, despite awareness of the limitations imposed by the government's minority status. Some 115 of the 136 trade union candidates had been elected and all 43 MFGB candidates went to Westminster. There had been much uncertainty over the likely outcome of the election and this added to the feeling that a great victory had been achieved.[23] The unions were now eager to see this success extended to the parliamentary arena. The GC compiled a list of legislative demands divided into fifteen major areas of policy.[24] For many union leaders this was a time to reflect on the remarkable progress Labour had made since 1900, to believe that 'the inevitability of gradualness' was a reality and that Labour's future success was guaranteed.[25] It was now time for the working classes to 'share a place in the sun'.[26] MacDonald's popularity amongst the trade unions had never been higher. Even *The Miner*, not noted for its praise of the Labour leadership, spoke of the Prime Minister's 'great all-round intellectual gifts' and of 'his personal integrity'.[27]

There were, of course, some who did not share this optimism. Trade unionists on the left felt that Labour would be powerless to implement real change through a parliamentary system devised to preserve capitalist control.[28] A small minority felt that after the failures of the first Labour government, MacDonald should never again accept office without a majority.[29] A number of union leaders feared that the minority position would prove a serious handicap. John Bromley, the General Secretary of the Amalgamated Society of Locomotive Engineers and Firemen (ASLEF), and MP for Barrow, warned that: 'Only the foolish will expect all at once the Eldorado of our dreams will be here'.[30] Yet the overriding mood was one of high expectation. The election result was felt to represent a victory not only for the Labour Party but also for the union movement which had helped to secure it. The vast majority of trade unionists eagerly awaited events at Westminster and expected significant improvements in their own trades and for the working classes in general.

Local Labour parties

> The local parties are the living and growing units of the steadily advancing strength of Labour in the nation. They are the great training schools of service and of idea ... it is there that elections are won and gains consolidated. It is there, above all, that the Socialist personnel is created on which the working-out of large-scale plans for social transformation depends. Socialist machinery will not work unless there are Socialist minds to drive, direct and co-operate with it.
> M. A. Hamilton, *The Labour Party Today* (1938)[31]

Local party development in the 1920s

Without the development of an extensive local party organisation from 1918, Labour would not have been in a position to have become the official opposition at Westminster in the 1920s, let alone a party of government.[32] Labour's national success depended largely upon its ability to win parliamentary seats, and with the rapid increase in the number of constituencies which it contested in the 1920s, it was essential that the party should have extensive, well-organised and permanent local machinery. The return of a Member of Parliament was seen both by the parties themselves and by national Labour headquarters as the primary function of local organisations. This, however, was far from being their only objective. The election of Labour figures to local councils and poor law committees was also regarded as important; not only did this raise the prestige of the party and improve its chances of electing a national representative, but it also constituted a source of local influence at a time when local government still exercised extensive responsibilities.

Local parties had a further key function in the eyes of the national party: to create the mass membership needed to facilitate a socialist society and in the meantime to develop the financial security essential to the movement's consolidation and expansion. The 1918 constitution had sanctioned individual members officially for the first time,[33] with the intention of creating a broadly based membership amongst not only the working but also the middle classes.[34] It was intended that local parties should become the focus of local activity in place of the trades councils (essentially federations of local trade union branches) that had previously dominated in many constituencies.

Henderson and Webb calculated also that a more homogeneous network would enable head office to achieve increased control of the localities.

These grandiose ambitions, however, were not translated into reality in the 1920s. Rather, what continued to exist was a diverse local structure still dominated by the party's affiliated membership. There was certainly a rapid rise in the number of local organisations; by 1924 there were nearly 3,000 divisional or local Labour parties and only three constituencies existed in which there was no form of local party. This impressive achievement was paralleled by a tremendous increase in the party's women's sections: Woolwich and Barrow-in-Furness both had over 1,000 members in their women's groups and by 1924 there were 1,332 separate organisations with a total membership of 150,000. In 1923 the National Executive set up a sub-committee to investigate the question of youth sections and by 1925 150 such groups had been created to cater for members between the ages of fourteen and twenty-one.[35] Equally, many local parties in the 1920s made significant inroads in the creation of neighbourhood organisation.[36]

Yet there was no dramatic increase in general individual membership. In 1924 the *Labour Organiser* was able to find only two local parties with large individual memberships: Ardwick in Manchester and Woolwich in London. By 1929 the situation had changed little; the 578 divisional parties between them had only 227,897 individual members, a mean of less than 400 per party. In contrast, the unions affiliated over two million members to the national party in the same year, which constituted nearly ten times the number of individual members.[37] This was despite a national drive in 1925 to increase membership and a new scheme which allowed individual members to pay fees in instalments.

There were many factors involved in this failure to create the mass party envisaged in 1918. Most of the male members of the working classes sympathetic to Labour were already affiliated to the party through a trade union. The most spectacular increase in individual membership was achieved in the women's sections principally because most women had no access to union organisation.[38] Labour never succeeded in dominating the social life of the British working classes as, for example, the SPD had done in Germany before 1914. Although many parties did have their own darts leagues, social clubs and so on, the majority continued to go outside for their entertainment: to the cinema, the football match or the public house. In many non-industrial localities, it was difficult for individuals to join their local party for fear of abuse from non-sympathisers and victimisation from employers. Hence, even as late as the 1920s and beyond, it was not unknown for individuals to participate either anonymously or under a false name.[39]

National success was important in attracting new members, and since Labour's rise in the 1920s was far less inexorable than is often suggested, local membership was consequently subject to ups and downs.[40] Membership levels were linked also to economic circumstances, and the major recession of 1920–21, together with consistently high unemployment throughout the 1920s, was detrimental to party growth. The Trade Disputes Act was a further handicap; local parties lost a significant number of affiliated members and experienced a corresponding fall in income. Finally, and most importantly perhaps, the Labour leadership overestimated the extent to which the working classes were interested in spending precious leisure time engaged in political activities. Only the truly dedicated were prepared to work an eight-hour day or more and then spend the bulk of their evenings on routine committee work.

Local party members

Since most party members remained sympathisers, rather than becoming activists, the vast majority of local parties were run by a small group of devoted members. This could have negative repercussions. Sidney Webb described local parties in 1930 as 'little nonentities dominated by fanatics and cranks and extremists', a statement containing much exaggeration but also an element of truth.[41] Often those involved in local politics, in parallel with those who stood for Parliament, were attracted by the opportunity to exercise power, however limited that power might have been. Many local parties were turned into power bases for prominent individuals who could make or break a political career. Nepotism was rife in a number of areas, for example on the Clydeside, where the patronage of John Wheatley and his brother Patrick was of great significance for an individual seeking a political career.[42]

It would be misleading, however, to give the impression that all local party activists were power-crazed empire-builders. In contrast, the motivations of the majority were far more altruistic; they believed passionately in Labour's cause and devoted so much of their time to it in the belief that their contribution would help to shape the socialist millennium. Yet the rapid conversion of many in the immediate post-war period was dependent upon a sense of religious fervour and a belief that their actions would produce immediate results. Perhaps the party's greatest problem in the 1920s was that the 'New Jerusalem' was not as imminent as many had believed, and the result of Labour's inevitable setbacks was all too often local disillusionment. Whilst success at a local level was important to local parties, particularly when they were able to win control of the town or city council, as happened for example in Sheffield in 1926 and Derby in 1928, it was essentially to the national stage that party members looked for the achievement of real change.

The inclusion of women's sections in the 1918 constitution owed much to the anticipated enfranchisement of women in the post-war period. Direct attempts were made thereafter to attract women through the pledging of

17

support for equal partnership and for full emancipation. *Labour and the New Social Order* included passages on female unions and equal pay, and the 1918 constitution had given women the option of joining the party either as members of women's sections and/or through their local parties. It had also guaranteed them four seats on the NEC, a Chief Women's Officer and a Women's Advisory Committee.[43]

To begin with this strategy appeared to have been very successful. By 1921, there were 70,000 women in the party and 650 women's sections by 1922. The reality of continuing male dominance, however, created tensions. The 1921 National Conference of Labour Women passed a motion calling for the Women's Conference to be given some executive power and for the four women on the NEC to be elected by the women's sections alone, rather than by the whole Labour conference. At the 1921 Labour Conference, a number of male delegates supported these proposals. They were opposed, however, by their national leaders, including the few prominent female figures in the party, like Margaret Bondfield, who argued that they would split the party on gender lines. Although the issue was raised once again at both the 1922 and the 1926 Labour Conference, the inferior national status of women in the party was to remain a reality throughout the inter-war period and beyond.[44]

None the less, many women during the 1920s involved themselves in local party activities with tremendous fervour, and were an important component in the vitality of local organisation. The character of the local party and 'the nature of practical working-class politics' tended to influence the role of women in the local organisation.[45] For example, in heavily industrial areas with few women workers, they tended to be restricted to supportive, traditionally female roles. In textile areas, with much higher levels of female employment, the designation of roles tended to be less rigid, and the women's sections were able to enjoy greater input into policy-making.[46] In most divisional local parties, however, women were responsible primarily for fundraising, the organisation of social events, and routine party activities, such as canvassing and attendance at polling stations. Despite frequent opposition from Labour men, many women did stand for the local councils and served as poor law guardians.[47]

Diversity in organisation

In 1929 there remained a tremendous diversity in local party organisation. To a large extent this was a reflection of the regional diversity of the British Isles. Contrary to the perspective of Labour's head office, Britain was not a homogenous mass but rather a mix of different cultures, traditions and dialects. Labour's 1918 constitution hardly reflected these differences. Although Henderson paid lip-service to them through the creation of regional organisers (of whom there were nine by 1929), head office viewed regional differ-

ences essentially as obstacles to be overcome on route to the monolithic structure that it wished to create. The localities, however, were often less ready to
give up the personalised structures of their party organisation than
Henderson had credited.

In industrial areas many local parties remained little more than 'glorified
Trades Councils with little non-trade union membership to speak of', and a
number were dominated by one union, for example Wansbeck in Northumberland, where the miners constituted 70 per cent of the electorate.[48] Most
parties in Scotland remained under the domination of the ILP, despite the fact
that the 1918 constitution had set out to remove this control. In the 1929
election, Scottish DLPs stood only twenty candidates as opposed to the
twenty-nine ILP candidates.[49] Conversely, in areas where the Co-operative
movement was strong, for example in Nottinghamshire, the local parties
would often be jointly run by Labour and the Co-op. In predominantly agricultural areas the nature of local parties was different again. Usually created
only in 1918, and because unionisation was limited, these parties tended to
consist almost entirely of individual members. Chichester in West Sussex was
one such party.[50]

It was also still the case in 1929 that a significant number of parties
functioned almost solely as electoral machines and scarcely operated outside
general and local election periods. This was often the case in constituencies
occupied by former Liberal MPs, who had no wish to create organisations
which would limit their freedom of manoeuvre. This was certainly the case in
Newcastle-under-Lyme, where Josiah Wedgwood undermined attempts to
make the party anything more than his private organisation. He wished to
appeal to his constituents on the basis of his own personality and policies, and
since he was so electorally successful, local members were unlikely to question the wisdom of this approach.[51] In addition, some local parties failed to
follow the 'model rules' laid down in 1918. For example, according to these
rules, Woolwich Labour Party should have split into two separate divisional
organisations to contest the two parliamentary seats in the borough, and
created a borough party to co-ordinate the two. The Woolwich Executive,
however, resisted this course and insisted the party remain one entity. Judging
by the steady growth of the party throughout the 1920s and its solid record in
general elections, it appears that this resistance was justified.[52] Clearly, then,
activists often understood their constituencies better than the officials at head
office and the control of the national party over the localities was greater on
paper than it was in practice.

Trade union control of many local parties remained as total in 1929 as it
had been in 1918. The unions continued to contribute the bulk of affiliation
fees and campaigning expenses and consequently had the greatest input into
organisation and strategy, especially in the winnable seats. The extent of

union dominance, however, acted as a barrier to the attraction of individual members. Many constituencies in single-industry areas had a small proportion of non-union members,[53] and it is arguable that unions had a vested interest in keeping it this way. This would explain union resistance to any attempts to finance local parties through head office. On three separate occasions in 1920–22, a proposal for the pooling of funds, in order that all parties could receive equal finance, was rejected by the national conference. The consequence was that throughout the 1920s local organisation was financed most heavily in unionised areas, which added further to the diversity in the structure of local parties.

Finance and benefactors

Finance was the single most important consideration in the affairs of all local parties. Any extension of organisation was dependent upon the availability of sufficient financial resources. In a real sense, it was money as much as effective campaigning that was needed to secure both votes and members. Mass meetings, propaganda, day-to-day administration, and, above all, election campaigns all required a great deal of money. The financial strain upon local parties was tremendous and increasing. As the national party set about contesting ever more seats in the four general elections between 1922 and 1929, so local parties were forced to stretch themselves to their financial limits and beyond. Set against a background of national economic problems and a serious decline in union membership, together with the handicapping effects of the Trade Disputes Act, it was remarkable that the majority of local organisations managed to remain solvent.

Ideally, all local parties would have liked a full-time agent, a party car, their own premises, speakers of national standing to address their meetings, and their own newspaper. All were a major boost to a local party, since it would be able to organise more effectively, put its message over to its constituents more successfully and translate its higher profile into the all-important votes at the ballot box. Only the most successful, however, had achieved all of these ambitions by 1929, and the majority were pleased if they had managed two or three. They all represented a major undertaking for organisations with paltry incomes and all involved some element of risk. The decision to purchase the party's own premises was one which could not be undertaken lightly, for it entailed the negotiation of a mortgage which might take twenty years to pay back. Most hazardous of all was a venture into a party newspaper. Any successful newspaper required the attraction of sufficient advertisers and this was a difficult proposition for a political party which called for major reform of the industrial system.

Fundraising activities were a permanent feature in the activities of all local parties and an essential component in the balancing of a party's accounts. Bazaars, whist drives and raffles were the most popular methods and were often very effective means of raising money, but some party members also devised more unusual schemes. Competitions to predict how many votes candidates would receive and the selling of shares were not unheard of.[54] It was hardly surprising, therefore, that parliamentary candidates with money, whether through union-sponsorship or personal wealth, were attractive to local parties. Indeed, so strong was this attraction that an assessment of a potential candidate's financial credentials was often of more importance to a local selection committee than his or her political views. Many local activists perhaps felt uneasy about this trend, but, set against a background of economic difficulties, they recognised that the parties had little choice. Head office did little to discourage this tendency, recognising that this was the only manner in which the national party could increase its parliamentary representation with haste. The NEC, no doubt, was able to convince itself that the bringing of non-working-class candidates into the party was essential to the extension of Labour's national appeal; that many of these individuals possessed personal wealth was merely coincidental. In truth, however, it was as much their money as their 'respectability' which encouraged the party to welcome into its ranks so many ex-Liberals and ex-Conservatives in the 1920s. The rapid expansion of the number of seats contested by Labour (363 in 1918 to 561 in 1929) in a period when affiliated union membership halved (4,317,537 in 1920, 2,011,484 in 1930) would have been impossible without them.[55]

The difference a wealthy individual could make is best illustrated by the example of Sir Oswald Mosley and Birmingham Borough Labour Party. After his unsuccessful candidature in the Ladywood division of the city in November 1924, the wealthy aristocrat turned Birmingham into his private political base. Not only did he heavily subsidise the party and its newspaper, the *Birmingham Town Crier*, but he also brought in the capable Allan Young as local organiser.[56] His input was of tremendous importance in the transformation of this previously lacklustre party; by 1928 Labour had become the second largest party on the city council and at the 1929 election the number of Labour MPs increased from one to six (of a total of twelve).[57] So great an influence was Mosley that local newspapers reported that children went through the streets chanting 'Oswald is merciful! Oswald will save us!'[58]

The influence of other individuals on local parties was less dramatic but still significant. For example, Earl De La Warr helped to create a party in East Grinstead and not only subsidised its development but also allowed its Executive to use his estate at Buckhurst Park for fêtes and other fundraising activities.[59] Sir Stafford Cripps used his wealth from his highly successful legal career to contribute large sums to Bristol East DLP throughout the 1930s after his return at a by-election in January 1931. J. F. Horrabin, a successful author and journalist, gave substantial amounts to Peterborough Labour Party and Josiah Wedgwood did likewise in Newcastle-under-Lyme.[60] In return, however, these individuals expected that these parties should conform to their requirements. As will be seen, this could be highly detrimental to local parties in the longer term.

Religion

The continuing influence of religion in the Labour movement after 1918 has been much underestimated.[61] The commonly held notion that the conversion of the working classes to 'socialism' or to Labour after 1918 led them to reject organised religion is too simplistic.[62] Rather, the allegiance to a political party and to the Church tended often to exist in parallel. Although the First World War dealt a major blow to religious belief and attendance declined over the inter-war period as a whole, the 1920s was a period of limited religious growth. In 1930 8.5 million individuals were members of a church, out of a population of 45 million.[63] As such, religious perspectives on social, political and economic issues were something all political parties had to consider seriously. For the Labour leadership, they presented a real obstacle to the universal appeal that it wished to create. Since Labour support was drawn from all religious denominations – Anglicans, Nonconformists, Catholics, Presbyterians and Jews, and also from many atheists and agnostics – the party was forced to tread a very fine line if it was to avoid alienating any of these groups. The often vague socialism of MacDonald was an asset in this respect, but, on a number of occasions, religious divisions would prove more deep-seated than the Labour leadership recognised and could create considerable friction in many local parties. Birth control, divorce, the laws on blasphemy, temperance and education were chief amongst the likely sources of tension in domestic policy. Foreign policy concerns, not least Anglo-Soviet relations, could also create friction.

Of all the denominations, it was Catholicism which was the greatest potential source of religious tension. Clustered principally in north-western England and in Scotland, the majority of the Catholic communities in Britain had grown up through immigration from Ireland in the nineteenth century. In 1918, of 2.5 million Catholics in Britain, the vast majority were from the poor working class. Lancashire alone contained over 900,000 Catholics, and London, Tyneside, Leeds and Birmingham also contained sizeable Catholic communities.[64] In the cities of Liverpool, Manchester and Glasgow, sectarian divisions remained strong throughout the inter-war period and beyond. The majority of the immigrants held on to their religion as a means of identity in a society where they were seldom accepted as equal citizens by their Protestant neighbours and, as such, the hold of the Catholic Church upon its adherents was far greater than that of the Church of England or of the 'Free

Churches'.[65]

It was not surprising that many working-class Catholics were attracted after 1918 to a Labour Party which promised to improve their living standards. To the Labour leadership in the early 1920s it appeared there were few obstacles to the party's total annexation of the working-class Catholic vote. The Catholic hierarchy had declared it acceptable for Catholics to join Labour and many of those who had done so were clearly very committed to its cause. Whilst, however, the hierarchy and the Labour leadership accepted the other's right to exist, considerable mutual suspicion remained and essentially the two bodies were in competition for the loyalty of the Catholic working classes.

The Catholic hierarchy, both in Britain and abroad, viewed socialism as a tremendous threat. Socialism, it was believed, would lead to the creation of an omnipotent state apparatus which would intervene in spheres which the Church viewed as its own, for example health care, education and birth control.[66] The Church felt also that it had much to fear from an ideology which aimed to create a form of 'heaven on earth'. The extent of this underlying conflict was masked in the 1920s because the Catholic hierarchy largely refrained from public attacks on the party. The hierarchy was afraid that if it condemned Labour it would drive away members of it own Church and provoke anti-Catholic sentiments. It also saw Labour as a bulwark against communism, a creed which it viewed with abject horror. Privately, however, the hierarchy by the late 1920s was ill-at-ease with substantial sections of Labour's programme, and was fearful that Labour was becoming more hardline socialist, particularly the Maxtonite ILP. Many Catholic Labour members and supporters shared this fear that there was a conflict between their religion and an allegiance to Labour. Clearly, then, there was considerable potential for a serious conflict of interests, not least once Labour was in office.

The 1929 election

Local parties approached the 1929 election campaign in a general mood of optimism. The larger parties were pleased by the number of activists who came forward. Bristol East, for example, used over 700 volunteers in the month before the election. Many executives were pleased to report that such intensive campaigning was having positive effects on membership levels.[67] Parliamentary candidates addressed a large number of well-attended meetings, and the audiences for the national leadership were often into the thousands. Over 15,000 heard MacDonald speak in Birmingham at the end of May.[68] A 'Bid for Power Fund' was launched in many constituencies and was successful in raising significant sums of money for the campaign.

The results of the election, which saw the return of a Labour MP in many constituencies for the first time, and a great increase in Labour's majority in many others, created an atmosphere of general elation. Many activists felt that their endeavours over the turbulent years since the war would be rewarded; finally, a Labour government would be able to implement at least some of the reforms for which they had been campaigning for so long. There was also general satisfaction that Labour's strategy of gradualness had now been justified.[69] The editorial of the *Nelson Gazette* of 4 June described the great excitement amongst Labour supporters in the town. Returning to address a victory celebration after securing a majority of over 10,000, Arthur Greenwood was scarcely able to reach the platform as he was mobbed by the jubilant crowd. One old man was so overcome that 'Tears of joy trickled down his face, for he knew that his work had been worthwhile.' After the meeting had finally broken up, the still exhilarated crowd pulled Greenwood's car through the streets.[70] Such scenes were far from uncommon; all of those local parties who returned MPs held celebrations and treated their candidates as heroes. This cult of personality reached phenomenal levels in the case of MacDonald, who was widely held to have been Labour's 'true prophet'.[71] On his return to London on 31 May, he was met by an overwhelming demonstration at King's Cross Station.[72] He received a similar reception at a meeting of 20,000 Labour women in Durham in mid-July,[73] and also when he was honoured in his birth place, the small fishing village of Lossiemouth, on 13 June.[74]

As with the trade unions, expectations amongst the local party members were tremendous. This was a source of great inspiration to the local and national leaderships, but it had unfortunate implications for a minority administration bound to suffer frequent difficulties. Unlike the unions, who had their own separate organisation and philosophy to fall back upon, local party activists' commitment to the success of the government was total and any setbacks would be deeply felt.

The Parliamentary Labour Party

The Labour Party ... was made up largely of strongly assertive men who had, mainly in the trade union movement, pushed themselves up from obscurity to sufficient prominence to be elected as MPs.

E. Thurtle, *Times Winged Chariot* (1945)[75]

What I was totally unprepared for was the behaviour of the solid rows of decent, well-intentioned, unpretentious Labour back-benchers.... Again and again an effort was made to rouse them from their inertia. On every occasion they reacted like a load of damp cement. They would see nothing, do nothing, listen to nothing that had not first been given the seal of MacDonald's approval.

J. Lee, *This Great Journey* (1942)[76]

From the time of its inception, the PLP was troubled by two major issues. The first was the degree of independence which it should enjoy. Should the PLP remain largely free of outside interference or should it be subordinate to the wider movement outside of Parliament? The second concern was one of coherence. What was the PLP to stand for and how should unity of purpose be maintained?[77] By the early 1920s, progress had been made upon both of these issues but it is misleading to give the impression that they had been resolved.[78] Rather, the role of the PLP remained an area of considerable disagreement and uncertainty.

Prior to 1914, there was continual debate in the movement over the purpose of the PLP and a number of attempts at party conference to restrict PLP autonomy. During the First World War, the extent of its influence was reduced, demonstrated most clearly when the decision to leave the Lloyd George Coalition was taken against PLP advice. The 1918 constitution was ambiguous on the role of the PLP. The PLP complained that it had been given insufficient input into the drafting process and only after an amendment at the party conference was it accepted that election programmes should be worked out by both the NEC and the PLP.[79] The constitution stated explicitly that 'the work of the Party [would] be under the direction and control of the Party Conference'.[80] It has been argued that the sovereignty of the party conference was thus stated clearly.[81] Others, however, propose that the 1918 constitution served in the long term to strengthen the position of the PLP and that extra-parliamentary control was more extensive on paper than it was ever to be in reality.[82] The formal commitment to socialism in the constitution did help to give the PLP a unity it had previously lacked. Nevertheless, the degree of uncertainty which remained regarding both the function and the power of the PLP should not be underestimated.

The return of Labour's most able figures to Parliament in 1922 increased PLP authority in the movement considerably, but the experience of the first Labour government demonstrated that the issue of PLP power was still a contentious one. In the context of the disappointment following the government's defeat, there was renewed discussion of the PLP's role. There was widespread support outside Parliament for greater external control of the PLP and of any future Labour government. There was also discussion of turning the PLP Executive Committee into a back-benchers' committee to exclude party leaders.[83] None of these proposals was ever implemented, and they were to recede in the context of MacDonald's renewed hold over the party from 1927, which encouraged a belief amongst the parliamentary leadership that the PLP was an autonomous entity, free from extra-parliamentary control. Such a degree of independence was unusual amongst European socialist parties; the PLP was 'not a function of the party nor its expression of political power, but a party in itself'.[84] Again, however, it is incorrect to assume this interpretation was accepted by all in the movement and could not be re-evaluated in the light of subsequent events. Predictably, it was the party's radical wing which was most at odds with the notion of PLP autonomy.

Theoretically, the function of the PLP was to represent the interests of the Labour movement in Parliament, but within this definition there was considerable room for interpretation. Individual Labour MPs had to juggle a number of different loyalties and responsibilities. First, according to the traditions of the British constitution, they were the representatives of their constituents. Secondly, in party terms, they had a duty to voice the interests of their local parties. Thirdly, they had to consider the best interests of the party as a whole. Fourthly, when Labour was in office, back-benchers, excluding occasions when they could invoke grounds of conscience, were expected to support the government at all times.[85] Fifthly, many felt themselves to have a duty to consider the interests of the nation, particularly in relation to foreign affairs and the economy. Finally, all felt the need to be true, as far as possible, to their own beliefs and ideologies. For much of the time, the Labour MP was able to rationalise that all these various ends and responsibilities were served equally by one course of action. It was inevitable, however, that there would be some conflict between these differing ends, not least when Labour was in office in a minority government.

The most striking feature of the 1929 PLP was that, with 287 members of Parliament, it was by far the largest it had ever been.[86] From the early 1920s, its increase in size had been truly phenomenal: before the 1922 General Election it had contained only around seventy MPs. The PLP, then, had grown fourfold in only seven years. Such a rapid increase had major implications for party management. Labour's leaders and party whips had no experience of controlling a group of this size, yet, because of the government's minority status, it was imperative they should do so. In terms of composition, the PLP also underwent a fundamental change in the 1920s. As noted above, there had been a dramatic increase in the number of MPs who had run their campaigns with DLP backing, from only 25 in 1924 to 128 in 1929.[87]

Attempts to define groups within the PLP created after the 1929 election are problematic. There was tremendous diversity within the parliamentary party and considerable crossovers between any sub-groups that can be determined. The notion of a left/right dichotomy is of little help. Whilst this concept of a political spectrum is arguably universally problematic, it does appear to be particularly flawed in the context of the late 1920s. Although it is possible to argue that the Maxtonite ILP formed Labour's left wing, it is more difficult to determine who would fit into the notion of a right wing. The majority of the PLP cannot be easily slotted either into one or the other. On some issues, like disarmament, MPs who might otherwise be regarded as being on the right appear to be anything but.

Despite these problems, however, it is possible to divide the June 1929 PLP loosely into three sub-groups. First, the trade union group, that is, those 114 MPs who had been sponsored by a trade union. Whilst different unions had different priorities, and union-sponsored MPs placed varying degrees of stress upon their responsibilities to their unions, there were important unifying features in their outlooks. They all placed a strong emphasis upon the need for industrial legislation, were wholly from the working classes and were all deeply imbued with the ethos of Labourism. Many were elderly, retired union officials, particularly within the forty-two sponsored by the MFGB. It was likely, then, that this group would be most susceptible to appeals from the government for the need for party loyalty and solidarity.

The second group which can be determined is the Maxtonite section of the ILP.[88] This group included by no means all the thirty-seven ILP-sponsored MPs elected in 1929, but rather a solid core of around twenty who disagreed fundamentally with the Labour leadership's gradualist strategy. The position of the ILP in the movement after 1918 had been anomalous. Wishing to pose as 'the intellectual spearhead' of the Labour Party,[89] and to justify its continuing existence, the ILP attempted to create a separate political programme. *The Living Wage* of 1926, based upon J. A. Hobson's theory of underconsumptionism, had proposed that, by increasing the purchasing power of the workers, a living wage would provide the solution to unemployment.[90] Under the influence of the Maxtonites (Maxton becoming the new chairman of the ILP in 1926) the living wage came to be seen as a transitional tactic: a means of bankrupting capitalism by forcing industries to pay a minimum wage they could not afford. Such militancy had created growing tensions between the Maxtonites and ILP moderates, which included the bulk of MPs with ILP membership. Some, like Snowden in 1927, resigned, whilst others, such as Charles Trevelyan and Clement Attlee, transferred their candidacies in 1929 to DLP sponsorship.[91] With a Labour leadership reluctant to address the issue, however, the anomalous position of the ILP remained.

Labour's electoral victory of 1929 did nothing to alleviate these tensions. In contrast, with Labour's taking of office the ideological debates became more than theoretical, and all the more heated in consequence. The Maxtonite group of twenty or so MPs believed that the ILP should have more control over those 142 MPs who were ILP members,[92] whereas the majority of these individuals saw themselves primarily as members of the PLP and did not accept that the ILP should be pushing a separate political agenda. The Maxtonites argued that Labour would only be justified in taking office if the government acted boldly to alleviate unemployment and made significant strides in the advancement of socialism. From the beginning, it was determined to push the government into a more radical policy. For a minority government, in need of every vote it could muster, the possibility of twenty of its own MPs voting regularly against it, and forming an effective 'party within a party', was a very serious one.

The final group which one can identify can only be defined negatively, that is, those MPs not in the union group or the Maxtonite ILP. This constituted the largest of the three groups and within it there existed a great diversity: in terms of age, class, religion, character, ideology and policy priorities. It also contained individuals with a wide range of former vocations: doctors, priests, lawyers, schoolteachers, soldiers, journalists, writers, factory workers, agricultural labourers, civil servants, bank clerks, academics and so on. Clearly, with such a diversity of background and belief it is difficult to define this group in any collective sense. What united them ultimately was their belief that Labour's socialism offered the answer to Britain's and the world's problems.

In terms of their potential loyalty to the government, it can be suggested, again tentatively, that this diverse group of individuals was less imbued in the Labourist ethos than the trade union group and was perhaps therefore more likely to be critical of the government. Many had given up careers to become MPs and in that sense had personally staked more on the success of the government than trade unionists, who, on leaving Parliament, could return to trade union duties or enter retirement. Many had no job to return to if they lost their seats, particularly those who were working-class. In a time of depression and because of a strong possibility of victimisation by employers, their chances of finding employment outside of the Labour movement were slim.[93] Paradoxically, however, whilst this group was in some respects more liable to be critical of the government because their livelihoods depended upon its success, they were perhaps also more committed than the union group to keeping the government in office. In June 1929 their expectations for the government were considerable, their belief in the logic of socialism total, and, very aware of the hopes placed in them by those who had elected them, they were prepared to back the government to the hilt in its mission to improve the conditions of the working classes.[94] For the whole PLP, the potential for disillusionment was considerable, and was perhaps to be all the more painful as they observed the government's limitations from close at hand.

Socialist intellectuals

The statesman on the modern stage is inevitably a pigmy; the writer who knows his business, even more the teacher, watches hundreds who never heard of him rediscover the truths he has uttered.

Harold Laski to Oliver Wendell Holmes, 16 June 1923[95]

> I think that I am the only one who knows how to handle these chaps. I get them to come and see me and have a talk. And then I ask them to write me a memorandum. That pleases them and keeps them quiet for a time. And I often learn quite a lot from what they write.
>
> Arthur Henderson, in conversation with Hugh Dalton[96]

One of the dictionary definitions of the term 'intellectual' is 'a person who uses his intellect'. Perhaps one of the major weaknesses of Labour in the 1920s and beyond was that it was a party that did not use its intellectuals. The quotations above illustrate the vastly differing perceptions which one intellectual and the Party Secretary held with regard to the importance of ideas. For Laski, and his fellow Labour intellectuals, ideology was more important than individuals and party politics. The role of the party intellectual in Laski's eyes was to construct the ideology upon which the party's policy would be formulated, and to amend that ideology in the light of changing experience. For Henderson, ideas were subordinate to political practicalities, and those who devised them were just another group which had to be managed in the best interests of the movement. The Labour Party in the 1920s was not ideally suited to the aspirations of the socialist intellectuals, and yet it was, nevertheless, highly influenced by their writings.

Labour's emphasis upon class and its suspicion of outsiders did not make the party very welcoming to intellectuals, who had to endorse its general ethos and play by its well-defined rules.[97] The party that emerged in 1900 was conceived essentially as a vehicle for representing the interests of trade unionism. Despite the involvement of the Fabians, the ILP and the Social Democratic Federation (SDF) in its creation, these groups were very much in the shadow of the unions, and in spite of them Labour before the First World War had no real political ideology. Instead, its policy was best defined as 'Labourism': policies were to be shaped around the furtherance of trade union ends.[98] As such, there was not even any great need for intellectuals in the movement at this time, since Labourism was not a doctrine which required a great deal of definition.

The developments during the First World War initially seemed to create an atmosphere more congenial to the input of an intelligentsia. The emergence of the Labour Research Department and the need to construct a new constitution resulted in Henderson bringing in not only Sidney Webb and the Fabians, but also a number of younger and more left-wing individuals, like G. D. H. and Margaret Cole. Yet little improvement was made to the status of the intellectual. The famous reference to workers 'by hand or by brain' was largely tokenistic; and, whilst there was a small increase in middle-class members of the party during the 1920s, those who used their hands to earn their livelihoods continued to dominate overwhelmingly. Shortly after the end of the war, the opportunities for intellectuals to change the party's direction began to close up. Having used them for its own purposes, the leadership was not keen to define a permanent role for the intelligentsia.

The nine advisory committees set up in 1918 proved to be less than dynamic, as did the joint departments created with the TUC in 1921, which, as shown above, began to break down by the mid-1920s. In the wake of the creation of the CPGB the leadership were keen to stamp down upon any activities they considered to be too 'extremist' and it was in this spirit that the role of the Labour Research Department was undermined in the party reorganisation of 1922. Similarly, the formerly militant *Daily Herald* became more moderate after the party had taken control of it in the same year. The party leadership was essentially content with the 1918 constitution and with *Labour and the New Social Order*, and had little desire to tinker with the ideology defined within them. Webb's comment at the 1923 Labour Conference that anyone who wished for details of Labour's policies should send for a copy of *Labour and the New Social Order* was indicative of this notion that policy debates were now closed.[99] As such, therefore, the intellectual fluidity of the period at the end of the war had been replaced by a leadership-induced ideological dogmatism. G. D. H. Cole later wrote of the 1920s party:

> there was a failure to appreciate brains and a suspicion of 'cleverness' which prevented service in the party machine from offering attractions to the younger people who could have helped to provide it with the driving force that it manifestly lacked. Its propagandist literature ... was ... dully written and most unattractively presented ... outside volunteers ... were often given as many kicks as thanks in return for their trouble.[100]

Equally, as has been shown, the union dominance of the movement continued in the 1920s and this also worked against the attraction of intellectuals. Labourism and suspicion of non-working-class 'intellectuals' pervaded. Hardly surprisingly, many trade unionists distrusted the motives of those from outside the movement who sought to push it in directions of their own choosing. The attitude of Bevin was perhaps typical: it was all very well for middle-class writers to tell the workers what they should do when it was not they who would have to endure any ill-consequences.

It was not until 1918 that Labour's constitution made possible the direct entry of 'intellectuals' without them having to join through one of the three affiliated socialist societies: the ILP, Fabian Society and SDF. Not until 1937, with the development of a specific constituency party section of the NEC to be voted for only by the local parties, was it possible for an intellectual to get elected to the Executive without representing one of the socialist societies.[101] Of these societies, the Fabian group offered the best opportunity in the 1920s to influence party policy, but by the middle of the decade it was not the dynamic force that it had once been. The ILP's increasingly confrontational and dogmatic stance from the same date ensured that it was not an attractive vehicle for those seeking freedom of thought. Consequently, the socialist intellectual wishing to influence the party's ideology without seeking election to Parliament, aside from relying upon teaching and writing, was essentially forced to seek the patronage of powerful figures in the movement.

The potential for this avenue, however, was also very limited, since the leadership was not particularly inclined to use the skills of the intellectual. Clynes and Thomas were both moderate trade unionists, the latter of whom did not even consider himself to be a socialist. Henderson, whilst he recognised that intellectuals could be of use, was more concerned with party management than ideological debates. Finally, Snowden and MacDonald saw such figures as an intellectual threat. Both men considered themselves to be socialist theorists; MacDonald had written a number of pamphlets and books outlining his embryonic socialism, chiefly *Socialism and Society* (London, 1905) and *Socialism: Critical and Constructive* (London, 1921), and Snowden had produced *The Living Wage* (London, 1912) and *Socialism and Syndicalism* (London, 1913). Snowden wished to consolidate his position in the 1920s as the party's recognised financial expert, and MacDonald never seems to have been comfortable in the presence of intellectuals. It is possible that the Labour leader was jealous of their education, he having largely educated himself, and their intellectual self-confidence tended to feed his insecurity.[102] Equally, he liked to avoid being tied down to detailed programmes in order that he might retain considerable room for manoeuvre. In 1928 he considered *Labour and the Nation* to be the last word for the foreseeable future upon the party's long-term strategy. Clearly, then, it was difficult for intellectuals to gain access to the corridors of power during MacDonald's tenure as party leader, or to influence policy except in those areas dictated by the leadership.

Sidney and Beatrice Webb, R. H. Tawney, Harold Laski and G. D. H. Cole were five of the most important intellectual figures in the first fifty years of the Labour Party's history. Although they reached their zenith at different junctures, all had considerable influence on the Labour Party of the late 1920s. By this date, they were all loyal party members and had won the confidence of the movement. Despite the fact that they all experienced frustrations with it, they were all very much party intellectuals. Although ideologically and individually diverse, all five had the intention not only of defining socialist theory in the long term, but also of directly influencing the next Labour government.

The Webbs

The Webbs have often been portrayed in a negative light. Their socialist ideology is said to epitomise the worst features of collectivist, mechanistic and bureaucratic socialism.[103] Leaving aside the validity of these claims, however, there can be no doubt that their work had a lasting impact on the Labour movement. Not only did their numerous writings influence a whole generation of socialists, but the Webbs succeeded in imposing much of their Fabian ideology upon the Labour Party that emerged from the First World War. Sidney Webb formed a close partnership with Henderson in 1917 and drafted much of the new constitution of 1918, including the famous 'Clause IV'. He also wrote the policy document of that year, *Labour and the New Social Order*, which set the tone for the party of the 1920s and beyond. Beatrice could justifiably comment in 1917 that her husband had become 'the intellectual leader of the Labour Party'.[104] Furthermore, it was Sidney Webb who coined the phrase in 1923 that encapsulated the party's ideology in the 1920s, 'the inevitability of gradualness': the belief that radical social improvement could be achieved through piecemeal reform. Such an approach was ideally suited to the requirements of the Labour leadership since it would allow Labour to implement socialism via parliamentary means and without a period of transitionary upheaval.

Although they incorporated some of the ideas of pluralism, which were strong on the Labour left at that point in time, into *A Constitution for the Socialist Commonwealth of Great Britain* (London, 1920), the Webbian ideology continued to spotlight the role of the expert and of the state. It was nationalisation controlled by technocrats that would be the chief avenue to the socialist utopia. For the Webbs, socialism was about scientific efficiency and it was the inefficiency and not the immorality of capitalist society that provided the impetus for their desire to change it.

In 1929 Sidney Webb was seventy and Beatrice seventy-one. Since 1926 they had grown increasingly distant from the heart of Labour politics. This was due in part to old age but it was also a result of disillusionment with the party and with MacDonald in particular. Sidney had entered Parliament in 1922 and had become the President of the Board of Trade in 1924, but had not proved to be a great success. Both he and Beatrice were looking forward to a retirement in which they could concentrate upon their writing and had little inkling of the significant role which Sidney would play in the next Labour government.

R. H. Tawney

The philosophy of Tawney has survived historical re-examination more successfully than the work of the Webbs. Like them, Tawney was a versatile figure, for he was able to combine the roles of the teacher, the economic historian, the educational reformer and the socialist intellectual. His socialism, expressed most famously in *The Acquisitive Society* (London, 1921) and in *Equality* (London, 1931), continued to appeal after his death to figures on both the left and the right of the Labour movement. In both his personal life as well as his teaching, Tawney shunned materialism and was noted for his humility and his asceticism: attributes which many Labour members would admire, even if they found it a little more difficult to achieve them personally. Tawney was also very much the loyal party man and the arch-democrat. Whilst the majority of Labour thinkers had toyed with undemocratic means of implementing socialism, particularly in the 1930s, Tawney remained largely true to his democratic socialist credentials.[105] Tawney's writings provided the central moral foundation of Labour's political thought in the 1920s, and therefore merit extensive attention.

The Acquisitive Society

Margaret Cole was later to describe *The Acquisitive Society* as 'perhaps the most powerful of all post-war appeals for Socialism'.[106] Its critique was based upon an abstract moral rejection of the materialistic and self-interested nature of capitalist society and, as such, the book has taken on something of a timeless quality. The central problem with it, however, is that Tawney was better at diagnosing the maladies of capitalism than in recommending a cure.

The Acquisitive Society was written at a time when there seemed a real danger that society was falling apart, and throughout the work there is a sense of apocalyptic urgency. Tawney believed the growing gulf between the top and the bottom of society was a direct result of the emphasis of capitalism both upon the concept of individual rights, as opposed to duties or services, and upon the accumulation of wealth. He proposed that since the industrial revolution, the concept of the common good had been gradually eroded and replaced by the ideas of private rights and individual interests, with the state serving to protect existing property and to legitimise the religion of materialism.[107] The means by which this 'acquisitive society' attempted to preserve some semblance of social harmony was by appealing to individual self-interest.[108] Since everyone was attempting to obtain the maximum for themselves, however, social peace could be achieved only through a precarious balance of power, which was doomed to continual collapse. The chief consequence was inequality, which was not only morally indefensible but also economically inefficient. Labour was degraded and seen merely as a means to the acquisition of wealth, and the creation of luxury goods for the rich meant that basic necessities were being produced in insufficient quantities. Above all, industrialism had created a 'parasitic rentier class' who were concerned only with profit.[109]

Tawney felt that the means to correct this situation lay in the creation of a 'functional society'. This concept was not a new one, being derived both from Ruskin and from the guild socialists.[110] For Tawney, it meant that: 'Society should be organised primarily for the performance of duties, not for the maintenance of rights.'[111] Rights were to be made conditional, not absolute, and each section of society would be judged upon the contribution that it made to the common good. On the question, however, of how this transformation would be achieved, Tawney was noticeably less clear-headed. He felt neither guild socialism nor nationalisation offered an absolute answer to industrial organisation. He proposed that professional societies should form the basic unit of the new society, since they had integrity and were always conscious of their duty to serve. Any capital involved would be paid only a fixed rate of interest and all excess profits would be reinvested, and the choice of nationalisation or guilds would depend upon the requirements of the particular industry.[112] Essentially, therefore, Tawney's approach to socialist organisation was utilitarian and he always held the reorganisation of society to be secondary to a moral change in the behaviour of individuals.

There were considerable difficulties with these proposals. First, Tawney did not have any great respect for trade unionism and, indeed, regarded it as an obstacle to the socialist society he wished to create. This dislike stemmed from the belief that the unions represented sectional interest groups and had little concern with the common good. Whilst he implies that the unions would be the embryo of the professional societies, he gives little indication of how this transformation would be achieved. Secondly, Tawney was guilty of romanticising early industrial society and of seeing its structure as suitable for emulation, regardless of the fact that with mass production and the extension of markets an entirely new set of problems had been created. Thirdly, Tawney's view of professional societies and of working-class altruism is idealised. He assumed that professional societies would recognise their duty to the common good when, in fact, it seems likely that the British working classes would have been as keen as their middle-class contemporaries to protect their interests. Fourthly, Tawney pays little attention to the economic functioning of a socialist society. He essentially accepted the process of capitalist production, did not see private property as wrong in itself, and believed there was no conflict between employers and employees that could not be overridden by social reorganisation.[113]

Finally, and perhaps most importantly, Tawney does not define what the common end of society was. It has been argued that this end was a Christian one, that is, to ensure eternal salvation in the kingdom of God.[114] Whether this was true or not, his belief that a social consensus for socialism was latent within society had major implications for the Labour strategy of the 1920s. Perhaps most significantly, as with the input of the Webbs, it made Labour believe the attainment of socialism would be easier than was in fact the case. The use of semi-religious terminology was not out of place in a movement that still had an evangelical feel to it, and whose socialist philosophy was for many a quasi-religion. Equally, in some respects the vague nature of the common end was a definite asset, since it could mean whatever the reader or the listener wished it to mean. At the same time, however, the lack of coherent guidelines to the implementation of socialism was potentially disastrous.

Equality

Tawney developed many of the themes of *The Acquisitive Society* in his 1931 work, *Equality*, the product of a series of lectures given in 1929. Some commentators have seen this as his most impressive political discourse.[115] Tawney set out to illustrate how inequality dominated Britain and to demonstrate the manner in which people's destinies were decided by their place in the social system. He proposed that individuals were denied the opportunity to fulfil their true potential in a society in which, in 1919, over two-thirds of the wealth was held by less than 1 per cent of the population.[116] In the socialist society envisaged by Tawney, equality would be achieved in the form of equal consideration and opportunities for all, and through a move away from the evaluation of people according to their wealth.[117]

Once again, Tawney was more convincing in his analysis than he was at prescribing a remedy. Many of the criticisms made of *The Acquisitive Society* could be applied to *Equality*. What is most interesting is the manner in which Tawney's alternative to capitalism had changed during the period 1921–29. Most striking is the complete absence from the later work of the notion of professional societies and the move from guild socialism towards state collectivism as the tool for socialist transformation. In particular, Tawney now devoted a great deal of attention to comprehensive healthcare and an extensive and equal education system for all, to be paid for through progressive taxation.[118] Whilst he still advocated a mixed economy and did not believe all private property should become state-owned, Tawney now favoured the implementation of some form of public control in the areas of banking, transport, power, coal, land, armaments and agriculture. Once again, however, he did not commit himself to a detailed programme for this transformation, and, although he did not state it categorically, the implication seems to be that it would be left to experts to decide these questions.

What is apparent, therefore, is that Tawney's thought had become more Fabian in tone by 1929. He was still wary of seeing nationalisation as a panacea for all industrial problems and of the danger of too much bureaucracy,[119] but his previously low regard for the work of the Webbs had developed into a position of mutual respect by this date, and it was to them that he dedicated the book.[120] Further, his previous optimism with regard to the working classes had been tinged with a greater element of Webbian doubt by 1929. In particular, he was beginning to question whether the workers would perform the high moral role he had previously assigned for them and whether they had either the ability or the desire to reject the capitalist system.[121]

The failure of the General Strike appears to have deeply affected Tawney's view of the unionised working classes.[122] After joining the Fabian Executive in 1921, he had become a prominent adviser to the Labour leadership, and was chiefly responsible for the development of Labour's education policy in the 1920s.[123] Tawney's personal relations with MacDonald were a little uneasy. MacDonald apparently dismissed urgings in 1922 that he should put Tawney in the Lords as Labour's education spokesman because of Tawney's notoriously unkempt appearance.[124] Nevertheless, in ideological terms the two men were largely in agreement. Tawney was chosen to redraft *Labour and the Nation* in 1928, which had originally been written by MacDonald.[125] This lengthy document contained many of his stylistic trademarks and can be said to have been a synthesis of the ideology of MacDonald, Tawney and the Webbs. Tawney agreed with MacDonald's central premise that the programme should have a national and not a sectional appeal. This involvement in turn influenced his own socialist writing; it is possible to detect many of its central tenets in the pages of *Equality*. By 1929, then, the ideology of Tawney and of the Labour Party had become intrinsically intertwined.

The election campaign

Tawney was involved in the process of scaling down *Labour and the Nation* to create a Labour election manifesto. In January 1929 he was concerned that the Liberals were stealing Labour's thunder on unemployment and wrote to Henderson to push for a more definite Labour statement in its employment proposals.[126] This letter may have been influential in the decision of the Labour leadership to invite G. D. H. Cole to write *How to Conquer Unemployment*. Tawney held similar misgivings with regard to the final version of the manifesto, however, which he felt was still too vague on unemployment.[127] In March 1929 he had placed his own draft manifesto before a special NEC committee, but had to leave the meeting early. Consequently, he wrote to MacDonald to inquire what had been concluded. With characteristic prevarication, MacDonald attempted to convince Tawney that he personally felt the manifesto was 'excellent' but had not noticed that Tawney had left and when he 'turned to get a definite decision of the use to be made of it, [he] found that [Tawney] had gone'.[128] None the less, MacDonald valued Tawney's intellectual abilities, for he was invited to join MacDonald on his election campaign as his principal adviser.[129] Due to his London School of Economics (LSE) commitments, Tawney was unable to take more than one week off, but agreed to meet MacDonald for the English leg of his campaign. This relationship seems to have worked reasonably well since Tawney was asked by MacDonald to draft his key speech for radio broadcast at the end of May.[130]

Harold Laski

Unlike Tawney, Harold Laski is not a name one is likely to see invoked by contemporary Labour Party leaders. Until the recent, and long overdue, reassessment provided in two biographies, Laski's reputation had dropped to a point of near obscurity.[131] Yet his contribution to the Labour movement and its political thought is, once again, indisputable. Laski published more than twenty books and thousands of essays and worked tirelessly to further the ends of the Labour Party. He was heavily involved in workers' education for three decades and served for twenty-four years from 1926 as a member of the Industrial Court, set up in the post-war period to arbitrate in industrial disputes. Of all the Labour intellectuals of the period, Laski was the most popular amongst the party membership, later being elected to the new exclusive constituency section of the NEC created in 1937 and for every year for the next eight years. In the year of his greatest public exposure, when he served as Party Chairman in 1945, Laski's profile was such that Churchill would attempt to portray him as the personification of all the worst aspects of hardline socialism.

Pluralism

It was during his period in America during the First World War that Laski developed the political theory for which he remains most noted, the concept of pluralism. Laski believed that sovereignty had been chiefly responsible for the outbreak of the war, and held that excessive state power suppressed the liberty both of individuals and of the multifarious associations in society. He argued that the state should be regarded as only one entity to which individuals gave their allegiance, and should be judged upon the same grounds as all other associations. He developed these arguments most convincingly in his first book, entitled *Studies in the Problem of Sovereignty* (Yale, 1917). However, despite his earlier toying with syndicalism, Laski at this point was still in essence a left-wing liberal. Liberty, rather than equality, or a central role for workers in a new society, remained his prime concern.[132]

It was the Russian Revolution and the intensification of class conflict in Europe that convinced Laski that the ends of capital and labour could not be reconciled. In a brave attempt to marry his pluralist beliefs with the ends of syndicalism, Laski produced *Authority in the Modern State* (Yale, 1919). His attitude to Cole's guild socialism was ambivalent; whilst he suggested that it was 'the most significant development in English political thought in the last decade', Laski did not propose that workers' councils should replace the parliamentary system but only supplement it.[133] Essentially, he feared that industrial councils would become too powerful and thereby undermine his pluralist objectives by overriding the ends of other groups in society. Ironically, therefore, Laski now appeared to be arguing that the sovereignty of the state *was* necessary, in order that the liberty of associations might be protected.

Fabian pluralism

By the mid-1920s, Laski had come to believe that state power was more formidable than he had previously believed and that nationalisation could promote the development of a more equal society. This ideological shift was allied to his increasing closeness to the Webbs, who effectively became his patrons in the Labour movement. He became a prominent figure in the Fabian Society and, at this stage, a great admirer of MacDonald.[134] By 1925 Laski appeared to have become the Fabian intellectual *par excellence*. Yet he had not abandoned his earlier pluralism entirely, but rather was attempting to achieve a synthesis between this earlier doctrine and his new-found belief in collectivism. The result was the work many regard as his *magnum opus*, the 1925 *Grammar of Politics*.

Laski's earlier emphasis upon the importance of associations and workers' councils was now toned down and replaced by a more limited vision of local participation and decentralisation. He now conceived a powerful state which would have obligations to its citizens and would be subject to their constant scrutiny. The state was now defined in utilitarian terms; it would be an 'organisation for enabling the mass of men to realise social good on the largest possible scale', and would be assessed on how successfully it achieved that end. What Laski proposed was a form of corporatism, in which state power would be shared with society's interest groups. The influence of Tawneyism upon Laski's thought is obvious. Although he suggested individuals had rights, Laski proposed they had duties also. He favoured also the notion that 'industry ... must be made a profession'.[135] Finally, he was also largely pragmatic over the question of public ownership and supported the idea of a mixed economy.[136] Whilst he believed some reform was needed to both the legal and the political apparatus of the nation, chiefly the abolition of the House of Lords, essentially Laski believed that the existing state machinery could be harnessed for the purposes of fundamental social and economic reform.[137]

Despite its length (over 650 pages), *Grammar* had a significant and lasting impact.[138] It continues to impress through its emphasis upon the need to combine collective control with the greatest possible degree of devolution. There were, however, problems with it. First, once again, Laski says little about how the economic transformation of society would be achieved. Like Tawney, he places his emphasis upon the moral justification for socialism and the need for a change in attitudes rather than upon a change in economic structures. Secondly, in line with most British socialists, Laski viewed the state as class neutral and did not see a need for a fundamental overhaul of the administrative apparatus. Thirdly, the tension between pluralism and collectivism is not always resolved; now that he accepted the supremacy of the state it was not always clear how large a role associations would have in the governing process. Finally, whilst he recognised that there was a danger of resistance from the propertied classes,[139] Laski believed that compromise could override this danger. In optimistic mood, Laski argued that reason would triumph. The events of the next six years would shake this confident prediction.

The General Strike led Laski to question his belief that socialism could be achieved peacefully. Although uneasy with regard to the revolutionary implications of the strike and privately relieved it had failed,[140] the new mood of class hostility led Laski to question the viability of gradualism.[141] It is apparent, then, that Laski was already sowing the seeds of doubt that would lead him to reject gradualism after 1931. In the short term, however, this uncertainty led Laski to reassess Marxist socialism in *Communism* (London, 1927), almost as if by so doing he could reassure himself that gradualism offered the only way forwards.

Yet while he still held to his belief that peaceful change was both desirable and practicable, it is clear that in 1927 he was increasingly questioning the ability of the Labour leaders to achieve it. In particular, he had begun to doubt the capability of MacDonald, and wrote a highly critical article on the 1927 Labour Conference for *New Republic* in November. He gloomily concluded that: 'Mr MacDonald himself has something like a horror of ideas.... Mr Snowden has largely ceased to be a Socialist ... and Mr Thomas never was a Socialist.' He warned that if the Labour Party was 'merely to become the alternative to the Conservative Party with a philosophy that is as related to Socialism as a jerry-built house to Westminster Abbey, it will not continue to attract those who still venture to dream of a new world built by high courage and arduous effort'.[142]

Despite his reservations, Laski endorsed the leadership line on non-affiliation of the Communist Party and applause for the Mond–Turner talks,[143] and, casting his doubts to one side, worked hard to see Labour's return at the 1929 election. He campaigned in over thirty constituencies and was asked by MacDonald to speak in Seaham Harbour, somewhat ironically in view of his later reputation, specifically to counter the communist threat that was being mounted in the constituency.[144] Laski believed a small Conservative victory could be the best result for Labour in the long term, but was none the less visibly excited by the possibility of a Labour success.[145] He had decided once again not to stand for Parliament himself, preferring to remain a teacher and an independent thinker. Like Tawney, he saw his role as to advise on policy whilst preserving a high degree of intellectual freedom, and he believed that, in the long term, the party theorist was more influential than the politician. In 1924 he suggested that to disentangle successfully the relationship between liberty and equality was 'worth all the Cabinet offices a man was ever able to enjoy'.[146]

The ambitious Laski relished the opportunity to obtain the direct influence upon government policy which a Labour victory would place within his grasp; in a revealing letter to his wife, Frida, on 17 April, he justified his decision to work for MacDonald because 'we may sometime need something from him ... I felt that if we *do* form a government, I want to sit on commissions and things and I better have MacDonald in my debt.' Arguably, therefore, Laski's ambition, coupled with a sense that the tide could be moving in Labour's direction, led him to cast aside his doubts with regard to both the leadership and its strategy, and the result was that he was to find himself uncomfortably close to a government whose chances of success he had long had grounds to doubt.

G. D. H. Cole

The contribution of G. D. H. Cole to the Labour movement was at least as significant as that of his fellow socialist intellectuals and greater than is generally credited.[147] Like Tawney and Laski, he was a remarkably eclectic figure, combining successfully the roles of the academic, the economist, the historian, the philosophiser, the journalist and the politician. His greatest claim to ideological originality is to be found in the theory of guild socialism which he developed from 1910 to 1922, most impressively in *The World of Labour* (London, 1913). A philosophy born of a period of pre-1914 trade union militancy, guild socialism was a reaction against Fabian collectivism. In opposition to the emphasis placed by the Webbs upon the role of the state and of the expert, guild socialism was the expression of a desire to return to the direct democracy advocated by Rousseau with its roots in the Greek Republic of ancient times. It was Cole who succeeded in shedding the philosophy of its romantic notions of a return to medieval society and in developing guild socialism into a formidable theory which synthesised syndicalism and state socialism. Like Laski, Cole suggested that the state was only one of a number of organisations in society and that if socialism was to succeed it would require foundations in a plurality of institutions. He saw the trade unions as embryonic self-governing workers' guilds which would reunite the worker with the fruits of his labour and form the basis of a new, and truly functional, democratic socialist society.[148]

The socio-political changes brought about by the First World War initially seemed to be very conducive to the spread of guild socialism.[149] As has been noted, Cole's ideas had a major impact on a number of other prominent socialist thinkers, including Tawney, MacDonald and the Webbs, and a number of guild committees were created in 1919 in the building trade. Yet

the period of success was to be short-lived; the collapse of this National Building Guild in 1923 and the serious split in the National Guilds League over its
attitude to the Russian Revolution, particularly after the formation of the
CPGB, put an end to any further inroads which guild socialism might have
made.[150] Most importantly, the dependence of guild socialism upon trade
union strength and militancy meant that it had been dealt a fatal blow by the
sudden ending of the post-war boom in 1920 and the deep recession which
followed. The effect on Cole's political theory was fundamental; never again
would he recapture the unity of theory and practice of the period 1910–22.

In consequence, Cole was left ideologically stranded by 1923. A number
of his contemporaries from the National Guilds League had joined the Communist Party and had accepted the 'democratic centralism' of the USSR, but
Cole rejected this line as incompatible with his democratic beliefs. He resigned
from the Labour Research Department in 1924, where he had been a major
contributor, because of its increasingly communist leanings. As such he was
left without both an organisation and a coherent philosophy.[151] Increasingly
frustrated by his isolation, however, Cole began reluctantly to accept that Labour offered the only realistic vehicle for socialist transformation and consequently the period 1925–29 witnessed his gradual move back towards the
mainstream Labour Party. He came to realise that the party's electoral prospects were becoming ever brighter and that a Labour government with a majority could potentially achieve a considerable degree of socialist change. Of
fundamental significance to this changing attitude was the General Strike.
Webb recorded on 5 September 1926 that Cole was 'disillusioned about workers' control'.[152] In 1928 he rejoined the Fabian Society and accepted the centrality of the state in implementing socialism.[153] Parliamentary action was
now regarded as a necessary preliminary to workers' control.[154] He supported
the Mond–Turner talks and rejected the Cook–Maxton Manifesto as the work
of a group who were 'trying to make the trade union movement an appendage
of the Communist Party'.[155] Similarly, he largely endorsed *Labour and the
Nation*, describing the document as 'moderate and evolutionary in its method,
but at the same time drastic and comprehensive in its aim'.[156] Indeed, such
was the extent of Cole's change of emphasis that in April 1929 he was fearful
that the TUC would attempt to dictate policy to a future Labour government
and argued that a move away from union dependence could only be beneficial
to the party.[157]

The Next Ten Years

Cole, however, was beginning to develop his own ideas as to how the Labour
Party should best go forward, ideas which in many instances conflicted with
the strategy of the leadership. He outlined these new proposals at considerable
length in *The Next Ten Years in British Social and Economic Policy*, written in

1928 and published in March 1929. This book represented a brave attempt to outline a comprehensive approach for Labour to pursue in all areas of economic and social policy in the immediate future. Throughout the work, Cole stressed that Labour needed to construct a practical political programme to address the problems of the present if it was ever to succeed in creating socialism in the long term.

It has been argued that *The Next Ten Years* was perceived by Cole in limited terms only, that is, solely as a political programme for an immediate purpose, and that therefore the book did not signify any fundamental change in Cole's theoretical approach. According to this line of argument, Cole still saw himself as a guild socialist and held on to this philosophy throughout the 1930s, justifying his new acceptance of the role of the state as a temporary expedient necessitated by the circumstances of the time, in particular the economic problems and the threat of fascism.[158] This is misleading. Whilst it is correct to propose that Cole considered *The Next Ten Years* primarily as a short-term programme for a future Labour government, significant sections of the text would suggest that Cole's whole approach to socialist theory had undergone a fundamental change. Cole now admitted that many of the tenets which he had previously expounded were no longer defensible and he adopted a view of the working classes with which the Webbs themselves would have concurred. Principally, Cole felt that he had misread the psychology of the working classes on two key levels. First, he now accepted that the workplace was not necessarily the central interest in the worker's life and that a great deal of work was unavoidably dull and would always remain 'primarily an obligation', no matter how the workplace was organised.[159] Secondly, Cole now suggested that the worker was not so much of 'a political animal' as he once thought and was not interested in spending his non-working hours in setting up a great number of committees.[160]

Cole did not abandon the ideas of workers' control altogether. In a section which sat somewhat incongruously with the emphasis of the rest of the book, however, he now replaced the concept of self-governing guilds with the more limited idea of 'work councils'. As opposed to the central role previously envisaged for the guilds in creating the new social order, these work councils would not *run* but merely *advise* industry. Essentially these councils would only help to guide the Webbian enlightened 'experts' whom Cole now proposed should run British industry.[161] In what represented a complete departure from the ideas of *The World of Labour*, Cole emphasised the central role of the state and of its appointed commissioners to oversee policy changes on its behalf. In all areas of policy from industry to education it was the state which would implement the changes needed to facilitate the gradual development of socialism out of a better functioning capitalist society. If Cole did believe that he was still a guild socialist, then he was deluding himself on a grand scale. The central propositions of guild socialism, that the workplace would be the key institution of socialist transformation and that legislation from the centre was incapable of achieving real socialist change because it did not directly involve the voice of the worker, were nowhere to be found in *The Next Ten Years*. What was to be found in their place was one of the most powerful discourses yet advanced for the intervention of the state in Britain's economy and society on an unprecedented scale.

The most important factor in Cole's new collectivist approach was his belief that only state action could solve Britain's major economic problem, namely unemployment. Cole felt that one million out of work represented an intolerable waste of human and economic resources: 'A society that acquiesces in the presence in its midst of a vast permanent army of unemployed is a society that has ceased to believe in itself.'[162] In a thesis highly influenced by the Liberal 'Industrial Inquiry' of 1928, Cole argued that long-term unemployment was detrimental to the country as a whole and that the state should recognise a moral duty to provide work rather than the cheaper option of maintenance.[163] As opposed to the often half-hearted relief work that governments had previously initiated, Cole proposed the idea of a 'national labour corps' which would be 'a national organisation of workers available for any useful form of national service'.[164] Although this scheme appears to the modern eye to be impressively forward-looking, in view of the subsequent success of similar programmes in Roosevelt's 'New Deal' in the USA from 1934, it is clear that it would have encountered considerable problems. Cole was certainly not unaware of a number of them; he realised that many trade unionists would detest the proposal as representing the militarisation of labour and as a potential weapon for the destruction of the Labour movement, but his rejoinders to these weaknesses were not altogether convincing. Essentially, he argued that a Labour government must be prepared to override the objections of the unions and that the risk of a conservative reaction was one which it had to be prepared to take.[165] This was a highly dubious stance for an avowed advocate of workers' control to adopt, and it would appear unlikely that the unions would have endorsed a policy which might threaten their very existence.[166]

The most impressive proposals in *The Next Ten Years* were Cole's calls for the socialisation of banking and finance. Cole argued that socialist control of capitalist financial organisations was far more important to Labour than the nationalisation of industry. After outlining the manner in which the banks currently controlled credit for the ends of Big Business and financial speculators, he proposed that a Labour government should immediately nationalise both the Bank of England and the joint-stock banks.[167] As a result of these reforms, together with the nationalisation of insurance and the development of a board of national investment along the lines proposed by the Liberal Party to administer public loans, a Labour government would hold the power necessary to aid suffering industries and, more importantly, develop new ones.[168] Rather than take the form of a public corporation as *Labour and the Nation* had advocated, Cole believed that these financial organisations should best be run by independent experts who did not have vested interests in the financial world.[169]

With regard to the socialisation of industry, Cole attempted to play down the long-standing Labour belief in the importance of nationalisation. Cole argued that *control* and not ownership was the key to socialist transformation; as such he proposed that the mining industry should remain privately owned initially although the state would supervise compulsory amalgamation of the mines into more economic units. Similarly with the railways, he proposed that gradual socialisation after a 'state of transition' was needed.[170] As such, Cole astutely hoped to avoid many of the potential problems associated with immediate and complete nationalisation: most importantly, the passing on to the state of financial responsibility for industries which were suffering severe economic problems. Cole's ideas from as early as 1929 can be viewed as a precursor of both the corporate socialism and the mixed economy that dominated Labour's strategy in the 1940s and 1950s.

Cole believed that any rejuvenation of British industry would depend upon an extension of the home market, since the possibilities for an upturn in overseas trade were severely limited. He emphasised the unpalatable truth that British staple industries would never again enjoy the level of prosperity of the pre-war period. Neither the process of rationalisation, nor the extension of economic ties with the Empire, offered any real solution to Britain's economic ills.[171] Control of finance and investment was therefore vitally important. In addition, Cole advocated family allowances and the creation of trade boards to increase wages and thereby extend the purchasing power of the workers.[172] As such, Cole attempted to tie in the under-consumptionist ideas of Hobson with his new emphasis on the need for state action, but rejected the 'Living Wage' proposals of the ILP because they would force the state to take over the running of those inefficient industries which were unable to pay such a wage. Unlike the ILP's strategy, Cole's was not a transitional one; like the Labour leadership he wished to see a socialist society evolve through a period of peaceful transition, not from a deliberate precipitation of capitalist collapse.

Unfortunately for Cole, and arguably for the Labour movement, *The Next Ten Years* arrived too late to have any real impact on the policy of MacDonald's second government. Although Cole sent a copy to both MacDonald and Snowden, there is no suggestion that they ever read the book.[173] Whilst it provoked considerable interest in the Labour movement and in the Labour press, at over 400 pages long the work was unlikely to achieve a very wide readership.[174] It would seem that Cole himself had not envisaged a Labour government in 1929 when he embarked upon the project and had expected that his ideas would have time to be discussed widely before Labour's next term of office. The book was seen by the right as the work of a new convert, and by the left as a betrayal.[175] Beatrice Webb fell into the former category and believed that Cole had finally accepted the inevitable hegemony of Fabianism.[176]

Cole certainly felt himself to be close enough to the official Labour Party line to write *How to Conquer Unemployment*, a short rejoinder to the proposals of Lloyd George, which claimed that the Liberals had stolen their ideas from Labour and that only MacDonald's party was committed to implement them.[177] He also spoke in a number of constituencies during the election campaign.[178] He was convinced that only Labour's programme provided 'both an emergency programme and at least the outline of a sound plan of permanent economic reconstruction'.[179] Cole was pleased by the election result and felt that Labour had won 'every seat in which it could reasonably have been supposed to ... stand a tolerable chance'.[180] Although he held no delusions about how difficult Labour's task would be, he had no reservations with regard to MacDonald's acceptance of office. He realised that the government would be hampered by its parliamentary difficulties but still believed that it was Labour's duty to accept the opportunity to do all that it could to improve Britain's economy and society within these constraints.[181]

NOTES

1 D. E. McHenry, *The Labour Party in Transition, 1931–1938* (London, 1938), p. 309.
2 Note that this was the lowest percentage in the movement's history at that point in time.
3 See, for example, British Library of Political and Economic Science (hereafter BLPES), Passfield Papers, B. Webb's Diary, 28 July 1927.
4 L. Minkin, *The Contentious Alliance: Trade Unions and the Labour Party* (Edinburgh, 1991), p. 11.
5 BLPES, Citrine Papers, I/1/1, 'Notes and Memoirs 1924–35', pp. 16–17.
6 V. L. Allen, *Trade Unions and the Government* (London, 1960), p. 237.
7 Ibid., p. 240.
8 Modern Records Centre, University of Warwick (hereafter MRC), MSS 126/ T&G/4/2/7, B. Tillett, 'Report on the TUC', *The Record*, September 1929, p. 38; MRC, MSS 127/NU/1/1/17, C. T. Cramp, Report to National Union of Railwaymen (NUR) AGM, July 1929, p. 26; MRC, MSS 127/NU/5/12/92, P. H. Collick, *The Locomotive Journal*, October 1929, p. 453.
9 The level of personal antipathy reached such levels that it became a source of great embarrassment to the other members of the GC, who occasionally, but without success, attempted to improve relations. See T. Evans, *Ernest Bevin* (London, 1946), p. 118; BLPES, Citrine Papers, I/7/4, Review of Alan Bullock's biography of Bevin 1960 for *New Dawn*; Lord Citrine, *Men and Work: An Autobiography* (London, 1964), pp. 234–5.

10 MRC, MSS 126/T&G/4/2/5, *The Record*, April 1924.

11 BLPES, Citrine Papers, I/1/1, 'Sidney Webb and the TUC', 29 December 1924.

12 Harvester Press, TUC Pamphlets and Leaflets, Series II, 1897–1930 (Brighton, 1977), *The Future of Trade Unionism*, July 1929.

13 For a brief discussion of the varying viewpoints on the corporatist overtones of the Mond–Turner talks see G. Phillips, 'Trade Unions and Corporatist Politics: The Response of the TUC to Industrial Rationalisation 1927–33', in P. J. Waller (ed.), *Politics and Social Change in Modern Britain* (Brighton, 1987), pp. 192–4.

14 There were of course some fiercely hostile exceptions, most notably the views of sections of the left, voiced in dramatic terms in the Cook–Maxton Manifesto of 21 June 1928.

15 Phillips, 'Trade Unions and Corporatist Politics'.

16 H. Pelling, *A Short History of the Labour Party* (London, 1961), chapter 5.

17 British Newspaper Library (hereafter BNL), *The Miner*, 9 March 1929.

18 South Wales' Coalfield Archive, University of Swansea (hereafter SWCA), A1, Annual Volume of Proceedings 1929–30, Executive Committee, 12 April 1929, Appendix A, 'A. J. Cook's report on meeting with the PLP, 26 March 1929', p. 10.

19 P. Davies, *A. J. Cook* (Manchester, 1987), pp. 167–8.

20 MRC, MSS 126/T&G/4/2/7, *The Record*, September 1928, p. 45.

21 BNL, *The Miner*, General Election Supplement, 25 May 1929, p. 3.

22 MRC, MSS 126/T&G/1/1, General Secretary's Report, 22 May 1929. Bevin's commitment to the success of the campaign is documented elsewhere, for example Public Record Office (hereafter PRO), MacDonald's Papers, PRO 30/69/1174, Bevin to Henderson, 19 March 1929.

23 See, for example, PRO, MacDonald Papers, Diary, PRO 30/69/1753/1, May 1929, and for the rank-and-file view, H. T. Edwards, *Hewn for the Rock* (Cardiff, 1967), p. 75.

24 TUC, *Report of the Sixty-First Annual Trades Union Congress* (London, 1929), p. 254.

25 SWCA, A1, Annual Proceedings 1929–30, President's Address, 22 July 1929, p. 27; MRC, MSS 126/T&G/4/2/7, *The Record*, Editorial, June 1929, p. 323.

26 MRC, MSS 127/NU/1/1/17, NUR Minutes, AGM, President's Address, 'Agenda and Decisions', p. 6.

27 BNL, *The Miner*, 8 June 1929, Editorial, p. 3, and 'Secretary's Review', p. 5.

28 See letter columns of trade union journals, for example MRC, MSS 78/ASW/4/1/9, Journal of the Amalgamated Society of Woodworkers, July 1929, letter from H. V. Davy, Hull, pp. 427–8; MSS 78/NASOHSPD/4/1/9, Journal of the National Amalgamated Society of Operative House and Ship Painters and Decorators (NASOHSPD), September 1929, p. 15.

29 See, for example, MRC, MSS 78/NASOHSPD/4/1/9, NASOHSPD Journal, September 1929, letter from J. Moss, p. 15.

30 MRC, MSS 127/NU/5/12/92, *The Locomotive*, Editorial, July 1929, p. 3.

31 M. A. Hamilton, *The Labour Party Today* (London, n.d., 1938), pp. 62–3.

32 Many regional studies have useful things to say about individual local Labour parties after 1918, but there have been few attempts to assess the overall development of local organisation in the 1920s. The notable exceptions are R. McKibbin, *The Evolution of the Labour Party, 1910–1924* (Oxford, 1974); C. Howard, 'Expectations Born to Death: Local Labour Party Expansion in the 1920s', in J. M. Winter (ed.), *The Working Classes in Modern British History:*

Essays in Honour of Henry Pelling (Cambridge, 1983); M. Savage, *The Dynamics of Working-Class Politics: The Labour Movement in Preston, 1880–1940* (Cambridge, 1987)

33 Although a number of local parties had previously created *ad hoc* individual memberships, officially party members had had to affiliate either through the trade unions or through one of the socialist societies.

34 See Howard, 'Expectations Born to Death', p. 75.

35 G. D. H. Cole, *A History of the Labour Party from 1914* (London, 1948), pp. 140 and 143–4.

36 Savage, *Dynamics of Working-Class Politics*, pp. 194–7.

37 Cole, *History of the Labour Party*, Appendix III, 'Labour Party Membership 1900–46', p. 140.

38 For women and trade unions, see S. Boston, *Women Workers and the Trade Union Movement* (London, 1980) and N. C. Soldon, *Women in British Trade Unions, 1874–1976* (Dublin, 1978).

39 Author's interview with Jack Barnes, former activist in Worthing DLP, Sussex, and district organiser for the NUR, April 1993. A prominent member of the Worthing Executive went under a false name for over a decade.

40 For example, F. Williams, *Fifty Years' March: The Rise of the Labour Party* (London, 1949).

41 BLPES, Passfield Papers, B. Webb's Diary, 19 May 1930.

42 Howard, 'Expectations Born to Death', p. 80.

43 P. M. Graves, *Labour Women: Women in Working-Class Politics, 1918–1939* (Cambridge, 1994), pp. 5–29.

44 Ibid., pp. 30–3.

45 Savage, *Dynamics of Working-Class Politics*, pp. 51–6.

46 For example, Preston, noted by Savage, *Dynamics of Working-Class Politics*, pp. 174–9. Savage argues that in Preston, the women's sections played a key role in the adoption of statist politics by the local party, i.e. support for increased state intervention in health, welfare, education and so on.

47 Graves, *Labour Women*, pp. 156–78.

48 McKibbin, *Evolution*, p. 138; Celia Minoughan, 'The Rise of Labour in Northumberland: The Wansbeck DLP 1918–32', University of Leeds dissertation, Northumberland Record Office, NRO 2973/186, p. 9.

49 Cole, *History of the Labour Party*, p. 220.

50 D. Howell-Thomas, *Socialism in West Sussex: A History of the Chichester Labour Party* (Chichester, 1983), p. 5.

51 F. Bealey, J. Blondel and W. P. McKann, *Constituency Politics: A Study of Newcastle-under-Lyme* (London, 1965), pp. 85–9. It also important to note that Wedgwood played on local issues by allying himself to the strong desire of many in the town not to become part of Stoke.

52 Woolwich Labour Party, E.P. Microfilm (1982), Reel 1, Introduction by Dr R. Eatwell. Of course in boroughs with two seats it was usually one two-member constituency with a single party anyway, so this was not intolerable to head office.

53 Savage, *Dynamics of Working-Class Politics*, p. 198.

54 Sheffield City Archives, Sheffield Brightside DLP, LP(B)5, EC, 30 December 1929; West Sussex Record Office, Chichester DLP, LA/1CH/1/1/1, EC, 18 January 1931.

55 Cole, *History of the Labour Party*, Appendix III, 'Labour Party Membership

1900–46', pp. 480, 87, 223.

56 In 1928 Mosley was giving £450 to the Ladywood division of Birmingham alone, as well as £337 to pay for the Agent's salary in Smethwick; see Borthwick Institute of Historical Research, York, W. Whiteley Papers, UL6/4, Mosley to Whiteley, 25 January 1928.

57 Despite the fact that he left the city to fight Smethwick at a by-election in 1926, and won that seat again in 1929, Mosley's influence on the Birmingham party remained pronounced.

58 N. Mosley, *Rules of the Game: Sir Oswald and Lady Cynthia Mosley, 1896–1933* (London, 1982), p. 91.

59 West Sussex Record Office, Minutes of East Grinstead Labour Party, LA/2MS.

60 Bristol Record Office, Bristol East DLP, ACC 39035/29, Finance Committee 1931–33; Peterborough DLP, E.P. Microfilm (1982), Reel 1, Introduction by K. Laybourn; Bealey, Blondel and McCann, *Constituency Politics*, pp. 85–9.

61 A sizeable proportion of this section is taken from N. Riddell, 'The Catholic Church and the British Labour Party, 1918–1931', *Twentieth Century British History* 8: 2 (1997), 165–93, which explores the relationship between Labour and the Catholic Church in greater depth.

62 S. Fielding, *Class and Ethnicity: Irish Catholics in England, 1880–1939* (Buckingham, 1992).

63 J. Stevenson, *British Society 1914–45* (Harmondsworth, 1984), p. 357.

64 Ibid., p. 357, and A. Hastings, *A History of English Christianity, 1920–1990* (London, 3rd edn, 1991), p. 135.

65 Fielding, *Class and Ethnicity*, pp. 40–8.

66 Ibid., p. 58.

67 Bristol Record Office, Bristol East DLP, ACC 39035/54, Annual Report, 14 February 1930; Greenwich Local History Library, Greenwich DLP, Annual Meeting, 18 July 1929, recorded that membership was up by 1,500 to 2,783 over the previous year,.

68 BNL, *Birmingham Town Crier*, 31 May 1929.

69 South Shields Labour Party, E.P. Microfilm (1979), Reel 1, Minutes of the Party and Council, 4 June 1929, pp. 373–4.

70 Working Class Movement Library, Salford, *The Nelson Gazette*, Editorial, 4 June 1929, p. 2.

71 BNL, *Birmingham Town Crier*, 'From the Watchtower', 7 June 1929, p. 1.

72 PRO, MacDonald Papers, Diary, PRO 30/69/1752/1, 1 June 1929.

73 BNL, *Leeds Weekly Citizen*, 19 July 1929.

74 *Daily Herald*, 14 June 1929.

75 E. Thurtle, *Times Winged Chariot: Memoirs and Comments* (London, 1945), p. 111

76 J. Lee, *This Great Journey* (New York, 1942), p. 118.

77 R. T. McKenzie, *British Political Parties: The Distribution of Power Within the Conservative and Labour Parties* (London, 2nd edn, 1963), pp. 386–91.

78 Ibid., pp. 407–12. McKenzie argues that, as a consequence of its acceptance of the conventions of the Cabinet and parliamentary system, it was inevitable that effective power in the Labour Party would pass to the PLP and to the parliamentary leadership in particular.

79 Ibid., pp. 405–7, and Cole, *History of the Labour Party*, p. 52.

80 1918 constitution, 5.1, in Cole, *History of the Labour Party*, p. 74

81 L. Minkin, *The Labour Party Conference: A Study in the Politics of Intra-Party*

Democracy (London, 1978), pp. 8–9.

82 McKenzie, *Political Parties*, pp. 407–8.

83 Ibid., pp. 431–2 and 417.

84 E. Wertheimer, *Portrait of the Labour Party* (London, 1929), p. 10.

85 The Standing Orders of the PLP included a 'conscience clause' which allowed MPs to refrain from voting with the party in particular instances. Members were also allowed to have a free vote on Private Members' Bills and on the few motions that did not affect party policy; see McHenry, *The Labour Party in Transition*, pp. 167–8.

86 Note that 287 is the correct figure for the number of seats won by Labour at the May 1929 General Election; 288 or 289 is often given, but this is derived from the inclusion of Neil Maclean, who fought Govan as an 'Independent Labour' candidate, and was not endorsed by the NEC until August 1930, and Sir William Jowitt, who fought Preston as a Liberal before coming over to Labour in June.

87 Cole, *History of the Labour Party*, p. 220.

88 For the purpose of brevity, the term Maxtonite is used to refer to the radical core of the parliamentary ILP, although John Wheatley was of at least equal import as a leader of the group before his death in May 1930.

89 R. E. Dowse, *Left in the Centre: The Independent Labour Party, 1893–1940* (London, 1966), p. 35.

90 G. Foote, *The Labour Party's Political Thought: A History* (London, 1985), pp. 133–7.

91 Dowse, *Left in the Centre*, pp. 124–7 and 136.

92 Ibid., p. 152.

93 Brynmor Jones Library, University of Hull (hereafter BJL), D. Chater, *Autobiography*, unpublished, p. 35, describes the problems encountered in finding an occupation after losing his Hammersmith South seat in 1931. Lee, *This Great Journey*, p. 140, also comments on this problem.

94 See, for example, Thurtle, *Times Winged Chariot*, p. 111; BJL, D. Chater, *Autobiography*, unpublished, p. 157; Lee, *This Great Journey*, p. 115, P. Snowden, *An Autobiography, Vol. 2: 1919–1934* (London, 1934), p. 755.

95 Laski to Holmes, 16 June 1923, in M. D. Howe (ed.), *Holmes–Laski Letters, Vol. 2* (Cambridge, 1953).

96 H. Dalton, *Call Back Yesterday: Memoirs, 1887–1931* (London, 1953), p. 195.

97 D. Marquand, *The Progressive Dilemma* (London, 1991); D. Blaazer, *The Popular Front and the Progressive Tradition: Socialists, Liberals and the Quest for Unity, 1884–1939* (Cambridge, 1992).

98 Foote, *The Labour Party's Political Thought*, pp. 1–14.

99 Labour Party, *Annual Report 1923* (London, 1923), p. 178.

100 Cole, *History of the Labour Party*, p. 124.

101 Under the 1918 constitution, local parties were able to nominate their own candidates to the NEC, but, since there was a joint vote with the trade unions, it was the unions who had monopolised these elections.

102 D. Marquand, *Ramsay MacDonald* (London, 1977), p. 410.

103 Much of this caricature derives from H. G. Wells's caustic portrayal of the Webbs in *The New Machiavelli* (London, 1910). Two generations later, Anthony Crosland was similarly damning with his famous remark that 'total abstinence and a good filing system are not now the right signposts to the Socialist Utopia'; quoted in L. Radice, *Beatrice and Sidney Webb* (London, 1984), pp. 1–2. More

recently, K. O. Morgan has suggested that the Webbs were the archetypal middle-class bureaucrats who saw socialism as being more about order than about people: *Labour People: Hardie to Kinnock* (Oxford, 2nd edn, 1992), p. 60.

104 M. Cole, *Beatrice Webb's Diaries, 1912–24* (London, 1952), p. 99.

105 N. Dennis and R. H. Halsey, *English Ethical Socialism: Thomas More to R. H. Tawney* (Oxford, 1988) are open admirers of Tawney's work and award him the epithet of 'the great modern master of ethical socialism' (p. 2). R. Terrill, *R. H. Tawney and His Times: Socialism as Fellowship* (Cambridge, 1973) and A. Wright, *R. H. Tawney* (Manchester, 1987) are a little more critical, but the only major critical reappraisal has been that of W. H. Greenleaf, *The British Political Tradition, Vol. 2: The Ideological Heritage* (London, 1983), pp. 439–63. Greenleaf suggests that Tawney's work was almost wholly derivative, and quotes approvingly the comment of A. MacIntyre, 'The Socialism of R. H. Tawney' (1964) in *Against the Self-Images of the Age: Essays on Ideology and Philosophy* (London, 1971), pp. 38–41, that Tawney's philosophy was characterised by 'cliché ridden high-mindedness and banal earnestness'.

106 M. Cole, *The Story of Fabian Socialism* (London, 1961), p. 187. By 1948, the book had been reprinted fourteen times.

107 R. H. Tawney, *The Acquisitive Society* (London, 1921), pp. 17–32.

108 Ibid., p. 33

109 Ibid., pp. 36–58.

110 Greenleaf, *The Ideological Heritage*, p. 454.

111 Tawney, *The Acquisitive Society*, p. 80.

112 Ibid., p. 82–127.

113 Foote, *The Labour Party's Political Thought*, p. 79.

114 Greenleaf, *The Ideological Heritage*, p. 452.

115 Foote, *The Labour Party's Political Thought*, p. 76.

116 R. H. Tawney, *Equality* (London, 1931), p. 68.

117 Ibid., p. 87.

118 Ibid., pp. 126–50.

119 Ibid., p. 185.

120 Tawney and his wife were on good social terms with the Webbs in the 1920s. See BLPES, Passfield Papers, B. Webb's Diary, 2 January 1928.

121 Tawney, *Equality*, pp. 40–1.

122 BLPES, Passfield Papers, B. Webb's Diary, 1 December 1926.

123 Tawney had been a key player in the landmark report on adult education published by the Lloyd George government's Social Reconstruction Committee in 1919 and was the most dynamic individual on Labour's new Advisory Committee on Education.

124 Ibid., p. 71. Tawney, in line with his general rejection of materialism in his private life, was famous for the continual wearing of a pair of khaki army trousers. If MacDonald had made the offer, however, it seems highly unlikely that Tawney would have accepted since he had a lifelong aversion to the honours system, and turned down the offer of a peerage on at least one subsequent occasion, in 1935.

125 BLPES, Passfield Papers, B. Webb's Diary, 5 July 1928.

126 PRO, MacDonald Papers, PRO 30/69/1174, Tawney to Henderson, 31 January 1929.

127 PRO, MacDonald Papers, PRO 30/69/1174, Tawney to MacDonald, 22 March 1929.

128 PRO, MacDonald Papers, PRO 30/69/1174, MacDonald to Tawney, 22 March 1929. In the final outcome, it would seem that most of the election manifesto was written by Snowden. See PRO, MacDonald Papers, PRO 30/69/1174, Tawney to Arnold, 25 May 1929.

129 MacDonald was looking for someone 'with an experienced political mind and who has the facts of our main issues pretty well at his finger ends – one also who has a little bit of imagination so as to give me suggestions how to handle the same subject in a fresh way day after day'. PRO, MacDonald Papers, PRO 30/69/672, MacDonald to P. Noel-Baker, 10 April 1929.

130 PRO, MacDonald Papers, PRO 30/69/1174, Tawney to Arnold, 25 May 1929.

131 I. Kramnick and B. Sheerman, *Harold Laski: A Life on the Left* (London, 1993) and M. Newman, *Harold Laski: A Political Biography* (Basingstoke, 1993). These two studies have provided a wealth of new information upon Laski and have superseded K. Martin's personal assessment, *Harold Laski* (London, 1953), G. Eastwood's work of near hagiography, *Harold Laski* (London, 1977) and B. Zylstra, *From Pluralism to Collectivism: The Development of Harold Laski's Political Thought* (Assem, 1968), which concentrates upon the changed emphasis in Laski's political ideology in the inter-war period. W. H. Greenleaf, 'Laski and British Socialism', *History of Political Thought* 2: 3 (1981), 573–90, argues that there is more consistency in Laski's political thought than is often suggested.

132 Newman, *Harold Laski*, p. 48.

133 Quoted in Kramnick and Sheerman, *Harold Laski*, p. 123.

134 Ibid., p. 212.

135 H. Laski, *A Grammar of Politics* (London, 1925), p. 25. Laski and Tawney were very different in their temperaments and were never to be close friends. However, Laski clearly had a great deal of respect for his LSE contemporary and for his work; in a 1925 review article, Laski described *The Acquisitive Society* as 'the most influential English book of the last fifteen years'; Kramnick and Sheerman, *Harold Laski*, p. 238.

136 Laski, *Grammar*, chapter 9, 'Economic Institutions', pp. 433–540.

137 Ibid., chapter 10, 'The Judicial Process', pp. 541–86.

138 S. Webb was so impressed by it that he told Laski that he was intending to celebrate his birthday in July 1925 with 'another read of your great book'; BJL, Laski Papers, DLA/8, S. Webb to Laski, 13 July 1925. J. Callaghan later recalled the tremendous impact which the book had on him as a youth; foreword to Eastwood, *Harold Laski*.

139 Laski, *Grammar*, pp. 534–5.

140 Newman, *Harold Laski*, p. 99.

141 'Present Tendencies in British Politics', *New Republic*, 13 July 1927, cited in Newman, *Harold Laski*, pp. 100–1.

142 *New Republic*, 24 November 1929, cited in Kramnick and Sheerman, *Harold Laski*, pp. 256–7. Not surprisingly, the Labour leader was far from pleased by this attack and wrote to Laski both to refute his criticisms and to berate him for publishing such critiques in foreign publications; BJL, Laski Papers, DLA/43, MacDonald to Laski, 21 November 1927.

143 Ibid., pp. 257, 259.

144 PRO, MacDonald Papers, PRO 30/69/1714, MacDonald to Laski, 16 April 1929.

145 Laski to Holmes, 21 May 1929, in Howe (ed.), *Holmes–Laski Letters*; BLPES, Passfield Papers, B. Webb's Diary, 1 June 1929.

146 Cited in Newman, *Harold Laski*, p. 77.
147 See the introduction to N. Riddell, '"The Age of Cole"? G. D. H. Cole and the British Labour Movement 1929–1933', *Historical Journal* 38: 4 (1995), 933–57, from which the bulk of this section is taken.
148 We still unfortunately await a comprehensive study of this much-overlooked socialist theory; the best available treatment is to be found in A. W. Wright, *G. D. H. Cole and Socialist Democracy* (Oxford, 1979). Foote, *The Labour Party's Political Thought*, pp. 102–25 is a useful summary.
149 For more detail, see Riddell, '"The Age of Cole"?', p. 936.
150 See M. Cole, *The Life of G. D. H. Cole* (London, 1971), pp. 120–3.
151 BLPES, Passfield Papers, B. Webb's Diary, 17 May 1924.
152 BLPES, Passfield Papers, B. Webb's Diary, 5 September 1926.
153 Cole, *G. D. H. Cole*, p. 162.
154 'Trade Unionism and the Future', *New Statesman* 31 (1928), 688.
155 'Trade Unionism and Politics', *New Statesman* 31 (1928), 721.
156 'The Labour Party and the Nation', *New Statesman* 32 (1928–29), 4.
157 'Trade Unionism and the Labour Party', *New Statesman* 33 (1929), 74.
158 Wright, *G. D. H. Cole*, pp. 119–22.
159 G. D. H. Cole, *The Next Ten Years in British Social and Economic Policy* (London, 1929), p. 17.
160 Ibid., pp. 19–20 and p. 160.
161 Ibid., pp. 164–70.
162 Ibid., p. 46.
163 In an attempt to revitalise their flagging fortunes, the Liberal Party led by Lloyd George had set up an Industrial Inquiry in 1928 composed of politicians and economists which resulted in the famous 'Yellow Book' or *Britain's Industrial Future*, a grandiose scheme for government intervention in the economy. Cole differed from most of their suggestions in that he wanted the scope of intervention to be much wider and to be aimed at a redistribution of wealth.
164 Cole, *The Next Ten Years*, p. 50.
165 Ibid., pp. 55–64.
166 For a typical union response to the idea of the national labour corps see the review of *The Next Ten Years*, BNL, *Cotton Factory Times*, 3 January 1930.
167 Cole, *The Next Ten Years*, pp. 226–42.
168 Ibid., pp. 219, 74.
169 Ibid., p. 242.
170 Ibid., pp. 130–56.
171 Ibid., pp. 32–5, 108–9.
172 Ibid., pp. 178–88.
173 Cole, *G. D. H. Cole*, p. 165.
174 See, for example, reviews in *Glasgow Forward*, 10 August 1929; BNL, *The Miner*, 1 June 1929, and BNL, *Cotton Factory Times*, 10 January 1930.
175 See *Labour Monthly*, July 1929; H. Gaitskell in *Highway*, November 1929, and H. Laski, 'If G. D. H. Cole were Premier', *New Leader*, 7 June 1929.
176 B. Webb, *Fabian News*, December 1929.
177 Marquand, *Ramsay MacDonald*, p. 485.
178 Cole, *G. D. H. Cole*, p. 167.
179 'The Two Problems of Unemployment', *New Statesman* 32 (1928–29), 784.
180 'Second Thoughts on the Election', *New Statesman* 33 (1929), 205.
181 'Mr Thomas's Task', *New Statesman* 33 (1929), 297.

2

The trade unions

The honeymoon

The trade unions were generally contented with the record of the government during its first months in office. Whilst some unionists felt that legislation was insufficiently bold and that the government was taking too long to introduce vital reforms, their leaders urged the need for patience. At the TUC in September 1929, Arthur Hayday urged the membership not to harass the government too soon, stressing that it must be given time to implement its programme.[1] A. J. Cook and William Thorne, the General Secretary of the NUGMW, both placed a similar emphasis on the need for restraint, as did Bevin.[2] The confident outlines which ministers gave of their plans at the Labour Conference in October were well received by the trade union delegates. The National Amalgamated Society of Operative House and Ship Painters and Decorators (NASOHSPD) journal wrote of 'a good, a happy, useful and a largely unanimous conference, composed of men and women who ... felt that their ends and aims were in the right hands',[3] and *The Miner* described the addresses of Henderson and Snowden as 'two of the most remarkable speeches ever heard'.[4] *The Locomotive* compared the government to 'a hive of industrious bees'.[5] *The Record*'s 'Man in the Gallery' implied that a new era had arrived: 'The House of Commons is sometimes called the House of Patience, but Labour is altering this and with the help of its rank-and-file will make it a "House of Performance".' Further, the journal predicted that: 'nothing is more certain than that if there were a General Election tomorrow Labour would be returned with an overwhelming majority'.[6]

A number of unions also expressed satisfaction with the change in government departments. The Admiralty, War Office and the Ministries of Health and Labour were singled out for their more favourable approach towards complaints and receiving deputations.[7] A. J. Cook was impressed by the 'human touch' of Margaret Bondfield and by the fact that the miners had been able to meet the Minister of Health, Arthur Greenwood, within twenty-four hours of the government's formation and the Prime Minister in less than forty-eight hours.[8] In the field of domestic legislation, the unions were pleased with the Bill to end profiteering and with the abolition of the seven-year limit on war pensions.[9] Even Bevin, although frustrated already by the limitations imposed by its minority status, was pleased with the government's achievements during its first six months. In a mood of astounding optimism, he confidently predicted that Labour would secure at least ten million votes at the next general election.[10]

The major disappointment in the first six months was housing legislation. Both the Amalgamated Society of Woodworkers (ASW) and NASOHSPD had hoped to see a return to the 1924 Wheatley subsidy for house-building, but Greenwood, no doubt constrained by Snowden, was only able to reintroduce the subsidy at a reduced rate. For two unions suffering badly from the lack of house construction this represented a considerable blow. Frank Wolstencroft, General Secretary of ASW, felt that the full subsidy could have been introduced without major Tory and Liberal resistance.[11] None the less, even the ASW was prepared to accept that the government had achieved a considerable amount in its first six months in office.[12]

Government successes in foreign affairs attracted considerable union attention and praise. Many unions had a strongly internationalist outlook.[13] This was the result of both moralistic and materialistic calculations. Besides a genuine belief in the need for workers' solidarity, the unions also looked forward to the positive effects that international 'pacification' could have on their own trades. Henderson was applauded for his work on disarmament, the signing of the 'Optional Clause' at the League of Nations and for the re-establishment of relations with the USSR.[14] MacDonald's visit to the USA in the summer of 1929 attracted similar acclaim. Even Citrine marvelled at the Premier's skilful handling of the Americans, writing in February 1930 that 'businessmen who are supposed to be insured against the tricks of the orator were more or less helpless against MacDonald's masterly personality'.[15] The piece of 'diplomacy' which really caught the imagination of the unions, however, was Snowden's stand at The Hague in the summer of 1929. Snowden's refusal to allow a reduction in Britain's share of reparations appealed to the 'John Bull' spirit often found in abundance in many unions. *The Record* enthused that Snowden had 'proved to the people of Great Britain that their interests were far safer in Labour's hands than in those of its predecessors'.[16] Many union journals spoke in similarly reverential tones and W. M. Pickles of NASOHSPD suggested that 'generations of our own class still unborn will benefit by Snowden's diplomacy in spite of capitalist exploitation'.[17]

With the abrupt ending of the government's honeymoon period in early 1930, however, there was a rapid deterioration in trade union/government relations. Faced with economic depression, and the difficulties associated with implementing more contentious legislation, the government's relationship with the unions became more uneasy and the fundamental tensions, outlined in Chapter 1, now rose to the surface. Initially, the unions were prepared to suppress and rationalise their dissatisfactions in the interests of the government, but during the course of 1930 they were to find it progressively more difficult to remain silent.

Government appointments

The unions had not been altogether satisfied with the composition of the Cabinet. Only six members of the Cabinet were union-sponsored, as opposed to seven in 1924: Henderson; Thomas; Clynes; Bondfield; William Adamson, the Secretary of State for Scotland; and Tom Shaw, who became Secretary of State for War (see Appendix 2). Whilst these included three of the five most important positions in the government, the two highest offices of state, namely Prime Minister and the Chancellor of the Exchequer, were in the hands of non-trade unionists. Most controversial of these appointments was the placing of Margaret Bondfield in the Ministry of Labour. Although a prominent union figure for many years and a former TUC President, many in the GC doubted Bondfield's suitability for this most difficult of roles. No doubt there was an element of chauvinism here, but, in addition, some had never forgiven Bondfield for her participation on the Blanesburgh Committee from November 1925.[18] The TUC had hoped to see either Thomas or Henderson placed in the role, but Citrine's protests to MacDonald were not well-received.[19]

The appointment of Emanuel Shinwell to the position of Parliamentary Secretary to the Mines Department in June 1930 proved to be equally unpopular with a number of unions, not least the MFGB. Shinwell had made a number of speeches before the 1929 election guaranteed to arouse TUC hostility, in which he condemned the General Strike and suggested there was no guarantee that the Trade Disputes Act would be repealed by a future Labour government.[20] It is possible that this influenced MacDonald's initial decision to make Shinwell junior War Minister, rather than return him to the Mines Department where he had been in 1924, although it would seem unlikely in view of the fact that MacDonald did not take kindly to any form of TUC interference. What is clear, however, is that the move in June 1930 was badly received by the MFGB. In an article in *The Miner*, Cook stressed the strong belief of the union that a miner should be placed in this position.[21]

Poor relations

As outlined in Chapter 1, the GC held firm expectations of close government/
TUC relations. The TUC was felt to have a right to regular and direct consultation on industrial policy and to be given a general outline of the government's legislative timetable and its wider policy aims. It was expected that
requests for consultation and representatives for committees would be
directed through the GC and it was hoped that ministers would consent to
easy access for trade unionists. The unions believed this was asking the bare
minimum of a government they had been instrumental in creating.

Citrine was particularly concerned that the deterioration of relations
which had occurred in 1924 should not be repeated. Consequently, immediately the government was formed, he tried to establish a defined format for
contacts. On 5 June he met Henderson and expressed his desire for regular
meetings with the Cabinet. The Foreign Secretary, however, was keen to avoid
any commitment. Although he responded with some interest to Citrine's idea
that the General Secretary and Chairman of the TUC should meet MacDonald
regularly on an informal basis, Henderson concluded that Citrine should
write to the Prime Minister on the subject.[22] In the subsequent letter of 5
June, Citrine argued that close co-operation was in everyone's interest.[23] Privately, he summed-up the TUC outlook in simple terms: 'Everyone knows that
we are connected with the Labour Party ... Why try to hide it?' MacDonald's
reply, however, was dismissive, suggesting that such a close relationship would
leave the government open to the criticism that it was being run by an 'outside body'. In a typical piece of temporisation, the Prime Minister asked
Citrine to raise the matter 'later ... when I have time to attend to it'.[24]

MacDonald's fear of accusations of TUC dictation was shared by his colleagues. When Henderson put Citrine's request for liaison before the NEC on 5
June, the meeting agreed unanimously that it should be rejected.[25] There was
some justification for the government's fears; newspapers such as the *Daily
Mail* and, more subtly, *The Times* were quick to interpret any TUC contacts
with the government as evidence that the unions were pulling MacDonald's
strings, and ministers were understandably concerned to retain a degree of
freedom in a difficult parliamentary situation.[26] None the less, the Prime Minister's outlook did appear to be bordering on paranoia. If he had consented to
regular informal meetings he would not have been committing the government to anything but would have gone a long way to pacify the TUC regardless, and it is difficult to conceive that the opposition would have brought the
government down on the issue.

By refusing to allow regular meetings the government undoubtedly created more problems than it solved; not only did Citrine feel slighted but it
fuelled GC suspicions that the government had something to hide. On 12

August 1929 Walter Milne-Bailey concluded that MacDonald's fears were unfounded and with regard to industrial policy he found it 'almost incredible that the government should propose to go ahead on any of these matters without prior discussion of an informal kind with representatives of the General Council'.[27] Bevin was equally perturbed by the prospect of what he referred to as a 'slipshod arrangement' and believed that the TUC should be treated as a 'consultative body on industrial questions'.[28] Citrine had little choice but to accept the government's attitude for the time being, but would continue to press for consultation and use any contacts inside the government, even civil servants, to attempt to keep abreast of events.[29] Despite a tacit arrangement made at the 1929 Labour Conference that a small group from the GC should meet occasionally with Clynes for informal talks, this too failed to develop into a permanent arrangement.[30]

As a result of its refusal to make a formal commitment, government procedure for the drafting of industrial legislation took on a spontaneous dimension and varied according to the department and the minister concerned. The unions continued to press for the issue of draft Bills but on most occasions their appeals were rejected. Citrine tried in vain to persuade Clynes to release the details of his Factories Bill.[31] Bondfield was similarly reluctant to release draft proposals, yet Herbert Morrison allowed the TUC to see his proposed Road Traffic Bill, and William Graham, President of the Board of Trade, was prepared to let the miners see the general outline of his Mines Bill in November 1929.[32] This inconsistency of attitude understandably added to the TUC frustration towards those departments which refused consultation and did imply a definite lack of co-ordination from 10 Downing Street.

In addition to meetings with the government, theoretically the unions had their own MPs to keep them aware of government policy. Union-sponsored MPs, however, were generally more committed to the PLP than to the union movement and some unions complained of an increasing detachment.[33] For some of these individuals the pomp and prestige of parliamentary life proved attractive and a number enjoyed the opportunities for the high life which the position offered. J. H. Thomas was the paradigm of this phenomenon, portrayed perpetually by the cartoonist, Strube, in the evening attire of the social climber.[34] Those who were in the government had little time to devote to union matters. For a union like the NUGMW, the election of the government meant the loss of its two most prominent officials, which was considered a sizeable sacrifice on the union's behalf. The slow emergence of a trade union group in the Commons also suggested a lack of solidarity. Citrine was uncertain whether such an arrangement existed by July 1929,[35] and the meetings of this group thereafter proved to be erratic.[36] Moreover, since a considerable number of prominent unionists were not to be found within this collective, the TUC did not regard its existence as in any way a substitute for regular GC consultation with the government.

Informal social contacts were even less satisfactory. MacDonald and Snowden did not find the idea of small talk with trade unionists very appealing, Thomas was busy wrestling with unemployment, and Henderson, the one Cabinet minister most likely to be concerned to maintain social links, spent a great deal of his time wrapped up in foreign affairs. It is clear that MacDonald hoped that Henderson, with his long experience as Party Secretary, would be able to play the co-ordinating role in the movement in which he had been so successful since 1918. Henderson was not able to do so, however, not because he was alienated by what he regarded as the increasing unreasonableness of the TUC, but through lack of time.[37] The rest of the Labour leadership feared that small talk would turn to business and their wish to avoid this scenario became more intense as government problems became more formidable. Significantly, this was a Cabinet whose members were loath to socialise with each other, never mind the rest of the movement. For a time, MacDonald did seem concerned to maintain links. In November 1929 he expressed his regret over detachment from 'old friends' and the result was a GC dinner party at 10 Downing Street on 27 November. Ironically, however, the Prime Minister seems to have spent little time in attendance.[38] Despite his repetition of such sentiments of detachment to Citrine in January 1931, MacDonald made no overtures for similar social gatherings.[39] In truth, his growing contempt for a number of unions by 1931, together with the fact that his already full agenda was occupying all of his waking hours, would suggest that dinner parties for the GC were pretty low on his list of priorities.[40]

During its dealings with the government, the TUC developed varying opinions of the different ministerial departments. Bevin was often to emphasise what he saw as the destructive effect of civil servants on government legislation. He was deeply distrustful of the Ministry of Labour, in particular, and felt that Bondfield had done little to reduce its hostility to the TUC. Privately, he felt that she was in the hands of her civil servants, particularly the formidable Permanent Secretary, Sir Horace Wilson, who Bevin suggested was 'paralysing t[he] Government'.[41] Citrine and others on the GC shared Bevin's reservations and this was detrimental to the atmosphere in which relations were conducted.[42]

Committees

Government inconsistency over the appointment of trade unionists to committees was glaring. The TUC expected the government to respect the protocol that all requests for union representatives should be submitted to the GC. Yet in July 1929 the government sent invitations direct to Bevin and Arthur Pugh requesting them to join the Colonial Development Committee and the Consultative Committee on Employment Schemes. In August etiquette was again ignored when Snowden issued a personal invitation to the Assistant General Secretary of the TUC, A. S. Firth, to sit on the Royal Commission on the Civil Service. As a sign of protest, the GC rejected the offer, with the result that protocol was observed when Snowden asked the GC for representatives to sit on the Macmillan Committee on Finance and Industry in October 1929 and when MacDonald wanted trade unionists appointed to the Economic Advisory Council (EAC) in February 1930. Yet the TUC was once again to be angered by the ill-considered approaches of Bondfield to secure trade union representatives for the Holman Gregory Commission in December 1930, and, in protest, resolved to boycott the commission. Not until 28 January 1931 did the GC consent to give evidence to the commission, and then only with extreme reluctance.[43]

The GC was aggrieved also by several non-union appointments made to government committees. Citrine was dismayed to discover that in December 1929 MacDonald was considering the appointment of Sir Lynden MacCassey to the EAC.[44] MacCassey had been involved in labour dilution during the First World War as head of the Shipyard Labour Department and had also been appointed to oppose Bevin during the Shaw Inquiry of 1920. As such, it is difficult to conceive of a figure more unpopular in union circles. This was not the only instance of MacDonald paying no attention to union sensibilities. In September 1930 the ASW journal complained bitterly that the present Chairman of the Public Works Loans Committee, Lord Hunsdon, who had suggested in 1926 that it was legitimate to starve the miners into submission, was to be reappointed by the government for a further five years.[45] The GC was uncomfortable also with some of those appointed to the EAC, the Holman Gregory Commission and especially the 1931 May Committee, which did not appear to be constituted in order to consider all viewpoints.[46] This dissatisfaction with appointees to committees was both a cause and a reflection of a growing government detachment from the concerns of the union movement.

The use of joint trade union and Labour Party committees by the government can best be described as erratic. A few were set up or continued after the formation of the government, principally to discuss disarmament, unemployment insurance, family allowances and the 'living wage'. It was also agreed that the GC would meet the NEC every month, but as time went on the gaps between the meetings became notably longer. At the final meeting of the two executives before the fall of the government on 23 June 1931, there had been no joint meeting for seven months.[47] Increasingly it appeared that Henderson was the only prominent government member concerned that these meetings should take place. On 29 May 1930 the GC and NEC met over the Trade Disputes Bill only as a result of the Foreign Secretary's suggestion.[48]

MacDonald predictably disliked the concept of the joint committee.[49]

The history of the National Joint Council (NJC) illustrates better than anything else the woeful lack of government/union co-ordination. Deeply concerned over the lack of consultation, in February 1930 the GC wrote to J. S. Middleton, the Acting Secretary of the Labour Party, urging a revitalisation of the NJC and a radical alteration of its constitution. Wishing to ensure the maximum possible union input, the GC called for the reconstruction to include six members of the TUC and six drawn from the NEC and PLP, together with the Chairman of the TUC and the Secretary of the Labour Party.[50] This would represent a doubling of union membership at the expense of party representation. Predictably, MacDonald was quick to take this opportunity to step down as one of the representatives.[51] On 24 March 1930 the GC received a letter from the NEC agreeing to the reconstitution, and finally on 27 May 1930 the NJC met for the first time since 8 December 1927. In a brief meeting, the new constitution was discussed and agreed upon and the hope was expressed by the TUC that the NJC would enable 'Labour to speak with one voice on all questions of national importance'. The NJC would aim to consider all questions relevant to the Labour movement and resolve a common policy through discussion. In addition, it was agreed that meetings were to be held 'at least once each quarter', and the next meeting was arranged for 22 July 1930. Yet ironically, the next meeting of the Council occurred in very different circumstances, for the NJC was not to meet again until 7 December 1931.[52]

The chief reason for the failure of the NJC was a lack of government will to make it an effective co-ordinating body. Despite its rhetorical promises, it was not prepared to devote the necessary time to achieve this transformation. At the TUC of 1929, the Fraternal Delegate, J. Compton, MP, had talked of the 'development of the machinery of the NJC' and had stated that the Congress should look forward to it becoming 'a cabinet of the Labour movement'.[53] It is difficult to comprehend how Compton could make such high-minded predictions for a body which had not even met for two years; what is clear is that the real commitment of the government to the NJC was nowhere near as strong as he suggested. When Henderson proposed on 23 October 1929 that the issues of disarmament and unemployment should be passed over to the NJC to discuss, 'it was felt in some quarters that this would occasion delay'.[54] Essentially, the NEC was loath to discuss these issues with members of the GC for fear of the difference of opinion that would result. Whilst the government had little time to ensure that the body functioned effectively, union resentment is easily comprehensible in light of the promises that had been made. The failure to rejuvenate the NJC was deeply symbolic of the gulf which was opening up between the two halves of the Labour movement by the middle of 1930.

Legislation

By mid-1930 the trade union movement was extremely disappointed with the lack of government success on domestic policy. As early as 24 January 1930 Citrine told the Prime Minister:

> We cannot disguise from ourselves that our movement is uneasy. The Government's very notable achievements in matters of foreign policy have been brought into parallel with its achievements in domestic policy and a rather invidious comparison is being made ... so frequently and so pointedly that it is very difficult indeed to explain to the lay mind why the Government has been so limited.[55]

In particular, the GC was dismayed by the lack of progress on the Trade Disputes Bill and the ratification of the Washington Convention. Although appreciative of the limitations imposed by lack of parliamentary time, which MacDonald was eager to impress upon them,[56] and of the obstacles created by its minority position, the GC still felt the government was not doing everything that it might to honour its election pledges. Bevin believed that a lack of courage was to blame and was already commenting on low union morale by January 1930:

> If the Washington Convention ... and the Trade Disputes Act is not introduced this session ... there will be terrible disappointment in the ranks of the real solid Trade Unionists. They have been led to expect it.... If you are defeated on any issue and if you go to the country again, you will have a very poor defence after all the speeches we have made.... We want something to fight about.... What we want is a first-class Parliamentary scrap ...[57]

The GC feared that the government was not going to proceed on the Factories Bill, the Trade Disputes Act or the Washington Convention. As Bevin's comments reveal, the GC was concerned not only that the government would be tarnished in the eyes of the rank-and-file, but also that its own reputation would be damaged. The TUC decided, therefore, that it must continue to pressurise the government on these issues at every opportunity. In addition, the GC was concerned that the government was not prioritising the right bills. In January 1930 Citrine expressed disquiet that the government was moving ahead on slum clearance and land reclamation whilst the Trade Disputes Act and the Washington Convention, which remained top of the TUC's list, remained absent from the legislative programme.[58] Speaking on behalf of the whole GC, Bevin concluded in his statement to MacDonald on 24 January 1930:

> No one desires to see the impossible.... None of us have criticised you publicly ... but what we are concerned with ... is our fate ... because it is comparatively easy to defend a Labour Government, having regard to its difficulties, in the first seven

months, but it is not quite so easy to defend the disappointment in the second seven months.[59]

Despite the cathartic benefits of this meeting, however, and the government's assurances that it was pleased to hear the attitudes of the TUC so frankly expressed, the practical repercussions were limited.

Coal-mining

The difference in legislative priorities was potentially a great source of conflict between the unions and the government. The unions generally expected that the government would be able to manoeuvre the promised reforms through Parliament undiluted and true to the principles on which they were founded. Although they understood the government's parliamentary situation was problematic, the TUC was often guilty of a failure to understand just how difficult a task the government faced. The problems encountered in the implementation of legislation for the coal industry illustrate these tensions most vividly. Not only had the government to consider the position of the Conservatives and the Liberals, but also of the coalowners and the miners, two of the most inflexible organisations in British industry. Amicable compromises were extremely difficult to obtain, with the consequence that on more than one occasion the failure to reach agreement on coal threatened the very existence of the government.

The need for reform of the British coal industry had been evident to most informed observers since 1918. The reasons for the decline of the industry were connected not only with the shortcomings in organisation, but also with a structural fall in the demand for British coal around the world. Drastic reorganisation was essential if British mining was to have any chance of halting its long-term decline. Few of those in the industry, however, accepted the inescapable reality that, however efficient, coal-mining would never be able to employ as many individuals as it had done in 1914. Although it believed nationalisation offered the only real solution, the government decided, in view of its minority position, that a process of 'rationalisation' would be the best policy in the short term. This would involve a streamlining of production processes through the creation of large industrial units, together with the limitation of unnecessary labour and old machinery, and had already been apparently successful in Germany and the United States. This approach had been accepted tentatively by the Labour movement as a general industrial policy during the period 1927–29. By late 1929 and early 1930, however, union attitudes had changed fundamentally.[60] The rapidly deteriorating economic situation meant that retention of employment had once again become the top union priority and any job losses were now regarded as unacceptable.

The major stumbling block to the implementation of mining legislation was the Mining Association of Great Britain, a notoriously conservative body representing mineowners, which was opposed to the reintroduction of a seven-hour day, national wage agreements and a National Wages Board. It believed that any reduction in the working day would not aid the industry, and the maximum that it was prepared to concede was a half-hour reduction. In return, it expected the right to reduce wages where it was felt necessary, the introduction of a national quota system to avoid over-production and an export subsidy for coal to improve its international competitiveness. In addition, many of the owners favoured an extension of the 'five counties scheme' employed in Yorkshire, Lancashire and the Midlands to control prices on a national basis.[61]

The government decided to construct a Cabinet committee under the chairmanship of William Graham. It proved impossible to sit all parties around one table and therefore consultation had to be conducted with the MFGB and Mining Association separately.[62] Such was the level of suspicion that it was decided to take verbatim minutes at all meetings in order that there might be no discrepancy over what had been said.[63] As a result proceedings became very protracted and the original plan to introduce a Bill by November had to be dropped. This produced some frustration but the majority of miners accepted that it was the owners and not the government who were the obstacle to progress. Delegates at the MFGB Annual Conference at the end of July agreed that the seven-hour day policy was the ideal one but differed over their attitudes to compromise. Some felt the miners must ensure the survival of the government, but others felt that the principle was too important to allow it to be undermined. Some expressed dismay at the atmosphere of 'servility and obedience to the politicians' and were adamant that the government should stand or fall by a bold policy. At the end of a very long debate the conference passed a non-committal resolution calling for the repeal of the Eight Hour Act which made no mention of proposed replacement hours. In addition, the Federation continued to hope for the socialisation of the industry in the not too distant future; at the same conference a unanimous resolution was passed calling for nationalisation at 'the earliest opportunity'.[64]

Dissatisfaction with the lack of progress soon grew more obstreperous. Although speculation that the government was turning its back on the seven-hour policy was dismissed, the MFGB came to believe that the government was allowing the owners too much scope to be obstructive.[65] In October *The Miner* launched an open attack upon the perceived procrastination of the Cabinet. Herbert Smith urged MacDonald to force an agreement upon the owners and the journal proposed that the patience of the miners had now reached breaking point. The government should tackle the problem 'over a wide front', with courage, and not fall 'too much under the influence of the coalowners', or else it risked losing the miners' support.[66]

At a meeting with the miners on 16 October, the committee finally made

the unpalatable announcement that, as a result of the opposition of the owners, the government was able only to introduce the 7½-hour day. The response
was one of predictable displeasure; Cook accused the government of having
'disregarded everything that ... [it had] pledged to the miners'. He was angered also by the shallow nature of the proposed reorganisation proposals,
particularly the lack of provision for miners' involvement. Smith was even
more vociferous, believing that the Bill 'belong[ed] to the coal owners absolutely'. He was disappointed above all that the government had made no commitment to protect wages and urged the government to lay down a minimum
wage. The MFGB Executive continued to push the government for a commitment but the Cabinet was not amenable, despite the fact that Snowden had
made a statement in early October suggesting that no reduction in wages
would occur.[67]

The issue of whether or not to accept the 7½-hour day created seismic
internal tensions within the MFGB which almost split it irrevocably. At a
special November conference, the MFGB had to decide whether to accept or
resist the compromise. The issue was complicated greatly by the actions of the
delegation from Yorkshire. Since they already possessed a working agreement
for the 7½-hour day, and were dissatisfied with the limited scope of the proposals, the Yorkshire delegation tried to undermine any possibility of compromise with the hope of forcing the government to examine the situation
afresh.[68] The pretext they chose to walk out of the conference was to protest
that there had been insufficient discussion of the scheme in the districts.
Smith was placed in a highly uncomfortable position, but, feeling that his first
responsibility lay with his own association, he resigned the chair. Thomas
Richards, the 72-year-old Vice-President, was forced to assume the Presidency and attempted to calm down an agitated and militant conference.
Amidst a general feeling of crisis, fierce criticism of the government was un-
leashed by the more radical delegates. Noah Ablett of South Wales summed
up the inner frustrations of the whole conference when he declared that the
politicians should be told 'get it done. Do it now. It is your job. We pay you for
it.' After much discussion, the conference finally voted in favour of acceptance.[69]

This decision, however, was not accepted by Yorkshire delegates, who
decided to attempt to push their own agenda upon the government. In a
detailed memorandum sent to Thomas and MacDonald, Yorkshire's General
Secretary, Joseph Jones, called for reduced hours to be linked to reorganisation
and for the creation of a public corporation to include representatives of both
employers and unions. Most importantly, Jones suggested that hours must be
linked to wages and that any scheme to restore the seven-hour day should be
deferred until such time as it was possible to persuade the employers to introduce wage agreements lasting at least five years. This far-sighted policy, which

recognised that any reduction in hours in the current economic climate would have been accompanied by employers' demands for wage cuts, was directly opposed to the policy of the Federation and bears witness to the size of the gulf which had opened up between Yorkshire and the rest of the MFGB.[70]

The completed Mines Bill was finally published in December 1929. Cook called for the loyalty of the miners to the government and urged members to accept the unanimity of their cause: 'We are working together. We are in the same team – your own Labour Party.'[71] Yet the miners were not even to see the achievement of the unconditional statutory 7½-hour day. The Coal Bill's passage was a stormy one, with the opposition taking every available opportunity to stall its progress. After a number of all-night sessions, and largely due to the supreme effort of Graham, the Bill was finally passed by eight votes.[72] It was not to survive intact through the Lords, however, where Lord Gainsford introduced an amendment which would permit a 'spreadover' system. This would allow employers to enforce ninety hours of work over a two-week period, which could include a number of eight-hour days. The reaction of the miners was one of despair; the MFGB Executive declared that a spreadover would negate the 7½-hour day and 'defeat the purpose of the Bill'.[73]

Although highly appreciative of the efforts of Sankey, just as they had been of the supreme efforts of Graham,[74] the miners were greatly perplexed by the situation in the Lords. Graham proposed that the government should table its own amendment to the Gainsford proposition to the effect that any operation of a spreadover system would require the approval of both the Mining Association and MFGB. After many hours of anxious discussion, the MFGB Executive decided reluctantly they would have to accept this proposal, or else lose the whole Bill, but only by ten votes to nine. The narrowness of this decision demonstrates the extreme disquiet in the MFGB over this level of compromise. If the Executive had voted to reject this proposal, at best the whole Bill would have been lost, at worst the government would have been placed in an unworkable position and forced to resign. As it was, the decision provoked considerable protests from a number of districts, once again led by Yorkshire.[75]

The August 1930 Annual Conference of the MFGB was consequently a troubled affair. The breach between the Executive and the Yorkshire delegation led by Smith grew ever wider, with the latter standing for the Presidency against Richards, and blaming the government for the lack of progress. In his Presidential Address, Richards defended the Executive's decision against the background of a general atmosphere of disillusionment. In proposing a resolution urging the government to fulfil its election pledges, the Yorkshire delegation was singularly unimpressed by the excuses of the minority position: 'Minorities don't count with us at all.... It is by persistence on the floor of the House of Commons [that] reforms are obtained.' Cook continued to defend the administration from these accusations of betrayal, suggesting that the government had done all that it could and that the miners should 'eulogise those who got this matter through in a Minority Government'. These remarks provoked an angry response from Smith, who suggested that Cook had forgotten what the policy of the MFGB was.[76]

After a short discussion, the Yorkshire resolution was passed unanimously, and despite the proposer's denial, this represented a vote of censure not only on the government but also on the Executive. This was followed by a further Yorkshire resolution calling for the minimum wage which again passed unanimously. Yorkshire's tactics were clearly wrecking ones; they knew that the government was not going to introduce seven hours and that the possibilities for a minimum wage were extremely limited. Essentially then, Yorkshire was prepared to accept the real possibility that their line of action could bring the government down. In a further discussion on the Coal Mines Bill later in the conference, more criticism was made both of the government and the Executive. One Yorkshire delegate now expressed the opinion that the government was no longer worth supporting and that, 'If I had thought that a Labour Government would have brought in anything like this in an Act of Parliament, before I would have supported them I would have committed suicide.'[77] Despite Richards's explanation of insufficient time, a number of delegates were still resentful that no national conference had been called on the issue of the spreadover, and there was a vote on whether the Executive's report should be referred back. Although this proposal was defeated 346 to 185, it was clear that the Executive was under tremendous pressure. The MFGB had become a deeply troubled organisation as a direct consequence of the government's problems.

Negotiations with the owners for the 7½-hour day and the spreadover proved to be difficult, particularly as they were conducted against a background of wage cuts. Strikes and lockouts were the result in a number of areas, most notably in South Wales and Scotland. The government did nothing to prevent these cuts and this had the effect of turning against it many who had previously remained loyal. Amongst this number was Richards himself.[78] At a special conference in November 1930, Richards spoke of his great dissatisfaction. Convinced that it had promised to protect wages, he felt that 'the Government must not refuse to accept responsibility for the position created'. After all the compromises which the Federation had accepted, Richards felt it was the duty of the government to give the miners 'a fair deal'. His disillusionment was now complete; he was sorry that the miners would have to fight their battles alone, but he could see no other alternative.[79]

At a further Special Conference, the delegates had to decide whether or not to allow the districts to accept spreadover proposals from employers. Led by Yorkshire, and to the extreme dismay of Cook, it was decided by 304 votes to 177 not to grant this right. In a passionate plea for unity, Cook expressed his 'anxiety for the future of the Federation'.[80] Cook's apparently 'wonderful transformation'[81] from the militant rabble-rouser of 1926–27 to the last leading member of the MFGB Executive to defend the government is clearly in need of explanation. In the first place, the militancy of Cook's pre-1927 position can be exaggerated.[82] Secondly, although fervent in his desire for the seven-hour day, Cook was devoted to his membership and was troubled deeply by the fissures emerging in the organisation. Above all, he did not want the Yorkshire Mineworkers' Association to become another Spencer Union.[83] Consequently, he tended to emphasise the limitations of the minority position, once suggesting that the government should best be regarded as 'an ambulance brigade doing rescue and relief work', and stressing that the government was better than the Conservative alternative.[84] He also held a real fear that democracy would collapse and be replaced by fascism.[85] Finally, by 1929 Cook was a very ill man; possibly this reinforced his commitment to the government in order that his life's work might not appear futile.[86]

Others in the Federation did not share Cook's pragmatism, and did not react kindly to MacDonald's suggestion in December 1930 that the only solution to preventing a situation in which 210,000 miners would be forced to work the spreadover illegally was to remove the veto of the miners and the owners and to accept the spreadover unconditionally for a temporary period of three months.[87] On 4 December the MFGB met to decide whether to accept MacDonald's proposal or to call a 'General Strike'. Cumberland, Kent, Lancashire, Scotland and Yorkshire all voted for a national strike, and the proposition was only defeated by 230 votes to 209.[88] Finally it was decided to put the issue back to the districts and by the smallest of margins, 271 votes to 265, the MFGB accepted the continuation of the spreadover. Once again, the alternative may have been the bringing down of the government.[89] At this juncture, even Cook felt that the miners had taken too much ill-treatment from the government. In a very bitter letter to MacDonald on 9 January 1931, written from his sickbed, Cook wrote:

> I did think a Labour Government would defend its own Mines Act ... but no – we are left to battle alone.... We have had nothing but lavish promises which makes it ... impossible for some of us to defend in the future. It appears to me that our only hope is in our trade union movement.[90]

The condition of the industry continued to deteriorate during the first part of 1931 as unemployment increased and wages fell, and it was in a mood of despondency that the MFGB met in March 1931. In an emotional speech, Richards bemoaned the dashing of union hopes and the dire fate to which the government had abandoned them. Miners had been the victims of either the spreadover or wage reductions and the leaders of the Federation had been let down. The general mood of the conference concorded with the sentiments of the President, and it voted 401 to 134 against the extension of the spreadover beyond 31 March.[91]

The MFGB had one last hope for the protection of wage levels. Unfortunately for the government, the Eight Hours Act of 1926 legislated for a five-year period only and was due to expire on 8 July 1931. As a result, unless legislation was passed to supersede the Act, the seven-hour day would become law. The MFGB saw this as a potential lever in negotiations in pressing for an amendment of the Minimum Wage Act of 1912. Otherwise they felt the owners would introduce a general attack on wages in July when the seven-hour day was reintroduced. A joint sub-committee with the mining MPs drew up proposals for a minimum wage and even accepted an invitation from Lloyd George to put its proposals before the Coal Committee of the Liberal Party, a clear sign of its desperation.[92] The Executive also had the continuing problems of internal disunity. Despite the decision not to continue the spreadover past the end of March, by the end of April both the Scottish and North Wales districts were continuing to operate the system. Despite its great disillusionment with the government, then, paradoxically the MFGB was largely powerless to prevent wage cuts itself and therefore still looked to Parliament. On 30 April Richards told the Prime Minister: 'If you cannot come to our salvation there is no salvation anywhere.'[93]

The suggestion of what amounted to wage increases was a practical impossibility for the government and was anathema to Snowden. MacDonald refused to accept that wages were the government's responsibility and was angered by the tactics of the MFGB. He felt that the MFGB had to accept either shortened hours or reduced wages and the spreadover, informing Cook that he was 'sick and tired of the way that some of you get your men into difficulties and then turn to the Government and say, "If you do not get us out, we will tell you how disgusted we are with you."'[94] Government officials calculated that the miners' proposals would add three to four shillings to the cost of a ton of coal,[95] and the majority of the Cabinet agreed that wage negotiations were not the government's job.[96]

An increasingly ailing Richards[97] became angered by what he saw as government evasion and on 30 April warned Henderson, 'You may depend upon it that if the government fails us it is going to have a serious effect.'[98] On 25 June a further Special Conference was dismayed by the lack of progress. The left-wing S. O. Davies of South Wales summed up the general bitterness when he remarked that the government's true intention was 'that they shall introduce legislation in the interests of the coal-owners'.[99] This remark brought an angry reply from Cook who was still concerned that the miners should not bring the government down for fear of the alternative. Finally, on 2 July 1931, the MFGB accepted reluctantly the government's proposals for a 7½-hour day for another twelve months and assurance of no reduction in basic wage rates, although Yorkshire, South Wales, Cumberland and the Forest of Dean dissented. Only Cook could summon any enthusiasm for the settlement. The majority of miners were bitter that the high hopes of 1929 had been shattered and their only consolation was to look forward to that far off time of a majority Labour government. The conference of 2 July unanimously passed a resolution calling for nationalisation at the earliest opportunity and for an assurance from Labour that it would be 'the chief plank in its next election programme'. For the MFGB the second Labour government was now effectively otiose.

Cotton, iron and steel and transport

The government had expended much time and energy upon the mining question, for little satisfactory gain, and this did not encourage it to undertake similar projects in other industries.[100] In November 1930 Graham stated categorically that the government had 'no desire' to become involved in any further legislation on reorganisation.[101] There were also external factors which worked against rationalisation. Increasingly unions saw the process as an excuse for wage cuts, and were concerned that employers would exploit the opportunity to undermine working arrangements. Fear of the short-term effect on unemployment was also important in influencing both government and unions, particularly those that were connected to the staple industries.[102] Consequently, the Coal Bill was the last attempt at industrial reorganisation through legislation and the promised investigations into iron and steel and the cotton industry proved to be lacklustre.

The textile workers had hoped for a full-scale government inquiry but had to be satisfied with a small sub-committee set up by the EAC, chaired by Graham, Alexander and finally Clynes from February 1930. Although it remained Britain's largest export industry in 1929, cotton had experienced growing problems in the 1920s. Once again, the principal reason for decline was the growth of foreign competition. The Depression led to a fall in the world demand for cotton and for the finer quality goods in which Britain had remained dominant. In 1930 British exports of cotton piece goods amounted to only two-thirds of the level of 1913.[103] The industry also had considerable internal problems to cope with. After the war a great shortage of cotton goods had created a wave of reckless speculation which resulted in mills being recapitalised at too high a rate and a legacy of debt throughout the 1920s.

The most obvious solutions to the problems faced by British cotton were twofold: the cancellation of debts and reorganisation through the amalgamation of small concerns. It was to both these ends that Thomas encouraged the Bank of England to back a Lancashire Cotton Corporation in 1930, which would aim to combine spinners of coarse and medium cotton into one great productive unit. The report of the cotton inquiry in June 1930, however, proved to be a great disappointment to the cotton workers. The *Cotton Factory Times* on 11 July 1930 commented that it had failed to come up with anything 'sensational or original'.[104] The main reason for disquiet was the report's negative attitude to government intervention in the process of reorganisation; whilst the report favoured technological improvement and amalgamation, no government money would be provided to this end.[105] Amalgamation proved to be a slow process. With the Depression deepening in 1930, resulting in a 40 per cent fall in prices over twelve months, owners were reluctant to take such bold financial risks.[106] As there was little union pressure, with the cotton workers divided into a dozen independent unions, and pressed by its many other problems, the government did little more. Graham came out in favour of compulsory amalgamation in August 1930 but both MacDonald and Snowden rejected his proposals.[107]

The story with iron and steel was a similar one. Although the industry was maintaining its export levels in expensive special steels in 1929, the 1920s had been a period of long-term decline, with Britain falling behind its competitors in the output of mass-produced cheap steel. Britain remained the world's fourth largest producer in 1928, but also imported more steel than the USA, France, Belgium, Luxembourg and Germany, some 3,700,000 tons on average in 1926–28.[108] The chief reasons for decline were the use of newer technology and cheaper labour costs overseas, together with a continental cartel which excluded British steel and forced a greater dependence upon exports to the Empire. As with cotton, many of the firms were heavily in debt, and were unable to attract the fresh capital needed for new plant.

A government committee set up under Sankey finally published the international part of its report in August 1930.[109] The British Iron and Steel and Kindred Trades Association (BISAKTA) was less than pleased with the main body of the unpublished report. No reference was made to the proposals of BISAKTA for a Central Board to control the industry or for an Imports and Exports Board to fix prices, nor were any proposals made for displaced labour. Instead the report concentrated on the creation of integrated regional units, and BISAKTA was afraid that the report had strengthened the case for lower wages, longer hours and safeguarding, all of which it opposed.[110] Despite a Commons debate, no legislation was introduced, and BISAKTA and the manufacturers were greatly frustrated. As with the cotton industry, the unionised workforce favoured compulsory amalgamation, and calls for government intervention became ever more pronounced. Imports for 1930 were up by 10 per cent on the previous year, whilst exports had fallen by 50 per cent, which meant that for the first time in the industry's history imports exceeded exports by 114,000 tons.

Employers' demands for protection grew ever more vocal; the Executive

Committee of the National Federation of Iron and Steel Manufacturers urged MacDonald in January 1931 to undertake 'the immediate adoption of some policy for the regulation of imports'.[111] BISAKTA tried to increase public awareness of its own policy, publishing a pamphlet entitled *What is Wrong with the British Iron and Steel Industries*, and holding a number of public meetings. Despite Graham's statements in 1931, however, that the best way forward in the long term was a public utility corporation, a view shared by Arthur Pugh, General Secretary of BISAKTA, and discussions between the government and the Bank of England in May 1931,[112] nothing concrete developed. Essentially, as was the case with coal and cotton, the government had left the trade unionists in iron and steel to fight their battles alone.

One of the few successful pieces of domestic Labour legislation was the London Passenger Transport Bill of 1931, passed finally by the National Government, which reorganised the London transport system and represented the one government attempt at nationalisation. The scheme, however, did not meet with unanimous trade union support. The issue of union representation on the new London Passenger Transport Board provoked a fierce clash between Bevin and Herbert Morrison. Morrison felt that the Board should be composed of experts appointed on their own merits and rejected Bevin's demands for a minimum number of union representatives. Bevin appealed directly to the Prime Minister in June 1931 but made no ground except for a minor concession on the number of Labour representatives on the Advisory Committee.[113] John Bromley of ASLEF summed up union disbelief: 'Heaven help us when a Labour Government cuts out all idea of Socialist ideals, and tells the world that only businessmen can secure our future.'[114] The other major Bill on transport, the Road Traffic Act of 1929, resulting from the Royal Commission on Transport to which the TGWU had submitted evidence, did not go as far as Bevin wanted but was welcomed as a major improvement.[115]

The Trade Disputes Act

The failure of the government to repeal the Trade Disputes Act was a tremendous disappointment for the unions. As already noted, repeal had been a top TUC priority in May 1929. By as early as September 1929, the TUC was disappointed by the lack of progress. Clynes was subject to considerable heckling whilst he tried to defend government inactivity, which resulted in a number of individuals being forcibly ejected from the hall, and a unanimous resolution was passed calling for immediate repeal.[116] Wary of the difficulties it would encounter, in particular Liberal hostility to the idea of a restoration of the pre-1927 position, the government proceeded slowly. The two major areas of difficulty were general or sympathetic strikes and the return to contracting out of the political levy. The TUC wished to see a complete repeal of section one of the Act, which had defined illegal strikes. It feared these restrictions would be open to abuse in the hands of an unscrupulous Conservative or Liberal government, and felt that the laws relating to treason and sedition were already adequate to cover the event of any real revolutionary activity.[117] A return to contracting out was held to be less important and the GC was prepared to compromise on the issue. The chief concern was that a Bill should be introduced quickly; even if it had to be dropped the government 'would ... have kept its word'.[118]

Concerns that the government was not fulfilling its commitment were voiced at the deputation of the GC to the Prime Minister on 24 January 1930. In a tone of some frustration, Citrine stressed that the GC had tried to make life easier for the government by pressing for no more than a return to the pre-1927 position and he highlighted the work which the TUC had done to secure repeal:

> We spent several thousands of pounds in 1927 on a campaign to arouse the country to a realisation of what this Bill meant to the trade unions, and some of us are egotistical enough to imagine that the campaign largely resulted in the advent of the present Government.[119]

Snowden had made a speech as long ago as 23 October announcing that the Bill was completed, but Citrine claimed to know that this was not the case. Both he and Bevin were suspicious that the government lacked courage on this issue.[120]

None the less, not until April 1930 was a Cabinet committee appointed. Aware of the potentially damaging effect of a Liberal amendment, and claiming that Labour would be portrayed as favouring revolutionary strikes, Henderson informed the GC that the government would have to concede a clause making political or revolutionary strikes illegal. For the Labour leadership, the General Strike had been a source of much embarrassment and privately they had no objections to such strikes remaining illegal. The TUC, however, wished to stand by its earlier position.[121] Henderson suggested a joint meeting of the GC and NEC to discuss the Bill. At this meeting on 29 May, the key issue remained the revolutionary strike. Bevin complained once again of the lack of progress, and MacDonald once more put the delay down to the problems of 'the Parliamentary Machine', but no progress was made on the point at issue. Instead, it was decided that a draft amendment would be prepared by the Law officers and submitted to the two national executives for consideration.[122]

After a number of attempts by the GC, a meeting of the TUC sub-committee with the government was finally arranged for 20 June. The discussion followed familiar lines, with Henderson trying his hardest to win GC consent for a government amendment on illegal strikes should the Liberals push the point. The GC remained reluctant to agree to any concession in advance, and to the exasperation of the government it made little effort to grasp the parliamentary realities. An increasingly frustrated Henderson decided to play his final bargaining chip; although the government would not 'pursue any course of action without the agreement of the TUC', he warned that the probable outcome without the acceptance of an amendment would be the government's resignation.[123] This plea finally paid off, for on 25 July the GC consented reluctantly to the clause making revolutionary strikes illegal.[124]

Henderson aimed to ensure that close consultation on the Bill continued and was prepared, despite his many engagements, to devote time to that end; on 25 July he wrote to Citrine offering his services on the Act if the GC should require them.[125] None the less, formal contacts became less frequent now the government had obtained TUC consent for the key amendment. On 7 November Citrine wrote to MacDonald, ostensibly regarding a rumour that the Act might be introduced in the Lords, but also to complain of the lack of government contact with the TUC sub-committee.[126] Meanwhile, the wider union movement was growing restless. The Sixth Annual Conference of Trade Councils called for immediate repeal in May 1930, as did the Annual Conference of the National Federation of Building Trade Operatives in June.[127] The journal of the NUGMW suggested in October 1930 that repeal would engender 'greater confidence of the industrial side in its political counterpart'.[128] Bevin was critical not only of government hesitation but also of what he viewed as MacDonald's poor handling of the situation.[129]

Unfortunately for both unions and government, however, even with the leverage of the agreed amendment on illegal strikes, Jowitt's attempts to secure Liberal support proved wholly unsuccessful. In an informal interview with Citrine in December 1930, Jowitt outlined the possibility of government defeat and asked for the TUC's opinion on further action. MacDonald wanted to drop the Bill, but Henderson felt that after the 'definite promise' made there was no alternative but to proceed.[130] The TUC was certainly not ready to give up yet. Its research department undertook extensive inquiries into the effect of the Act upon the unions and even compiled a detailed study of the Liberals who had voted against it in 1927.[131] A circular was issued to all unions and trades councils asking them to exert the utmost pressure,[132] and to write to their MPs and those Liberals and Conservatives who were on the standing committee for the Bill.[133] Local Labour parties were also employed in this task and the local response was enthusiastic.[134] The GC was consequently hopeful of success and declared in belligerent tones on 25 February 1931 that if the Liberal amendments were carried it would be 'regarded as a declaration of war on the Trade Union movement'.[135]

Ultimately, however, these efforts were futile. Not content with the illegal strike clause, the Liberals tabled further amendments, one of which would endanger the future of all strikes by making unions liable for inconveniences suffered by individuals during stoppages. A TUC delegation met the government members of the committee on 28 February 1931, where it was decided that the PLP could not agree to this amendment and if a division was forced the government should drop the Bill. Yet, to the disbelief of Citrine, who was observing in the Gallery, when it came to the forecasted division two Labour MPs said they wished to continue the discussion and, despite the earlier agreement, the majority of the PLP concurred. As a result, the Liberals and the Conservatives combined and the amendment was predictably carried. Only after this humiliating defeat did the government drop the Bill.

A bitterly disappointed Citrine spoke to Arthur Greenwood immediately afterwards and the two agreed that proceedings had been atrociously mishandled. What followed, however, was an extraordinary scene of confrontation, in which Citrine became involved in an explosive argument with Archibald Gossling, the ASW-sponsored MP for Yardley, Birmingham, and A. S. McKinlay, MP for Glasgow Partick, which almost resulted in the exchange of physical blows. This dispute illustrates well the different priorities of the TUC and PLP and many of the grievances which were seldom voiced so explicitly. Gossling, absent when the initial agreement was made, told Citrine that the TUC had no right to interfere in the matter. Further, he accused the TUC of having 'no political sagacity at all' for pushing the government to introduce the Bill. McKinlay was even more vitriolic, and accused the unions of 'dictation'. Citrine retorted that the TUC had every right for consultation on the issue and 'had not asked Labour members for very much'. He accused McKinlay of cowardice and of being more concerned with holding on to his job than with principles.[136]

The post-mortem, however, was far from complete. On 6 March a dispirited John Bromley wrote to Citrine informing him of a conversation with the Reverend R. M. Kedward, Liberal member for Ashford, during which a charge of an 'exceedingly serious nature' had been levelled. Kedward had claimed that the amendments which had finally defeated the Bill had been 'drafted for them by the leaders of the Labour Party', namely Tom Shaw, Lord Sankey and J. H. Thomas.[137] Both Citrine and Bevin were concerned sufficiently to press MacDonald for a meeting to discuss the matter,[138] and the TUC requested that a delegation should be arranged 'without delay'.[139] These requests were met by Prime Ministerial disdain, which served only to inflame the GC's wrath and encouraged a belief that the allegations were true. MacDonald suggested that Citrine should have approached Tom Shaw in the first place 'before writing to him a letter of this kind, based on lobby gossip'.[140] Citrine's further attempt of 30 March met with a similarly hostile response.[141] MacDonald, of course, did have more pressing concerns, but such an off-hand reply to a highly agitated GC was another example of MacDonald's often disastrous mismanagement of his own supporters, and another sign of an increasingly disintegrating Labour movement.

Not until 21 April did MacDonald agree finally to meet the TUC and then only after the intervention of Jowitt, who wished to clear his name of the allegations made against him in *Truth*, which claimed he had entered into a conspiracy with the Liberals to trick the TUC.[142] A number of GC members felt that the TUC should turn down MacDonald's invitation because he had not consented to meet them on their original grounds and a resolution to this effect was defeated only by thirteen votes to seven.[143] On 28 April the TUC sub-committee on the Trade Disputes Bill finally met to discuss the long-standing rumours.

It was clear from the explanations of Jowitt and Shaw that there was no truth in the allegations.[144] Kedward and the Liberals had their own reasons for creating tensions between the government and the TUC; the TUC was furious with Liberal attitudes to repeal and determined to frustrate electoral reform proposals.[145] The key point, however, is that relations between the government and the unions were so poor that the TUC was prepared to believe there was substance in the allegations. Ultimately more unnecessary time and effort were expended by MacDonald's continuing refusal to meet a deputation and the cost in terms of TUC goodwill was considerable. The TUC's report on the meeting of 28 April, although accepting the government's denial, makes clear GC dissatisfaction with the manner in which it had been treated. At the meeting Swales had asserted 'that no previous Government, whatever its party, had ever declined to meet TUC representatives'. They were deeply dismayed by the Prime Minister's priorities, feeling that 'a letter from the General Council should be at least as important to the Prime Minister as a paragraph in *Truth*'. Equally, the GC was annoyed that conversations with the Liberals should take priority over consultation with the TUC. The report concluded that 'this unfortunate accident would never have arisen had the Joint Sub-Committee ... functioned in the way that was intended. It never met, and from this initial breakdown in machinery arose considerable misunderstandings.'[146]

The attempt to repeal the Trade Disputes Act had resulted in disaster in every sense. The government was unable to get the Bill through the Commons and succeeded only in creating a disillusioned, distrustful and resentful trade union movement. By its mishandling of the TUC and, above all, its failure to observe the joint machinery, created by Henderson with the intention of avoiding the very situation which ultimately resulted, the government had alienated the majority of trade unionists. What is equally apparent is that this breakdown in relations was a harbinger for the events of August 1931. By failing to observe the warning signals of union discontent whilst they were still resolvable, the government was steadily undermining the already fragile foundations that were crucial to its survival.

Washington Hours, factories and compensation

The other areas of industrial legislation so confidently proposed in *Labour and the Nation* met with a similar fate. Most important of these was the failure to ratify the Washington Hours Convention, which called for a maximum 48-hour week and an eight-hour day for all industries. Citrine personally regarded this piece of legislation as more important even than the Trade Disputes Bill.[147] Unfortunately for the government, a conference of the International Labour Organisation (ILO) was due to meet at Geneva within a matter of days of Labour's acceptance of office, and a reluctant MacDonald was pressurised by his colleagues and the TUC into authorising E. L. Poulton, head of the British delegation, to make a statement committing the government to ratification at the earliest opportunity. Before agreeing to this course of action, MacDonald had obtained assurances from the Ministry of Labour that there would be no difficulties in drafting a Bill, but on closer investigation the government discovered that the obstacles were numerous.[148] Once again, Labour was guilty of failing to do sufficient homework before coming into office. The major problem was that the Bill would have to override the various hours agreements already in existence, with the added problem that some unions, most notably those involved in the railways, were opposed to any ban on overtime.

Consequently, progress was slow. Bondfield had little time to devote to the measure and the lack of parliamentary time added to the inertia. The TUC became ever more agitated, not only for domestic reasons. At the meeting of the GC with MacDonald on 24 January 1930, Citrine spoke of the effect that the government's pledge had had 'in raising the prestige of the International Labour Organisation' and emphasised the great embarrassment that would accrue if nothing was achieved.[149] Initially the railway workers wished to be excluded but eventually a special railway clause was inserted into the draft Bill which would allow an agreed level of overtime.[150] Yet once the railway workers had received special treatment, sections of the TGWU also requested concessions and as a result negotiations were still being conducted as late as April 1931.[151]

On 16 April 1931 Bondfield received a deputation from the TUC which again emphasised the international dimension. The ILO was due to meet again in May and the GC requested a definite timetable for ratification.[152] Unimpressed by pleas of lack of parliamentary time, Citrine wrote to Bondfield warning that, unless a definite date was set, Hayday, the TUC delegate to the conference, would be forced to vote for the approval of the report of Albert Thomas, the Director of the ILO, which criticised the British government for failing to carry through its promises.[153] In desperation, Bondfield turned to MacDonald but was told there was there was no parliamentary time. Despite a personal appeal not to add to the government's difficulties, Hayday proceeded to carry through the TUC threat.[154] Albert Thomas's bitter attack on the government for its lack of commitment to social reform was widely reported in the international press, and provoked a very angry response from MacDonald, who told the Director of the ILO that he should mind his own business.[155] Once again, the government had badly tarnished its reputation through a failure to examine the practicalities of a promise before making a commitment.

No parliamentary time was ever found for the proposed Factories Bill. This caused considerable union dismay and suspicion that Clynes was deliberately stalling.[156] In January 1930 the GC expressed a desire for more consultation, but despite Clynes's pledge to do his utmost, no Bill reached the Commons.[157] A similar situation developed with regard to the Workmen's Compensation legislation promised before the election. This was of particular concern to the MFGB because of the dangerous nature of their trade,[158] and a resolution passed at the 1930 Annual Conference called for the pressurisation of the government to introduce the Bill.[159] Again, no parliamentary time was found and the unions were left to wonder why the government had made pledges it was unable to fulfil.

Industrial disputes

Government handling of industrial disputes had been a major bone of contention in 1924, but was not such a serious issue during the second Labour government. On no occasion did MacDonald have to resort to the preparation of emergency powers. The major problems occurred in the cotton and wool trades and in coal-mining, but the majority of the 1,250 disputes which began during 1929–31 were of a strictly minor character.[160] The unions were not in a position to be militant; with unemployment high and funds low, strikes were usually a practical impossibility. Initially, the unions were concerned not to provide the government with industrial problems and expected a favourable hearing without having to resort to strike activity. When the Depression provoked employers into tabling wage cuts, however, the government continued to adopt a stance of impartiality. Largely paralysed by their circumstances, there was often little that unions could do beyond protesting verbally.

Employers in the cotton industry began to call for wage cuts even before the economic situation deteriorated, and their demands were met by resistance from the unions. Sir Horace Wilson was sent by the government to promote a settlement, but was unsuccessful. On 29 July 1929 the bulk of the industry ground to a halt and 350,000 workers were locked out. On 6 August MacDonald appealed for a settlement,[161] and on 15 August the two sides agreed to arbitration. The rapid decision of the Board of Arbitration, under the aptly named Sir Digby Swift, to impose a reduction of half the cut demanded by the employers, was poorly received. The cotton workers believed the Board had failed to analyse the evidence in detail.[162] In a letter to MacDonald, one union official suggested that, had there been an immediate election in Lancashire, Labour would have been bottom of the poll in every seat.[163]

In the wool textile dispute of early 1930, Bondfield again went out of her way to demonstrate government neutrality. In June 1930 she commented, 'It is not for me to express any views upon the merits of the dispute.'[164] The cause of this strike was once again a call for wage cuts, to which the government responded by appointing a Court of Inquiry under Lord Macmillan, whose report recommended cuts of 9 per cent. The unions went out on strike, but despite the support of other unions,[165] and the creation of a TUC strike fund, the stoppage failed to retain a national coherence and a number of local agreements were reached.[166] None the less, heavy police reinforcements had to be drafted into West Riding and violence occurred in Bradford.[167] Many workers were dismayed by Bondfield's apparent lack of concern for their plight, but a second round of wage cuts in wool textiles in August 1931 met with no resistance from a demoralised workforce.

The second major dispute to occur in the cotton industry was also a lock-out, this time over the attempt of employers to increase the number of looms attended by each weaver to eight. Originally based in Burnley, the dispute spread in January 1931, despite Bondfield's efforts to contain it. The threatened increase in looms was seen by workers as a move towards further unemployment and offered a particular threat to the large numbers of married women who worked in the industry. Bondfield, clearly far from an advanced feminist, angered many women textile workers by suggesting that they should seek work as domestic servants or canteen waitresses in order to reduce unemployment and underemployment in Lancashire. So unpopular were these statements that calls were made subsequently for her resignation.[168] MacDonald's attempts at intervention proved unsuccessful on this occasion,[169] and in private he was annoyed by what he saw as the 'unreasonable and unintelligent' behaviour of the cotton workers.[170] Essentially, the government was at a loss to know what to do next, since they realised that another Court of Inquiry would be immensely unpopular with the unions. Yet the increasing likelihood that the workers might win their case alone was considered by MacDonald with trepidation. On 9 February he told Clynes that: 'If this happens there is a grave danger that the government will be turned upon by the victorious operatives', meaning that the workers' requests for legislation to improve the textile industries would be heightened.[171] Not only, then, did the government do little to aid workers threatened by wage cuts, but also on occasions hoped privately that the unions would lose their fight. In the long term the unions' victory proved to be of little significance since the eight looms scheme was reintroduced in the autumn of 1931.

The other major stoppages occurred in coal-mining; in 1931 three million working days were lost in protest against the failure to secure the seven-hour day and the spreadover.[172] The National Industrial Board, set up under the Mines Act, attempted to reach a compromise wherever possible and this strategy proved to be generally successful. Although the MFGB came close to the calling of a national strike at the end of 1930, strike activity was limited to a few specific areas.[173] In January 1931 there was a stoppage in South Wales, another in Scotland for three weeks in July, and miners in Cumberland were out from late June until mid-August. The MFGB Executive was satisfied that the Board had ruled fairly in the disputes brought to it; the problem was that the owners had generally ignored its recommendations.[174]

Rising unemployment naturally brought with it a considerable fall in union membership. The NUGMW, for example, lost over 23,000 members during the period 1929–31.[175] Consequently, most unions were forced to accept wage cuts, although they were angered by government neutrality at a time when their standard of living was being attacked from all sides. In line with its gradualism, the government accepted that the wage cuts were inevitable and necessary for the continuing health of the capitalist system, a system which had to achieve prosperity once more if it was to provide the finance needed for socialist reform. Such a philosophy was bound to clash heavily with the long-standing trade union ethos which saw the protection of wage levels as the primary aim. It was over unemployment that this tension was to reach a level of grave proportions.

Unemployment

Unemployment represented a significant drain on union members and finance, since those who remained in work had to contribute a greater proportion of their wages to support those who were unemployed. The Boiler-maker's Society, for example, reported in 1931 that some 60 per cent of its membership was either unemployed, sick or on a pension.[176] From late 1930, all unions began to fear a cut in unemployment benefit and those with a degree of economic knowledge recognised that Snowden's financial orthodoxy made this a real possibility. An attack on what were perceived as the already low living standards of the unemployed was viewed as intolerable, especially when being contemplated by a Labour government. Aside, however, from concern for the effect financial retrenchment would have upon the unemployed, the unions feared that it would act as a trigger for a general wage-cutting policy. Unemployment benefit would be the issue over which the national responsibilities of the government and the sectional interests of the trade unions were to come into the most serious conflict in 1931.

Until 1931, however, the TUC had no alternative to the government's orthodox economic policy and the majority of trade unionists were prepared to leave matters in the government's hands. Few union complaints were made over Thomas's largely futile attempts to deal with unemployment through limited public works schemes and increased trade with Canada. Unions accepted the government reasoning that unemployment was the result of capitalism, and since the government was not sufficiently strong to implement a socialist programme, there was little it could do.[177] Most were prepared to rationalise the government's efforts for most of 1930. *The Record* of March 1930 wrote that the 'Government has done more in nine months to grapple with unemployment than the Liberals and Tories did during their years of absolute power.'[178] Most felt that only a Labour majority would ever have a chance of solving the problem and of eliminating the 'Siamese twins' of capitalism and unemployment.[179] The Seventh Annual Conference of Trade Councils, for example, passed a unanimous resolution calling for nationalisation as the only solution.[180]

The unions did have proposals for the administration of unemployment benefit they wished to impress upon the government. On 25 July 1929 the government appointed the Morris Committee on Unemployment Insurance, to which Hayday was nominated to represent the TUC. Before submitting its evidence, the GC sent a circular to all affiliated unions asking for their views on the administration of the unemployment exchanges.[181] Clearly this was an issue of great concern, since the GC received detailed replies from all of the major unions. The top priority was to see the repeal of the 'Not Genuinely Seeking Work' clause which made it compulsory for claimants to prove they were looking for work through the production of documentary evidence. The GC called for a return to the spirit of the 1920 Act such that the unemployed could only be disqualified if they had definitely turned down a suitable offer of work, a solution which became known as the 'Hayday Formula'.[182] It wished also to see the unions take on more of the administration from the exchanges and requested changes in the qualifications for benefit. Yet neither Bondfield nor the October report of the committee accepted the Hayday Formula. Instead, the report recommended that a claimant should be disqualified if there was 'evidence that suitable work was available and [the claimant] fails to prove that he had made reasonable efforts to obtain such work'.[183] The unions were resentful that their recommendations had not been accepted and that claimants would still have to submit documentary evidence.

The report of the Morris Committee formed the basis of the Unemployment Insurance (No. 2) Bill, the text of which was published in November 1929. A joint GC/NEC delegation met with Bondfield on 7 November and called for an increase of benefit, an inclusion of agricultural workers and domestic servants, a reduction in the waiting period and the repeal of the 'Not Genuinely Seeking Work' clause.[184] Hayday wanted TUC participation in the drafting of the Bill but Bondfield was only prepared to concede a joint consultative committee to discuss the Bill's progress. This did not pacify the TUC, which felt that it had far greater knowledge of the administration of benefit than the Labour Party, and in December 1929 it rejected the joint committee.[185] The final Bill did not propose any increase in benefit – Snowden would not even contemplate the suggestion – and neither did it accept any reduction in the waiting period or the repeal of the 'Not Genuinely Seeking Work' clause. Will Thorne was so incensed that he decided to appeal directly to MacDonald and this was followed by a petition from fifty-five trade union MPs.[186] This pressure paid off, for eventually, on 5 December, Bondfield agreed to the Hayday Formula. Even then the trade unions only saw the Bill at best as 'a temporary stop-gap'.[187] For the National Union of Agricultural Workers its continued exclusion from the unemployment insurance was a source of great bitterness. Despite the backing of the GC on the issue and a number of meetings at the Ministries of Agriculture and Labour, they were to find no joy. The agricultural workers felt their case had been neglected and 'their patience was exhausted'.[188] Yet in January 1931 Bondfield announced she was unable to find any parliamentary time for the issue, and despite a TUC protest, that was how it was to remain.[189]

As already noted, the GC had been greatly displeased by the manner in which the Holman Gregory Commission was established. It was perturbed by the proposal to set up a Royal Commission in the first place, feeling that its terms of reference were too narrow and conceived solely in the context of strengthening the case for benefit cuts.[190] The TUC felt it should have been consulted about the terms of reference before they were drawn up. On 17 November 1930 Citrine received a telephone call from Bondfield informing him that the Cabinet was to decide the issue in half an hour, and could representatives be sent to discuss the matter immediately. At a meeting with the government on 2 January 1931 Citrine recounted his reaction to this request:

> We were not prepared to come down to see you within half an hour of the Cabinet meeting ... without knowing what the subject was, without knowing what you wanted to discuss ... and without giving us any chance to find out the opinion of our people, so that you in turn could communicate to the Cabinet a point of view that we ourselves did not know would be supported by our members. That is not the way to do business.[191]

In this long and often bitter meeting with MacDonald, Bondfield and the new Lord Privy Seal, Vernon Hartshorn, the GC expressed union grievances at length. Not only did it reject the terms of reference, but it objected to the fact that the opposition parties had been consulted. Hayday was at a loss to understand why another committee was necessary; there had been three major investigations since 1920, including the recent Morris Committee. The GC was able only to conclude that the commission was 'deliberately intended to strike off at least 300,000 of the present recipients from Unemployment Insurance Benefit', and warned that the TUC was no longer prepared to 'blindly stand by and be ignored' when the livelihood of so many trade unionists was threatened. MacDonald's vague and somewhat condescending reply, in which he spoke of the urgent need to reduce the borrowing of the Unemployment Insurance Fund, not only lacked financial clarity but failed to convince the GC that the government's intention was not to facilitate cuts.[192]

It was only with extreme reluctance that the TUC agreed to give evidence. Circulars were again sent to all unions asking for evidence, particularly on the administration of benefit for short-time workers and married women, but this time few replies were received. The suspicions of the GC were clearly shared by the rank-and-file and a general feeling of futility influenced their inertia. In the evidence submitted in April 1931, following the Chairman's extension of the deadline, the GC obstinately resubmitted its previous proposals, knowing full well that the commission would scarcely even look at them.[193] They did succeed, however, in greatly irritating MacDonald, who felt they could best be summarised as the 'irresponsible proposals of responsible men'.[194] The interim Majority Report published on 4 June 1931 realised all of the TUC's worst fears. It was proposed to limit benefit to twenty-six weeks in the year; raise worker, employer and state contributions; reduce benefits and introduce a means test to reduce the annual borrowing of the Unemployment Fund from £40 million to only £8 million.

The union response was pugnacious; unions everywhere expressed antipathy and the GC decided to organise a publicity campaign against the report. A pamphlet entitled *Fair Play for the Unemployed* condemned not only the report but also the whole manner in which the commission had been established.[195] It was claimed that the objective had been a reduction in the Insurance Fund and that the commission had not even considered the wider issues, or the effect of its proposals on the unemployed. The pamphlet reiterated the call for increased benefits, an action which can only be construed as an attempt to create a climate of opinion which would make it impossible for the government to implement the report.[196] In addition, preparations were begun for a series of district conferences and demonstrations for 21 June.[197]

The GC did not believe that the government would accept the report's recommendations but was in favour of pressurising the government to make doubly sure. In a meeting on 12 June, Hayday outlined the seriousness of the situation, suggesting that if the government dared to go ahead there 'would be a serious revolt in the minds of the people'. Citrine unsuccessfully attempted to secure the involvement of Labour head office in the demonstrations. After a long talk with Henderson, Citrine felt it unlikely that the government would do more than attend to the alleged abuses.[198] Nevertheless, he was as relieved as the rest of the GC when MacDonald announced in June that the government would not reduce benefits, increase contributions or decrease the period of entitlement. Yet this did little to improve government popularity. At the eight conferences held by the TUC and the two organised by the trade councils from 20 to 27 June, the government was widely criticised for establishing the commission and resolutions were passed condemning the report and urging the government to legislate along the lines of the GC demands.

The meeting at Newport on 20 June was marked by a blistering attack by the young Aneurin Bevan, MP, on both the commission and the Unemployment (No. 3) Act, better known as the 'Anomalies Bill'.[199] This Bill was something of an obsession for MacDonald, who, adopting a Victorian attitude to idleness, could not bear to think there were individuals claiming benefit to which they were not entitled. In what can only be judged as a rather misguided use of his time, he wrote an array of letters to his friends to ask them whether they knew of any cases of benefit abuse.[200] His attitudes were shared by Bondfield, who introduced a Bill on 18 June which dealt with casual, intermittent and seasonal workers and married women. Whilst doing little to ease the burden on the Unemployment Insurance Fund, this act took away benefit from many legitimate cases, particularly married women.[201]

Economic policy

TUC dissatisfaction with unemployment was paralleled by a growing questioning of economic policy in general. Prior to 1929, few trade unionists possessed any extensive economic knowledge and many regarded economic decisions as outside their jurisdiction. Both Bevin and Citrine, however, had been influenced by Keynes's attack upon the gold standard and had felt that it was important that the GC should have a general position on economics. The outcome was the creation of the TUC Economic Committee in 1929, a body finally to construct the alternative economic policy of August 1931.

In the course of the Mond–Turner talks, the TUC had found itself in agreement with the employers that a monetary policy was needed that considered the interests of industry rather than the City. This was instrumental in the formation of the Macmillan Committee on Finance and Industry in November 1929. Although his appointment by Snowden was largely an act of tokenism, Bevin's involvement in its discussions was a crucial stage in his economic thinking. He was fascinated by the proceedings of the committee, and not only did his knowledge of the wider issues increase, but also his innate intellectual curiosity led him to develop a considerable admiration for Keynes and his critique of classical economics. Having been the leading critic of the government's economic policies at the Labour Conference of 1929, Bevin now adopted a philosophy which enabled him, with an intellectual coherency he had previously lacked, to question the sanctity of the gold standard and, as he saw it, the reactionary dogma of the Bank of England. Essentially, Bevin felt that financial policy should be directed to the real needs of industry and to the millions of workers whose lives were affected by the decisions of a small group of faceless figures in the banking community. In a separate statement attached to the report of the inquiry in July 1931, Bevin called for the Bank of England to become a public corporation, and for a managed currency characterised by state planning and economic reorganisation. In addition, he was convinced that the devaluation of the pound was essential to the welfare of British trade and, although he continued to hold reservations, that tariffs would be preferable to a general reduction in wages. In keeping with his continuing commitment to the need for functional policies, Bevin felt that the TUC had a duty to consider the immediate welfare of its members rather than fall back on dogmatic socialist excuses.[202]

The reaction of Citrine to events was again remarkably similar to that of Bevin. Although he did not devote so much time to the issues, Citrine also grew instinctively impatient with the perceived economic orthodoxy of the MacDonald administration, feeling that it displayed a want of courage.[203] He felt an economic general staff should have been appointed to aid Thomas in his task and was also prepared to countenance protection.[204] Although welcoming the creation of the EAC, he was unhappy with its vague job description and hesitated before accepting MacDonald's invitation to join it.[205] His reaction to the preliminary meeting of 9 December was highly critical; if it was to be at all effective the EAC should have a large permanent staff and should also be responsible to the Cabinet.[206] In February 1930 he called for a clear definition of the council's role in order that it should not become a dumping ground 'for all the odds and ends that the government likes to turn over to us'.[207] Moreover, he felt that it should contain no politicians since their continual absence through other commitments made sustained discussion difficult. By July 1930, both he and Bevin were dissatisfied with the shortcomings of the EAC. Not only was it failing to perform the advisory role assigned to it, but it was also disorganised and overcrowded.[208] Despite a private meeting with MacDonald to discuss these criticisms, no consensus was reached with the wider council as to what its role should be.[209]

In line with Keynes, Bevin supported increased government spending to raise general purchasing power and, more specifically, he called for the immediate nationalisation of iron and steel and for Britain to leave the gold standard. If the government was to pursue a policy of cuts, it was imperative to

Bevin and Citrine that there should be equality of sacrifice. Both men were frustrated by the refusal of Snowden to consider in any depth some of the alternative proposals the report of the economists had suggested in September 1930.[210] By 1931, they had given up hope of the EAC influencing government policy and were little surprised when its meetings became ever more infrequent. For the GC, the demise of the EAC was symbolic of an increasingly defensive and incommunicative government which seemed ever more ready to countenance the need for extensive cuts in expenditure.

An alternative TUC economic strategy was slow to emerge. The rank-and-file, together with many union leaders, were less amenable to unorthodox economics than Bevin and Citrine, and seldom considered the wider implications of economic policy. From union journals, one can discern little comment on economic policy beyond the basic questions of wages and unemployment. Early in the course of the government, the majority were prepared to give unconditional support to Snowden and Thomas. The Chancellor's first budget met with general approval and a TUC research document of February 1930 felt that Thomas was doing all that he could.[211] From 1930, increasing calls for a more radical policy were heard from some union leaders, but such statements seldom articulated any coherent alternative.[212] It was more common for unions to deal with specific issues relevant to their own industries. For example, ASW favoured land nationalisation and was pleased by Snowden's land tax of June 1931, and BISAKTA pushed the government for reorganisation of the iron and steel industry.[213] Not until the tariff issue found its way on to the TUC agenda did the whole union movement enter any meaningful debate on wider economic issues.

Set against a background of conversion to protectionism, it was inevitable that the TUC should debate the issue in 1930.[214] Many older trade unionists, often former Liberals, maintained that free trade had been responsible for Britain's economic supremacy and were reluctant to accept that changed circumstances might necessitate a new policy. Equally, those with a strong commitment to international socialism saw tariffs as detrimental to working-class solidarity across the globe and as a symbol of capitalist competition and corruption.[215] In addition, many feared tariffs would lead to a general increase in prices, particularly of food. Attitudes, however, did vary with the industry. Many unionists in the iron and steel industry would have welcomed a protective tariff, whereas those in the building industry and most textile workers did not wish to see the price of raw materials increased.

In May 1930 the Economic Committee of the TUC presented a report to the GC which recommended the development of fuller economic relations with the British Commonwealth. To the council's great annoyance, the *Daily Express* saw the report as an opportunity to link the TUC with the Empire Free Trade campaign then under way in the Beaverbrook Press.[216] Despite the rapid appearance of an appendix to the report to distance the TUC from this implied alliance, the whole tariff issue remained divisive. On 25 June 1930 an attempt was made by A. G. Walkden of the Railway Clerks' Association to commit the GC to tariffs, but his proposal was rejected by seventeen votes to five.[217] At the Nottingham Congress in October 1930, a full-scale debate developed on the tariff and Empire issue. The wide range of views expressed illustrates the lack of consensus. Some delegates denied the validity of the Commonwealth as an economic unit. Others felt that the Economic Committee's report had not gone far enough in support of a Commonwealth economic bloc. T. E. Naylor, MP (London Society of Compositors), expressed the view that the issue had little to do with the unions and should be left to the Labour Party, and opposed the report as a free trader.[218] The MFGB was opposed on the grounds that only 2 per cent of coal exports were destined for the Empire.[219] Both ASLEF and the ASW rejected the report and the NUGMW was so divided that it did not vote at all.[220] In the final outcome, the report was only narrowly accepted, with 1,878,000 voting for acceptance and 1,401,000 in favour of referring it back.

Predictably, the government was little interested in the economic attitudes of the TUC. It took Citrine nearly six months to arrange a meeting to discuss the economic decisions of the 1930 TUC. The GC wished particularly to call attention to the resolution which had urged MacDonald to offer employment to the able-bodied unemployed, and Citrine also requested a government body with both union and employer representation to investigate credit given to foreign trade. Both requests met with a negative response from MacDonald and Graham, with the former most concerned to emphasise the government's serious financial situation.[221] MacDonald and Snowden felt that financial policy should be the sole responsibility of the government and did not wish to complicate further their already difficult parliamentary situation through a close consideration of the views of the unions as well as those of the opposition, the Treasury, the Bank of England, the City and the industrialists. Recognising the government's difficulties, together with their own indecision and lack of understanding, the vast majority of unionists were prepared to refrain from criticism throughout 1930.

The resignation of Oswald Mosley in May 1930, in protest at the government's lack of economic innovation, created little excitement amongst trade unionists. It did, however, prove to be a little uncomfortable for Bevin, who agreed with many of the proposals of the 'Mosley Memorandum' but distrusted Mosley's motives. Cook, who together with seventeen MPs signed the 'Mosley Manifesto' in October 1930, tried to get the GC to allow Mosley an opportunity to present his case, but was wholly unsuccessful. In light of Mosley's resignation and in the interests of unity, Bevin refrained from criticism at the 1930 Labour Conference, although it is clear that he was already suppressing considerable frustration.

The greatest fear of the union movement by 1931 was a general attack on wage levels and unemployment benefits. As such, the TUC's economic outlook was characterised increasingly by defensiveness and this overshadowed the already low level of interest in alternative economic strategies. Opposition to rationalisation had hardened by this date; it was now seen as a policy favouring only the employers and facilitating more unemployment.[222] By November 1930, the TUC felt that rationalisation could only be acceptable if conceived as part of a general nationalisation policy.[223] Deeply suspicious of government intentions, Citrine told MacDonald in January 1931 of information he had received from W. J. Brown, MP, that Snowden and the Treasury 'had written to the Banks suggesting that a movement should be undertaken by them for the purpose of reducing wages'.[224] By August 1930, Bevin considered that over two million unemployed constituted a state of national emergency and was unrestrained in his criticism of the government's failure to deal with it. He felt that 'the best brains of the country should be mobilised for the purpose of really tackling the problem instead of "footling" about in the manner we are at the moment'. Further, he warned that, 'Unless the Government is vigorous and less fearful during the coming year ... it is going to be bad for us at the next General Election.' Fearful of a general attack on wages and government acceptance of cuts, Bevin called upon the workers to rally to the only thing that could save them: trade unionism.[225]

Disillusionment and distrust

At the end of 1930 disillusionment was the pervasive sentiment within the trade union movement. By as early as August, Bevin held out little hope for the government and was concerned primarily with creating an independent TUC economic line to distance it from the policy of cuts which the government seemed ever more likely to adopt. In addition, he had become involved in the activities of G. D. H. Cole, who from late 1930 was working on the creation of the Society for Socialist Inquiry and Propaganda (SSIP) and the New Fabian Research Bureau (NFRB), with the intention of constructing a new long-term socialist policy for the Labour Party. Bevin quickly became one of the key members of these two groups, becoming Chairman of the SSIP in early 1931. Citrine had long held serious reservations with regard to the ability of the government and doubted it would achieve much after mid-1930. As early as February 1930, he confessed that he was 'disillusioned with the Labour world' and in January 1931 told MacDonald that 'we have a long way to go before we can feel that we have the right administrative talent'.[226] His belief that the union movement was the best custodian of working-class improvement was reinforced and he was frustrated intensely by the breakdown in consultation with the government. In January 1931 he told MacDonald that, 'For a period it did appear that cohesion was present, certainly in greater measure than had previously existed, but of late that cohesion has disappeared, and as far as I am personally concerned scarcely exists.'[227] MacDonald's attempt in November 1930, on the advice of Henderson, to neutralise the two most powerful and troublesome figures in the union movement by offering them peerages was unsuccessful.[228] Both men considered the invitation seriously but independent of each other decided their commitment to the unions should prevail.

The attitude of the rest of the union movement was one of similar dissatisfaction and in some cases one of utter despair. William Westwood, the Glaswegian General Secretary of the Shipconstructors' and Shipwrights' Association, declared in August 1930 that he was not prepared to stand again for the Sutton division of Plymouth, a seat he had narrowly lost in 1929. Westwood felt the government had 'play[ed] fast and loose with the loyalty of its supporters' and should 'have tried to implement at least some of its promises'. He suggested that many other union leaders felt the same but were too loyal to contemplate outright criticism.[229] John Bromley, the idealistic General Secretary of ASLEF, felt similarly dispirited and announced in January 1931 that he would not be recontesting his seat in Barrow. In a letter of 27 January to MacDonald, he stated that the principal reason for his decision was the sectarian activities of the Catholics in defeating the government's Education Bill, but his reasoning went deeper than that.[230] Bromley was disillusioned by the lack of fight within the Labour Party and by the government's lack of socialist commitment. In April 1931 he wrote that the administration was 'afraid of attempting anything progressive, and will either have to go to the country or die like a sick sheep under the hedge'.[231]

A number on the left shared Bromley's apocalyptic vision and spoke in terms of the crisis within capitalism and even of the inevitable victory of communism. One correspondent in *The Locomotive* in February 1931 felt that the workers should stick by Labour until the government had 'definitely failed' and then they would be fully justified in turning to the CPGB.[232] Others remained pessimistic with regard to the revolutionary potential of the British working class. Writing in July 1931, one dispirited ASLEF socialist felt that the British worker would never turn to revolution, not even in the dire circumstances within which most now found themselves.[233]

Despite their disappointments, throughout 1930 the majority of trade unionists had been loath to give up entirely on the government. In the bleak environment at the turn of the decade, the government still seemed to offer the one avenue for improvement. Like the drowning man, then, trade unions clung desperately on to the only available branch of hope, even if it was drifting randomly downstream towards an uncertain fate. Even Bevin refrained from using his new economic philosophy as a focus within the TUC for organised opposition to the government partly because he felt that a poor Labour government was better than the alternative.[234] Yet disillusionment by the beginning of 1931 was more complete and defence of the government was a less popular pastime. Indeed, it is discernible that the amount of space in union journals devoted to political affairs began to diminish, indicating a lack of desire to comment on what was an increasingly disheartening subject.[235] The upturn in the economy in the months March to May, during which time unemployment dropped for three consecutive months, did lead to a brief spate of renewed optimism in government circles, but had little effect on the despondency which pervaded the union movement.[236] This is illustrated by the reluctance of trade unions to pay their affiliation fees to the Labour Party. In August 1931 union affiliation fees received by Transport House amounted to only half the figure for the previous year.[237]

Conclusion

For the trade unions the high expectations of May 1929 were dashed irreparably by mid-1931. Of the fifteen trade union demands identified by Citrine in January 1930, only one, regarding housing and slum clearance, had actually been met by July 1931. The Trade Disputes Act had not been overturned and thus 'contracting in' and the illegality of sympathetic strikes continued, and the Washington Hours Convention and legislation on workmen's compensation had not even been brought to Parliament. No Factories Bill had been introduced and nothing had been done for agricultural workers. The MFGB was highly dissatisfied by the failure to achieve the seven-hour day and workers in all industries were disappointed by the unsympathetic attitude of the government towards industrial disputes. In the administration of unemployment benefit, the 'Not Genuinely Seeking Work' clause had been removed only after a great deal of pressure and not only had the government not extended the range of the scheme but was clearly toying with the idea of doing the exact opposite by July 1931.

The readiness of the unions to rationalise these disappointments, and accept them as the consequence of the formidable difficulties which the government faced, was severely undermined by the government's failure to treat the unions with the respect they felt they deserved. The extreme reluctance of the government to concede any notion of regular consultation with the TUC; its failure to observe TUC protocol over the appointment of trade unionists to government committees; and the neglect of joint TUC/Labour committees, not least the NJC, all had a highly detrimental effect on relations. By 1931, as union distrust of the Labour leadership became more pronounced, the distance between the TUC and the government was growing ever wider. Although loath to see the government collapse, for fear of the alternative, by mid-1931 the trade unions were largely disillusioned with an administration to which, only two years previously, they had looked with such high hopes. Predictably, by this date, union/government differences were beginning to manifest themselves in policy terms, most visibly in the area of economic policy and, in particular, attitudes to unemployment. By July 1931, then, it was already possible to predict the likely opposition of the TUC to proposed government requests for cuts in unemployment benefit, regardless of pleas that they were vital to 'the national interest'. It was clear also that, given the opportunity to voice its opinion, the TUC would be more than ready to make the government's task a difficult one.

NOTES

1 Trade Union Congress Report 1929, p. 304.
2 South Wales Coalfield Archive, University College, Swansea (hereafter SWCA), A1, MFGB Annual Proceedings 1929–30, Annual Conference, 22 July 1929, pp. 61–2; South Wales Miners' Library, Swansea (hereafter SWML), Journal of NUGMW, January 1930, p. 2; Modern Records Centre, University of Warwick (hereafter MRC), MSS 126/T&G/4/2/7, *The Record*, September 1929, p. 38.
3 MRC, MSS 78/NASOHSPD/4/1/9, NASOHSPD Journal, 'Report on the Labour Party Conference', November 1929, p. 16.
4 British Newspaper Library, Colindale (hereafter BNL), *The Miner*, 13 October 1929, p. 3.
5 MRC, MSS 127/NU/5/12/92, *The Locomotive*, Editorial, August 1929, p. 349.
6 MRC, MSS 126/T&G/4/2/7, *The Record*, November 1929, p. 111.
7 SWML, Journal of the NUGMW, 'Parliamentary Notes', October 1929.
8 SWCA, A1, MFGB Annual Proceedings 1929–30, Annual Conference, 22 July 1929, p. 61.
9 MSS 127/NU/5/12/92, *The Locomotive*, December 1929, p. 352.
10 MRC, MSS 126/T&G/4/2/7, *The Record*, January 1930, p. 176.
11 MRC, MSS 78/ASW/4/1/9, ASW Journal, 'Address', August 1929, p. 452.
12 MRC, MSS 78/ASW/4/1/10, ASW Journal, 'Address', January 1930, p. 1.
13 This can be seen from the sizeable sections in union journals devoted to the work of their counterparts abroad.
14 MRC, MSS 127/NU/5/12/92, *The Locomotive*, December 1929, p. 352; SWML, NUGMW Journal, January 1930, p. 2.
15 British Library of Political and Economic Science (hereafter BLPES), Citrine Papers, I/7/8, 'Ramsay MacDonald and Lloyd George', 17 February 1930.
16 MRC, MSS 126/T&G/4/2/7, *The Record*, August 1929, p. 3.
17 MRC, MSS 127/NU/5/12/92, *The Locomotive*, September 1929, p. 401; MRC, MSS 78/ASW/4/1/9, ASW Journal, letter from F. W. Brown, November 1929, p. 666; MRC, MSS 78/NASOHSPD/4/1/9, NASOHSPD Journal, October 1929, p. 9.
18 Bondfield had signed a unanimous report on unemployment in 1927 containing clauses that not only watered down the policies of the Labour movement but in some instances directly opposed them.

19 BLPES, Citrine Papers, I/7/8, 'Cabinet Making', 5 June 1929.
20 *Manchester Guardian*, 23 April 1929, discussed, Harvester Press, Microfilm, GC Minutes, 24 April 1929.
21 BNL, *The Miner*, 31 May 1930, p. 4.
22 BLPES, Citrine Papers, I/7/8, 'Cabinet Making', 5 June 1929.
23 MRC, TUC Papers, MSS 292/190/4, Citrine to MacDonald, 5 June 1929.
24 BLPES, Citrine Papers, I/7/8, 'Cabinet Making', 5 June 1929, and MacDonald's reply, 7 June 1929.
25 BLPES, Citrine Papers, III/1/13, 'Labour Government – Early Contacts', 10 June 1929; P. Snowden, *An Autobiography, Vol. 2: 1919–1934* (London, 1934), p. 762.
26 *Daily Mail*, 29 January 1930; *The Times*, 25 January 1930; *Evening Standard*, 27 June 1929.
27 MRC, TUC, MSS 292/190/4, Research Department Document, 12 August 1929.
28 MRC, MSS 292/190/4, 'Report of Discussion of General Council on Relations with the Labour Government', 26 June 1929, pp. 1–2.
29 BLPES, Citrine Papers, I/7/8, 'Cabinet Making', 5 June 1929.
30 Public Record Office (hereafter PRO), MacDonald Papers, PRO 30/69/371, H. B. Usher to Thomas, 5 November 1929. This letter was sent also to Greenwood, Clynes, Bondfield and Lansbury.
31 MRC, TUC, MSS 292/145.8/3, correspondence Citrine and Clynes, 25 January to 5 February 1930.
32 MRC, TUC, MSS 292/190/4, 'Deputation to the Prime Minister', 24 January 1930, pp. 21–2; SWCA, A1, MFGB Annual Proceedings 1929–30, Special Conference, 5 November 1929, p. 18.
33 A. Clinton, *Post Office Workers: Trade Unions and Social History* (London, 1984), pp. 405–7.
34 See Strube Collections for 1929, 1930 and 1931, published by the *Daily Express*.
35 MRC, TUC, MSS 292/753/2, Citrine to G. P. Blizzard, 3 July 1929.
36 MRC, TUC, MSS 292/753/2, J. Gibbons, MP, to Citrine, 25 June 1931.
37 R. McKibbin, 'Arthur Henderson as Labour Leader', *International Review of Social History* 23: 1 (1978), 93–5.
38 BLPES, Citrine Papers, I/7/8, 'Anecdotes at Downing Street', 27 November 1929; PRO, MacDonald Papers, PRO 30/69/1753/1, 27 November 1929.
39 BLPES, Citrine Papers, I/7/8, 'The Prime Minister', 29 January 1931.
40 See PRO, MacDonald Papers, Diary, PRO 30/69/1753/1, for early 1931 period.
41 BLPES, Citrine Papers, I/7/8, 'The Prime Minister', 29 January 1931.
42 BLPES, Citrine Papers, I/7/8, 'Cabinet Making', 5 June 1929.
43 MRC, TUC, MSS 292/157.83/4a, Memorandum interview Citrine with Bondfield, 21 November 1930, and Citrine to Holman Gregory, 28 January 1931.
44 BLPES, Citrine Papers, I/1/11, 'Economic Council', 9 December 1929.
45 BNL, *The Miner*, July 19, p. 5; *The Miner*, correspondence, August 1929.
46 BLPES, Citrine Papers, III/1/13, extract of report in *Daily Mail*, 29 January 1930; MRC, TUC, MSS 292/157.83/4a, Citrine to Holman Gregory, 28 January 1931, and Citrine to MacDonald, 18 December 1930; Harvester Press, Microfilm, GC Minutes, 17 December 1930, p. 28a.
47 MRC, TUC, MSS 29/33/2, Joint Meetings, 26 November 1930 and 23 June

1931.

48 MRC, TUC, MSS 292/46.52/6a, Joint Meeting NEC and GC, 21 May 1930; MSS 292/46.52/7, Henderson to Citrine, 25 July 1930.

49 PRO, MacDonald Papers, PRO 30/69/1176, MacDonald to Henderson, 24 July 1931.

50 MRC, TUC, MSS 292/24.1/4, GC Finance and General Purposes Committee (hereafter FGPC), 10 February 1930, p. 46.

51 Labour Party Archive, National Museum of Labour History, Manchester (hereafter LPA), CC Minutes, 25 March 1930.

52 MRC, TUC, MSS 292/32.1/2.

53 TUC Report 1929, p. 351

54 MRC, TUC, MSS 292/33/2, 23 October 1929, p. 2.

55 MRC, TUC, MSS 292/190/4, Deputation to the Prime Minister, 24 January 1930, p. 10.

56 Ibid., pp. 15–20.

57 Ibid., p. 10.

58 BLPES, Citrine Papers, III/1/13, TUC Report on Discussion of the General Council, 22 January 1930, pp. 2–4.

59 MRC, TUC, MSS 292/190/4, 24 January 1930, p. 31.

60 For Bevin see TUC Report 1929, p. 385, and for Citrine, see H. A. Clegg, *A History of British Trade Unions since 1889, Vol. 2: 1911–1933* (Oxford, 1985), p. 385.

61 Clegg, *A History*, p. 483.

62 SWCA, A1, Special Conference, 7 November 1929, p. 49, and Chairman's Report of Meeting with Government, 6 November, pp. 67–8.

63 PRO, MacDonald Papers, PRO 30/69/248, R. B. Howarth to MacDonald, June 1931.

64 SWCA, A1, Annual Conference, 23–25 July 1929, pp. 71–126.

65 BNL, *The Miner*, Editorial, 21 September 1929, p. 6.

66 BNL, *The Miner*, 19 October 1929. The articles in this edition would have been written before the meeting of the Coal Committee of 16 October.

67 SWCA, A1, Report of Meetings with the Government on the Coal Mines Bill, 16 October 1929, pp. 8 and 55; 25 October, pp. 61–2; 12 and 13 November, pp. 90–117.

68 PRO, MacDonald Papers, PRO 30/69/559, Jones to MacDonald, 13 November 1929.

69 SWCA, A1, Special Conference, 5 November 1929, pp. 72–91.

70 PRO, MacDonald Papers, PRO 30/69/559, Jones to MacDonald, 13 November 1929, and copy of memorandum to J. H. Thomas, sent 26 October, enclosed.

71 SWCA, A1, adjourned Special Conference, 20 November 1929, p. 129.

72 T. N. Graham, *Willie Graham: The Life of the Rt. Hon. William Graham* (London, n.d., 1948), p. 181.

73 SWCA, A1, Executive, Resolution 1, 10 April 1930, p. 4.

74 SWCA, A1, Annual Conference, President's Address, 11 August 1930, p. 23; BNL, *The Miner*, 12 April; SWCA, A1, Executive, 6 May 1930, Cook to Sankey; Bodleian Library, Oxford, Sankey Papers, MSS Eng. Hist. C508.

75 SWCA, A1, Executive, 11 August 1930, p. 5.

76 SWCA, A1, Annual Conference Report, 11 August 1930, pp. 22–72.

77 SWCA, A1, Report of Executive Committee on Conference, p. 87.

78 The government had seen Richards as a moderate to this point, see PRO,

MacDonald Papers, PRO 30/69/248, Memorandum from H. G. Usher, 10 January 1931.

79 SWCA, A1, President's Address to Special Conference, 20 November 1930.

80 Ibid., Special Conference, 28 November 1930.

81 PRO, MacDonald Papers, Diary, PRO 30/69/1753, 8 November 1929; MacDonald was greatly pleased by Cook's new elasticity. P. Davies, *A. J. Cook* (Manchester, 1987) unfortunately sheds little light on the motivations for his turnaround during 1929–31; the lack of primary source material does make explanations difficult.

82 BLPES, Passfield Papers, B. Webb's Diary, 10 September 1926, suggested that Cook was 'drunk with his own words, dominated by his own slogans'. Despite his subsequent denials, during the 1926 lockout Cook had negotiated with people close to the owners and the government without informing the Executive Committee.

83 In November 1927, disliking the militancy of the national leadership, G. R. Spencer formed a breakaway union from the Nottinghamshire Miners' Association to secure a district settlement with the coalowners. The split lasted until 1937 when the two amalgamated; A. R. Griffen, *The Miners of Nottinghamshire, 1914–1944: A History of the Nottinghamshire Miners' Unions* (London, 1962).

84 BNL, *The Miner*, 4 January 1930, p. 8, and 1 November 1930, p. 4.

85 Bodleian Library, Oxford, Sankey Papers, MSS Eng. Hist. C508, Cook to Sankey, 31 August 1931.

86 Cook had his right leg amputated in March 1931 and died in November.

87 SWCA, A1, Executive Committee, 3 December 1930.

88 Ibid., Adjourned Conference, 4 December 1930, pp. 106–41.

89 Ibid., Executive Committee, Appendix 3, 'Result of District Voting on PM's suggestion', 16 December, pp. 39–40.

90 PRO, MacDonald Papers, PRO 30/69/674, Cook to MacDonald, 9 January 1931.

91 SWCA, A1, Special Conference, 19 March 1931, pp. 2–4 and 42.

92 Ibid., Executive, 17 April, pp. 2–3.

93 Ibid., Report of Conference at 10 Downing Street, 30 April 1931, p. 21.

94 PRO, MacDonald Papers, PRO 30/69/674, MacDonald to Cook, 12 January 1931.

95 PRO, MacDonald Papers, PRO 30/69/248, J. R. Willis to C. P. Duff, 21 March 1931.

96 In a Cabinet discussion of January 1931, only Lansbury disagreed; PRO, MacDonald Papers, PRO 30/69/248, Report on the Cabinet, 7 January 1931.

97 Richards resigned the Presidency in July 1931 on grounds of ill health, and died in November 1931.

98 SWCA, A1, Conference, 30 April, p. 26.

99 Ibid., Special Conference, 25 June 1931, pp. 34–5.

100 The extensive nature of the files on coal-mining in MacDonald's papers bear witness to this fact.

101 *House of Commons Debates*, Vol. 244, 3 November 1930, col. 527.

102 For a fuller discussion see A. Thorpe, 'The Industrial Meaning of "Gradualism": The Labour Party and Industry, 1918–31', *Journal of British Studies* 35: 1 (1996), 84–113.

103 PRO, MacDonald Papers, PRO 30/69/413, Report of the Cotton Committee,

June 1930.

104 BNL, *Cotton Factory Times*, 11 July 1930, p. 1, and letter from 'Sentinel', 25 July 1930. See also A. Fowler, 'Cotton Trade Unionism: Lancashire Trade Unionism in the Inter-War Years', in J. A. Jowitt and A. J. McIvor (eds), *Employers and Labour in the English Textile Industries, 1850–1939* (London, 1988).

105 PRO, MacDonald Papers, PRO 30/69/413, Report of the Cotton Committee.

106 PRO, MacDonald Papers, PRO 30/69/413, Memorandum of Clynes to the Cabinet, CP 319(30).

107 BNL, *Cotton Factory Times*, report on Graham's speech, 1 August 1930; PRO, MacDonald Papers, Diary, PRO 30/69/1753/1, 12 January 1931.

108 PRO, MacDonald Papers, PRO 30/69/412, L. Replogle, New York, to C. G. Dawes, Ambassador to Great Britain, on the steel industry.

109 The government, and Snowden in particular, resisted full publication for fear it would increase pressure for safeguarding; see PRO, MacDonald Papers, PRO 30/69/412, Memorandum Usher to MacDonald, June 1930.

110 MRC, BISAKTA papers, MSS 36, I14 (General), Executive Council A.P. L1 19/8/30, pp. 2–3.

111 PRO, MacDonald Papers, PRO 30/69/412, W. J. Larke to MacDonald, 15 January 1931, and Larke to MacDonald, 30 April 1931.

112 PRO, MacDonald Papers, PRO 30/69/412, Notes of Meeting of Snowden, Graham and the Governor of the Bank of England, 11 May 1931.

113 MRC, TGWU Papers, MSS 106/T&G/1/1/9, 'Assistant General Secretary's Quarterly Report', 20 May 1931.

114 MRC, MSS 127/NU/5/12/94, *The Locomotive*, General Secretary Remarks, June 1931, p. 238.

115 MRC, MSS 126/T&G/4/2/7, *The Record*, 'Road Transport', December 1929, p. 153.

116 MRC, MSS 78/ASW/4/1/10, ASW Journal, October 1930, p. 577.

117 MRC, TUC, MSS 292/46.52/6a, Research Department Document, 8 April 1930.

118 MRC, TUC, MSS 292/46.52/6a, TUC Memorandum of Interview, 13 November 1929.

119 MRC, TUC, MSS 292/190/4, Report on Deputation, 24 January 1930, p. 12.

120 Ibid., p. 27.

121 MRC, TUC, MSS 292/46.52/6a, TUC Memorandum of Interview with the Cabinet Committee, 3 April 1930, pp. 2–3.

122 MRC, TUC, MSS 292/46.52/6a, Minutes of Joint Meeting, 29 May 1930, pp. 18–19.

123 MRC, TUC, MSS 292/46.52/6a, Memorandum of Interview with the Government, 20 June 1930, pp. 2–3.

124 MRC, TUC, MSS 292/46.52/6a, Report on Joint Meeting, 25 July 1930.

125 MRC, TUC, MSS 292/46.52/7, Henderson to Citrine, 25 July 1930.

126 MRC, TUC, MSS 292/46.52/7, Citrine to MacDonald, 7 November 1930.

127 Harvester Press, Microfilm, TUC Pamphlets and Leaflets, Series II, 1897–1930 (Brighton, 1977), Report of the Sixth Annual Conference of Trade Councils; MRC, MSS 78/ASW/4/1/10, ASW Journal, Report on the NFBTO Conference June 1930, August 1930.

128 SWML, NUGMW Journal, October 1930, p. 247.

129 MRC, TGWU, MSS 106/T&G/1/1/8, Bevin's Quarterly Report, 17 November 1930; PRO, MacDonald Papers, PRO 30/69/359, Bevin to MacDonald, 27

August 1930.

130 PRO, MacDonald Papers, PRO 30/69/359, MacDonald to Henderson, 5 December 1930, and Henderson's reply.

131 MRC, TUC, MSS 292/46.52/6b, Research Document, 28 January 1931.

132 MRC, TUC, MSS 292/24.1/5, GC FGPC, 26 January 1931, p. 34.

133 MRC, TUC, MSS 292/23.1/9, TUC Circulars, 3 February 1931.

134 MRC, TUC, MSS 292/23.1/9, H. V. Tewson to J. S. Middleton, 5 February 1931; MRC, TUC, MSS 292/46.1/2.

135 Harvester Press, Microfilm, GC Minutes, 25 February 1931, p. 38, min. 112.

136 BLPES, Citrine Papers, Notes and Memoirs I/1/1, 'Trade Union Bill', 28 February 1931, p. 254.

137 MRC, TUC, MSS 292/46.52/7, Bromley to Citrine, 6 March 1931.

138 MRC, TUC, MSS 292/46.52/7, Bevin to Citrine, 2 April 1931 and Citrine to Bevin, 8 April 1931.

139 MRC, TUC, MSS 292/46.52/6a, Citrine Circular to all members of the GC.

140 MRC, TUC, MSS 292/46.52/6a, Citrine to MacDonald, 25 to 31 March 1931.

141 MRC, TUC, MSS 292/46.52/6a, Citrine to MacDonald, 30 March 1931, and Usher to Citrine, 31 March 1931.

142 MRC, TUC, MSS 292/46.52/7, MacDonald to Citrine, 21 April 1931. This story was made credible by the fact that Jowitt had been elected as a Liberal in 1929 and had transferred to Labour when offered the position of Attorney General.

143 Harvester Press, Microfilm, GC FGPC 12 May 1931, item 118, 22 April 1931.

144 MRC, TUC, MSS 292/46.52/6b, TUC Report of the Meeting. The Liberal amendment had never been discussed and neither Kedward nor Thomas had been involved in meetings between the Liberals and the government. Tom Shaw had worded another proposed Liberal amendment so that the government could see what the Liberal's position was.

145 MRC, TUC, MSS 292/46.52/7, Bromley to Citrine, 6 March 1931.

146 MRC, TUC, MSS 292/46.52/6b, Report of the Sub-Committee on the Meeting, 28 April 1931.

147 BLPES, Citrine Papers, I/4/2, Speech to the TUC Summer School, 5 July 1931.

148 PRO, MacDonald Papers, PRO 30/69/359, MacDonald to Snowden, 27 September 1929.

149 MRC, TUC, MSS 2292/190/4, Deputation to the Prime Minister, 24 January 1930, p. 11.

150 MSS 127/NU/1/1/18, NUR Quarterly meeting, 3–14 March 1930, p. 121, and NUR General Secretary's Report, AGM, 7 July 1930, pp. 5–6.

151 MRC, TUC, MSS 292/127.51/2, 'History of the Industrial Employment Bill', 10 August 1931.

152 PRO, MacDonald Papers, PRO 30/69/359, Bondfield to MacDonald, 7 May 1931.

153 PRO, MacDonald Papers, PRO 30/69/359, Citrine to Bondfield, 21 and 22 May 1931.

154 PRO, MacDonald Papers, PRO 30/69/359, Bondfield to MacDonald, 7 May and 30 May 1931, and MacDonald's reply, 8 May; Bondfield to Citrine, 26 May 1931.

155 *The Times*, 4 June 1931, and PRO, MacDonald Papers, PRO 30/69/359, MacDonald to Thomas, 9 June 1931.

156 MRC, TUC, MSS 292/190/4, Meeting with the Prime Minister, 24 January

1930, p. 13.

157 BLPES, Citrine Papers, III/1/13, GC Discussion, 22 January 1930.

158 SWCA, A1, Report of the Executive for year ending June 1930, p. 33.

159 SWCA, A1, Annual Conference Report, August 1930, p. 73.

160 V. L. Allen, *Trade Unions and the Government* (London, 1960), p. 240.

161 PRO, MacDonald Papers, PRO 30/69/672, Greenwood to MacDonald, 7 August 1929.

162 BNL, *Cotton Factory Times*, 30 August 1929, p. 1.

163 PRO, MacDonald Papers, PRO 30/69/1174, H. Pickles to MacDonald, 25 July 1929.

164 A. Hutt, *A Post-War History of the British Working Class* (London, 1937), p. 202.

165 SWCA, South Wales Miners' Federation Minutes, 12 May 1930.

166 MRC, TUC, MSS 292/23.1/8, TUC Circular on 'Wool Textile Dispute', 23 April 1930.

167 Hutt, *Post-War History*, p. 202.

168 Fowler, 'Cotton Trade Unionism', p. 115, and BNL, *Cotton Factory Times*, 2 January, 30 January and letters 6 February 1931.

169 PRO, MacDonald Papers, PRO 30/69/413, letters sent 2 February 1931 to A. Naesmith of the Northern Counties Textile Federation and to J. Grey of the Cotton Spinners Manufacturers' Association.

170 PRO, MacDonald Papers, Diary, PRO 30/69/1753/1, 1 February 1931, complained that, 'Disputes like this in lean times are of the nature of revolutions'.

171 PRO, MacDonald Papers, PRO 30/69/677, MacDonald to Clynes, 9 February 1931.

172 Clegg, *A History*, p. 493.

173 SWCA, A1, Adjourned Special Conference, 4 December 1930.

174 SWCA, A1, Annual Report for year ending June 1931.

175 E. A. and G. H. Radice, *Will Thorne, Constructive Militant: A Study in New Unionism and New Politics* (London, 1974), p. 113.

176 J. E. Mortimer, *History of the Boilermakers' Society, Vol. 2: 1906–1939* (London, 1982), p. 213.

177 MRC, MSS 126/T&G/4/2/7, *The Record*, June 1930 and August 1930; SWML, NUGMW Journal, July 1930; MRC, MSS 78/ASW/4/1/11, ASW Journal, March 1931.

178 MRC, MSS 126/T&G/4/2/7, *The Record*, March 1930.

179 MRC, MSS 126/T&G/4/2/7, *The Record*, August 1930.

180 Harvester Press, Microfilm, TUC Pamphlets and Leaflets, Series II, 1897–1930 (Brighton, 1977), TUC Pamphlet of the Conference, 30 May 1931.

181 MRC, TUC, MSS 292/157.82/1, Morris Committee Circular, 1 August 1929.

182 Harvester Press, Microfilm, TUC Pamphlets and Leaflets, Series II, 1897–1930 (Brighton, 1977), *Genuinely Seeking Work*, evidence submitted to the Morris Committee, 27 August 1929.

183 R. Skidelsky, *Politicians and the Slump: The Labour Government of 1929–31* (London, 1967), Morris Committee Report, paragraph 43, p. 115.

184 Harvester Press, Microfilm, GC Minutes, 17 November 1929, pp. 19–19c.

185 Harvester Press, Microfilm, GC Minutes, 18 December 1929, FGPC Report, Item 61, letter from Middleton, 10 December 1929.

186 PRO, MacDonald Papers, PRO 30/69/1176, W. Thorne to MacDonald, 3 December 1929, and letter from fifty-five MPs to the Chairman of the Consulta-

tive Committee on Unemployment Insurance Bill, n.d.

187 SWML, NUGMW Journal, December 1929

188 PRO, MacDonald Papers, PRO 30/69/4, Greenwood to MacDonald, 20 December 1930.

189 Harvester Press, Microfilm, GC Minutes, 28 January 1931.

190 MRC, TUC, MSS 292/157.83/1, Citrine to Holman Gregory, 28 January 1931.

191 MRC, TUC, MSS 292/157.83/4a, Deputation to Prime Minister, 2 January 1931, p. 36.

192 MRC, TUC, MSS 292/157.83/4a, Transcript from Treasury Report of Meeting of the GC with the PM, 2 January 1931.

193 MRC, TUC, MSS 292/157.83/1.

194 PRO, MacDonald Papers, PRO 30/69/677, MacDonald to Bondfield, 6 May 1931.

195 SWCA, A1, Executive, 5 June 1931; MRC, MSS 78/ASW/4/1/11, ASW Journal, 'Parliamentary Report', July 1931.

196 Harvester Press, Microfilm, TUC Pamphlets and Leaflets, Series II (Brighton, 1977), *Fair Play for the Unemployed*, June 1931.

197 MRC, TUC, MSS 292/23.1/9, TUC Circular, 6 June 1931.

198 MRC, TUC, MSS 292/157.83/1, Citrine to Hayday, 8 June 1931.

199 MRC, TUC, MSS 292/157.83/3, TUC Report on the Conferences, 27 July 1931.

200 PRO, MacDonald Papers, PRO 30/69/677.

201 Hutt, *Post-War History*, p. 199; BLPES, Passfield Papers, B. Webb's Diary, 28 October 1931; 'The PLP has not been defeated but annihilated: largely we think by the women's vote'. See Chapter 4 for a more detailed discussion of the Bill.

202 *Macmillan Committee Minutes of Evidence and Report*; for Bevin see A. Bullock, *The Life and Times of Ernest Bevin, Vol. 1: Trade Union Leader, 1881–1944* (London, 1960), pp. 425–34, and for Keynes see P. Clarke, *The Keynesian Revolution in the Making, 1924–1936* (Oxford, 1988).

203 MRC, TUC, MSS 292/135.4/6, Deputation to the Prime Minister, 20 April 1931, p. 4.

204 Harvester Press, Microfilm, GC Minutes, Report of Meeting with Thomas, 28 November 1929, p. 28c.

205 BLPES, Citrine Papers, I/1/11, 'The Webbs', 1 February 1930.

206 BLPES, Citrine Papers, I/1/6, 'Economic Council', 9 December 1929.

207 BLPES, Citrine Papers, I/7/8, Diary, 17 February 1930.

208 S. Howson and D. Winch, *The Economic Advisory Council 1930–1939: A Study in Economic Advice during Depression and Recovery* (Cambridge, 1979), p. 39.

209 K. Middlemas (ed.), *Tom Jones. Whitehall Diary, Vol. 2: 1926–1930* (London, 1969), pp. 267 and 270.

210 Howson and Winch, *Economic Advisory Council*, pp. 74 and 81.

211 MRC, MSS 127/NU/5/2/93, *The Locomotive*, Editorial, May 1930, and SWML, NUGMW Journal, May 1930, p. 115.

212 MRC, MSS 127/NU/5/2/93, *The Locomotive*, Editorial, September 1930, p. 406; SWCA, A1, Annual Conference 1930, President's Address.

213 See MRC, MSS 78/ASW/4/1/10, ASW Journal, July 1930, pp. 413–14, and MSS 78/ASW/4/1/11, June 1931, Parliamentary Report, p. 343.

214 By the end of 1930, the Federation of British Industries and the National Council of Employers' Organisations, the Conservative Party, J. M. Keynes and a number of prominent Liberals had announced their support for protection in

some shape or form; P. Williamson, *National Crisis and National Government: British Politics, the Economy and Empire, 1926–1932* (Cambridge, 1992), chapter 6.

215 SWML, NUGMW Journal, C. Dukes, MP, November 1930.

216 Harvester Press, Microfilm, GC Minutes, 28 May 1930, p. 74, min. 224.

217 Harvester Press, Microfilm, GC Minutes, 25 June 1930, p. 83, min. 256.

218 Harvester Press, Microfilm, TUC Pamphlets and Leaflets, Series II (Brighton, 1977), *Commonwealth Trade: A New Policy*, September 1930, pp. 13–42.

219 SWCA, A1, Annual Conference, 11 August 1930, p. 26.

220 MRC, MSS 127/NU/5/12/94, *The Locomotive*, Report on TUC, October 1930, p. 456; MRC, MSS 78/ASW/4/1/11, ASW Journal, Report on NFBTO Annual Conference, July 1931; SWML, NUGMW Journal, November 1930, 'TUC Economic Policy'.

221 MRC, TUC, MSS 292/135.4/6, Meeting with the Prime Minister, 20 April 1931.

222 Harvester Press, Microfilm, GC Minutes, 22 October 1930, Report of the FGPC, p. 15, article 44.

223 G. Phillips, 'Trade Unions and Corporatist Politics', in P. J. Waller (ed.), *Politics and Social Change in Modern Britain* (Brighton, 1987), pp. 199–208.

224 MRC, TUC, MSS 292/57.83/4a, TUC Meeting with the Prime Minister, 2 January 1931.

225 MRC, TGWU, MSS 126/T&G/1/1/8, Bevin's General Secretary's Report, 19 August 1930; see also PRO, MacDonald Papers, PRO 30/69/461, Bevin to MacDonald.

226 BLPES, Passfield Papers, B. Webb's Diary, 5 February 1930; BLPES, Citrine Papers, I/7/8, 'The Prime Minister', 29 January 1931.

227 MRC, TUC, MSS 292/157.83/4a, Deputation to the Prime Minister, 2 January 1931, pp. 5–7 and 14–15.

228 Lord Citrine, *Men and Work: An Autobiography* (London, 1964), p. 281; T. Evans, *Ernest Bevin* (London, 1946), p. 140; PRO, MacDonald Papers, Diary, PRO 30/69/1753/1, 26 November 1930. Note, however, that this offer can be interpreted also as the action of a Prime Minister desperate to solve the problem of lack of Labour representation in the Upper House. See P. Williamson, 'The Labour Party and the House of Lords, 1918–1931', *Parliamentary History* 10: 2 (1991), 317–41.

229 Taken from the *Evening World* and quoted in D. Dougan, *The Shipwrights: The History of the Shipconstructors' and Shipwrights' Association, 1882–1963* (Newcastle, 1975), p. 235.

230 PRO, MacDonald Papers, PRO 30/69/1176, correspondence Bromley and MacDonald, 26, 27 and 28 January; 27 and 29 May 1931.

231 MRC, MSS 127/NU/5/12/94, *The Locomotive*, April 1931, p. 137.

232 MRC, MSS 127/NU/5/12/94, *The Locomotive*, February 1931, p. 91.

233 MRC, MSS 127/NU/5/12/94, *The Locomotive*, correspondence, entitled 'When?', July 1931.

234 There were other reasons. First, he doubted he would be successful. Secondly, he was too busy at the TGWU and with the campaign to relaunch the *Daily Herald*. Finally, with the serious threat to living standards by the end of 1930, theoretical economic policies ranked low compared to the immediate need to protect wage levels. Bevin saw himself as a trade unionist and not a politician; attempts to get him to stand in by-elections were rejected.

235 See, for example, MRC, MSS 127/NU/5/12/94, *The Locomotive*; MRC, MSS 78/ASW/4/1/11, ASW Journal; SWML, NUGMW Journal.

236 This renewed spell of hope is clearly illustrated in PRO, MacDonald Papers, Diary, PRO 30/69/1753.

237 R. Shackleton, 'Trade Unions and the Slump', in B. Pimlott and C. Cook (eds), *Trade Unions in British Politics* (London, 1982), p. 123.

3

Local Labour parties

Organisational matters

The enthusiasm instilled by the election result was slow to subside, and local parties continued to enjoy its positive effects for many months. Whilst some were disappointed with the moderate programme announced in the King's Speech, general satisfaction was expressed with the government's initial activities and with party fortunes in the localities. Many continued to pick up new members and the November 1929 municipal elections were generally a great success; nationally the party gained 100 seats and lost only a handful.[1] The October Labour Conference witnessed few local party criticisms of the government or the national leadership.

Eager to take advantage of this general feeling of goodwill, the NEC made a further attempt to improve local organisation and the national party's finances. A revised constitution was submitted to the October 1929 conference which proposed that the local party affiliation fee to head office should be doubled to 4d per member and that, in order to extend membership, a third class of member should be introduced, to be called 'national affiliated members'. This latter proposal would constitute a radical change to the manner in which individuals were recruited; in place of a necessity to become involved on a local level, a prospective member would be able to affiliate directly to head office. Both suggestions were resisted fiercely by local party delegates. G. R. Shepherd, the National Agent, suggested that the key advantage of national affiliated membership would be to attract those professional people who felt that they could not afford to associate directly with the movement.[2] The chief concern of local parties, however, was that these members would be unaccountable and consequently untrustworthy. E. H. Parker of Bristol

Labour Party summed up these sentiments: 'If you take these people in, who have been shy of coming in until we get respectable, what is going to happen the next time you stand up against a crisis? They will "rat" immediately.' Others were concerned that existing members would cut their ties with their local organisation.[3] In consequence, the NEC decided to withdraw rather than experience inevitable defeat in a vote. Effectively, then, an amendment that could have had a positive effect on widening the party's membership base was defeated by the desire of local parties to retain their current status within the movement's hierarchy.[4]

Reactions to the proposal to raise affiliation fees were similarly hostile. J. A. W. Douglas of Bermondsey West Labour Party argued that the implementation of this reform would undermine the party's ability to attract new members and to retain its existing ones.[5] Councillor E. Allan Robson of Cardiff Trades Council and Labour Party (TCLP) argued that the increase would effectively bankrupt his and many other local parties. Henderson's defence offered a revealing insight into the differing perspectives of the local parties and head office. He reminded the delegates that the NEC's contribution to local parties in the form of propaganda and financial assistance amounted to more than £5,000 each year, a sum which exceeded the total annual affiliation fees from the localities. He displayed his party management skills to their full effect and conference was able to agree upon a compromise figure of 3d per member.[6]

Many non-union party members had long resented the degree of union control at local level and at the national conference. The union block vote was a major bone of contention; at every conference local party delegates were forced to watch helplessly as decisions were made by the mass vote of the union representatives. At the 1930 conference the 356 delegates from trades councils and local parties wielded only 394,000 votes, whereas the 354 union attendants claimed to represent some 2,047,000 members.[7] This was a situation which many non-union members wanted to see changed. During the debate at the 1929 conference on the issue of affiliation fees, E. Allan Robson requested that 'for the first time in this Conference the Labour Parties themselves may be allowed to vote on their own question', in order that:

> The block vote of the trade union representatives will not wipe us out as it has on every resolution which was of any value to us.... Although this is a Labour Party Conference, Labour Party delegates have no voice. The Trade Unionists have their own Trades Union Congress, but here we get snowed under by the block vote on practically every issue.[8]

Such sentiments were not confined to Cardiff. The delegate from Nottingham South later complained that 'it was hopeless for a divisional delegate with one vote to get a fair chance sitting beside [a] trade union delegate, who could up [*sic*] hundreds of votes' and therefore he proposed that the best solution would be 'a series of regional conferences from which a few delegates [would] be appointed to attend a National Conference'.[9] The NEC decision in October 1929 to reduce the increasingly unwieldy conference structure through the limitation of local representation to one delegate per 5,000 individual members was therefore predictably met by unified local party resistance, but, since the unions had already consented to a reduction in their own delegation (from a former figure of 3,000 to around 400–500), the constituency delegates were again defeated by the union block vote.[10]

This amendment was resented particularly by the women's sections, who believed it would undermine further the already low level of female representation at conference. Previously, local parties had been eligible to send a second delegate if they had 500 members in their women's section, but it was now proposed that there had to be 2,500 women in a local party to allow it to qualify for this privilege. Mrs Thomson, a delegate from Coventry, pointed out that 'one does not need any spectacles or any super intelligence to know that when only one delegate has to be chosen, it is the man who is sent by the Constituency Party'. A number of male delegates from local parties were also critical of the proposed change; a Mr Setchell from Bermondsey expressed his disgust with the party's hypocritical attitude towards its women members. Whilst it eulogised them for their hard work it continued to deny them any responsibility in the running of the party. Yet Susan Lawrence defended the decision and urged women to abolish their existing privileges and work to get to the party conference by 'fighting and scrapping with male comrades on terms of perfect equality'. The effect that the passing of this amendment had upon the attitudes of female members is difficult to assess. What is apparent is that the fears of the women's sections were well-founded, since the appearance of female delegates at the national conference became thereafter a rare occurrence. The number of women's sections declined significantly during the period 1930–32, from 1,969 sections in 1930 to 1,824 in 1931 and 1,704 in 1932. Economic depression was central to this decline, but a negative reaction to the changes described, together with disillusionment over the party's unwillingness to improve the national status of women, may also have played their part.[11]

Relations with Members of Parliament

Good relations between local parties and their Labour MPs was necessarily an important component in the maintenance of loyalty to the government. Once again, both sides had basic expectations with regard to the duties of the other. Local parties expected their MP to inform them regularly of events at Westminster, participate in occasional local public meetings, take account of local policy priorities and, perhaps above all, pay any contributions they had pledged to party finances. The MP expected to receive the party's support and to be granted a degree of flexibility over his or her constituency duties.

Relations between local parties and their MPs, however, took on a variety of forms. It was often the case that those elected for the first time in 1929 expended the greatest effort in ensuring that relations were harmonious. J. Chuter Ede in South Shields and J. Walker in Newport were two examples. Ede won the confidence of South Shields Labour Party through the sending of regular parliamentary reports, and Newport DLP was very satisfied with the extensive efforts of Walker on its behalf.[12] Both men attended party meetings at regular intervals, and not only was this appreciated by the party, but it also served to combat any local opposition to the government.[13] It was a truism that local parties were far less likely to be critical of the administration in the presence of their MP. It was equally the case, however, that as government problems increased, MPs were ever more reluctant to face their constituency parties.[14]

Elsewhere, relations were far less harmonious. Darlington, Wrexham and Penistone DLPs all recorded their growing dissatisfaction over the infrequent contacts with their respective MPs and no doubt this only served to fuel their disagreements with the government.[15] The more prestigious figures in the national party were able to avoid fulfilling duties to their local parties. Snowden, for example, attended only one local party event in his constituency of Colne Valley during the course of the government, and that was to visit the 1930 AGM. Other attempts to secure him to speak at public meetings were fruitless, although the party was able to take advantage of his connections to secure other prominent figures to attend its 1931 May Day Rally. Colne Valley, then, accepted that Snowden had many demands upon his time and felt that having an MP of national standing was more than sufficient compensation for any deficiency in the carrying out of local duties.[16]

When it came to financial obligations, however, they were far less forgiving. Even the likes of Snowden were unable to escape this constituency duty; Colne Valley DLP felt strongly after the 1929 campaign that Snowden had not paid the share of the election expenses agreed beforehand, and the Executive wrote to inform him accordingly. Ironically for a Chancellor not noted for his financial generosity, after an initial refusal, Snowden paid the promised sum in early August.[17] Rennie Smith had a two-year disagreement with Penistone DLP on the subject of election expenses, with the MP refusing to pay the sum the party claimed he owed.[18] The situation that developed between Nottingham South DLP and G. W. Holford Knight, KC, was more acrimonious still. Finding itself increasingly in debt from mid-1930, the Executive decided to set up a fighting fund and felt that, since he was a wealthy man, Knight should contribute £100 per annum. Upon discovering this decision, a very annoyed

Knight protested that, since he was no longer paid barrister fees, he could not possibly afford to pay such a sum. At a special meeting of the MP with the Executive on 20 July 1930, it was apparently agreed that Knight should pay only £50. Yet, on reflection, the Executive decided this was insufficient and that if Knight could not afford the £100 then another candidate would have to be found. Knight refused to accept this decision, which he claimed had been reached by a small section of the Executive keen to 'undermine his prestige'. Thereafter, the party became increasingly divided between those who supported Knight and those who did not. Not until 9 October 1930 did a quarterly meeting of the whole party agree finally to accept the offer of £50 and attempt to end the poor relations by passing a vote of confidence in Knight.

This was not to be the end of the dispute. The Party Secretary resigned in January 1931 and in February the Executive reported that Knight had still not paid any of the £50 owing. Not until March did the money finally arrive. Relations remained sufficiently sour for the National Organiser in the Midlands Area to be called in April to investigate this damaging situation. The antipathy between the MP and his local party was to culminate in Knight's support for the National Government in August 1931, an outcome which was no doubt viewed with considerable relief by the Nottingham South Executive, since it presented the party with the ideal opportunity to part ways with a candidate who had proved to be a disastrous choice.[19] It was somewhat ironic that such a confrontational situation should develop between a local party and a candidate who had been chosen primarily for his wealth.

Disagreements over policy were another potential source of tension, but on the whole these were rare. As has been noted, the majority of local members were keen to support their government and it was not until 1931, when disillusioned party activists were daring to become more critical, that local parties were prepared to pass anything which amounted to votes of censure on their MPs. The piece of legislation that provoked the greatest tension was the government's 'Anomalies Bill' of June 1931. Both Greenwich DLP and Llanelli DLP were unhappy with the stand that their MPs had taken on this issue. E. T. Palmer, MP for Greenwich, had voted for the Bill, and Dr J. H. Williams had abstained, which his local party regarded as 'tantamount to agreement'.[20]

Legislation

Local party legislative priorities depended both upon the make-up of their constituencies and the outlook of their members, and consequently there was considerable variation from place to place. Agricultural DLPs, like Cambridgeshire and Chichester, tended naturally to prioritise agricultural reform. The *Cambridge Elector*, Labour's 1929 election paper in Cambridge, made its appeal on the basis of what a Labour government would do to improve the lives of agricultural workers, through the extension of unemployment insurance, increased wages and the control of imports.[21] Both Chichester and Cambridge were disappointed by the government's failure to implement any major agricultural reform and sent a number of resolutions to the 1930 and 1931 Labour Conferences, calling for the nationalisation of land, import boards and a specific housing act for agricultural areas.[22] The latter proposal was passed at the 1930 conference but had no effect on the government's legislative programme. Similarly, in those areas dominated by textiles, local parties were very concerned that the government should reform the cotton industry. Nelson and Colne Borough Labour Party (BLP) passed a unanimous resolution at its annual conference on 25 May 1930 urging the government 'to legislate in the interests of the worker in the cotton industry', and the *Nelson Gazette* gave extensive coverage to the textile disputes and consistently advocated the need to put the cotton industry on a sounder organisational basis.[23]

The policy concerns of those parties in mining areas were dominated by events in the coal trade. Broxtowe Labour Party in Nottinghamshire sent a resolution to Ben Turner on 19 October 1929 calling for nationalisation of royalties, the enforcement of a national wage agreement and for workers' representatives on the marketing board, and passed a further resolution on 1 February 1930 expressing 'disapproval to the negotiations being carried on with the Liberal Party on the Mines Bill'.[24] Wansbeck DLP, which was dominated by members of the Northumberland Miners' Association, was similarly preoccupied, but despite their obvious disappointment with legislation, its members remained loyal and were more reluctant to be critical than their Nottinghamshire contemporaries.[25] Those parties in railway towns naturally prioritised the nationalisation of transport; for example, York Labour Party sent a resolution to the Prime Minister on 17 December 1930 calling for the government to resist cuts in railway wages and for public ownership of both rail and road transport.[26]

Criticism of legislation not directly related to local issues was less overt. The avenues open to local parties to influence the government's legislative programme were clearly limited. Aside from impressing upon their MP (if they were fortunate enough to have one) the importance of a particular issue, or attempting to pass a resolution through the annual conference, the only other course was to send a grievance to the Prime Minister or to the government department concerned. None of these avenues had any real chance of success. Unless their MP was a prominent figure then he was unlikely to be able to change the government's decision. The passing of a resolution through conference required, first, that the party's motion be selected and, secondly, that it could command enough support, particularly from the unions. Even then, of course, the government could not be mandated to implement it. The Prime Minister and the various government departments received thousands of letters on particular issues and a resolution passed by a local party was scarcely likely to be top of the Cabinet's list of priorities.

Some local parties were more prepared to criticise the government in this fashion than others. No doubt many party members felt it was not the local party's function to question the wisdom of the leadership; rather it was its duty to remain steadfastly loyal and not add to the government's already sizeable difficulties. Perhaps others felt that since the effect of their criticism would be minuscule it was pointless to waste local party time when other issues nearer to home were more pressing. Routine business took up the bulk of local party time; they had plenty enough with which to concern themselves without undertaking long discussions on national issues. This must certainly have been the case from 1930 when many began to confront serious problems of declining membership, financial difficulties and local election defeats. Much again depended upon both local traditions and the nature of their membership. Whilst it is difficult to generalise, there is enough evidence to hypothesise that the longer established and often heavily working-class parties, like Woolwich (formed 1903) and Wansbeck (1910), were less ready to be critical than some of the newer and less working-class organisations, like Cambridgeshire and Birmingham DLPs. These older local parties were perhaps not only less impatient for change but more imbued with the ethos of loyalty to their national leaders.

The area of legislation which provoked the greatest number of resolutions in local parties was that of educational reform. The extension of educational opportunity was an issue to which all party members were firmly committed and many were dismayed to discover that it was not included in the King's Speech. York, Darlington, Leeds, Birmingham and Penistone and Holmfirth Labour parties all sent resolutions to the government regretting this omission.[27] The continuing delay through late 1929 and early 1930 caused considerable frustration and led to further resolutions urging the government to proceed immediately.[28] The Bill which was finally put forward in 1930 did not altogether satisfy the local parties, with the issue of the means test for child maintenance grants causing particular unrest. Such was the level of feeling on the issue that a Bath Labour Party resolution to the 1930 Labour Conference favouring the complete removal of the means test was defeated only by 1,336,000 to 872,000.[29] The education issue had been given a high profile during the 1929 campaign in most constituencies and all local parties had been led to believe that the implementation of Labour policy in this area would be relatively straightforward. As such, party members were ill-prepared for the protracted negotiations that Trevelyan was forced to undertake and the final defeat of the Bill in March 1931 was a heavy blow to morale. Thereafter, local parties remained largely silent on this painful issue, partly because they were aware that the cause was lost for the foreseeable future, but more importantly, as will be shown, because the reform had created so much religious division.

The demand for adequate pensions also received strong support. A number of local organisations passed resolutions urging the government to introduce pensions at the age of sixty.[30] More financially realistic was a motion passed at the 1930 Labour Conference which called for adequate pensions at the age of sixty-five.[31] Once again, however, a resolution passed at conference failed to influence the government. Disarmament was a topic which also provoked a high degree of local party discussion. Fear of the potential consequences of poor relations with the USA, still vivid memories of the First World War, and the continuing association between socialism and peace, were the chief reasons for this concern. Many parties noted the progress of the Naval Conference from February to April 1930, and of the Foreign Secretary at Geneva.[32] Some members, however, believing that the government was not doing enough on an issue they considered central to the future of world peace and to socialism, called for the British government to act unilaterally. At its February 1931 AGM, for example, Sowerby DLP carried a unanimous resolution proposing that 'the time ha[d] come when [the government] should take steps to secure a reduction in armaments irrespective of what other governments may do'.[33]

The failure to repeal the Trades Disputes Act caused general local frustration, most notably in industrial areas. A number of resolutions had been sent to the government calling for greater haste,[34] and a TGWU resolution to the 1930 Labour Conference along similar lines was passed unanimously.[35] Many local parties participated in the TUC campaign of early 1931 by writing to those Liberals and Conservatives on the standing committee for the Bill.[36] The failure to ratify the Washington Hours Convention created similar displeasure and a number of localities were equally dismayed by the government's limited reforms for housing. Greenwich Labour Party passed a resolution for submission to the 1931 Labour Conference calling for a National Housing Board,[37] and Nelson and Colne BLP proposed in May 1931 that the government should provide grants to local authorities in order to build houses for the aged.[38]

Birth control

Birth control, as noted in Chapter 1, was an issue which created serious religious tension within the Labour movement. By 1918, the belief had begun to develop amongst sections of the Labour movement that the party should adopt a pro birth control policy as a means of improving working-class quality of life through the limitation of family size. The most vocal support came from the party's women's sections, who pushed the leadership in the early 1920s for a commitment that all maternity and welfare centres should offer birth control information to married women who requested it. This issue was to become a focal point for the gender struggle waged in the 1920s by the women's sections,[39] but throughout the decade, despite continuing pressure, the NEC was able to avoid committing itself to any birth control policy.[40] One of the central motivations of the Labour leadership had been to avoid alienating Catholic opinion, which it was well aware was fervently opposed to birth control.[41]

Birth controllers had continued to press MacDonald in the 1929 election campaign but he was only prepared to concede the possibility of a free vote in the Commons on the issue.[42] Unfortunately for the Labour leadership, however, on a local level a number of Labour organisations decided to act unilaterally and a group of local authorities, led by Shoreditch, threatened from 1929 to defy the Ministry of Health. In consequence, in a number of areas the tension between Catholics and birth controllers reached breaking point. In many parts of Lancashire, Catholics disrupted Labour meetings and the Catholic hierarchy was often involved directly in these activities. When in January 1930 Bootle Town Council voted to join some fifty other local authorities demanding autonomy on the issue, the local priest, Monsignor O'Brien, threatened to rally 30,000 Catholic voters and declared confidently that 'knowing the Catholic women of Bootle as I do, I am perfectly safe in saying that rather than receive that knowledge they prefer even death itself'.[43] Unfortunately for 'the Mussolini of Bootle', as one local council referred to him, O'Brien does not seem to have known his flock as well as he claimed, because in the end a number of Catholics on the council endorsed the decision to demand autonomy.[44]

As a result of this pressure, the Minister of Health, Arthur Greenwood, felt compelled to make a significant concession. It was decided by the Cabinet in July 1930 that contraception could be provided to mothers where further pregnancies could be physically detrimental, but not until March 1931 did the Ministry of Health finally issue a discreet memorandum to local authorities.[45] Whatever its effects on the behaviour of local authorities, Greenwood's action had hardly been conducive to conciliating Catholic opinion.

Religion and foreign policy

Aspects of the government's foreign policy were watched with particular interest by religious groups. The Catholic Church was greatly displeased by the government's support in March 1931 for a suspension of the constitution in Malta on the grounds that it was biased towards the Catholics of that country.[46] This decision added to the distrust which the Catholic hierarchy felt towards the Foreign Secretary, principally because he was a Nonconformist lay preacher. More significant was Catholic hostility to the resumption of diplomatic relations with the USSR. In line with its tremendous antipathy towards Communism, the Catholic hierarchy condemned any agreements with what it saw as 'a red-handed, anti-God state'.[47] The Catholic press attempted to publicise the persecution of religious groups in the USSR and was outraged by the government's claims that the reports from mid-1929 of anti-religious atrocities amounted to no more than Conservative propaganda.[48] Subjected to repeated questioning in the Commons, Henderson was placed in a very difficult position. Aware, however, of the need for trade with Russia, together with the strong support in the movement for a restoration of relations, the Labour leadership suppressed any doubts it might have had that the reports were genuine.[49] Catholic opinion continued to criticise the government's stand in 1930 and 1931, and the issue was used by the Catholic press in late August 1931 to propose that a Henderson-led Labour Party was a great threat to Catholic interests.[50]

Equally serious for the government was Jewish outrage at the events in Palestine and at the proposals of Lord Passfield for dealing with them. In August 1929 trouble had flared between the Jews and the Arabs in Palestine, culminating in anti-Jewish riots, and Passfield was inundated by 'Jews and the admirers of Jews, great and small, in a state of violent grief and agitation demanding revenge and compensation'.[51] Webb was widely seen to be pro-Arab because he doubted the legitimacy of a Jewish 'National Home' in Palestine and because he felt that the Arab case had not been fully heard. The publication in October 1930 of Webb's fair-minded White Paper on Palestine, which included the suggestion that the poorest Arabs should be settled on reclaimed land, resulted in 'a storm of anger from Jewry throughout the world'.[52] This included the 250,000 Jews in Britain, many of whom turned away from Labour.[53] The Secretary of Leeds Labour Party noted that one of the reasons for the loss of seats in the municipal elections in November 1930 was the 'very large Jewish electorate who strongly rejected the Government's policy in Palestine' and this reaction must have occurred in many other Jewish areas.[54] Hugh Dalton recorded in November 1930 that 'the Jews all over the world, and in Whitechapel particularly, where a by-election is pending, are off their heads with indignation', and this was instrumental in the reduction of Labour's majority in the constituency on 3 December.[55]

A religious education?

It was the issue of Catholic schools which had been the principal concern of organised Catholicism during and after the 1929 election campaign. Parish schools were regarded by the Catholic Church as much more than places of education; they were held to be the chief means of ensuring the continuation of a Catholic culture.[56] Under the 1902 Education Act, Catholic schools, together with other 'voluntary'/'non-provided schools', were supported partially by local authority grants, and this dual system of state and voluntary schools remained in existence in the 1920s. In 1929 there were 1,164 Catholic schools in existence, which served over 400,000 Catholic children.[57] Many, however, were in a poor state of repair and had been 'blacklisted' by local education authorities for failing to meet the recommended standards of accommodation.

The Catholic hierarchy wanted increased state aid for Catholic schools, and was encouraged by statements from Lord Percy, the Conservative President of the Board of Education, that, if re-elected in 1929, the Conservatives would provide money to improve the blacklisted schools. Throughout the 1920s, the Church had held the hope of achieving an educational settlement in England and Wales on the lines of the 1918 Scottish Education Act. This had relieved Catholics almost entirely from the funding of education, but had guaranteed their right to appoint teachers and supervise religious teaching in their schools. The Catholic Church decided in 1929 that it would press all the political parties very hard on the question of equal treatment for Catholic schools. Catholic confidence was running high as a result of events on the Continent. In February 1929 Pope Pius XI had signed the Lateran Pacts with Benito Mussolini, which ended the long-running feud between the Catholic Church and the Italian state. The reaction of the English hierarchy was one of jubilation and perhaps the guarantees which the treaty contained with regard to Italian Catholic education encouraged the English hierarchy to push harder.[58] By great coincidence, the signing of the treaty also corresponded with the centenary of Catholic emancipation in Britain and it is clear from a joint letter issued to the churches in February that the hierarchy was keen to mark these two events by pushing for further equality.[59]

The hierarchy devised a strategy of sending small Catholic delegations to address candidates at the 1929 election to obtain a statement from each on the schools issue, and Cardinal Bourne presided over a mass meeting at the Albert Hall to publicise the cause.[60] Labour was placed in a difficult position; whilst it did not wish to alienate Catholic voters it was also aware that the National Union of Teachers favoured strongly the abolition of the dual system, as did many of its secular and Nonconformist party members. In these circumstances it decided to fudge the issue; whilst the party claimed to support 'fair treatment' for the Catholic schools, it fell back upon its usual method for dealing with difficult issues: the promise to set up a committee, in this instance to 'work out an agreed policy between the representatives of the non-provided schools and the State'.[61] Despite this official line, however, a number of Labour candidates in heavily Catholic areas did make statements supporting equality of funding.[62]

The issue was greatly complicated by Labour's commitment to raise the school leaving age to fifteen. At the end of July 1929 Sir Charles Trevelyan, the new President of the Board of Education, announced that the school leaving age would be raised from April 1931, but made no mention of the voluntary schools issue.[63] Catholics were concerned that they would not be able to afford the cost of the extra year and wanted the state to provide the finance needed to expand and carry out repairs to their schools. They were suspicious of Trevelyan, who as a Liberal had supported the ending of the dual system in 1906, and were outraged when an education circular appeared at the end of 1929 pledging building grants for the local education authorities but not for the non-provided schools.[64]

It is clear from Trevelyan's papers that he intended to ignore Catholic opinion and push his proposals through Parliament with Anglican and Nonconformist support. During the 1929 election campaign he had written privately that he was opposed to building grants for Catholic schools:

> I am absolutely determined that the Labour Party shall not get into the hands of any religion, least of all the Catholics. I represent a constituency swimming with Irish Catholics. I would rather lose the seat than give the priesthood a bigger power in the schools.[65]

His friend Bertrand Russell had suggested astutely that the Labour Party was 'not very good at understanding things which are not class issues'[66] and it does seem that Trevelyan exemplified this observation. He later described religion as nothing more than 'a pretty fairy story'[67] and he seems to have had little idea of how great an issue denominational schools would be for the government. His strategy of moving quickly was undermined immediately by the failure of the government to find time for the Education Bill, and this gave the hierarchy time to organise its opposition. When Trevelyan published his White Paper in April 1930, which proposed that grants to voluntary schools would be paid for three years only and that local authority control of teaching in Catholic schools would be increased, Bourne was quick to condemn it. Catholic opinion now considered that raising the school leaving age had become a guise for the destruction of Catholic schools.[68]

The hierarchy participated openly in a growing Catholic campaign in the country against the Bill. In March 1930 the *Preston Catholic News* recorded that over thirty town councils had passed resolutions in support of the Catho-

lic education policy, from as far afield as Folkestone and Jarrow, and the issue
was creating serious splits in a number of local Labour parties. Liverpool TCLP
expelled a Catholic for pushing the schools issue too far and Chorley DLP did
likewise with two members. Bishop Bidwell addressed a private meeting of
150 in the House of Commons in May 1930, and Archbishop Downey of
Liverpool addressed 150,000 in June to warn Catholics that the Education Bill
was 'an invidious attempt to destroy the Catholic character of our schools',
and to urge them to show the Labour ministers that 'they are your servants
and not your masters'. John Scurr, MP for Mile End, and head of the Catholic
Labour Members group, led the campaign in the House and the dropping of
the Bill in June 1930 was heralded in the Catholic press as a great victory for
Catholics.[69]

It was clear, however, that Trevelyan intended to reintroduce the Bill and
therefore the Catholic hierarchy continued its campaign, with disastrous
effects for a number of local parties. Catholic Labour members now began to
advocate a 'freedom of conscience' clause for all Catholics on issues where
religion was more important than political loyalties, and the refusal of others
to accept this proposal led to a number of resignations. George Clancy
resigned from Gorton Labour Party in Manchester in October 1930 and contested the November municipal elections as an independent. In Chorley, Councillor Charles Williams stood as an 'expelled Labour' candidate, and in
Manchester two further Catholics resigned, including the Chairman of the All
Saints ward branch, after a meeting broke up in 'fisticuffs'. Labour undoubtedly lost a large section of the Catholic vote in many areas in the November
municipal elections, particularly in the north-west. Whilst only a couple of
breakaway Catholic Labourites won their seats, the splits in the Catholic vote
aided a number of Conservative gains. In Chorley, the Conservatives won all
eight seats contested and a very prominent local Labour figure was defeated,
and in Salford Labour lost six seats.[70]

At this juncture, sections of the Catholic press were becoming increasingly anti-Labour and revelled in the effect that their divisionary tactics were
having upon the party. The editorial of the *Preston Catholic News* on 22 November 1930 declared that Labour was now revealing its 'anti-Catholic policy
of persecution' and that all Catholics should be aware that 'the gravest danger
to the Catholic cause in this country comes from the Labour Party'.[71] The
hierarchy was also becoming more hostile towards other religious denominations. In October the Archbishop of Canterbury, Cosmo Lang, had criticised
the Catholic Church for its uncompromising attitude to the Education Bill and
had provoked a spirited defence from Cardinal Bourne.[72] In December two
more Catholics were expelled and a third was suspended from Chorley DLP,
and in Ashton-under-Lyne a councillor and the Party Secretary both
resigned. One complained that 'atheists and extremists' had too much control

in the local party because the Executive was afraid to deal with them.[73] Whilst he had the full backing of the Archbishop of Canterbury for his proposals,[74] Trevelyan was concerned increasingly that the Catholics would succeed in wrecking the Bill again,[75] and in December he managed to get all sides to agree to a conference, which was to meet before the report stage of the re-introduced Bill. Whilst he was prepared to concede some ground to the Catholics, however, this annoyed the Nonconformists and the conference collapsed without agreement. The Catholic Labour MPs threatened to move an amendment calling for equal grants for non-provided schools and the hierarchy organised a further series of meetings around the country in January 1931. MPs were bombarded with postcards from Catholics, with 60,000 being sent from the Archbishop's House, Westminster alone.[76] The result was that the 'Scurr amendment' was carried as a result of the Conservatives joining with thirty-six Labour MPs, the '36 Holy Innocents' as MacDonald referred to them,[77] to defeat the government. The Nonconformists were highly critical of the Catholics' wrecking tactics; the Free Church Assembly described them as an attempt by 'a single religious denomination ... to dictate the policy of a nation, 19/20s of whom did not share the distinctive beliefs of that denomination'[78] and it was afraid that the defeat of the Bill would herald a national advance for Roman Catholicism.[79] The Bill was finally lost and the Catholic press acclaimed a great victory.

This Catholic victory, however, served only to exacerbate tensions within the Labour movement. The *Preston Catholic News* was highly critical of those Labour MPs whom it claimed had failed to honour their pledges, and tried to persuade its readers that 'conscientious Catholic workers' should 'resign from the party' in order to teach the 'intolerant government a lesson'.[80] Understandably, this growing opposition from Catholic quarters, which seems to have contributed to the loss of the Sunderland by-election in April, was of major concern to Labour's head office. It would appear that the decision of Ashton-under-Lyne to select John William Gordon to stand in a by-election in April 1931 was at least partly influenced by a desire to pacify the 4,000 Catholics in the constituency. Whilst Gordon was the official candidate of the National Union of Railwaymen (NUR), he also had the advantage of being a Catholic and an Irishman.[81] The Catholic press and the local priesthood in Ashton, however, were not entirely content with Gordon and the loss of the Catholic vote, as well as the New Party's interjection, was instrumental in Labour losing the seat. The NEC was disturbed sufficiently to instruct Labour's candidate in a by-election in June to tell voters that if he was elected he would 'give a pledge to vote against [an] Education Bill unless it contain[ed] the principles embodied in the amendment moved by Mr John Scurr, MP'.[82] It appears also that Joseph Cleary was deselected and replaced by a Catholic in the East-Toxteth by-election in February 1931,[83] and that the schools issue cost Catholic votes at a May by-election at St Rollox.

The hierarchy's already strong antipathy to Labour was greatly fuelled by Pope Pius XI's Encyclical on social and labour questions, *Quadragesimo Anno*, broadcast in May 1931, which declared that socialism and Catholicism were wholly incompatible.[84] A number of small breakaway Catholic groups were formed on a constituency level, most notably in Lancashire,[85] and the sectarian divide which resulted in Liverpool was highly damaging to the local party for the next decade.[86] Sections of the Catholic press now felt free to declare that 'Socialism is the Devil'.[87] Both the Catholic hierarchy and the Catholic press were to offer their wholehearted support for the National Government after August 1931. Whilst it is impossible to determine the extent to which Catholic voters followed this advice, it would seem likely that, due to the perceived tensions between the ideology of socialism and the Catholic faith, the Labour Party lost a substantial number of Catholic votes at the 1931 general election.[88]

The *Daily Herald*

The most remarkable piece of local party campaigning during the lifetime of the government was connected to the re-launching of the *Daily Herald* in 1930. Asked by Odhams and the TUC to secure new readers for the paper, the local parties responded with great enthusiasm and through the dedicated work of local members succeeded in enrolling many thousands of new subscribers. In its Annual Report for 1931, Woolwich Labour Party reported that over 2,000 new readers had been found, and Wolverhampton, Colne Valley and Greenwich Labour parties had all achieved over 1,000 readers by May 1930.[89] It was this dedication that enabled the *Daily Herald* to reach its target circulation figure of one million by as early as April 1930, and to go on to become the first daily in the world to reach a circulation of two million two years later. Somewhat ironically, however, a significant number of local party activists were soon unhappy with the new paper which they had done so much to promote. They felt that the *Herald* had become too populist and seemed more concerned to report on film stars and sporting events than to undertake serious political journalism. A number wrote to William Mellor to make this point but, unsurprisingly, the editor was not prepared to alter a style which was very successful. This was only the beginning of a move towards increased trivia in the paper under the instructions of Julius Elias, the head of Odhams Publishers, which was later to provoke the acerbic comment from one party activist that: 'the only way to get socialism into the official Labour daily was to write it on the back of a bathing beauty'.[90]

Unemployment

As with the unions, it was the issue of unemployment which caused the greatest degree of debate and unrest. All local organisations had campaigned hard on the issue during the campaign and had believed that even a minority Labour government would be able to do a great deal to relieve the problem. The resolution which was passed by York Labour Party on 17 July illustrated how important the issue was to all Labour supporters when it urged the government to 'go forward encouraged by the knowledge that the workers are behind them in their efforts to deal with this great problem'.[91] They were forced, however, to watch helplessly as unemployment increased dramatically through 1930 and the first months of 1931 (see Appendix 3). The effects of this rising unemployment on all local parties were direct; they all experienced a fall in membership, not only because many of their supporters were laid off and could no longer afford affiliation fees, but also as a result of the disillusionment with the failure of the government to deal with unemployment. The effect on women's sections was also substantial, not least in areas of previously high female employment.[92] The unemployment issue was also clearly losing the party local votes; the Secretary of Leeds Labour Party cited the 'Government's inability to cope with unemployment' as a major factor in the loss of Labour seats in the 1930 municipal elections.[93]

The majority of local parties were disappointed by the partial reform of the unemployment benefit procedure. The initial omission of any repeal of the 'Not Genuinely Seeking Work' clause from the Bill of late 1929 was met with considerable dismay in local parties and Newport DLP was so angered by it that it passed a resolution in December which criticised the government for its handling of the issue, despite the presence of its MP, J. Walker, who defended Bondfield. Local parties were also displeased that Bondfield did not propose to reduce the waiting period for receipt of benefit.[94] A number of individual resolutions were sent to the Prime Minister and Bondfield calling for an increase in benefit and a widening of the eligibility of the unemployment insurance scheme.[95] This discontent culminated in a motion passed at the 1930 Labour Conference, proposed by Bootle TCLP and seconded by Falmouth DLP, which demanded that the minimum allowance should be as laid down in the joint TUC and Labour Party evidence given to the Blanesburgh Committee.[96] Some local party demands went further than this, for example Darlington DLP, whose call in June 1931 for universal unemployment benefit to the age of seventy, on a non-contributory basis, was clearly a transitional proposition aimed at bankrupting the capitalist system. It was also a sign of the radicalising effect that two years of government failures on unemployment had induced amongst a number of party members.

All local parties were disappointed by the failure of the government on this foremost economic and social issue. Delegates to the 1929 Labour Conference already felt that the government was not doing enough and were instrumental in a proposal to refer back a PLP report on unemployment. This effective vote of censure was defeated by only 1,100,000 votes to 1,027,000.[97] Once again, some local parties were more willing to be critical than others and only a few parties sent resolutions to the government urging a bolder strategy. Few local parties had any coherent alternatives to offer, which was not surprising when the same could be said of the majority of politicians, whose access to information was far greater than for party members. In addition, the majority of members would have possessed little economic knowledge and would not have felt qualified to comment upon issues which they saw as solely for statesmen to decide. Consequently, those parties which did pass resolutions gave few indications as to what exactly the new departures should be. Greenwich Labour Party's motion for the 1931 conference, sent in June, which urged the government to undertake a 'National Plan of Work', was unusual in this respect. More common was the vague resolution passed by Broxtowe Labour Party in July 1930, which urged its MP, F. J. Seymour Cocks, to 'do all in his power in the Parliamentary Party to substitute *socialism* for capitalism'.[98]

The ILP

Whilst ILP membership had fallen from its peak in the mid-1920s of 34,000 to 27,000 in 1929,[99] and had also suffered a relative decline in its share of MPs (only thirty-seven in May 1929), the ILP continued to exert a strong influence upon many local parties. In those areas where this influence was most marked, the highly confrontational relationship that developed nationally between the Maxtonite section of the ILP and the mainstream Labour Party was mirrored locally. This friction was heightened by the recession from 1930, which hit the ILP local organisations very hard. It has been estimated that by the end of 1930 at least 50 per cent of the ILP's members were unemployed.[100] Such tension was certainly not confined to Scotland, where the grass roots of the ILP were not as radical as has often been believed. Whilst the ILP's greatest area of control of local parties was undoubtedly in Scotland, which contained seventeen of its thirty-seven MPs, Scottish ILP members were often less militant than the legendary Clydeside MPs, and in Glasgow the moderate Patrick Dollan, who was Secretary of the city's ILP, was more influential than Maxton.[101]

As early as November 1929, Wolverhampton West Labour Party reported that a number of ILP members were opposing official candidates in the forthcoming municipal elections and on 7 November it was decided that they should be expelled.[102] A resolution was put to Leeds City Labour Party on 17 September 1930 protesting against the arrangement by the ILP of a meeting with national speakers for the following month since it would compete with six divisional Labour Party meetings. In November 1930 the Secretary of Leeds Labour Party cited 'awkwardness and lack of energy from the ILP' as a major factor in the loss of municipal seats.[103] Clearly, then, the ILP was becoming 'a party within a party' on a local as well as a national level.

A number of local parties passed resolutions during the 1929–31 period expressing their support for a number of ILP policies, most notably the living wage proposals. Darlington, Stockport and Nelson and Colne Labour parties all passed resolutions in 1931 that urged the government to introduce a Living Wage Bill.[104] A number of others mandated their delegates to vote for ILP proposals at the Labour Conferences and purchased copies of ILP pamphlets on unemployment.[105] Opposed by the trade unions at conference, the ILP was largely unsuccessful in converting the rest of the movement to its proposals in 1929 and 1930. An amendment at the 1930 conference which called for 'Socialism Now', strongly endorsed by Manchester and Llanelli Labour Parties, was heavily defeated. An ILP resolution seeking to allow parliamentary members the freedom to express their own views on all issues met a similar fate.[106] The exception to this trend was the carrying of a motion at the 1929 conference supporting family allowances, despite opposition from Henderson, Clynes and a number of prominent union leaders, including Bevin. ILP policies, then, did appeal to many local parties. If the national ILP leadership had refrained from taking such a confrontational line during the government, which served to alienate many Labour members, these policies could perhaps have provided the focus of a new Labour programme in the aftermath of the 1931 crisis.[107]

Sir Oswald Mosley

Local party attitudes to the actions of Oswald Mosley present an interesting insight into the ethos of the Labour movement. As has been noted, Mosley's influence upon the Birmingham Labour Party had been profound and at the time of the 1929 election he was widely admired by party members for his presence, his oratorical abilities and his dynamism. Unimpressed by the government's handling of unemployment, many parties followed with interest Mosley's proposals for reforming Britain's political system and solving the country's economic problems. His subsequent resignation was seen by many as a brave and principled act. The *Birmingham Town Crier* and the *Leeds Weekly Citizen* both argued that his action would ginger up government handling of unemployment.[108] His resignation speech to Parliament on 28 May 1930 was acclaimed by much of the local and national press and a number of local parties decided to purchase up to 100 copies of the speech.[109] At this stage, then, Mosley was appealing to many local parties over the heads of the national leadership.

Many were clearly impressed by what they read, for at the 1930 Labour Conference in October, Doncaster DLP, supported by many other local organisations, moved that the Mosley Memorandum should be referred back to the NEC for greater consideration. Mosley's speech to the conference was an impressive appeal for the logic of his case and he received a tremendous ovation from a movement which clearly believed that there were more options open to the government than it had been prepared to consider seriously. Whilst the motion was narrowly lost, by 1,251,000 to 1,046,000, ultimately it would seem because the miners decided to vote against the advice of Cook, Mosley still enjoyed a very successful week at Llandudno.[110] He had been elected to the NEC in place of Thomas and many people both inside and outside of Labour circles were convinced that he was destined to be the next leader of the party.

As it became apparent from late 1930, however, that Mosley was considering a breakaway movement, local parties were less keen to associate themselves with him. Birmingham began to distance itself; the *Birmingham Town Crier* of 12 December 1930 criticised the 'Mosley Manifesto' for putting socialism in the background and for its support of tariffs.[111] In a symbolic move, Sheffield Brightside DLP, which had been previously eager to secure Mosley for a mass meeting in January 1931, now removed him from its list of potential speakers.[112] Yet, even at this stage, Mosley's following had not been wiped out. Darlington Labour Party, for example, was still eager to secure him to speak in the constituency as late as 12 January 1931.[113] His decision in March 1931 to form the New Party, however, served to destroy this support almost completely. Mosley had now committed the gravest of Labour sins, that of disloyalty to the party. All local parties endorsed the NEC's decision to expel him and there was clearly much surreptitious local party involvement in the disruption of New Party activities.[114] New Party meetings in Dundee and Hull were terminated successfully by such disruption and in April serious fighting broke out at a meeting in Hammersmith.[115]

The Ashton-under-Lyne by-election in Lancashire on 30 April 1931 proved to be a disastrous start for the New Party. Mosley himself had been very ill with pneumonia and Allan Young secured only 4,472 votes, which was only just sufficient to retain the deposit but more than enough to provoke angry responses from the local Labour Party, which felt that Young had allowed the Conservative candidate in by splitting the Labour vote. Clearly, any lingering hopes that Mosley might have had for taking large sections of the Labour movement with him had evaporated by as early as April 1931, only one month after the party's formation. In the eyes of the faithful, by choosing to operate outside of the Labour Party, Mosley was no longer the courageous figure offering an alternative socialist policy but the betrayer of the working classes and a man of uncontrollable personal ambition. This example above all others during 1929–31 demonstrates the importance of unwritten codes of practice in the Labour movement and the strength of its almost tribal emphasis on loyalty. Mosley had not played by the 'rules of the game' and as such his punishment was political and social ostracisation.[116]

For Birmingham BLP these events were devastating. Both John Strachey, MP for Aston from May 1929, and Allan Young, the Party Organiser, were fully behind Mosley's Memorandum, and the party was placed into a very difficult position, torn between a desire to support its MPs and chief patron and to be loyal to the government. It was the publication of the Manifesto which brought this tension to a head. Strachey, Young and the MP for Birmingham Erdington, C. J. Simmons, all endorsed it and the Executive Committee twice deferred the question of whether Mosley should be invited to address a party meeting. On 26 January 1931 it decided not to invite him since it was felt that this would serve 'no good purpose'; undoubtedly it was afraid that Mosley would succeed in taking a significant section of the BLP with him.[117] At the same time, the Executive would have been reluctant to condemn the man who had done so much to establish the party and whose financial contributions were an important factor in party budgeting. The creation of the New Party was catastrophic for the Birmingham BLP; whilst only a few ILP members went with Mosley, both organisation and morale were dealt a serious blow and this was instrumental in the swift reversal of fortune for Labour in Birmingham which lasted for over a decade.

The effects of Mosley's actions were equally, if not more, damaging for Wolverhampton West DLP. W. J. Brown, Secretary of the Civil Service Clerical Association (CSCA), was elected in 1929 and as the Secretary of the ILP group in Parliament swiftly became a prominent critic of the government. By as early as January 1930 his attitude was causing extreme disquiet amongst many members of his DLP. After a long discussion in January 1930, Brown was pushed into promising that he would not vote on any issue 'so as to endanger the life of the Government'. His support for the Mosley Manifesto in December 1930, however, created serious splits in the DLP and in January 1931 he was called in front of its Executive to defend his action. At the beginning of February, he held his own public meeting at the Wolverhampton Theatre Royal without the local party's endorsement and later in the month he announced his decision to resign from the PLP with 'the Mosley group'.[118]

Yet Brown did not join the New Party. He later claimed that he was aware even at this stage that Mosley had fascistic tendencies, but in truth he was threatened with expulsion from the CSCA and the loss of his union position.[119]

In an incident of high comic credentials, a still very ill Mosley was driven in an ambulance to Brown's house to confront Brown from his stretcher. What he discovered was that Brown's brave words had turned to tears and a confession that he could no longer carry through his intended course of action.[120] This lack of courage placed Wolverhampton West in a situation of tremendous confusion. It was now unclear whether by resigning from the PLP Brown had resigned from the party also, and a badly in debt local party was understandably loath to give up the £250 given at election time by the CSCA. There was also the real possibility of a fundamental split in the party, for, despite his erratic behaviour, Brown still commanded a sizeable local following. The Executive decided that it would wait for a lead from head office on an issue that was causing a great deal of concern on the NEC. On 25 March 1931 it met with Shepherd, who advised that Brown's resignation was to be regarded as the end of his association with the Labour Party and that the DLP should undertake immediately the task of securing another parliamentary candidate. A significant section, however, was not prepared to accept this decision and on 26 March a number of prominent members resigned, including current and former local councillors, the Secretary of the League of Youth and a number of members of the ILP.[121] Due to the loss of CSCA money the party was forced in April to give both its agent and the landlord of the Labour Rooms three months notice and by the end of May debts of £150 had been accumulated. Consequently, Wolverhampton West was unable to field a candidate at all in the October election, whilst Brown, although losing the seat, won over 17,000 votes when he stood for the 'Independent Labour Association' (ILA). This split remained until 1936, with ILA candidates opposing official Labour ones at all local elections, and there was a further disastrous result for Wolverhampton West DLP in 1935 when its candidate secured only 1,325 votes to Brown's 14,867 (Brown once again losing the seat to the Conservative candidate). Such then was the disastrous effect that the manoeuvrings of a prominent individual could have upon local party organisation.

Declining support and finances

By the end of 1930, the majority of local parties were in a poor state of health. The municipal election results of November 1930 had been very disappointing. For example, six seats were lost in Salford, seven in Liverpool, five in Birmingham and Labour had lost control of the City Council in Leeds.[122] Local parties cited the 'indifference and carelessness of previous Labour voters' and 'apathy' as instrumental in these defeats, as well as dissatisfaction with the government's performance, particularly on unemployment.[123] Parties were also suffering increasingly from the declining enthusiasm of their own activists. Greenwich TCLP Executive cited this as an important factor in their poor results in the London County Council elections of March 1931, and Gloucester was concerned in mid-1931 that a sizeable number of members were regularly absent from its meetings.[124]

This was paralleled by a growing problem of falling membership. York, which had hoped to attain 3,000 members by the end of 1930, had to struggle hard to maintain 2,000 and by June 1931 only 1,360 of these individuals remained.[125] Derby's financial sub-committee decided in March 1931 that the decline in its membership was so great that membership figures should not be published in its Annual Report for 1930.[126] Doncaster recorded a fall from 9,339 members in 1929 to only 6,694 in 1931, which was mainly due to a decline in miners' affiliation.[127] There were a few exceptions to this trend; Wansbeck DLP actually increased its affiliated membership during 1930–31 but this was counter-balanced by a significant drop of 333 in individual membership, a fall of some 30 per cent over the year.[128] Even Woolwich, one of the most successful local parties, could not escape this pervading decline; from 1929 to 1931 its total membership dropped from 4,424 to 3,280, a fall of 26 per cent.[129]

With this decline in membership came the corresponding problem of a fall in income. Local party affiliation fees to head office for 1931 amounted to only £3,160, as opposed to £4,363 for the previous year.[130] The majority of parties experienced a serious reduction in finance and had to find ways either of cutting expenditure or of increasing income. The chances of achieving the latter were limited and the only real option, as there was a finite amount that could be collected through fundraising events, was an increase in affiliation or individual membership fees. This approach was chosen by Wansbeck DLP and the result was a damaging fall in individual members in 1930–31.[131] The alternative was to try to raise a loan in order to meet current deficits in the hope that the party would be able to pay the money back in more prosperous times; Wolverhampton West decided to adopt this desperate measure in July 1931 and borrowed some £150.[132] A number of parties already had enormous liabilities, however, and had therefore reached their credit limit; for example, Woolwich recorded in April 1930 that the party owed more than £2,000.[133]

All parties had therefore to find means of cutting expenditure. A number were forced to relinquish a full-time agent, for example Darlington and Wolverhampton West.[134] Some were forced to sell the party car.[135] Many more had to reduce or abandon altogether a delegation to national conference.[136] Not standing candidates at local or even national elections was another desperate measure that some parties were forced to adopt, for example Wolverhampton West in the November 1930 local elections and in the 1931 General Election.[137] The danger of adopting these measures was that the party would descend into a vicious spiral of decline; not standing candidates or relinquishing a party's assets was damaging to a party's local profile and detrimental to its ability to win back those supporters it had lost. These difficulties also had a tendency to aggravate existing tensions within local parties. In Greenwich a long-running feud between the Party Secretary and the Agent became more acute, and in Gloucester in June 1931 the party's Vice-Chairman resigned against a background of dubious financial management.[138]

Newspapers were also seriously affected. As has been noted, local newspapers were a risky venture, since any fall in circulation or withdrawal of advertising could leave the party with a major financial liability. This was, of course, most likely to happen in times of economic depression, as is evident from many examples taken from the 1929–31 period. Doncaster DLP created a local news-sheet to be issued monthly from the beginning of 1929, and had hoped it would become self-supporting through the acquisition of sufficient advertising. Yet, by as early as August the party had decided that the financial burden was becoming too great and the venture had to be terminated.[139] Both York and Darlington Labour parties experienced similar problems, and had to consider seriously the possibility that their papers should be discontinued. York's Executive Committee recorded on 18 April 1931 that the *York Echo* had lost £10 since its creation in September 1930, a sizeable sum for an increasingly struggling organisation,[140] and *Darlington Labour News* was close to liquidation in August 1929 after having run up a debt of £58.[141] Both parties were reluctant to lose what they regarded as important assets and decided to subsidise the papers in the hope that the situation would improve, despite the fact that this course of action created a continuous financial drain. The *Greenwich Times* was beset with similar difficulties of insufficient advertising and a falling circulation, and after much debate, and a temporary suspension of publication at the end of 1930, it was finally decided in August 1931 to accept an offer from the Co-op to run the paper jointly. Whilst the new *Greenwich Citizen* was larger, the party had been forced to sacrifice a large part of its local character to a greater coverage of national events.[142] Even the most successful of the local newspapers, the *Leeds Weekly Citizen* and the *Birmingham Town Crier*, struggled. Whilst their circulations remained in the thousands throughout the lifetime of the government, both papers were forced to reduce in size and the *Weekly Citizen* resorted to cutting its price to 1d in an attempt to revive its ailing circulation.[143]

Despite the overwhelming impression from local records that membership was declining, however, the figures given by the national party state that total individual membership increased throughout the period 1928–32 (see Appendix 4). Beginning in 1929, Labour's Annual Reports printed a figure for the individual membership for the previous year, and this figure became set in stone effectively, since it was thereafter reprinted in all subsequent reports and has been accepted as correct by all who have written subsequently on the party.[144] For 1928, the first year when total individual membership was compiled, the figure given was 214,970; for 1929, 227,897; for 1930, 277,211; for 1931, 297,003; and for 1932, 371,607. Yet, further examination of these figures in relation to information found elsewhere in the reports suggests that the 1930 figure is very inaccurate, with a definite possibility that it was deliberately falsified to give the impression that individual membership rose steadily throughout the four-year period.

As well as printing the total membership for the previous year, each Annual Report gave a breakdown of the number of individuals affiliated by each local party in the current year. In theory, the sum of these figures should correspond to the figure given in the following year's report for total individual membership for the previous calendar year. For membership in 1929 and 1931 this does seem to have been largely the case. The 1930 figures, however, reveal a major discrepancy; the sum of the memberships for each party comes to some 319,715, and yet the figure given in the 1931 Annual Report for membership in 1930 is 277,211. This represents a difference of over 40,000 and can hardly be accounted for by an error in the addition. How, then, can this vast difference be explained? Initially, it might be concluded that the answer lies in the changes to affiliation fees passed at the 1929 conference, which meant that, from 1930, local parties were required to affiliate a minimum of 240 members, rather than the previous minimum of 180. At the same time, an individual party membership scheme was introduced for the first time. One might hypothesise that the figure of 319,715 is misleading because many of those parties who paid the affiliation fees for 240 actually had less than 240 members, and the 277,211 figure was based on the actual number of party cards given out. This theory, however, is nullified by a statement given elsewhere in the 1931 report that 'making deductions for the return of unused cards, the number issued for 1930 was 319,218'.[145] This figure is very close to the one obtained from the sum of the individual affiliation figures, and thus suggests that the only means the party had of calculating total individual membership was from the number of cards paid for.

There is further evidence that deliberate misrepresentation took place. In the 1930 Annual Report, the National Agent reported that the new membership card had been introduced successfully and that supplies issued to local parties up to 28 August 1930 represented a total individual membership of 345,544.[146] If the 277,211 figure was correct, this would suggest that between August and December 1930 there had been a drop in membership of over 75,000; such a rapid decrease does not seem to have been very likely. Not knowing how local party fees were paid, that is once a year or in instalments, is a problem. What is very clear is that a detailed examination of the 1930 and 1931 figures for all parties reveal that there was a general trend of declining membership. Leaving aside those parties who affiliated the minimum fee either in 1930 or 1931 reveals that whereas membership increased in 117 local parties, it declined in 214.

As such, in the light of the fact that a total membership of 277,211 for 1930 appears to be far too low and is contradicted by all other statistics, the only logical conclusion is that this figure was fictitious. When one considers the circumstances in which the figure was first stated, namely during the 1931 Labour Conference, it is perhaps not too great a leap of the imagination to suggest that the figure was fixed by the leadership in order to give the impression that, despite the movement's difficulties, membership had increased steadily throughout 1928–31 and was still on the way up. Bearing in mind that Labour had just suffered the ignominious collapse of its government, that morale was low and that there was a tangibly more militant mood throughout the movement, is it impossible to conceive that Arthur Henderson, party manager *par excellence*, would have sanctioned a misrepresentation of the figures to counter the impression that his was a party in a state of collapse? It is interesting to note that the 1931 conference went into a long private session in order to consider the proposed further increase in affiliation fees from 3d to 4d per member, and that none of the discussion is recorded in the report. Clearly, it is impossible to prove this hypothesis, but equally it is difficult to see how the figure of 277,211 can be substantiated.

Conclusion

All local parties were united in their condemnation of the Interim Report of the Holman Gregory Commission in June 1931 and many sent delegations to the regional conferences organised by the TUC to protest against its recommendations.[147] Like the unions, local parties rejected cuts in unemployment benefit both as an attack upon the unemployed and as the trigger for a general wage-cutting policy. Few, however, had any inkling of the significance of the May Report or any detailed knowledge of the nation's growing financial problems. Once again it was the case that few local members would have felt sufficiently knowledgeable to comment upon these complex issues. Moreover, local parties had more immediate issues with which to concern themselves, for, by that date, many were engaged in what was essentially a battle for survival.

By July 1931, disillusionment was widespread. Labour's election victory of May 1929 had led many party members to believe that Labour's future progress, on both a national and a local level, was guaranteed. The initial increase in membership and the significant gains made at the local elections in November 1929 had further reinforced this belief. Yet, as the government's domestic record faltered throughout 1930, local parties suffered a swift reversal in fortune, reflected both in membership levels and in local election results. Local members became ever more disappointed by the government's performance, and financial commitments undertaken in 1929, particularly in the realms of local newspapers and the purchasing of premises, began to look ill-conceived. The growing tension between the ILP and the national party proved to be disruptive in many local organisations and the religious controversy provoked by the Education Bill led to a growth in sectarianism in those organisations based in Catholic areas. Meanwhile, the activities of Mosley and the formation of the New Party had disastrous consequences in those local parties which had Mosleyite MPs, most spectacularly in Wolverhampton and, above all, Birmingham. By 1931 all local parties were confronted by the very great problem of how to reverse a pattern of falling membership and financial loss by convincing people that they should continue to give up both their time and their money to a party whose national leaders seemed to be incapable of offering any solutions to the key economic problems of the age. Some constituencies were radicalised as a result, but the most usual response to this disillusionment was far more damaging to the movement: apathy. All local parties depended upon the continual hard work of a dedicated hardcore and any reduction in the enthusiasm of this group was reflected immediately in party fortunes. Many of those who retained their commitment rationalised the government's failings as no more than a temporary setback on the road to Jerusalem, and continued to concentrate on the difficult local tasks which confronted them. Very soon, however, they would be forced to deal with the devastating consequences of the national events which threatened to turn their world upside-down.

NOTES

1 Working Class Movement Library, Salford, *Nelson Gazette*, 5 November 1929.
2 Labour Party, *Annual Report 1929* (London, 1929), p. 196.
3 Ibid., F. Hughes, National Union of Clerks, p. 97.
4 A minor reform to allow a further category of affiliated members, termed 'professional organisations', was allowed through but had limited implications for an extension of membership. Interestingly, the same proposal for national associate members was again defeated in 1939 on exactly the same grounds and the idea was only accepted finally by the party in very recent times.
5 Labour Party, *Annual Report 1929*, p. 245.
6 Ibid., p. 247.
7 Labour Party, *Annual Report 1930* (London, 1930), p. 150.
8 Labour Party, *Annual Report 1929*, p. 247.
9 Nottinghamshire Record Office, Nottingham South Labour Party, DD.PP7/1, Quarterly Meeting, 8 December 1929.
10 Labour Party, *Annual Report 1929*, pp. 222–5.

11 Ibid., pp. 222–6; Labour Party, *Annual Report 1931* (London, 1931), p. 34, and *Annual Report 1932* (London, 1932), p. 41.

12 South Shields Labour Party, E.P. Microfilm (1979), Reels 1 and 2, 14 July 1929, 14 January 1930, 12 August 1930 and 28 December 1930; South Wales Coalfield Archive, University College, Swansea (hereafter SWCA), Newport DLP, A5, 23 January 1930.

13 See also Borthwick Institute of Historical Research, York, UL5/9, Major David Graham Pole Papers, reports to constituents and Churchill College, Cambridge, and Philip Noel-Baker Papers, 2/5, Pethick-Lawrence correspondence with his constituents.

14 British Library of Political and Economic Science (hereafter BLPES), Dalton Papers, Diary, 29 December 1930; 'I am going to Bishop Auckland in the first days of January and hate the prospect of meeting my constituents again. It is all tragically different, so far as economic questions go, from what one had hoped and dreamed a Labour Government would be like.'

15 Durham County Archives, Darlington DLP, D/X 922/3, General Council (hereafter GC), 17 December 1930, complaint that A. L. Shepherd, MP, did not attend enough; Wrexham TCLP, E.P. Microfilm (1985), Reel 1, GC Meeting, 22 July 1930, unimpressed that MP, R. Richards, could not attend meeting, and EC 12 May 1931 when Richards did not turn up; Penistone DLP, E.P. Microfilm (1980), Reel 1, EC 18 April 1931, unhappy with Rennie Smith's absence.

16 Colne Valley DLP, E.P. Microfilm (1979), Reel 2, Minutes, AGM 1930 and 3 August 1930.

17 Colne Valley DLP, E.P. Microfilm (1979), Reel 2, EC, 7 July 1929 and 6 August 1929.

18 Penistone and Holmfirth DLP, E.P. Microfilm, Reel 1, EC, 17 May 1930 and 18 April 1931.

19 Nottinghamshire Record Office, Nottingham South DLP, DD PP7, EC, July 1930 to September 1931.

20 Greenwich Local History Library, Greenwich DLP, EC, 13 August 1931; Dyfed Archives, Carmarthen, Llanelli Trades Council, EC, 1 August 1931.

21 Cambridge and Cambridgeshire TCLPs, E.P. Microfilm (1980), Reel 5, Election Addresses and Newspaper Cuttings, *Cambridge Elector* 1929.

22 Cambridge and Cambridgeshire TCLPs, E.P. Microfilm, (1980), Reel 4, Cambridgeshire DLP AGM 1930; West Sussex Record Office, Chichester DLP, LA/1CH/1/1/1, 26 April 1931.

23 Working Class Movement Library, Nelson and Colne BLP, Annual Conference, May 1930.

24 Nottinghamshire Record Office, Broxtowe DLP, DP PP6/3, Council Minute Book, 19 October 1929 and 1 February 1930.

25 Northumberland Record Office, Wansbeck DLP, NRO 527/4/2, Minutes 1926–35.

26 York Record Office, York DLP, ACC 196/1/5, General Management Committee, 17 December 1930.

27 York Record Office, York DLP, ACC 196/1/4, 17 July 1929; Durham County Archives, Darlington DLP, D/X/922/3, Committee and General Meetings, 11 July 1929; West Yorkshire Archive Service, Sheepscar, City of Leeds Labour Party, 4/5, EC and GC Minutes, 11 July 1929; Birmingham BLP, E.P. Microfilm, Reel 1, Minutes, 11 July 1929; Penistone and Holmfirth Labour Party, E.P. Microfilm (1980), Reel 1, Minutes, 20 July 1929.

28 Cambridge TCLP, E.P. Microfilm (1980), Reel 2, EC Minutes, 5 March 1930.

29 Labour Party, *Annual Report 1930*, p. 249; see also Nottinghamshire Archives, Broxtowe DLP, DD.PP6/3, Council Minutes, 14 June 1930; and West Yorks Archive Service, Calderdale, Halifax, Sowerby DLP, TU51/4, EC, 24 June 1930.

30 South Shields Labour Party, E.P. Microfilm (1979), Reel 2, Minutes, 30 June 1931, Resolution to Conference; Bristol Record Office, Bristol East DLP, ACC 39035/60, Resolution to Conference, June 1931, and Correspondence, June 1931, H. E. Roger to Shepherd.

31 Labour Party, *Annual Report 1930*, p. 234.

32 For example, Penistone and Holmfirth DLP, E.P. Microfilm (1980), Reel 1, letter sent to MacDonald, 15 February 1930, and West Sussex Record Office, Chichester DLP, LA/1CH/1/1/1, Resolution, April 1930.

33 West Yorks Archive Service, Calderdale, Halifax, Sowerby DLP, TU51/4, AGM, 28 February 1931.

34 For example, Sheffield City Labour Party, E.P. Microfilm (1979), Reel 7, EC Minutes, 8 April 1930.

35 Labour Party, *Annual Report 1930*, p. 173.

36 South Shields TCLP, E.P. Microfilm (1979), Reel 2, EC Minutes, 8 February 1931.

37 Greenwich Local History Library, Greenwich DLP, GC Minutes, 4 June 1931.

38 Working Class Movement Library, Nelson and Colne BLP, Annual General Meeting, 1 May 1931.

39 P. M. Graves, *Labour Women: Women in British Working-Class Politics, 1918–1939* (Cambridge, 1994), pp. 81–6.

40 R. A. Soloway, *Birth Control and the Population Question in England, 1877–1930* (Chapel Hill, 1982), pp. 287–96.

41 N. Riddell, 'The Catholic Church and the British Labour Party, 1918–1931', *Twentieth Century British History* 8: 2 (1997), 179–81.

42 British Newspaper Library (hereafter BNL), *The Tablet*, 27 April 1929, p. 564. This proposal was met by great hostility from the Catholic press.

43 Soloway, *Birth Control*, p. 309, and S. Fielding, *Class and Ethnicity: Irish Catholics in England, 1880–1939* (Buckingham, 1992), p. 75.

44 Ibid., p. 309.

45 Ibid., pp. 310–11.

46 BNL, *Preston Catholic News*, 21 March 1931.

47 BNL, *The Tablet*, 4 May 1929.

48 Reaction to speech by Margaret Bondfield during the election, BNL, *The Tablet*, 15 June 1929.

49 A. J. Williams, *Labour and Russia: The Attitude of the Labour Party to the USSR, 1924–1934* (Manchester, 1989), pp. 103–8.

50 BNL, *The Tablet*, 29 August 1931.

51 BLPES, Passfield Papers, B. Webb's Diary, 2 September 1929.

52 BLPES, Passfield Papers, B. Webb's Diary, 26 October 1930.

53 A. J. P. Taylor, *English History 1914–1945* (Harmondsworth, 3rd edn, 1975), p. 222n.

54 West Yorkshire Archives, Sheepscar, City of Leeds Labour Party, /9, Secretary to G. R. Shepherd, 6 November 1930.

55 BLPES, Dalton Papers, Diary, 6 November 1930.

56 Fielding, *Class and Ethnicity*, pp. 61–4.

57 A. Hastings, *A History of English Christianity, 1920–1990* (London, 3rd edn,

1991), p. 134.

58 For a brief summary of the Lateran Pacts see M. Clark, *Modern Italy, 1871–1982* (London, 1984), pp. 254–5. For the English reaction, see BNL, *The Tablet*, 16 and 23 February 1929, and *The Universe*, 15 February 1929.

59 BNL, *The Universe*, 15 February 1929.

60 BNL, *The Tablet*, 18 May and 1 June 1929 for report on the meeting.

61 West Yorks Archives, Sheepscar, City of Leeds Labour Party, /10, Election address of Henry Slesser in South East Leeds Parliamentary Division 1929.

62 Brynmor Jones Library, Hull University, W. A. Jowitt Papers, DPB/12/2(b).

63 *House of Commons Debates* (hereafter *HC Debs.*), 18 July 1929, Oral Answers, col. 613.

64 BNL, *The Tablet*, 23 November 1929.

65 Robinson Library, University of Newcastle (hereafter RL), Trevelyan Papers, CPT.138, Trevelyan to Bertrand Russell (n.d.), May 1929.

66 RL, Trevelyan Papers, CPT.138, Russell to Trevelyan, 14 May 1929.

67 A. J. A. Morris, *C. P. Trevelyan 1870–1958: Portrait of a Radical* (Belfast, 1977), p. 178.

68 BNL, *The Tablet*, 3 May 1930.

69 BNL, *Preston Catholic News*, 8 March 1930; 5 April 1930; 31 May 1930 and 28 June 1930.

70 BNL, *Preston Catholic News*, 1 and 8 November 1930.

71 BNL, *Preston Catholic News*, 22 November 1930.

72 BNL, *The Tablet*, 25 October 1930.

73 BNL, *Preston Catholic News*, 6 December 1930.

74 *The Times*, Report of Archbishop of Canterbury's speech to a Diocesan Conference in Canterbury, 17 October 1930, p. 17, column e.

75 In a letter to his wife, Kitty, Trevelyan referred to the Catholics as 'intriguing beasts', RL, Trevelyan Papers, CPT. EX124(1), 18 November 1930.

76 BNL, *Preston Catholic News*, 24 January 1931.

77 Public Record Office, MacDonald Papers, MacDonald's Diary, 30/69/1753/1, 21 January 1931.

78 Speech of Principal Griffiths Jones, President of the National Council of Evangelical Free Churches, to the Free Church Assembly on 10 March 1931, reported in *The Times*, 11 March 1931, p. 11, column a.

79 Whereas other religions were declining, the Catholic faith was continuing to grow in the late 1920s and 1930s, not only as a result of immigration but also through a significant number of conversions; see Hastings, *English Christianity*, pp. 275–7. For the alarmist Nonconformist reaction to the Bill's defeat, see the *Methodist Times*, 5 February 1931, report on a meeting held at Westminster, where the prominent Liberal Walter Runciman described it 'as a definite step in advance for the Catholics' and the meeting called for an 'extensive plan of campaign' against the Catholic Church.

80 BNL, *Preston Catholic News*, 31 January and 21 March 1931.

81 BNL, *Preston Catholic News*, 25 April 1931, pp. 4 and 9.

82 National Museum of Labour History, Manchester, Labour Party Archive, NEC Minutes, 23 June 1931.

83 P. Catterall, 'Free Churches' (Ph.D. thesis, London University, 1989), p. 406.

84 BNL, *Preston Catholic News*, 23 May 1931, p. 9.

85 BNL, *Preston Catholic News*, 18 July 1931, p. 2.

86 P. J. Waller, *Democracy and Sectarianism: A Political and Social History of Liver-*

pool, 1863–1939 (Liverpool, 1981), pp. 324–8.

87 BNL, *Preston Catholic News*, 24 October 1931.

88 For a more detailed discussion of Catholic voting behaviour at the 1931 general election see Riddell, 'The Catholic Church and the British Labour Party'.

89 Woolwich BLP, E.P. Microfilm (1982), Reel 12, Annual Report 1931; Wolverhampton West DLP, E.P. Microfilm (1983), Reel 2, EC, 29 May 1930; Colne Valley DLP, E.P. Microfilm (1979), Reel 5, Annual Report 1930; Greenwich Local History Library, Greenwich DLP, General Council, 13 February 1930.

90 F. Williams, editor 1937–40, noted in S. Koss, *The Rise and Fall of the Political Press in Britain, Vol. 2: The Twentieth Century* (London, 1984), p. 496.

91 York Record Office, York DLP, ACC 196/1/4, Delegate Meeting, 17 July 1929.

92 M. Savage, *The Dynamics of Working-Class Politics: The Labour Movement in Preston, 1880–1940* (Cambridge, 1987), pp. 180–2.

93 West Yorkshire Archives Service, Sheepscar, City of Leeds Labour Party, /9, W. J. Armstrong to G. R. Shepherd, 6 November 1930.

94 West Yorkshire Archives Service, Sheepscar, City of Leeds Labour Party, 4/6, Resolution 19 November 1930.

95 Birmingham BLP, E.P. Microfilm, Reel 1, Borough Meeting, 11 July 1929; and Bristol Record Office, Bristol East DLP, ACC 39035/60, H. E. Roger to Shepherd, June 1931.

96 Labour Party, *Annual Report 1930*, p. 225.

97 Labour Party, *Annual Report 1929*, p. 186.

98 Greenwich Local History Library, Greenwich DLP, Minutes, 4 June 1931; Nottinghamshire Archives, Broxtowe DLP, DP PP6/3, Special Council Meeting, 5 July 1930.

99 G. D. H. Cole, *A History of the Labour Party from 1914* (London, 1948), p. 143. As Cole points out, it is difficult to put an exact figure upon membership because the ILP tended to deliberately underestimate numbers in order that it might pay less to Labour in affiliation fees.

100 A. McKinley and R. J. Morris (eds), *The ILP on Clydeside, 1893–1932* (Manchester, 1991), pp. 180–4.

101 J. McKinley and J. J. Smyth, 'The End of the Agitator Workman 1926–32', in McKinley and Morris (eds), *The ILP on Clydeside*, p. 186.

102 Wolverhampton West DLP, E.P. Microfilm (1983), Reel 1, EC, 5 November 1929 and General Meeting, 7 November 1929.

103 West Yorkshire Archives, Sheepscar, City of Leeds Labour Party, /9, GC, 17 September 1930, and W. J. Armstrong to G. R. Shepherd, 4 November 1930.

104 Durham County Archives, Darlington DLP, D/X 922/3, Executive Committee, 8 April 1931; Stockport TCLP, E.P. Microfilm (1980), 25 June 1931; Working Class Movement Library, Nelson and Colne BLP, Annual Conference, 1 May 1931.

105 West Yorkshire Archives, Sheepscar, City of Leeds Labour Party, 4/5, EC, 18 September 1929; Colne Valley DLP, E.P. Microfilm (1979), Reel 2, Minutes, 14 September 1930; SWCA, Newport DLP, A5, 8 September 1930.

106 Labour Party, *Annual Report 1930*, pp. 199 and 234.

107 This motion was carried by 1,253,000 to 866,000. See Labour Party, *Annual Report 1929*, pp. 159–70.

108 BNL, *Birmingham Town Crier*, 30 May 1930, p. 1, and *Leeds Weekly Citizen*, 6 June 1930, p. 4.

109 York Record Office, York DLP, ACC 196/1, Delegate Meeting, 18 June 1930;

Sheffield City Labour Party, E.P. Microfilm (1979), Reel 7, EC, 1 July 1930; South Shields DLP, E.P. Microfilm (1979), Reel 2, 29 June 1930; Cambridgeshire TCLP, E.P. Microfilm (1980), Reel 2, EC, 30 June 1930.

110 Labour Party, *Annual Report 1930*, p. 200; N. Mosley, *Rules of the Game: Sir Oswald and Lady Cynthia Mosley, 1896–1933* (London, 1982), p. 168.

111 BNL, *Birmingham Town Crier*, 12 December 1930, p. 1.

112 Sheffield City Archives, Sheffield Brightside DLP, LP (B)4, EC, 20 November 1930 and 4 December 1930.

113 Durham County Archives, Darlington DLP, D/X 922/3, 12 January 1931.

114 Nottinghamshire Archives, Broxtowe DLP, DP PP6, 14 March 1931; Durham County Archives, Jarrow DLP, D/X 33/2, 16 March 1931; Sheffield City Labour Party, E.P. Microfilm (1979), Reel 7, EC, 24 March 1931; Sheffield City Archives, Brightside DLP, LP(B)4, EC, 16 March 1931.

115 D. S. Lewis, *Illusions of Grandeur: Mosley, Fascism and British Society, 1931–1981* (Manchester, 1987), p. 20.

116 For an astute discourse on this aspect of Labour's psychology, see H. M. Drucker, *Doctrine and Ethos in the Labour Party* (London, 1979).

117 Birmingham BLP, E.P. Microfilm, Reel 1, EC, 29 December 1930 and 26 January 1931.

118 Wolverhampton West DLP, E.P. Microfilm (1983), Reel 1, EC, 19 January 1930 and 18 January 1931; General Meeting, 5 February 1931.

119 W. J. Brown, *So Far ...* (London, 1943), p. 159.

120 Mosley, *Rules of the Game*, p. 173.

121 Wolverhampton West DLP, E.P. Microfilm (1983), Reel 1, Special EC, 25 March 1931, and Delegate Meeting, 26 March 1931.

122 BNL, *Birmingham Town Crier*, 7 November 1930; West Yorkshire Archives Service, Sheepscar, City of Leeds City Labour Party, 4/6, Annual Report 1930.

123 BNL, *Leeds Weekly Citizen*, 7 November 1930; Working Class Movement Library, *Nelson Gazette*, 4 November 1930; West Yorkshire Archives Service, Sheepscar, City of Leeds City Labour Party, /9, Secretary to G. R. Shepherd, 6 November 1930.

124 Greenwich Local History Library, Greenwich DLP, Minutes, Agent's Report, 12 March 1931; Gloucester TCLP, E.P. Microfilm (1980), Reel 2, EC, 12 August 1931.

125 York Record Office, York DLP, ACC 196/1/4, Delegate Meetings, December 1929 to June 1931.

126 Derby Local Studies Library, Derby DLP, DL 116, Finance Sub-Committee, 16 March 1931.

127 Doncaster Archives, Doncaster DLP, D57/1/1, Annual Reports 1930 and 1931.

128 Northumberland Record Office, Wansbeck DLP, NRO 527/A/2, General Meeting, 28 March 1931.

129 Woolwich BLP, E.P. Microfilm (1982), Reel 1, Introduction.

130 Labour Party, *Annual Report 1932*, p. 80.

131 Northumberland Record Office, Wansbeck DLP, NRO 527/A/2, General Meeting, 28 March 1931.

132 Wolverhampton West DLP, E.P. Microfilm (1982), Reel 2, EC, 30 July 1931.

133 Woolwich DLP, E.P. Microfilm (1982), Reel 12, 1929 Annual Report, 2 April 1930.

134 Durham Record Office, Darlington DLP, D/X 922/3, GC, 17 December 1930;

Wolverhampton West DLP, E.P. Microfilm (1982), Reel 2, EC, 26 February 1931.

135 National Library of Scotland, Edinburgh, Roxburgh and Selkirk DLP, ACC 4145(1), 1 September 1929.

136 Sheffield Archives, Sheffield Brightside DLP, LP(B) 13, Quarterly Meeting, 26 July 1931; South Shields, E.P. Microfilm (1980), Reel 2, General Meeting, 17 June 1930; Canterbury DLP, Maidstone Record Office, U1760/A1/1, GC, 10 June 1931.

137 Wolverhampton West DLP, E.P. Microfilm (1982), Reel 2, General Meeting, 8 July 1930.

138 Greenwich Local History Library, Greenwich DLP, Minutes, 1929–31; Gloucester TCLP, E.P. Microfilm (1980), Reel 2, 10 June 1931.

139 Doncaster Archives Department, Doncaster DLP, D57/1/1, Annual Report 1929.

140 York Record Office, York DLP, ACC 196/2/3, EC, 11 February 1931 and 18 April 1931.

141 Durham County Archives, Darlington DLP, D/X 922/3, EC, 12 August 1929 and GC, 14 August 1929.

142 Local History Library, Greenwich, Greenwich DLP, Minutes, 8 October 1929, 14 August 1930, 11 September 1930, 24 January 1931 and 13 August 1931. This reflected the general inter-war trend of a demise in the provincial press as it struggled to compete with the mass circulation dailies.

143 BNL, *Leeds Weekly Citizen*, 3 October 1930.

144 For example, see H. Pelling, *A Short History of the Labour Party* (London, 8th edn, 1985), p. 193, and Cole, *A History of the Labour Party*, Appendix III, 'Labour Party Membership, 1900–46'.

145 Labour Party, *Annual Report 1931*, p. 39.

146 Labour Party, *Annual Report 1930*.

147 Greenwich Local History Library, Greenwich DLP, Minutes, 9 July 1931; SWCA, Newport DLP, A5, 23 June 1931; Sheffield City Labour Party, E.P. Microfilm (1979), Reel 7, EC, 9 June 1931.

4

The Parliamentary Labour Party

Reactions of new Members of Parliament

The PLP contained well over 100 new MPs, many of whom knew little about parliamentary procedure or the limited role the average back-bencher was able to play. Daniel Chater, elected for Hammersmith South, later recalled that none of the new Labour back-benchers found parliamentary life to be what they had expected:

> There were some who, like myself, had pictured ourselves making a great speech during the opening debate on the King's Speech. We soon found that it was not easy to get into the debate at all, and if one did succeed it was not the occasion for a fighting socialist speech, and that its finest quality would be its brevity.

Not until April 1930 did Chater finally make his maiden speech and even then he was forced to change drastically what he had prepared after having 'sat on the bench continuously for over five hours during a housing debate'.[1] Aneurin Bevan, elected for Ebbw Vale, later described in vivid detail the effect which the atmosphere of Parliament had upon a new Labour member:

> His first impression is that he is in church. The vaulted roofs and stained-glass windows, the rows of statues of great statesmen of the past, the echoing halls, the soft-footed attendants and the whispered conversation, contrast depressingly with the crowded meetings and the clang and clash of hot opinions he has just left behind in his election campaign. Here he is, a tribune of the people, coming to make his voice heard in the seats of power. Instead, it seems he is expected to worship; and the most conservative of all religions – ancestor worship.... The classic Parliamentary style of speech is understatement. It is a style unsuited to the representatives of working people because it slurs and mutes the deep antagonisms which exist in society.[2]

In light of the sparsity of documentary material, it would be rash to suggest these experiences were universal. Perhaps those sponsored by trade unions, and generally more advanced in years, would have accepted parliamentary conventions more readily than the passionate young Bevan. Yet he was certainly not unique; as early as 11 July in the Commons, the ILP MP for Liverpool, Kirkdale, Elijah Sandham, told the Commons that: 'I believe that we could do more of a practical nature in a City Council in a day than we could do here in a week.'[3] Frank Smith, Labour MP for Nuneaton, shared this frustration. On 16 July he complained:

> I came here fresh from the fighting line. I have been a long time trying to get here.... Now I am here I begin to understand why things move so slowly. I do not wonder at people outside asking what is the use of the parliamentary machine. What is the use of it?... Hungry people cannot wait and people who are suffering ought not to have to wait ...[4]

Relations with the government

Aside from the dealing with correspondence and constituency affairs, a responsibility which many new MPs treated very seriously, voting in Parliament was the prime duty of any government back-bencher.[5] The Labour leadership expected back-benchers to make voting for the government their top priority. In view of the considerable problems which the administration faced and the legislative compromises bound to result, it was imperative that Labour MPs retained their faith in the Labour Cabinet. Central to this continued faith was a conviction that the government was ready to listen to PLP grievances and justify its decisions to the PLP. Unfortunately, as with the trade unions, the machinery for consultation proved from an early date to be woefully inadequate. The result, once again, was an exacerbation of existing differences.

In opposition, the parliamentary party had its own Executive Committee (in today's terminology, the 'shadow Cabinet'), which reported to a weekly meeting of all members. In order to save government time, the PLP was persuaded to suspend this weekly meeting and accept a monthly one, and, as in 1924, a 'Consultative Committee' (CC) of twelve members was created to 'serve as a channel of communication between the party and the various Ministers'.[6] Meetings of the CC could be called by members of the committee, by the government or following a demand from at least twenty MPs. In the first elections held in July, Harry Snell and John Scurr were elected to be Chairman and Vice-Chairman respectively,[7] and Henderson, Clynes and Thomas Kennedy, the Chief Whip, were chosen to attend regularly on behalf of the government. As with the unions, it is apparent that Snowden, MacDonald and Thomas did not volunteer to justify the government's decisions.

Ministers and back-benchers could also meet each other socially in the Commons and at the National Labour Club, although, as Beatrice Webb noted, the Clyde group of the ILP and the party's aristocrats, like Oswald and Cynthia Mosley, Arthur Ponsonby, Lord Thomson and Earl De la Warr, never attended such functions.[8] Most new Labour MPs would not have known each other well, if at all, before arriving at Westminster, and social functions were an important means to gain some semblance of a group identity. It was for this reason that Beatrice Webb felt that it was her duty to hold a regular weekly lunch for the Labour MPs. Groups of MPs concerned with particular aspects of government policy could arrange to meet with the ministers concerned. On 9 November, for example, Lord Passfield and MacDonald had met a small deputation on Kenyan policy, headed by John Scurr and Josiah Wedgwood.[9] Such consultations, however, were few and far between. In the hectic day-to-day functioning of the government, and with MacDonald, Henderson and Snowden all away from Westminster for long periods, it was difficult to find time to arrange them. As such, it was all the more imperative that the formal machinery for consultation should function effectively.[10]

It was Henderson who predictably worked the hardest to reconcile the PLP to government policy. He did so, however, 'not always with success and sometimes testing his own temper in the process'.[11] With its parliamentary position so uncertain, it was difficult for the government to outline a long-term policy to its back-benchers. Meetings of both the PLP and the CC were often difficult affairs for ministers, with considerable back-bench bitterness often expressed. In these circumstances, it is not surprising that few ministers were keen to attend and the clear reluctance on behalf of both MacDonald and Snowden can have done little to encourage others.

MacDonald, leaving aside the Maxtonites, whom he believed impossible to reconcile to government policy, had a tendency to take the loyalty of the bulk of the PLP for granted.[12] As with the unions and the local parties, he believed it was Henderson's responsibility to deal with any difficulties that did occur. His attendance at PLP meetings was a rare occurrence; he addressed the first meeting of the PLP on 27 June 1929, and the first meeting of the CC on 15 July, but was not present at either again until he spoke to the PLP on 5 February 1930. During the period October 1929 to October 1930 he attended the NEC twice, and between October 1930 and the fall of the government he attended on only six occasions.[13] Instead, he relied on correspondence from H. Scott Lindsay, the Secretary of the PLP, to keep him informed of party feeling.[14] Scott Lindsay became increasingly concerned by the Prime Minister's non-attendance. On 26 March 1930 he wrote: 'I wonder if you could find it possible to attend a meeting soon. You have never yet given your new Party a general talk. If you do this it would inspire the members for their meeting during the Easter recess.'[15] MacDonald was taking a considerable gamble on party loyalty; despite his busy schedule, not to have given the PLP a general talk nine months after the government's formation seems truly remarkable. His lack of attendance did create some annoyance amongst MPs, particularly when it appeared that he had time to go to social functions. Nevertheless, as Morrison records, the majority still had 'high affection and regard for him in general'; such was MacDonald's status that he was able largely to get away with this continual absence.[16]

Yet this state of affairs was not good for the morale of a PLP forced to suffer continual disappointments and was highly damaging to party unity. Affairs were not improved by the continual absence of Henderson through his commitments abroad. By 1931, MacDonald appears to have held equally little regard both for Henderson and the bulk of the parliamentary party. Not only was he increasingly critical in private of Labour MPs and of many ministers, and disgusted by the disruptive behaviour of the Maxtonite ILP, but he also equated what he saw as Henderson's cultivation of the PLP with a desire to take his job. On 27 January 1931 MacDonald recorded with little regret that he had missed an important party meeting and had 'probably suffered.... My pushful friend ... was pathetic in his tale of the sacrifices he had undergone to attend, in view of the importance of the meeting to the Party.'[17]

The CC failed to carry out the function for which it had been created. Morrison later recalled just how ineffective it was. The committee was too large and its conclusions often vague. It met too often, at least once a week, and this gave little time for constructive thought. Many of its meetings were held after problems had developed, rather than having as their purpose the prevention of these tensions. Since people were often working at cross purposes, heated argument was often the result. Finally, not enough ministers attended its meetings. Morrison recalls that MacDonald was worried by these tensions but failed to do anything constructive about them. Instead:

> He got rather cross, irritated, bad tempered. He probably sometimes assumed that there were conspiracies where conspiracies did not exist. The result was he got himself into a state of somewhat settled antagonism as between himself and the Parliamentary Party of which he was leader.[18]

Once again, then, the party leadership often succeeded only in exacerbating the tensions that existed between the government and its supporters.[19] The bulk of the PLP were still loyal to MacDonald in early 1931 and a few well chosen words would have gone a long way towards their pacification. Dalton noted on 25 November 1930 that although MacDonald had 'talk[ed] woolly nothings' at a party meeting he had still got 'a good reception from the majority.... Surely that this is the easiest party that leaders ever had to lead, if it is treated frankly.'[20] This failure to treat it frankly was to prove ultimately costly.

Parliamentary opposition

As noted, the Labour's government's parliamentary position was a difficult one. Whilst it was clearly impossible to include anything like all of the proposals of *Labour and the Nation*, the King's Speech of July 1929 did propose a fairly ambitious series of measures for a minority government.[21] Completion of this programme would require that legislation was passed swiftly and with the minimum of opposition.[22] It is in this light that MacDonald's plea on 2 July 1929 for the parties to 'consider [them]selves more as a Council of State and less as arranged regiments facing each other in battle' should be read, and not as evidence for a supposed desire for a National Government.[23]

The government was soon confronted with the major problem of obstructionist tactics from the opposition parties, particularly from the Conservatives. In a number of important debates, the Conservatives made speeches calculated to do little more than waste government time. The most obvious early example occurred during the protracted debates on the Coal Mines Bill from December 1929, which culminated in a series of all-night sittings in March 1930.[24] During Snowden's first budget of April 1930, the Conservatives placed over 100 amendments upon the order paper, and again encouraged all-night sittings during the committee stage of the Finance Bill that followed. One sitting lasted over twenty-two hours without interruption and not until July 1930 did the Bill finally leave the committee stage.[25] Daniel Chater later recalled that the Conservatives also used other strategies to make the government's life difficult:

> They often caused the House to appear very thin by storing a large number of their own men in St. Stephen's Club which was right opposite the House, and when the question was put streaming out from the Club and racing for the division lobby. Their hope was that some Labour members were absent at the moment, and probably their whips had advised them that such was the case.[26]

The discontent felt by Labour MPs over these tactics was often expressed in a desire to change the parliamentary procedure that allowed such strategies to be used. This was more marked amongst newer members, like Chater, who felt a tremendous sense of frustration with the intricacies of the parliamentary game, none of which they believed aided the ends for which they had been returned to Parliament. Major David Graham Pole, elected in 1929 for South Derbyshire, proposed abolition of all-night sittings and looked forward to a majority Labour government able to reform the parliamentary machine.[27] Pole was not a radical Labour figure (in 1931 he became Parliamentary Private Secretary to the Minister for War) and this suggests that such sentiments were widespread in the PLP. At a PLP meeting in December 1929, E. F. Wise (Leicester East), a prominent ILP intellectual, proposed that a committee of the party should be established to investigate parliamentary procedure.[28] In keeping with his desire that Labour should appear 'respectable', however, and in no way a threat to parliamentary traditions, MacDonald was opposed to reform and viewed such demands as symbolic of political naivety.[29] Aware of the heavy programme to which the government was committed, the long and involved issue of parliamentary reform was not one in which MacDonald wished to become engaged.

Yet, in light of Conservative obstruction, growing revolts within the PLP, the increasing fragmentation of the Liberals, and the resulting legislative backlog, it was clear from 1930 that the government would have to consider the options for making its parliamentary life an easier one. It decided to follow two avenues: first, the use of the guillotine and, secondly, negotiations to attempt to ensure Liberal support for Labour's programme. On 24 November 1930 MacDonald declared that: 'There is nothing that is doing this House more damage, in public opinion, than the leisureliness of its deliberations in its workings.'[30] On 21 January 1931 he moved that government business should be given precedence over Private Members' time on every Wednesday for the remainder of the parliamentary session,[31] and on 2 March he was able to put through a guillotine motion to limit the time spent on the electoral reform Bill.[32] On 4 June he did likewise with regard to Snowden's 1931 budget.[33]

Despite the minority position, the Labour leadership and the bulk of the PLP were opposed on taking office to the forming of any close alliance with the Liberal Party. Having just secured the greatest electoral result in its history, Labour was reluctant to come to an agreement with a party which it intended to supersede. The ILP was particularly opposed to any Lib–Lab collaboration, which it saw as a betrayal of socialism. Distrust of Lloyd George remained strong and Labour was aware that, because Liberal reunification in the mid-1920s had been an uneasy process, there was a strong possibility that Lloyd George would not be able to maintain unity.[34] The Labour leadership, and particularly Snowden, disagreed with the financial reasoning of the 'Yellow Book' proposals, which had allocated extensive state borrowing in order to finance large schemes of public works. Finally, the Liberal price for support of the government was electoral reform. The majority of the party, with Snowden a notable exception, were opposed to any measure of proportional representation, particularly after Labour had just performed so well under the existing system.

In an attempt to woo Liberal support, however, MacDonald announced in July 1929 that the government would set up a committee to look into electoral reform. This became known as the Ullswater Committee, and provided the government with a convenient means to stall on the issue, on the calculation that the Liberals would keep Labour in office until electoral reform had been achieved.[35] Lloyd George was, unsurprisingly, not satisfied by this concession and attempted to make the government's life difficult in the hope of securing a firmer commitment. This was evident during the passage of the Coal Bill in February 1930, when the Liberals almost brought about the government's demise, ironically only avoided by a split in the Liberal vote. At this point, relations had deteriorated to a state of mutual antipathy.[36]

The narrowness of the government's majority on the Coal Bill, together with the growing backlog of legislation, forced an attempt to improve relations. On 18 March 1930 the government announced it would introduce electoral reform if it remained in office. Lloyd George was determined to push for full proportional representation, whilst a number of his colleagues were prepared to accept the 'alternative vote'.[37] The Labour Cabinet would accept only the latter and talks collapsed. Following Mosley's resignation, however, MacDonald put out an appeal for an all-party conference on unemployment on 18 June 1930, and, although Baldwin swiftly rejected the offer, Lloyd George accepted. The Liberal leader continued to press for proportional representation but only Snowden was at all amenable.[38] The Labour representatives on the Ullswater Committee were firmly opposed and in May 1930 the NEC voted by eleven votes to six against even an acceptance of the alternative vote. The Cabinet believed, however, that an agreement on the alternative vote might gain the government an extended life span; inevitable opposition from the Lords would ensure that putting the measure through Parliament would take over two years. The NEC was eventually convinced of the logic of this course of action.[39]

The PLP, however, was less ready to accept this reasoning. The government had presented an initial Bill at the end of 1930, but had abandoned it as too time-consuming and too controversial, and it was not until February 1931 that Clynes finally proposed a second reading for the Representation of the People (No. 2) Bill.[40] In its committee stage in March, J. M. Kenworthy (Kingston-upon-Hull) spoke out against the alternative vote as a sell-out to the Liberal Party.[41] Most Labour back-benchers were reticent, but did vote for it. On 16 March the government was defeated on Clause 4 of the Bill, which had proposed to abolish the university seats, through Labour apathy, some Labour opposition and divisions within the Liberals.[42]

Meanwhile, regular conversations between the Cabinet and the Liberal leaders developed, and rumours of a Lib–Lab coalition began to abound. By May 1931, some believed there would soon be Liberals on the government front bench.[43] Whether there was any truth in these rumours has been the subject of historical debate.[44] What is certain is that the Labour leadership would have had an almost impossible task if it had attempted to win the trade union movement around to a Liberal–Labour alliance, particularly after Liberal opposition had mangled the Trade Disputes Bill in early 1931. If the notion was considered seriously then it was yet another manifestation of the gulf which had opened up between the leadership and the wider movement. The PLP was highly concerned by these rumours. The Maxtonites viewed a Lib–Lab pact as the logical conclusion to an administration it believed had moved ever further from socialism.

Relations with the Liberals had proved to be a source of much friction between the PLP and the government. The Labour leadership initially shared the hostility of the movement towards any pacts, but its increasing awareness of the fragility of Labour's position, the growing disruption caused by its own radical wing and, in particular, the pressure to deal with the country's enormous economic problems, forced it to accept the need for closer collaboration. The precarious existence of the government worked against any long-term agreement, as did the growing divisions in the Liberals, and the leadership was naturally fearful of providing further 'grist to the Left Wing mill'.[45] Yet, arguably, by failing to address the issue earlier, the government added both to its legislative difficulties and to its problems of party management. As a result of its initial opposition to talks, when it did negotiate seriously with Lloyd George from mid-1930 the government provoked PLP fears that it had moved to the right.[46] The secretive nature of the 1931 talks added to this sense of PLP suspicion and would also take the rift between the government and the Maxtonites to breaking point.

The honeymoon period

The government's initial period in office, however, was a time of general satisfaction for the majority of the PLP. The debate on the King's Speech in early July saw few interventions from the Labour back-benches. Beatrice Webb noted on 28 July that Arthur Ponsonby was 'full of praise of the new Labour members and the general spirit of the Party'.[47] The PLP was clearly impressed by the energy and enthusiasm displayed by its front bench in this initial period and by its self-belief.[48] The early successes abroad were once again the greatest source of satisfaction. MacDonald's visit to the USA and Canada and his announcement of a conference on naval disarmament met with the general applause of the House on 5 November,[49] and on the same day Henderson carried with ease a motion to restore diplomatic relations with the Soviet Union.[50]

The Maxtonites, predictably, did not share in this early satisfaction. Maxton expressed his 'complete dissatisfaction' with the King's Speech, which he felt contained even less socialism than had been found in the pages of *Labour and the Nation*.[51] Nearly all Labour criticism of the King's Speech came from the party's Scottish contingent, to culminate in the most serious admonishment on 10 July. Neil Maclean, at this stage still an 'Independent Labour' MP for Glasgow, Govan, drew attention to the fact that the speech had contained 'not a single word about Scotland'. He claimed that during the election Labour had pledged itself to suspend the Conservative 1929 Local Government (Scotland) Act and quoted from MacDonald's election speech in Glasgow promising increased self-government. In his reply, MacDonald reaffirmed his commitment to this declaration but announced that the government did not have the time to implement its own Act before Scotland's local elections the following September. All he could promise was that the government might be able to amend the Act and institute a full inquiry in the future. Although fifty-one MPs voted for the amendment proposed by Maclean, no Labour MP did so, and MacDonald's pledge had been sufficient to convince even Maclean to vote for the government.[52] None the less, this early reproof did not bode well for the future; not only did it illustrate the damaging effects of the government not being able to implement everything promised in the election campaign, but it also demonstrated a worrying lack of solidarity between the government and its radical wing.[53]

Unemployment benefit

Almost immediately the government was formed, it was pressed by the PLP to reveal its intentions for the extension of unemployment benefit.[54] On 10 July MacDonald informed the House that the only Bill to be introduced in the immediate future would be one to increase borrowing on the Unemployment Insurance Fund. This provoked an angry response from Bevan and from George Buchanan (Glasgow, Gorbals) who stressed the urgency of repealing the 'Not Genuinely Seeking Work' clause.[55] The following day saw the introduction of the Unemployment Insurance [Money] Bill, in which Bondfield proposed that, as a short-term measure, the Exchequer contribution to unemployment insurance should be increased to half of the sum paid by the workers and the employers. The Maxtonites used this opportunity to criticise the inadequate nature of the scheme and to urge Bondfield both to increase unemployment benefit and to remove the 'Not Genuinely Seeking Work' clause. Buchanan told the Minister of Labour to withdraw the resolution and to return in three weeks' time with a 'proper financial resolution', and Campbell Stephen referred to the 'Not Genuinely Seeking Work' clause as 'administrative persecution'.[56]

The debate that ensued made it clear that such sentiments were not confined to the Maxtonites. In his maiden speech, J. Kinley (Liverpool, Bootle) expressed his grave disappointment with government policy and made an impassioned plea on behalf of the unemployed:

I imagine that few honourable members have ever risen to speak here for the first time feeling sadder than I do at this moment. If there was one thing we had a right to look for from the Labour Government it was an immediate improvement in the condition of the unemployed ... as far as the Labour Government is concerned, the condition of the unemployed is to show no change for another 12 months ...[57]

After a detailed description of the poverty rife in his constituency, he called for the unemployed to be given the benefit to which he felt they were entitled, and for a new Bill 'worthy of our name, worthy of our party, and worthy of the faith that we say is in us'.[58]

Jennie Lee, the 24-year-old Member for North Lanark, made a similarly humanistic appeal for the rights of the unemployed and urged the government to do something 'immediately' as it had promised to do at the time of the election. John Beckett (Peckham) warned the government of the depth of feeling that existed in the country on the issue. Only John Bromley (Barrow-in-Furness) and the Reverend Gordon Lang (Oldham) defended Bondfield and the government from the back-benches. Meanwhile, half a dozen Labour MPs intervened to condemn the proposed measure as inadequate and to express the fear that the government was losing its radical zeal in the face of an obstructionist civil service. T. Lewis (Southampton) also commented on the lack of communication between the government and the PLP.[59] Despite the fact that no Labour Members voted against the resolution, the government had been given a powerful warning that a bolder policy was expected on unemployment benefit. It does appear, however, that the government could have avoided a confrontational position had it spoken to the PLP before the measure reached the House.

The Maxtonites reiterated their criticisms during the second reading of the Unemployment Insurance Bill.[60] On 25 July the government formed the Morris Committee, the report of which led to the introduction of the Unemployment Insurance (No. 2) Bill in November 1929 and to further scenes of back-bench dissatisfaction. This was despite the fact that the government had attempted to learn from the earlier lack of consultation; on 31 October 1929 Snowden had addressed the PLP on the financial responsibilities of the government,[61] and on 5 November the CC had established a sub-committee to interview Snowden and Bondfield on unemployment insurance.[62] Yet, whilst Snowden had 'promised to go into the matter again', neither the Chancellor nor Bondfield found the time to address the whole party on the proposed Bill.[63] When the Bill was circulated on 19 November, it was clear that the bulk of the party was far from enthusiastic. A half-hearted motion welcoming the Bill as 'a substantial step in the reform of the present system' provoked a long discussion and fourteen MPs voted against it.[64] A general talk at this stage on the rationale behind the Bill might have done much to alleviate PLP criticisms.

Despite her plea that the Bill should be considered only as a stop-gap measure, Bondfield was immediately subjected to a bitter attack from Arthur Hayday, whose formula for the replacement of the 'Not Genuinely Seeking Work' clause she had failed to accept, and who was also discontented by the omission of any mention of a reduction in the waiting period.[65] The Maxtonites again used the opportunity to accuse the government of cowardice,[66] and once more were more in tune with party opinion than the government. The intervention of Lang, who had shown himself already to be a government loyalist, was revealing of the tension which back-benchers felt to exist between their loyalties to the government and to their principles. Lang rationalised his disappointment by accepting the government's argument that it was merely an instalment, but warned that 'If I felt it represented the last word of my own Government on this matter I should be in despair.'[67]

For its part, the government was discernibly irritated by the criticism. Tom Shaw reiterated that the Bill was only an emergency measure, and that it was as much as the government could get through the House. Turning to the Maxtonites, he asked them whether they truly believed that 'the things they have said could be passed through this House [even] by a majority [Labour government]?'. Following the inevitable reply in the affirmative, Shaw commented in exasperation, 'If you do, God help your intellect.'[68] He then accused the group of irresponsibility and of a failure to confront political realities.[69] Already, therefore, the completely irreconcilable nature of the perspectives of the government and of the Maxtonites had been exposed.

The Bill's committee stage on 2 December finally saw the Maxtonites taking their disagreements to the point of forcing a division. John Wheatley moved an amendment calling for a further £50,000 from the Exchequer to relieve the unemployed in the coming winter months and made a sophisticated attack upon the government's pleas of lack of finance. He asked Snowden: 'What has become of the £2,000,000 we won at The Hague?... we have not heard much about the unemployed in South Wales, in Scotland, on Tyneside or in Lancashire sharing in that £2,000,000.'[70] In seconding the motion, Richard Wallhead (Merthyr Tydfil) refused to accept the common perception that the government was in office but not in power: 'Three times already there has been a very powerful combination against them, but they have escaped defeat ... the only power in this country that can defeat this party is its failure to carry out its pledges.'[71] Yet the bulk of the PLP was not moved sufficiently by this reasoning, and the amendment was defeated by 222 votes to 33.[72]

A further amendment from David Kirkwood (Dumbarton, Clydebank) to increase benefit rates won only twenty votes, despite a claim by John Beckett that the amendment was carrying out Labour's election pledges and was in line with 'the instructions of the Labour organisations'. Beckett disagreed with the government's entire approach, which he believed to be jeopardising socialism by attempting to 'show how alike we are to the other two parties', and illustrated what he believed to be front-bench hypocrisy on the question of loyalty. Susan Lawrence had told him that if he pressed the amendment then she would 'vote for [his] expulsion with both hands', and yet, 'In 1924 she voted against the Government on almost an exactly similar Amendment'. Indeed, he proposed that some 'nine members of the present government and 43 back-benchers had gone into the Lobby against the Labour Government at some stage'.[73]

Two further ILP amendments to increase benefits for particular claimants were also rejected on the grounds of expense, but they did succeed in making life uncomfortable for the rest of the PLP. Whilst they accepted Bondfield's financial reasoning, the bulk of the party sympathised with the moral justifications for these amendments.[74] C. J. Simmons summed up the back-bench dilemma, admitting, 'Some of us during the past few days have been living a very miserable life. Our hearts have been with the Clydeside, and our heads have inclined us to go into the Government lobby.'[75] Moderate party opinion was clearly wavering; some thirty-seven Labour Members voted for Jennie Lee's proposal to increase the allowance for the children of unemployed workers and this included Philip Noel-Baker, MP for Coventry, and the Parliamentary Private Secretary to Henderson.[76]

Back-bench pressure was not entirely ineffective, for the government did accept one amendment to secure a minor increase in benefit,[77] and, as noted in Chapter 2, Bondfield did accept the 'Hayday Formula' eventually.[78] However, despite the CC's successful attempt to get MacDonald to agree to a special party meeting, and the memorandum signed by fifty members of the trade union group, the government refused to reduce the waiting period for benefit to three days.[79] At this meeting, Snowden painted a very gloomy picture of the financial position and warned that the Exchequer 'had gone as far as it could possibly go'. After a long discussion, the meeting accepted reluctantly a motion that the PLP would not proceed with any amendments of a financial character.[80] A serious effect of these events was to tarnish the PLP's attitude to Bondfield, who was widely felt to be not up to the job.[81]

Coal

As illustrated in Chapter 2, the government's attempts to reform the coal mines resulted in extensive difficulties and almost in defeat. Paradoxically, however, unlike the unemployment insurance legislation, the Coal Bill initially had a unifying, rather than a divisive effect. The bulk of the party accepted that nationalisation was not possible and that the Bill was the best that could be hoped for. Equally, they recognised that the proposals had been accepted by the miners themselves. Finally, the PLP was well aware that the government would be faced by powerful opposition and that unity was essential if the government was to survive. Even the Maxtonites endorsed this reasoning and the government was pleased by the extent of party unity in December 1929.[82]

This unity was largely retained during the committee stage of the Bill. On 11 February 1930 Maxton pushed an amendment to introduce a minimum wage but the bulk of the party recognised that this could destroy the Bill and only twenty-one voted for it.[83] On 27 February Wheatley summed up the overriding sense of commitment that the party felt to the miners. Whilst he believed in the need for nationalisation, he was going to vote for the Bill because 'it contains that half-hour for the miners'.[84] E. F. Wise introduced an amendment on 1 April that proposed compensation for miners who were losing their jobs through rationalisation. This provoked an angry response from J. M. Kenworthy, who accused Wise of threatening to upset what had been a long process of negotiation, and only twenty-eight voted for the amendment.[85] The Bill finally passed its third reading on 3 April and Graham told MacDonald privately how impressed he had been by the party's loyalty.[86]

Yet this fragile unity had been maintained only because the MFGB, however reluctantly, had decided the government must be supported on the compromised Bill. With the introduction of the spreadover and the threat of wage cuts, this unity was threatened, particularly once it was clear the miners were pushing for the minimum wage in 1931. MacDonald was very concerned in early July 1931 that the PLP might revolt over the government's proposal to do no more than protect basic wage rates and the 7½-hour day for another twelve months. In typical fashion, he informed Henderson that he should arrange a party meeting beforehand and attempt to pacify the critics, as he himself was otherwise engaged.[87] There is no record of any reply from Henderson, but what is clear is that he was not present at the meeting of 7 July, when it was left to Shinwell to ask Maxton, Brockway, Wise and Stephen to withdraw their proposed amendment to the Bill, which called for the increase of minimum wage rates.[88] Shinwell was successful, once again largely because even the Maxton group accepted the need to abide by the decision of the MFGB to accept the legislation. In sombre tones, Ebby Edwards, miners' MP for Morpeth, seconded the Bill on 6 July as a necessary temporary measure, and even Jennie Lee, despite her grave reservations and her appeal for the logic of nationalisation, accepted that all Labour MPs were duty-bound to vote for the Bill, because they knew 'that a conflict would be a calamity'.[89]

Pensions and housing

Pensions were another area which became a focus for the fundamental disagreement between the Maxtonites and the government. An increase in pensions for the old and for widows and orphans was a reform the whole party wished to see implemented. For the majority, this reform was advocated on moral grounds, but for the Maxtonites pensions were seen in the context of under-consumptionism. This was evident during the second reading of the government's Widows', Orphans' and Old Age Pensions Bill on 31 October 1929, which proposed to extend the terms of the existing 1925 Act. Although he conceded the measure was 'a considerable improvement on the Act of 1925', Wheatley believed it did little more than 'dot the i's and cross the t's of Conservative legislation'. He argued that increased pensions could be an important means of increasing the poor's purchasing power and of allowing workers to retire earlier. He scoffed at Snowden's claim that the country could not afford a bold Act, arguing that there was sufficient money in the possession of the country's highest earners: 'I submit that the country could afford it if we had a Chancellor of the Exchequer who was as determined to get it as he was to get money out of the foreigners during The Hague Conference.'[90]

At this stage, the majority accepted the Bill as a significant improvement, and were reassured by Susan Lawrence, who was Under-Secretary to the Ministry of Health, when she stressed that the Bill should be regarded only as a first instalment.[91] In the committee stage, Buchanan expressed his doubts that further measures would follow and urged the government to act boldly and immediately.[92] Campbell Stephen was similarly critical and was met by an angry response from James Sexton, the Member for St Helens, who accused the Maxtonites of 'little less than organised hypocrisy' and urged them to accept the Bill in the spirit in which it was intended, namely as an instalment.[93] Predictably, therefore, attempted ILP amendments to reduce the minimum pensionable age for women from fifty-five to forty-five met with little Labour support on 19 November.[94] The bulk of the PLP accepted the government's argument and rejected the Maxton–Wheatley case as both unrealistic and divisive. Yet, ultimately, and as Buchanan had predicted, the 1929 Act did prove to be the only piece of pension legislation passed by the second Labour government.

Housing policy produced similar reactions. Greenwood's proposal to return the housing subsidy to the 1926 level provoked an immediate call from Wheatley to return to the level set by the 1924 Act.[95] Once again, Wheatley wanted the government to introduce a bold measure, stressing the economic and moral need for more house-building. He warned the government that such 'halting ... half-way legislation' would lead to the administration's discredit in the country within twelve months.[96] As with the legislation on pensions, Susan Lawrence attempted to alleviate back-bench concerns by stressing that the measure was only a temporary one, and the PLP largely accepted it on this basis.[97] In April 1930 the government finally introduced its Housing (No. 2) Bill, which set up a large scheme of state-aided slum clearance. This measure met with the general satisfaction of the parliamentary party and even Wheatley and Buchanan had few criticisms. Both Greenwood and Lawrence, the architects of the Bill, were widely praised in the party for their skilful manoeuvring of the measure through Parliament.[98] The Maxtonites no doubt viewed this success as proof that the government was capable of introducing bolder measures.

Disarmament

As shown in Chapter 3, disarmament was an issue of great concern in many local parties and was one that could arouse equally strong passions within the PLP. This was first apparent on 17 March 1930, when W. J. Brown intervened in a debate on naval estimates to urge a course of unilateral disarmament rather than the multilateral strategy pursued by the government. A. W. Haycock (Salford West) shared Brown's pacifist sentiment and stressed that money could always be found for defence, but not for the social services. He urged the House to consider the belief of many in the 1920s that the First World War had been justified only as a war to end all wars.[99] The following day John Beckett moved an amendment to reduce naval armaments and the size of the armed services. He stressed that Labour had moved a similar amendment in 1928 which even MacDonald had voted for.[100] C. J. Simmons conceded that the government had 'done more for peace than [its] predecessors', but believed that disarmament was the only way to secure peace for the future.[101] Only twenty-two voted for the amendment, but this included a number who did not usually vote with the Maxtonites, like Dr Alfred Salter, Bevan and Simmons. On 24 March William Cove (Glamorgan, Aberavon) moved a similar amendment in a debate on the army estimates, seconded by Brown. Shinwell defended the government's line and argued that the pacifist group was deluding itself that unilateral disarmament could end the threat of war. Some twenty-one still voted for the amendment, including John Bromley and Ellen Wilkinson, but the majority were content to place their hopes for disarmament in the London Conference.[102] On 15 May MacDonald spoke to the House on the agreement reached at the conference and was well received by the Labour benches. Kenworthy congratulated the Prime Minister on his 'great personal triumph',[103] and even Fenner Brockway was ready to applaud the treaty.[104]

This general satisfaction, however, dispersed when the government announced its new naval estimates in July 1930. Kenworthy, who had never voted against the government, declared himself to be 'completely at a loss to understand' the front bench's policy, which represented a reduction of only £4,000,000 on the Conservative government's navy spending for 1929.[105] He accused Alexander, the First Lord of the Admiralty, of 'a betrayal of the pledges of the Labour Party' and cited the commitment of *Labour and the Nation* not to build unnecessary ships. So strongly did he feel that he candidly announced that he was prepared to bring the government down over it, arguing that: 'even the life of a government is not to be compared with the lives of millions of men who will be forfeited if we are involved in another great war'.[106]

Charles Ammon, the Parliamentary Secretary to the Admiralty, did not disguise his irritation. He defended the London Naval Treaty, which had reduced substantially the amount of shipbuilding in Britain, and he implied that Kenworthy was guilty both of false financial statements and of naive utopianism. He warned that, despite Henderson's best efforts, there was no guarantee there would be a world disarmament conference in 1931, and therefore the government should not cut its navy too drastically.[107] This explanation failed to convince G. W. Holford Knight (Nottingham South), who declared that he also would have to vote against the government.[108] Alexander was forced into a further defence and re-emphasised the belief that mutual international agreement was the only means to secure further reductions. He accused his critics of being 'not sufficiently appreciative of what the Government had already done' and pointed to the cancelling of £12 million worth of building programmes in 1929.[109] He suggested that Kenworthy was guilty of a complete 'lack of naval knowledge' and explained the government's policy of building a number of larger cruisers in order to stabilise work in the shipyards and to replace smaller ones built during the war.[110] What he did not mention, but what was clearly a strong factor in the reasoning of the government, was the importance of maintaining work in the shipyards at a time of rapidly increasing unemployment. Labour's long-term disarmament commitment, together with many other aspects of its programme, was now in conflict with the economic realities in which it found itself.

Simmons repeated that Labour had pledged to achieve world peace and claimed the issue was 'the thing which arouses more enthusiasm, especially among the women electors, than any other issue'.[111] He was not alone in this feeling, since Ben Turner (Batley and Morley), the ex-Minister for Mines, also felt himself honour-bound to oppose the estimates: 'It seems to me that we are running a mad race for armaments, we are doing the very thing that many condemned in 1918.'[112] Some twenty-seven Labour MPs voted against the government, including a number who had never before gone into the opposition lobby. Such, then, was the level of passion over disarmament, and, once again, so considerable was the gulf between the commitments of *Labour and the Nation* and the policies of the government. In 1931 similar criticisms of the administration's armaments policies were expressed, but, once again, the majority of the PLP accepted the government's gradualist disarmament strategy, were generally pleased by the reductions that the government had secured and placed great hopes in the plans for a world disarmament conference.[113]

Lord Hunsdon

Trade union opposition to the reappointment of Lord Hunsdon to the Public Works Loans Commissioners has been noted in Chapter 2; this was an issue which provoked a first-class political row between the government and the PLP. The dispute is revealing, for two main reasons. First, because it was symbolic of a growing feeling that the government was conceding too much for the cause of respectability and, secondly, because it illustrated the serious lack of communication between the administration and the PLP by that date.

On 27 June 1930 F. W. Pethick-Lawrence, the Financial Secretary to the Treasury, moved a Public Works Loans Bill which the government clearly expected would raise little political controversy. However, E. F. Wise stepped in to criticise not only the limit of £30,000,000 for public loans to local authorities, but also Labour's blanket reappointment of the Public Works Loans Commissioners for a further five years. Wise suggested that, although none of the members of this Board were in sympathy with the government's policies, they had the power to decide whether a loan to a local authority should be given. Of the eighteen members, ten were bank directors, thirteen were insurance directors and four were directors of private utility companies, which were in direct competition with the public utilities.[114] Richard Wallhead, MP for Merthyr, went further in his criticism, declaring that the majority of Board members were 'violently anti-Socialist and opposed to the advancement of municipal services'.[115] He then pointed to the first person mentioned on the list, Lord Hunsdon, who had said in 1926 that the miners should be starved back to work.[116]

Pethick-Lawrence was caught off-guard by these criticisms and in his response managed only to inflame back-bench opinion. Stating in classic terms the Labour leadership's belief in state neutrality, he declared that the Board had to 'act in accordance with the policy laid down by this House' and declared categorically that he would not accept any amendments. Although prepared to add one or two names to the Board, he would do so only on economic and not political grounds. He was not prepared to 'accept any proposal which would have the effect of casting a slur on the way the present members of the Board have discharged their duties'.[117] Simmons was unimpressed with this response and accused the front bench of being 'too much inclined to think that people on the other side have all the ability, and that the people on our side have none'.[118]

Yet, despite the evident discontent, the government made no attempt to address the PLP on the matter and the consequence was that Wallhead moved an amendment during the committee stage on 11 July to remove Hunsdon from the Board. Pethick-Lawrence again refused to budge and Simmons and John Joseph Tinker (Leigh) called for an open vote. Simmons suggested that: 'by retaining this man on this particular Board we are putting a halo around his head instead of a noose about his neck, and giving a kind of Government sanction to his actions in the past'.[119] Tinker stressed the point that he felt sure that the Conservatives would not hesitate to drop anyone from a committee whom they particularly objected to.[120] Such sentiments were widespread, with a number of government loyalists also expressing their discontent. Francis Alfred Broad (Edmonton) argued that the workers were 'just as capable of managing great affairs and large financial transactions ... as other people', and warned that he felt forced to vote against the government for the first time.[121] In these circumstances, and to opposition jeers, Pethick-Lawrence decided to adjourn the debate, having finally recognised the need to discuss the issues with the PLP.[122]

The result was a very heated special meeting of the PLP on 17 July, addressed by Snowden, who declared himself willing to add four new names to the Board, but stated that 'it would be impossible for the Government to accept the amendment which had been moved to exclude Lord Hunsdon'. Yet, despite the Chancellor's opposition, the meeting still moved a motion that Hunsdon be removed from the commission, which was defeated only by thirty-eight votes to thirty-three, with the majority abstaining.[123] Such was the depth of feeling, then, that even the intervention of a senior Cabinet member had almost failed to win over the party. Snowden's victory was only a partial one, however, for the tremendous tension continued. The resumption of the committee stage on 23 July saw Wallhead repeat his reasoning and Joseph Batey (Durham, Spennymoor) revealed what had been the government's chief objection to Hunsdon's removal: that the House of Lords would refuse to pass the Bill.[124] James Chuter Ede, the moderate MP for South Shields, declared that he would be betraying the large number of miners who had returned him to Parliament if he were to vote for the Bill, whilst Frederick Seymour Cocks (Nottingham, Broxtowe) skilfully linked his concerns over the government's attitude to a questioning of its whole political strategy: 'What is the meaning of the inevitability of gradualness? Does it mean the inevitability of Lord Hunsdon?'[125]

Snowden replied by suggesting that Hunsdon had withdrawn the comments made in 1926 and had a long record of public service. He then became embroiled in a bitter slanging match with Seymour Cocks.[126] The comments of Francis Broad illustrate well the essential dilemma for the government back-bencher: to vote against Hunsdon would be 'a vote of no confidence in our Government' and Broad attempted to rationalise the government's position, suggesting that Snowden could not possibly withdraw Hunsdon's name at this late date.[127] Presumably a significant number of other Labour back-benchers also got cold feet, but sixty-three Labour Members, many of whom represented mining areas, still decided to vote against, which represented the largest protest vote during the whole of the second Labour government.[128] Once again, the government had handled its parliamentary party very badly; not only had it failed to anticipate the conflict, but it had also failed to stem the tension. This conflict, however, was about more than the appointment of an individual to a committee; it was an outlet for more deep-seated frustrations, of which the most significant was growing PLP concern over unemployment policy.

Unemployment policy and Mosley

The PLP was aware that the government would be judged primarily on its ability to solve unemployment. As such, it eagerly awaited Thomas's proposals. As early as July 1929, Thomas introduced a Bill to enact an immediate extension of government loans to public utility undertakings. The response of Labour back-benchers was mixed. Michael Marcus, the new MP for Dundee, was quick to pay tribute to Thomas's 'remarkably strenuous efforts' and to express his full confidence in the Lord Privy Seal's abilities.[129] Kenworthy was not so impressed, both because he was unhappy that much of the administration would be assigned to committees and, more substantially, because he believed a new separate staff would be needed to deal with unemployment.[130] E. T. Palmer (Greenwich) shared Kenworthy's belief that unemployment could be solved only if it was treated as 'a national emergency' and urged the government to act swiftly to introduce more extensive schemes.[131] Yet the bulk of the PLP was firmly behind Thomas, including Bevan, who fully accepted the proposals as a welcome short-term improvement.[132] During the Bill's second reading, Frederick Messer summed up the typical Labour attitude, suggesting that since Labour could not deal adequately with unemployment until it could introduce socialism, such short-term tinkering to alleviate the worst excesses was the best the government could do.[133]

Yet by November 1929 there was growing unrest, fuelled by a belief that more could be done. Maxton used the opportunity of a vote on the Lord Privy Seal's salary to criticise the government's whole approach to unemployment.

He was unable to discover even a hint of socialism in Thomas's speech, and, rejecting the notion that small public works schemes provided any solution, he mocked the government's gradualist approach:

> One of my enthusiastic colleagues ... said that Labour was in for twenty years. Well, I hope so. God knows that at the rate of progress indicated in the Lord Privy Seal's speech they will need every minute of it![134]

Maxton's solution was formulated once more on under-consumptionist lines; he believed that Labour should increase benefit to increase the purchasing power of the masses and thereby create employment. John McShane (Walsall) emphasised the inhuman aspect of unemployment and appealed to the opposition to give the government the freedom to implement its policies. The more typical Labour view was expressed by J. H. Alpass (Bristol, Central) when he applauded the government for what it had done within the constraints of capitalism.[135]

A further debate on 20 December, in the context of Thomas's call for supplementary estimates, demonstrated that it was only the Maxtonites that were prepared to question the government's strategy. Wheatley suggested that, whilst he did not doubt Thomas's energy and enthusiasm, the government had 'to face the hard fact that the right hon. Gentleman is making no impression on the unemployment situation'. All schemes enacted had been based on the assumption that unemployment was a 'temporary crisis' when what the government really needed was a long-term plan and 'a big scheme of national organisation'.[136] D. J. Vaughan (Forest of Dean), in a very nervous first speech, expressed the anger which many Labour MPs clearly felt at the Maxtonites' constant undermining of the government, revealing that: 'Sometimes I wonder what need there is for a Conservative and Liberal Party, since the Labour Party supply the opposition as well as the Government.'[137] The next incident of overt Labour criticism in the House occurred on 21 January 1930, when Buchanan urged Oswald Mosley, representing the Lord Privy Seal in Thomas's absence, to 'return to his socialism and to his Labour pledges, for along that way lies a saner path than following the stupidities and follies of rationalisation and capitalism'.[138] Little did Buchanan realise that, although he defended the government's record, in private Mosley had become equally critical of the administration's unemployment policies.[139]

As early as 1925, Mosley had questioned the assumptions of nineteenth-century economic orthodoxies in the so-called 'Birmingham Proposals' which formed the basis of *Revolution by Reason*. The degree to which these ideas were Mosley's alone, and the extent of John Strachey's influence in their conception, has been the subject of some historical debate.[140] What is beyond question is that, through a synthesis of Hobson's under-consumptionism and Keynes's 1923 *A Tract on Monetary Reform*, these proposals were, despite a number of weaknesses, a major innovation in Labour thought. What was novel about them was the demand for a public banking system to increase purchasing power and for an economic council to co-ordinate production and regulate demand. Mosley had hoped for a Cabinet office in May 1929, but had to be content with the Chancellorship of the Duchy of Lancaster. This position did have the major advantage that it entailed few administrative responsibilities and therefore left him time to consider unemployment, which he felt to be his prime responsibility.

The Committee on Unemployment, comprising himself, Lansbury and Thomas Johnston, the Under-Secretary for Scotland, failed to function effectively, and Mosley believed he was being excluded from the key decision-making processes. In effect, 'Mosley was given carte blanche to make himself a general nuisance, but no power to do anything'.[141] Mosley felt that the programme of only limited financial assistance to local authority schemes was wholly inadequate, and, together with Johnston, began to push in the autumn of 1929 for large-scale national schemes. Morrison, with whom Mosley's relations had long been poor, provided the major stumbling block. He did not believe such schemes would be successful and objected to the threat they would pose to local government.[142] As unemployment increased at the end of 1929, Mosley decided to write a memorandum containing his proposals, and appears to have received some encouragement from MacDonald, who was keen to receive new ideas for consideration by his new Economic Advisory Council. It would appear again that Strachey's input, as Mosley's Private Parliamentary Secretary, was more substantial than is generally conceded, although it was Mosley who wrote the final document.[143]

The 'Mosley Memorandum' was divided into four main sections. First, Mosley called for a radical reform of the Cabinet, favouring a small but powerful executive, to be assisted by a 'think tank' of key economists and scientists. Secondly, the Memorandum emphasised the need to develop the whole economy, rather than place hopes on a revival in the export trade as Thomas and Snowden were doing. Rationalisation should not be left to the banks but should be controlled by a state finance corporation, which would prioritise the need to provide credit for the newer industries. Surprisingly, Mosley did not mention the theoretical 'multiplier effect' of increased government expenditure which lay at the heart of Keynes's unorthodox ideas, which may imply that it was Strachey who had truly grasped the radical implications of Keynes's work.[144] Thirdly, Mosley called for increased road-building in the short-term, to be financed by a central government loan at a cost of £200,000,000, which would employ 300,000 for three years. Finally, he emphasised the need for a more flexible finance and credit policy in order to assist the home market.[145]

The response of the Treasury was one of almost complete opposition; it felt the proposals were impractical, too expensive, would undermine the collective responsibility of the Cabinet to Parliament and would produce few positive results.[146] The Cabinet Committee on Unemployment, chaired by Snowden, produced its final report at the start of May 1930. It concluded that the government should avoid all schemes 'involving heavy additions to Budget charges or grandiose loan expenditure' and that it 'must not be rushed into shovelling out public money merely for the purpose of taking what must inevitably be a comparatively small number of people off the unemployed registers to do work which is no more remunerative and much more expensive even than unemployment'.[147] Despite a strong protest from Lansbury that Mosley's proposals on public works were in line with Labour's election manifesto, and a number of meetings between the Cabinet committee and the advisory ministers, the Cabinet endorsed Snowden's and the Treasury's rejection of the Memorandum.[148]

Meanwhile, however, PLP interest in the Memorandum was increasing. Unemployment was becoming a constant feature of discussions at party meetings from early 1930, and on 19 February the PLP called for a meeting with Thomas.[149] On 18 March Kenworthy brought a motion before the PLP which, while it 'appreciate[d] the efforts' of Thomas, 'trust[ed] that the government [would] consider a wider policy' for dealing with rising unemployment. This provoked a long discussion, with Thomas defending his position, and eventually the motion was withdrawn.[150] This was only the first of a series of debates, the result of which was a call for the government to produce a response to the Mosley Memorandum. On 26 March Scott Lindsay wrote to MacDonald to inform him that at the close of a PLP meeting, a resolution had been passed asking the Cabinet to communicate its conclusions on the Memorandum in two weeks time.[151] On 30 April the PLP complained that no such statement had materialised and again pressed the government to act.[152]

Impressed by this high degree of interest and frustrated by his failure to make any progress within the government, Mosley resigned his position at the end of May to make a direct appeal to the party. The Labour leadership was somewhat alarmed, not least MacDonald, and not only because he feared Mosley could mount a powerful assault on his leadership. The Prime Minister must have felt himself partially responsible for Mosley's rise and feared that Mosley's potential disloyalty would reflect badly on himself.[153] Mosley's resignation, however, was initially met by ambivalence within the PLP. He received a 'very quiet reception' in the Commons and was largely greeted with silence from the Labour benches.[154] Although many felt Mosley's ideas on unemployment should be explored further, they were fearful that his resignation was conceived as a preliminary to an attempt on the leadership. Both Lansbury and Johnston were annoyed greatly by Mosley's decision to resign, which they felt had destroyed their chances of winning the economic arguments in the government. Dalton also felt that Mosley had been mistaken. On 21 May he wrote: 'Lord Oswald has played his cards badly.... The Loyal Lump will rally against him ...'.[155]

Dalton was largely correct in this prediction. At the special meeting of the PLP on 22 May, Mosley made a long speech which impressed many of his listeners. In a 'difficult atmosphere, not very friendly to the Government', it took all of Henderson's skills of party management to at least partially win the meeting back around to the government's point of view. He appealed to Mosley to withdraw his motion in the interests of party unity, in return for which he promised further discussions. Mosley, however, decided to push for a decision that night. Dalton believed that Mosley had made 'An amazing blunder':

> He might have left the meeting a hero, the darling of the back-benches, a moral victor. But his last words provoke a growl of surprise and indignation. One can feel votes turning away from him. There are shouts for a straight vote.... On a vote Mosley gets 29 votes against 210. It is a crushing defeat.[156]

By demanding an immediate decision, Mosley appeared to challenge directly the authority of the leadership, rather than calling merely for a further investigation into unemployment policy; for the first time he had become culpable of the gravest Labour sin, that of disloyalty to the party.[157]

Yet his chances of success were not as completely destroyed as Dalton liked to believe. On 28 May the Conservatives tried to censure the government for its failure on unemployment.[158] After a poor defence from MacDonald, Mosley made a long and powerful speech reiterating the arguments of the Memorandum and warning of the dangers of 'a real crisis' if the government did not get control of the situation.[159]

Skidelsky has written that, in the moments following the speech, Mosley was 'the undisputed leader of his generation'.[160] Although this is pushing the evidence a little too far, it is clear that the speech did have a tremendous impact, not least on the Labour benches. Prolonged cheering broke out all over the House and the newspapers were unanimous that it had been a tremendous triumph for Mosley.[161] Tom Johnston followed with a speech of general support.[162] The comments of Josiah Wedgwood illustrated just how great an impact the speech had made, and the extent of back-bench concern over its implications: 'We have listened to one of the most eloquent and one of the most dangerous speeches I have ever heard in the House ... Man after Man was saying to himself: "That is our leader".'[163] He urged Thomas to resist Mosley's unorthodox economics, implying that they would lead the country to ruin. In contrast, E. F. Wise welcomed Mosley's critique and gave the government an ultimatum on behalf of the more moderate members of the ILP: 'If the Government cannot show greater initiative and drive in handling this problem ... we think it is about time they gave place to somebody else.'[164]

Mosley, however, had the problem of what to do next. MacDonald was sufficiently disturbed to remove Thomas from responsibility for unemployment, but if he was to be able to influence policy directly, Mosley needed to create a more substantial PLP following. He was still widely distrusted within the party and could count on few solid allies, aside from his wife, Cynthia, and Strachey. Beatrice Webb summed up Mosley's detachment on 29 May 1930, writing:

> He arouses suspicion – he knows little or nothing about Trade Unionism or Co-operation – he cannot get on terms of intimacy with working men or with the lower middle class brainworker, he is, in fact, an intruder.... [He] will be a great success at public meetings – but will he get round him the Arthur Hendersons, the Herbert Morrisons, the Alexanders, the Citrines and the Bevins, who are natural leaders of the proletariat ... it is they who will decide who shall succeed or supersede J.R.M. ...[165]

He also aroused resentment because of his often superior tone; after a heated meeting of the PLP on 20 November 1930, Clement Attlee commented, 'Why does Mosley always speak to us as though he were a feudal landlord abusing tenants who were in arrears with their rent?'.[166] Mosley was able to win over a small band of younger MPs: Bevan, Brown, Oliver Baldwin (MP for Dudley and son of the Conservative Party leader) and Robert Forgan (West Renfrewshire), but the trade union group remained deeply suspicious. Bevan brought a motion calling for a more radical employment programme on 8 July 1930, but on 16 July this motion was finally referred to the CC to consider and was effectively buried.

Mosley consequently decided to build bridges with individuals of all political persuasions disgruntled with the parliamentary process.[167] As a result, he began to emphasise increasingly the need for parliamentary reform and for increased economic ties with the Commonwealth.[168] Yet these outside links served only to inflame Labour suspicions. Not only did talking with the Conservatives smack of treachery to many Labour MPs, but his increasing emphasis on Empire lost him ILP support, for offending socialist internationalism. In July 1930 Dalton noted with great delight that Mosley polled only fifty-four votes in elections for the CC, which was some sixteen votes short of last place.[169] Mosley, in his continuing determination not to play by 'the rules of the game', had managed to dispel any sympathy with his economic policies by not being prepared to bide his time. As Dalton commented on 10 November 1930: 'Having joined the party last week ... [Mosley] wants to lead it tomorrow afternoon'.[170] As shown in Chapter 3, Mosley came close to winning a resolution at the 1930 Labour Conference, and did get elected to the NEC. Yet his continual attempts to get the NEC to accept a radical unemployment policy were repeatedly blocked, largely by Henderson.[171] This lack of progress fuelled Mosley's growing conviction that he should lead a radical alliance of his own creation.[172]

In December 1930 a four-page manifesto appeared entitled *A National Policy for National Emergency*. It was signed by seventeen Labour MPs and by A. J. Cook. It had been written mainly by Strachey, Bevan and Brown, who had attempted to make it more amenable to Labour by dropping the imperialist tone of Mosley's recent public speeches. In large part, it reiterated the policies of the Memorandum, calling for a Cabinet of five without portfolios, a national plan of modernisation and an Import Control Board to improve trade with all nations, not just the Commonwealth, and for public works financed by loan, with the emphasis now on houses rather than on roads.[173] Whilst this 'Mosley Manifesto' aroused considerable debate, by attempting to please everybody, it effectively satisfied no one. The Liberals disliked the protectionist overtones, the ILP still felt that its tone was not socialist enough and the Tories disliked its calls for public works. Its impact on the PLP was minimal; although over half the party was approached to sign it, the majority clearly felt that it was a plot to remove the leadership. Morrison expressed a widely held Labour belief that it was the work of 'swell-heads not of working class origin ... with Tory blue blood in their veins'.[174] Dalton dismissed its programme as amounting to no more than 'Five Dictators and a Tariff'.[175] The majority of Labour MPs continued to endorse the financial orthodoxies expounded by Snowden and considered that the measures proposed would place Britain's status as a world financial centre at risk.

Mosley's so-called 'New Labour Group' attempted to organise a campaign against cuts in wages and in public spending in early 1931, and in the Commons in February Mosley launched a comprehensive attack on Snowden's economic policy.[176] Aware of the growing financial problems facing the Chancellor, and having been handed £50,000 by the car manufacturer Sir William Morris, Mosley decided to form 'the New Party'.[177] His intention to gain the maximum publicity for his new venture misfired badly. It had been decided that to maintain public interest, the Mosley group would resign in instalments, but, as has been seen, Brown, who was due to resign first, subsequently got cold feet, and Mosley himself never resigned but was expelled by the party on 10 March 1931. Bevan's response symbolised the instinctive reaction of Labourism to the formation of a rival political organisation; he would now have nothing more to do with Mosley. As such, Mosley's only tenuous link with the trade unions was lost. The New Party became no more than 'another bubble on the surface of political life'.[178]

Skidelsky has painted a picture of Mosley as 'the great lost leader', believing that Mosley offered the Labour Party an alternative economic vision during 1929–31, which it was either too blind or too obsessed with notions of workers' solidarity to endorse. An alternative way of viewing Mosley is to suggest that he did more than any other individual to discredit Keynesian ideas in the Labour Party in 1930 and 1931. By using them as a weapon with which he could attack the leadership, rather than concentrating upon winning the economic arguments themselves, he raised the natural defences of the movement. Further, his continual tinkering with his programme at the end of 1930, when he appeared to adopt any economic argument likely to win support from those discontented with Parliament, implied that his adoption of Keynesian notions had been a means to an end, rather than an end in itself.

Education

As shown in Chapter 3, the government's proposed educational reforms created serious tensions in the Labour movement in the country. At Westminster, the story of the Education Bill was one of Cabinet disagreement, poor parliamentary management, ignominious defeat and subsequent resignations. The raising of the school age was a measure which the majority of the PLP was keen to see implemented. Dalton noted on 18 July 1929 that Trevelyan's announcement that the school age would be raised from 1 April 1931 was 'a triumph for back-bench pressure'.[179] Trevelyan, however, was unable to convince MacDonald that the Education Bill should be prioritised.[180] On 27 June 1929 his call for an early Bill was defeated in Cabinet by MacDonald, Snowden and Thomas.[181] By early 1930 he had come to see MacDonald as 'the one obstacle' to its introduction.[182]

By this stage, back-bench pressure was escalating. On 11 February 1930 the Chairman of the CC 'drew attention to a growing feeling amongst members that an effort ought be made' to get the Education Bill through in the present parliamentary session.[183] On 24 February Trevelyan wrote that 'The Party [was] turbid with agitation.'[184] At a further meeting of the CC on 4 March, it was reported that a meeting of over 100 MPs had passed a resolution asking for early progress.[185] On 18 March Trevelyan experienced a 'most unsatisfactory interview with Ramsay. He knows he ought to push the Bill now, but he is in a fearful tangle with Parliamentary time.'[186]

MacDonald gave way finally to this agitation, for on 22 May 1930 Trevelyan announced the second reading would take place the following Monday.[187] It is possible that, in view of Mosley's recent resignation, MacDonald felt that it necessary to pacify back-bench opinion.[188] During the Bill's second reading, however, Trevelyan was subjected to back-bench criticism, on two key issues. The first of these was the question of maintenance allowances. At the 1929 election, Labour had promised allowances to compensate families for income lost through children staying on at school for an extra year, but

Snowden had been concerned about the cost and Trevelyan was forced to accept the introduction of a means test.[189] In responding to back-bench questioning, Trevelyan admitted he would like to avoid the means test, but finance would not allow, and he defended Snowden's generosity in agreeing to provide 60 per cent of local education authority maintenance costs.[190] Although disappointed by this decision, the PLP majority decided they should not jeopardise the Bill after having waited so long for its introduction and accepted the compromise reluctantly.

A more substantial disagreement occurred over the question of nonprovided schools. In dealing with the proposals for the voluntary schools, Trevelyan expressed his belief that the war had produced 'profound change' with regard to religion and education.[191] The speech of John Scurr which followed demonstrated that things had not changed as much as Trevelyan had hoped. Scurr warned that if Catholic amendments to the Bill were not accepted then they might 'possibly have to go to the point of voting against it'.[192] William Cove, in seconding the Bill, called for compromise and warned Scurr and the representatives of other denominations that, as a member of the National Union of Teachers, he believed in the need for a single unified education system, and reserved the option of putting down amendments to increase further the degree of public control of education.[193] J. A. Lovat-Fraser (Stafford, Lichfield) endorsed the Bill on behalf of the Church of England, and hoped there would not be 'any revival of the religious struggle of the early years of this century'.[194] During the committee stage on 30 May, Ernest Thurtle expressed what he described as 'the view of the Rationalist' to the education question, and made an appeal for the removal of all state money from the financing of separate religious schools.[195] Not surprisingly, this demand provoked an angry response from two Catholic MPs, James Sexton (St Helens) and J. R. Oldfield (Essex, South-Eastern).[196]

As has been illustrated in Chapter 3, this level of controversy led to the dropping of the Bill at the end of June. Trevelyan was incensed with the Catholic Labourites and greatly discouraged. He admitted privately that he was 'disgruntled about politics' in general and was not optimistic with regard to the possibility of his reaching a settlement.[197] Yet, encouraged by others in the Cabinet, particularly Lansbury and Sankey,[198] he attempted to get the Bill back on the government's agenda. This proved to be easier than expected; he was pleased to note on 23 October that, because of a long discussion on imperial questions, he was able to put his new Bill through Cabinet with no discussion.[199] The second reading of the new Bill on 6 November, however, witnessed what was in large part a repeat of the earlier arguments, despite Trevelyan's claim that by removing Clause 2 of the initial Bill, the voluntary schools question had been omitted and the proposal was therefore wholly uncontroversial.[200] Scurr once again called for equal building grants for the non-provided schools.[201] On 30 November Trevelyan was 'in the dumps' with regards to the Bill's chances of success.[202]

The defeat of the Bill on 21 January 1931, following the 'Scurr Amendment', led Trevelyan to the conclusion that he had no course open to him but to resign from the Cabinet. Trevelyan blamed the Labour leadership, and in particular MacDonald, for the Bill's defeat. A number of other government figures believed that Trevelyan himself was to blame. Dalton suggested that Trevelyan had 'no brains and no negotiating skill'.[203] Even the generally uncritical Sankey believed Trevelyan 'had made a mess' of the Bill and had unnecessarily offended people.[204] Trevelyan wrote to MacDonald in February to announce his resignation, which he justified not only in terms of the defeat of his Bill, but also as an expression of his general discontent with the government's direction and, in particular, with its economic policy.[205]

In his speech to the PLP on 3 March, Trevelyan attacked both the government and its leadership for their moderation.[206] His speech was met, however, only by stony silence.[207] Despite the level of PLP disillusionment, the majority still believed the current leadership could not be improved upon and resented the fact that Trevelyan appeared to be blaming everyone but himself for the defeat of the Bill. As such, the repercussions of Trevelyan's resignation were minimal. He had little following in the party and his decision was vastly overshadowed by the activities of Mosley (which had no doubt provoked serious distrust of individuals calling for a more radical economic policy). He did receive letters of sympathy from Lord Parmoor, Arthur Ponsonby, Josiah Wedgwood, Clifford Allen and Lansbury, but there was no question of the formation of a 'Trevelyan group'.[208]

There were further outcomes from the defeat of the Education Bill. John Scurr had resigned as Vice-Chairman of the CC at the beginning of 1931, and J. R. Oldfield, by that date Private Parliamentary Secretary to the Minister for Air, Lord Amulree, also resigned.[209] John Bromley wrote to MacDonald to inform him he would not be standing at the next election as a result of the humiliating acceptance by the party of Catholic sectarianism.[210] He wrote in similar terms to Trevelyan, suggesting that Labour had 'allowed itself to be made a nest for the Catholic Party'.[211] Such resentment of the Scurr group amongst non-Catholic Labour MPs must have been common, and MacDonald was clearly worried by sectarian divisions within the PLP.[212] What is certain is that, as Dalton noted on 22 January, the party was 'very demoralised' after the defeat on education. Indeed, so low was morale on that day that there was 'A lot of talk about it being better to go to the country, than to continue to be humiliated'.[213]

The ILP

Aside from the Mosley group, the most constant criticism of unemployment policy emanated from the Maxtonites, although it should be noted that there was considerable overlap between the members of this group and the supporters of Mosley. As has been seen, this group used every opportunity to promote its under-consumptionist solutions, and in no area of policy was this more pronounced than on unemployment. On 6 March 1930 Lloyd George moved a motion of censure on government unemployment policy and Wheatley intervened to call for a radical redistribution of wealth through the living wage.[214] David Kirkwood expressed a similar conviction on 19 May and called for the immediate facilitation of socialism through the use of the Emergency Powers Act.[215] In the second day of the debate on the King's Speech on 29 October 1930, W. J. Brown, whilst calling for support for Mosley, took a line which was more intrinsically Maxtonite than it was Mosleyite, once again calling for immediate socialisation.[216]

The consequence of this increasingly critical stance was a steady deterioration in the relationship between the Maxtonites and the government. The leadership was understandably concerned by the effect this internal opposition was having upon government stability. Shinwell led an attempt to suppress the dissidents, aided by P. J. Dollan in the country, but his attempt to co-ordinate a majority of the moderate ILP at the meetings of the parliamentary ILP met with limited success. Although he was able to pass a resolution at a meeting on 19 November 1929 to the effect that all amendments to the forthcoming National Insurance Bill should be submitted to the CC, this failed to curb the Maxtonites who went ahead with their amendments regardless.[217] Likewise, whilst Dollan was sufficiently powerful in Scotland to get a vote against Maxton at the 1930 Scottish ILP Conference, every other divisional conference supported him and Dollan was defeated at the 1930 national conference on a proposal to refer back the report of the Parliamentary Group.[218]

Tension was further increased when the same conference passed a resolution which declared that the ILP was 'an independent Socialist organisation' and that it was 'unreasonable to ask members of the Party to accept without question all the proposals of the Government when those proposals are not themselves subject to the decisions of the Parliamentary Party, and in many instances do not comply with the programmes authorised by the Labour Party Conference'. Further, the conference called for a reconstruction of the ILP Group in Parliament such that membership would be conditional on the full acceptance of the policies of the ILP.[219] Labour's NEC invited the ILP to meet with it, but, whilst some progress was made, the ILP then sent out a letter to all its MPs calling for their primary loyalty to be to the ILP and to the policies of *Socialism in our Time*. Not surprisingly, only eighteen accepted these conditions.[220] Further meetings took place between the NEC and the ILP but revealed only that the differences between them were largely irreconcilable. Each believed that the other was responsible for the breakdown; the ILP continued to press MPs to obey its decisions and the NEC responded by refusing to endorse candidates who had expressed allegiance to the ILP Group. In November 1930 the NEC refused to endorse an ILP candidate at the East Renfrew by-election and the negotiations between the NEC and the ILP continued unsuccessfully until the fall of the government.[221]

It was perhaps unfortunate that the continuing deterioration in the relationship had the effect of cancelling out any serious examination of ILP criticisms. Arguably, by bringing itself into direct conflict with the NEC, the Maxtonites negated any chance they had of attracting those MPs who were beginning to doubt the government's gradualist strategy by mid-1930. Undoubtedly, they lost much of their direction after the death of John Wheatley in May 1930: 'Maxton with Wheatley to advise him and Maxton without Wheatley were two very different propositions'.[222] Maxton's political ideas displayed considerable confusion; at times he favoured revolutionary class war and yet *Socialism in our Time* had as its central tenet the creation of socialism through economic tinkering at the centre.[223] This was true equally of the strategy of the ILP as a whole by 1931.

The extent to which the bulk of the PLP felt any attraction to the arguments expounded by the Maxtonites in 1930 and 1931 is difficult to determine. The group's confrontational tactics upset many, including a number of prominent ILP members. Thomas Johnston, for example, wanted the ILP to abide by the tactical decisions of the Labour Party, and, through his capacity as editor of the *Glasgow Forward*, condemned Maxton's stand.[224] Nevertheless, there is a danger of underestimating the continuing importance of the ILP both inside and outside of Parliament in 1931. As has been seen, ILP support in the local parties remained pronounced and it would be wrong to see the opposition of the Maxtonites as solely to do with manoeuvrings at Westminster. In Parliament, one occasion in particular demonstrates that sympathy for the view that a bolder strategy was needed was not confined to the Maxtonites alone. On 6 February 1931 Maxton moved a Private Members' Bill calling for a living wage. Despite the total opposition of Bondfield to the measure, the Bill passed its second reading by 122 votes to 51, with such moderate figures as Chuter Ede, Fred Messer and Harry Snell voting for it.[225] This suggests that Maxton had more sympathisers than many accounts would concede and may imply that a more adept handling of this latent radicalism by the ILP leadership could have resulted in an expansion, rather than a contraction, in the number of those calling for immediate socialisation in 1931.

Dwindling morale

By the end of 1930 the PLP had been transformed from the enthusiastic and expectant group of individuals returned in 1929 into a collective characterised by pessimism and disillusionment. Frustrated by the limitations imposed by the minority position, concerned by the ever-increasing unemployment and by the apparent inability of ministers to reverse it, back-bench morale had dropped to a very low level. Dalton summed up this general feeling of despondency:

> The black cloud of the Unemployment Figures have overshadowed everything and robbed all the political field of every glimmer of light. Tired and timid Ministers. Discouraged private members. Depressed rank and file in the country.[226]

Adding further weight to the disillusionment was the knowledge that by-election results were going against Labour. From May 1930 to June 1931, Labour lost four of its marginal seats to the Conservatives and suffered a substantially reduced majority in six others. The general atmosphere of the PLP by early 1931 is nowhere better expressed than in the memoirs of Leah Manning. Entering Parliament following a by-election victory at East Islington in February 1931, Manning recalled her initial experience in the Commons:

> I arrived at Westminster fresh and euphoric from a totally unexpected by-election victory and I walked into an atmosphere which stung like a cold lash. Bitter hostility there was where there should have been comradeship. I was hurt by the cold contempt of old ILP friends, such as Jimmy Maxton, who treated me as a criminal for having dared to stand, let alone win; everywhere I found frustration and defeatism in place of hope and constructive ideas ...[227]

The reaction to Stafford Cripps's success in the Bristol East by-election in January 1931 revealed the low level of Labour expectation by that date. Lord Ponsonby wrote immediately to Cripps to inform him that his victory had 'given us all a much needed message of encouragement' and Cripps received many similar letters.[228] Candidates of the calibre of Cripps were increasingly hard to find. MacDonald wrote to Shepherd on 17 April 1931 to express his concern with the poor quality of candidates coming forward. In his reply, Shepherd concurred and also reported that: 'Financial difficulties are very troublesome at present. The Party is not in a position to finance By-Elections itself. Consequently the availability of money plays an increasing part in the selection of candidates when contests arise.'[229]

The extent to which PLP dissatisfaction fuelled a desire to change the leadership is difficult to quantify. Both Dalton and Webb believed Henderson's popularity was increasing through 1930 and early 1931, and that he would be the next leader of the party.[230] MacDonald was deeply suspicious that

Henderson was plotting to take the leadership in early 1931. Although this was unlikely, it would seem plausible that Henderson's popularity in the PLP did increase at the expense of MacDonald.[231] Not only had Henderson been successful in foreign affairs, but he was not tainted by any involvement with unemployment policy. He was also more concerned to hear the views of the PLP than the Prime Minister. Nevertheless, it is evident that MacDonald still had many loyal supporters. In January 1931 S. T. Rosbotham, MP, wrote to MacDonald to express his continuing loyalty and to inform him that, 'Many MPs have expressed themselves of terms of affectionate goodwill towards you, and trust that you will remain Prime Minister for some time to come however difficult the position may be.'[232] George Hicks, MP, returned at a by-election for Woolwich East in April, wrote a similar letter to the Prime Minister on 27 June, and spoke of the 'super-human demands' on MacDonald, and how he would be 'deeply honoured' by the attendance of such a 'distinguished and able leader' at a function which he was organising.[233]

Finance and economy

In May 1929 the majority of the PLP accepted that Snowden was the most suitable candidate for the position of Chancellor. His standing was sufficient for him to convince the PLP of the impossibility of further expenditure on unemployment benefit in November 1929, and, despite the growing financial problems facing the country by mid-1930, he retained the confidence of the majority of Labour MPs. The first budget of April 1930 was generally well received on the Labour benches. Faced by a prospective budget deficit of £14 million, he decided to increase income tax and death duties. He was able also to remove the last vestiges of the betting duties but could not afford to abolish the McKenna duties or the silk duties imposed by Churchill.[234] Mary Hamilton claimed to voice 'the feelings of the great majority' of the PLP when she thanked Snowden 'for a Budget which we value for its honesty, for its courage, and for its vital contribution to industrial and economic reconstruction'.[235] David Logan (Liverpool, Scotland) was even more enthusiastic, declaring that it was 'a magnificent Budget' and suggesting that Snowden was a Chancellor 'of whom we have never had the like before in this country'.[236] The only real criticism came from the Maxtonites, who wished to see more taxing of the rich and who were concerned that Snowden had predicted only a small budget surplus for the following year. W. J. Brown declared that the budget was 'bad finance from a Socialist point of view', since 'You cannot get very much social reform on two and a quarter million pounds, certainly nothing on the scale contemplated by "Labour and the Nation"...'.[237]

The extent to which Mosley's stand damaged Snowden's reputation is difficult to assess. Snowden himself later illustrated the manner in which he came to be seen as 'the hindrance to the raising of a large public loan'[238] and it also seems likely that, as more Labour MPs began to consider the possibility of protection at the end of 1930, Snowden came to be seen as the chief obstacle to any reconsideration of fiscal policy. The TUC was toying with greater ties with the Commonwealth from mid-1930 and this must have affected the attitudes of union-sponsored MPs. At the Imperial Conference of October 1930, both Thomas, who favoured tariffs, and Christopher Addison, the Minister for Agriculture, attempted to increase British import control, but were blocked by Snowden.[239] MacDonald was considering the notion of a revenue tariff from around the same time, but Snowden was able to count on sufficient Cabinet support to resist any such proposals, although he did lose the respect of a number of his colleagues through his stubborn behaviour.[240] Opposition to Snowden's intractability was also growing in the PLP; on 10 November 1930 Dalton noted a rumour that thirty to forty MPs had signed an ultimatum demanding the Chancellor's resignation.[241]

Not prepared to countenance tariffs, Snowden had decided by the end of 1930 that economies were the only means through which the budget could be balanced for the coming financial year. He intended to use the first available opportunity to impress upon his own party the seriousness of the financial position. In February 1931 'the House of Commons came to [his] assistance', for the Conservatives put down a vote of censure on the government for its 'reckless' public expenditure.[242] After having attacked what he saw as the hypocrisy of the opposition in bringing the motion, Snowden 'turned away from Party recrimination to speak seriously about the national financial position'.[243] He told the House:

> I say ... that the national position is so grave that drastic and disagreeable measures will have to be taken if Budget equilibrium is to be maintained.... Schemes involving heavy expenditure will have to wait until prosperity returns. This is necessary ... to uphold the present standard of living, and no class will ultimately benefit more by present economy than the wage earners.[244]

The effect of this speech upon the Labour benches was 'stunning', for, as Snowden later recalled, it finally ended any hopes they still retained that Labour would be able to find sufficient money for long-cherished reforms.[245]

George Benson (Chesterfield) was the first Labour MP to speak after Snowden's statement and his words exemplified the lack of back-bench desire to digest the Chancellor's warnings. Benson denied the country needed to reduce its expenditure on social services and accused the Conservatives of attempting 'to stampede the country against the Government', almost as if Snowden's speech had not occurred.[246] It was W. J. Brown who drew out the wider implications of Snowden's statement. Brown suggested that the speech had demonstrated that Labour's gradualist strategy was now bankrupt, that Snowden was more concerned to protect the interests of the City than to promote socialism and that the speech had been conceived in order to 'prepare the mind of this House for the sacrifice of the unemployed man and woman'.[247] Noel-Baker accepted there was a need for public economy but urged Snowden to consider the avenue of cuts in defence expenditure rather than in the social services.[248] It is apparent, then, that the battle lines of August were already being drawn within the PLP by as early as the previous February.

Although the Tory censure motion was defeated, a Liberal amendment proposing a committee to investigate means of reducing expenditure was carried by 468 votes to 21, no doubt to Snowden's great delight. Yet his desire to prepare the Labour benches for cuts was partially negated the very next day, when the government endorsed a Liberal motion calling for schemes of 'national development', to be financed partly by loans. It clearly did so, as Brockway suggested, only in order to keep Liberal support, and attempts by MacDonald and Thomas to reconcile this proposal with the need for economy were unconvincing. The effect on the Labour benches must have been to convince them that perhaps the financial situation was not so black as the Chancellor had painted it.[249]

On 17 February 1931 a special meeting of the PLP was called to discuss Snowden's speech. In his autobiography, Snowden states that he outlined the budget deficit and warned those present of the necessity for cuts.[250] The impression received from the minutes of the PLP, however, is that Snowden's primary aim was to reassure Labour MPs that he did not advocate wage-cutting and that when 'he spoke of sacrifices from all, he meant that the sacrifice the workers might have to undergo would be a temporary suspension of the schemes of social development'.[251] It is possible that this was the element of the speech the minute-taker wished to emphasise, but it would seem likely also that Snowden was not as emphatic in stressing the need for cuts as he later liked to believe. His intention at this stage was that the report of the May Committee would do the job of convincing the PLP for him. Whilst a 'substantial number' of MPs wanted another meeting, Snowden was not keen to explain himself further and this meeting never materialised.[252]

By March 1931, the Cabinet was 'divided hopelessly' on economic policy.[253] The growing sense of drift was enhanced when Snowden was taken seriously ill. The Chancellor's enforced absence gave MacDonald the ideal opportunity to remove Snowden, who was his chief opponent on the revenue tariff. MacDonald considered the option, but prevaricated. He was aware that removing Snowden could create a crisis in business confidence at a time of financial insecurity, and that pressing the revenue tariff could result in a serious Cabinet split and the loss of Liberal support.[254] Ultimately, he was not convinced sufficiently of the case for the revenue tariff, or certain enough on economic issues in general, to undertake these risks. Equally, of course, he was aware of the demoralising effect that dropping one of the party's most senior and respected figures would have on the Labour movement. In Snowden's absence, the Cabinet avoided any discussion of fiscal policy wherever possible.[255] In consequence, the Chancellor, on recovering sufficiently to consider the next budget, was largely given a free hand.

Remarkably, demonstrating just how detached from the movement and the party he had become, Snowden decided to make the long-standing radical demand for a land tax the chief plank of his budget. Despite his awareness of the controversial nature of the proposal, he did not inform the Cabinet until the day before his budget speech, when he knew it was too late for it to be removed.[256] Snowden had calculated that the measure would rally the Liberal Party, but in the outcome there was a great deal of dispute over the details of the tax, to the extent that it was widely predicted that the government would fall.[257] Both the rest of the Cabinet and the PLP were horrified by the possibility of having to fight an election on such a marginal policy.[258] MacDonald wrote to Snowden on 12 June to plead with him not to bring about the government's defeat, because the party would 'be furious with us.... The issue is not regarded by the great bulk of our Members as being big enough.'[259]

Ironically, and somewhat farcically, for all the controversy, the land tax was not in fact a means of balancing the budget at all. Since it was necessary to carry out extensive valuation before the land could be taxed, the measure would not have yielded any returns to the Exchequer in the short term. Even more ironically, the budget was 'balanced' by two methods for which Snowden had consistently condemned his predecessor, Winston Churchill. One was creative paper accountancy (Snowden took some £13 million from a government exchange account used to finance overseas obligations) and the second was an increase in what was effectively a revenue tariff: the duty on oil.

The tone of Snowden's budget speech was not so alarmist as his statement of 11 February. In part, this was a result of the slight upturn of the economy in the months of March and April, but it was due also to a desire not to give the impression that his budget was intended to provide the context for expenditure cuts. He told the Commons that the prospective deficit of some £37 million was not as high as his earlier prediction and, despite his warning that expenditure would have to be reduced if the world depression failed to lift, the psychological effect on the back-benchers must have been to encourage a belief that the drastic measures proposed previously would not now be needed.[260] Snowden's statement that an increase in taxation was not a viable option because of the increased costs for industry, however, left little doubt that he still believed that cuts in the social services would have to come.[261]

E. F. Wise certainly believed this to be the case, suggesting that Snowden's intention was that the Holman Gregory Commission should recommend the cuts in benefit that would enable him to truly balance the budget. Wise called instead for increased taxation of the rich and quoted from Snowden's book on the *Socialist Budget*, published in 1907, which had stated that, 'The Socialists look to the Budget as a means not only of raising revenue to meet inevitable expenditure, but as an instrument of redressing inequalities in the distribution of wealth.'[262]

The Holman Gregory Commission and the Anomalies Act

Throughout 1930, Bondfield had been forced to ask the Commons repeatedly for further increases in the borrowing level on the Unemployment Insurance Fund. On 1 December 1930 this was increased to a level of £70 million, and during the debate a number of Labour MPs had expressed concern over the intentions of the proposed Royal Commission on Unemployment Insurance.[263] On 9 December Buchanan launched a spirited attack on the commission, which he believed, with only two Labour members on it, would be bound to support the Conservative call for reduced benefit. This would place the government in the position of having to accept the recommendations, since Labour would not be able to attack the findings of a commission of its own creation.[264]

During the second reading of the Unemployment Insurance (No. 2) Bill on 18 February 1931, which proposed to raise the Fund to £90 million and to extend the transitional period by six months, Campbell Stephen warned the government to keep its 'Hands off the unemployed'.[265] On the following day, Buchanan accused Snowden of plotting to reduce benefit and repeated Stephen's warning.[266] These suspicions were well grounded, for at the beginning of February Snowden was attempting to get the Cabinet to agree to a reduction in unemployment benefit, with some support from MacDonald.[267] No doubt aware of the strong PLP opposition to the suggestion, the Cabinet did not endorse the notion, although 'some were much inclined thereto'.[268] Following growing PLP concern, MacDonald and Henderson announced at a party meeting on 10 June that there would be 'No cuts in benefit, no increase in contribution, nor change in conditions of transitional benefits'.[269]

On 22 June Bondfield announced that she proposed to increase the borrowing on the Fund to £150 million, but that she rejected all the recommendations of the interim report of the Holman Gregory Commission, with the exception of the removal of so-called 'anomalies'. In an attempt to reassure the Labour benches of the government's intentions, she told them, 'This is not the time to single out one class, and that the class which can least afford it, for a serious reduction in the already low level of subsistence.'[270] Yet, the announcement of the Anomalies Act led many Labour back-benchers to the conclusion that the government was singling out one class to bear the brunt of the sacrifice. Buchanan accused the government of being in agreement with the policy of the Conservatives and called for a more socialist attitude:

> Instead of robbing £5,000,000 from the poor, the Government ought to be looking to other channels. They spend 6d of the national taxation on unemployment relief and 9s 6d on interest on the war debt. If they must save money, why take it from the labourer's wife.... If you must save, go to the rich, go to the rentier, go to those who can afford it, and leave the poor people alone.[271]

Kenworthy, Wedgwood and Hayday all concurred with Buchanan that they would never accept any reduction in unemployment benefit, the latter calling for the government to implement the proposals of the TUC in its evidence to the Royal Commission.[272]

The introduction of the Unemployment Insurance (No. 3) Bill on 8 July brought the conflict between the Maxtonites and the government to the point of no return. As well as fiercely opposing the proposals in debate, the group resorted to a series of disruptive amendments which resulted in a number of all-night sittings.[273] Whilst Bondfield did concede some ground to the trade union group by ruling that not all short-term workers would be placed outside of the scope of the scheme, the Maxtonites were still outraged by the disqualification of seasonal workers and of married women.[274] The PLP as a whole was clearly concerned by the implications of the Bill for the future course of unemployment policy, but, annoyed by the disruptive tactics of the Maxtonites and forced to defend the measure in the country, the majority did come around to accepting the government's reasoning, albeit with reluctance.[275]

Conclusion

By July 1931, the PLP had endured two years of parliamentary uncertainties and disappointments. Aware that it had achieved few of the reforms it had been elected to implement and that support for Labour was declining in the country, both the morale and the unity of the party had been damaged severely. Tension between the Maxtonites and the government had become ever more acute and general confidence in the leadership had diminished. The level of communication between the parliamentary party and the Cabinet was poor from the beginning and deteriorated further as a government which was increasingly uncertain of itself was ever more loath to justify its actions to the

PLP. As had been the case with the trade unions, the machinery designed to maintain harmony between PLP and government had failed to achieve its objective. In consequence, suspicion of the Cabinet's intentions increased, fuelled by the government's increasing closeness to the opposition parties and by its readiness to establish commissions whose composition made them likely to recommend courses of action totally incongruous with deep-seated Labour beliefs.

Yet this high level of discontent failed to find any effective focus, either organisationally or ideologically. The two major attempts to channel this frustration – the Maxtonites and the Mosleyites – had foundered, in part due to their confrontational strategy, which ran up against the instinctive loyalty of most Labour MPs to the existing leadership, but also because neither offered an alternative held by the bulk of the PLP to be sufficiently convincing. By 1931, despite serious misgivings, having compromised increasingly on their socialist or Labourist ends, and possessing no alternative economic approach, the bulk of the PLP had little option but to hope that the leadership's strategy would succeed and that the world economy would improve. Even the Maxtonite ILP was loath to bring the government down since it believed the result would be a majority Conservative government. Nevertheless, this state of inertia was not reached without the creation of increasing doubts about the notion of PLP autonomy; there was a growing unease with the extent to which Labour MPs were becoming detached from the desires and aspirations of those who had sent them to Parliament. Many in the PLP, therefore, would be susceptible to the notion that they must pay attention to the feelings of the movement at a time of national crisis.

The attitude of the PLP in July 1931 to cuts in social expenditure is unclear; whilst the majority had been wholly opposed to the recommendations of the Holman Gregory Report, they had, with the exception of the Maxtonites, accepted the 'Anomalies Act'. If they had been put to the test by a Labour Prime Minister determined to win their support, it is possible that as many as half would have decided they should place 'the country' before the Labour movement and would have accepted the necessity for substantial cuts in social expenditure. Of the three groups defined within the PLP, it is arguable that the non-trade union, non-Maxtonite group would have been most open to persuasion, and the trade union group the quickest to fall into line with the opposition of the TUC. As it was, of course, the PLP was never faced by a direct appeal for loyalty from MacDonald, Snowden or Thomas, three men whose detachment from the movement had become more pronounced during the two-year period. The supreme irony was that this level of detachment, although highly damaging for the second Labour government, would ultimately enable the Labour movement to endure the greatest crisis in its history without a more profound split in its organisation.

NOTES

1 Brynmor Jones Library, University of Hull (hereafter BJL), D. Chater, *Autobiography*, unpublished, p. 36.
2 A. Bevan, *In Place of Fear* (London, 1952), pp. 5–7.
3 *House of Commons Debates* (hereafter *HC Debs.*), 5th Series, Vol. 229, 11 July 1929, col. 1204.
4 *HC Debs.*, Vol. 229, 16 July, col. 382.
5 BJL, D. Chater, *Autobiography*, unpublished, pp. 37–9.
6 Labour Party Archive, National Museum of Labour History, Manchester (hereafter LPA), PLP Minutes, 27 June 1929.
7 LPA, PLP Minutes, 12 July 1929.
8 British Library of Political and Economic Science (hereafter BLPES), Passfield Papers, B. Webb's Diary, 29 June 1929.
9 Ibid., 9 November 1929.
10 Note also that the Society of Labour Candidates, formed in 1926 to bring Labour candidates together, held a number of meetings during the lifetime of the government. It had 224 members in 1930, but does not appear to have functioned very effectively; Churchill College, Cambridge, Papers of P. Noel-Baker, 2/2, 1929 and 1930 Annual Reports of the Society.
11 P. Snowden, *An Autobiography, Vol. 2: 1919–1934* (London, 1934), p. 762; Nuffield College Library, Oxford (hereafter NC), H. Morrison Papers, original draft for autobiography, p. 30.
12 Public Record Office (hereafter PRO), MacDonald Papers, Diary, 30/69/1753/1, 21 November 1929.
13 Labour Party, *Annual Report 1930* (London, 1930), p. 69; Labour Party, *Annual Report 1931* (London, 1931), p. 70.
14 H. Scott Lindsay had been appointed Parliamentary Assistant to the Labour Party in 1906, later assuming the title of Secretary. Due to the PLP's tremendous increase in size, co-ordination was more formidable a proposition than it had ever before been.
15 LPA, CC Minutes, 26 March 1930.
16 NC, Morrison Papers, original draft for autobiography, p. 37.
17 PRO, MacDonald Papers, Diary, 30/69/1753/1, 27 January 1931.
18 NC, Morrison Papers, original draft for autobiography, pp. 35–6.
19 The 1945–50 Attlee government learnt from these mistakes by creating a small Liaison Committee which arranged for ministers to attend the party meeting itself and aimed at anticipating problems rather than waiting for them to develop; H. Morrison, *Government and Parliament: A Survey from the Inside* (London, 3rd edn, 1964), p. 136.
20 BLPES, Dalton Papers, Diary, 25 November 1930.
21 Besides tackling unemployment, partially through a revival of British exports, the Address announced that in its first parliamentary session the administration would repeal the Trade Disputes Act; introduce Bills on coal organisation, factory reform, the Washington Hours Convention, slum clearance, house-building and pensions; and would initiate inquiries into the iron and steel and cotton industries; *HC Debs.*, 5th Series, Vol. 229, 2 July 1929, col. 47.
22 For the major problems the government experienced with the House of Lords, see P. Williamson, 'The Labour Party and the House of Lords, 1918–1931', *Parliamentary History* 10: 2 (1991), 317–41.
23 *HC Debs.*, Vol. 229, 2 July 1929, cols 64–5. Snowden, *Autobiography*, was the

first to propose that this appeal was evidence that even at this stage MacDonald was toying with a National Government, and it has been the cause of historical debate ever since. See R. Skidelsky, *Politicians and the Slump: The Labour Government of 1929–31* (London, 1967), pp. 83–4.

24 *HC Debs.*, Vol. 229, 11 March 1930; Vol. 256, 20 March 1930; Vol. 257, 1–3 April 1930.

25 Snowden, *Autobiography*, pp. 858–60.

26 BJL, D. Chater, *Autobiography*, unpublished, p. 37.

27 Borthwick Institute of Historical Research, York, Private Papers of Major D. Graham Pole, UL5/9, Easter Report, p .1; August Report, p. 1; July 1931 Report, p. 1.

28 LPA, PLP Minutes, 10 December 1929.

29 PRO, MacDonald Papers, Diary, 30/69/1753/1, 16 July 1929.

30 *HC Debs.*, Vol. 245, 24 November 1930, col. 927.

31 Ibid., Vol. 247, 20 January 1931, col. 43.

32 Ibid., Vol. 249, col. 229.

33 Ibid., Vol. 253. The reasons why the government did not introduce the guillotine before late 1930 are not clear. Possibly it felt it could not risk so doing until fuller co-operation with the Liberals had been secured.

34 A. Thorpe, *The British General Election of 1931* (Oxford, 1991), pp. 47–9.

35 Snowden, *Autobiography*, p. 777.

36 MacDonald accused Lloyd George of having made an 'outrageous personal attack on Graham during the coal debate'; British Newspaper Library, Colindale (hereafter BNL), *Forward*, 4 January 1930. Morrison told the Liberals on 4 January they must decide whether to aid 'constructive legislation' or bring down the government; *The Times*, 6 January 1930.

37 BLPES, Dalton Papers, Diary, 12 May 1930. The alternative vote was a system under which voters would be requested to nominate a second choice of candidate. These second choices would only be taken into account should the victor not gain an overall majority. Lloyd George was wise to have initially rejected this option, described memorably by A. J. P. Taylor, *English History, 1914–1945* (Oxford, 1965), p. 353 as 'a device for distributing the Liberal vote between the other two parties'.

38 Snowden, *Autobiography*, pp. 879–86.

39 BLPES, Dalton Papers, Diary, 20 May 1930 and 17 December 1930.

40 *HC. Debs.* Vol. 247, 2 February 1931, col. 1468.

41 Ibid., Vol. 249, 4 March 1931, cols 495–6.

42 BLPES, Dalton Papers, Diary, 15 March 1931.

43 BLPES, Passfield Papers, B. Webb's Diary, 31 May 1931.

44 Skidelsky, *Politicians and the Slump*, pp. 328–31, believes MacDonald considered this option seriously. Thorpe, *The British General Election of 1931*, p. 56, does not believe that a Lib–Lab coalition was ever a realistic possibility.

45 BLPES, Dalton Papers, Diary, 20 May 1930.

46 Henderson seems to have been the prime mover in securing regular weekly meetings between the Cabinet leaders and the Liberals from May 1931. BLPES, Dalton Papers, Diary, noted on 28 April 1931 that 'Uncle has been trying to bring this sort of thing about for two years'.

47 BLPES, Passfield Papers, B. Webb's Diary, 28 July 1929.

48 E. Thurtle, *Time's Winged Chariot: Memoirs and Comments* (London, 1945), p. 111.

49 *HC Debs.*, Vol. 231, 5 November 1929, col. 885.
50 For a comprehensive study of Labour's attitudes to the Soviet Union, see A. J. Williams, *Labour and Russia: The Attitude of the Labour Party to the USSR, 1924–1934* (Manchester, 1989).
51 *HC Debs.*, Vol. 229, col. 164.
52 *HC Debs.*, Vol. 229, 10 July 1929, cols 919–1034.
53 MacDonald soon decided the government had insufficient time to introduce a Bill amending the 1929 Local Government (Scotland) Act; *HC Debs.*, Vol. 230, 18 July 1929, 'Oral Answers'.
54 *HC Debs.*, Vol. 229, 9 July 1929, Oral Answers.
55 Ibid., 10 July 1929, Oral Answers, cols 874–5.
56 Ibid., 11 July 1929, cols 1134–42.
57 Ibid., col. 1146.
58 Ibid., cols 1149–50.
59 Ibid., cols 1174–210.
60 *HC Debs.*, Vol. 230, 15 July 1929, cols 139–57.
61 LPA, PLP Minutes, 31 October 1929.
62 LPA, CC Minutes, 5 November 1929.
63 Ibid., 7 November 1929. LPA, PLP minutes, 31 October 1929 noted that although the PLP was eager to discuss the unemployment scheme, it felt that the debate should be adjourned in the hope that Bondfield would be present at a future meeting.
64 LPA, PLP minutes, 19 November 1929.
65 *HC Debs.*, Vol. 232, 19 November 1929, col. 738, and resumed debate on the Bill, 25 November 1929, cols 795–800.
66 Ibid., G. Buchanan, cols 1066–74.
67 Ibid., col. 1038.
68 Ibid., col. 1089.
69 Ibid., cols 1090–1.
70 Ibid., 2 Dec. 1929, col. 2007.
71 Ibid., cols 2012–13.
72 Ibid., col. 2016.
73 Ibid., 2 December 1929, cols 2079–85.
74 Ibid., 3 December 1929, col. 2255, J. M. Kenworthy commented that he was tempted to oppose the government, but felt Snowden had a right to be cautious, and if they followed Maxton's course, 'The Government would go out.... There would be a coalition formed of the two parties opposite.'
72 Ibid., cols 2317–19.
76 Ibid., col. 2266.
77 Ibid., col. 2324.
78 Ibid., 5 December 1929, cols 2611–706. BLPES, Dalton Papers, Diary, 5 December 1929, suggested that if she had not done so, the government would have been defeated by the trade union MPs.
79 LPA, CC Minutes, 5 December 1929.
80 LPA, PLP Minutes, 6 December 1929. See also BLPES, Dalton Papers, Diary, 6 December 1929.
81 K. and J. Morgan, *Portrait of a Progressive: The Political Career of Christopher, Viscount Addison* (Oxford, 1980), p. 177; BLPES, Dalton Papers, Diary, 31 October and 6 December 1929.
82 BLPES, Dalton Papers, Diary, 19 December 1929.

83 *HC Debs.*, Vol. 235, 11 February 1930, cols 265–310.

84 Ibid., 27 February 1930, col. 2486.

85 *HC Debs.*, Vol. 237, 1 April 1930, cols 1230–40.

86 PRO, MacDonald Papers, PRO 30/69/1175, Graham to MacDonald, 4 April 1930.

87 PRO, MacDonald Papers, PRO 30/69/1176, MacDonald to Henderson, 3 July 1931.

88 LPA, PLP Minutes, July 1931.

89 *HC Debs.*, Vol. 254, 6 July 1931, cols 1767–79.

90 *HC Debs.*, Vol. 231, 31 October 1929, cols 401–11.

91 Ibid., col. 462.

92 *HC Debs.*, Vol. 231, 11 November 1929, col. 1646.

93 Ibid., 14 November 1929, cols 2326–50.

94 *HC Debs.*, Vol. 232, 19 November 1929, cols 327–62.

95 A 1926 Act had reduced the Wheatley subsidy and in 1928 it had been reduced further still.

96 *HC Debs.*, Vol. 230, 15 July 1929, cols 89–98.

97 Ibid., col. 130.

98 Bodleian Library, R. D. Denman Papers, Box 5, undated article, 1930.

99 *HC Debs.*, Vol. 230, 17 March 1930, cols 1799–801.

100 Ibid., 18 March 1930, cols 2029–44. Scrymgoeur also accused the government of letting down the No War Movement, a body formed in 1921 which had 3,000 members by 1927; see J. Hinton, *Protests and Visions: Peace Politics in 20th Century Britain* (London, 1989), pp. 80–1.

101 *HC Debs.*, Vol. 230, 18 March 1930, cols 2047–52.

102 *HC Debs.*, Vol. 237, 24 March 1930, cols 78–148.

103 *HC Debs.*, Vol. 238, 15 May 1930, col. 2120.

104 Ibid., cols 2149–50.

105 *HC Debs.*, Vol. 241, 21 July 1930, col. 1767.

106 Ibid., col. 1781.

107 Ibid., cols 1792–7.

108 Ibid., col. 1803.

109 Ibid., col. 1812.

110 Ibid., col. 1815.

111 Ibid., col. 1822.

112 Ibid., cols 1826–7.

113 See *HC Debs.*, Vol. 249, 10 March 1931, amendment proposed by Jennie Lee to army estimates; 11 March, response to Navy Estimates and amendment proposed by J. Kinley, col. 1349; 17 March, Sorenson amendment to Air Estimates, col. 1974; and Vol. 254, Supply Committee, 29 June 1931, cols 948–1000, for hopes for disarmament conference.

114 *HC Debs.*, Vol. 240, 27 June 1931, col. 1550–1.

115 Ibid., col. 1559.

116 Ibid., col. 1560.

117 Ibid., cols 1566–7.

118 Ibid., col. 1572–3.

119 *HC Debs.*, Vol. 241, 11 July 1930, col. 865.

120 Ibid., col. 867.

121 Ibid., col. 870.

122 Ibid., col. 873. MacDonald, Snowden and Henderson were all absent and this

may have encouraged more back-benchers to be openly critical.

123 LPA, PLP Minutes, 17 July 1930.

124 Ibid., Vol. 241, 23 July 1930, cols 2307–9.

125 Ibid., col. 2316.

126 Ibid., cols 2319–21.

127 Ibid., cols 2329–30.

128 Over half had never before voted against the government, including such noted moderates as R. D. Denman, James Chuter Ede, Ebby Edwards and Frederick Messer.

129 *HC Debs.*, Vol. 230, 16 July 1929, col. 315.

130 Ibid., cols 324–5.

131 Ibid., cols 357–9.

132 Ibid., cols 341–3.

133 Ibid., 19 July, cols 834–5.

134 Ibid., cols 702–3.

135 Ibid., cols 734–7.

136 *HC Debs.*, Vol. 233, 20 December, cols 1805–20.

137 Ibid., col. 1832.

138 *HC Debs.*, Vol. 234, 21 January 1930, col. 88.

139 Ibid., cols 97–101.

140 R. Skidelsky, *Oswald Mosley* (London, 1975), p. 138, claims Mosley was chiefly responsible for them; M. Newman, *John Strachey* (Manchester, 1989) believes Strachey was more important.

141 Skidelsky, *Mosley*, p. 190.

142 NC, Morrison Papers, Box E., Morrison to Thomas, 2 February 1930, and Skidelsky, *Mosley*, p. 189.

143 Skidelsky, *Mosley*, pp. 191–2

144 Dalton, who distrusted Mosley, believed that 'Lord Oswald' was only able to 'take in the cruder arguments' of Keynes's theories; BLPES, Dalton Papers, Diary, 23 October 1930.

145 PRO, MacDonald Papers, PRO 30/69/445, Mosley Memorandum, with letter Mosley to MacDonald, 23 January 1930.

146 Skidelsky, *Mosley*, pp. 202–6.

147 PRO, Cabinet Papers, CAB 24/CP 134, report of Unemployment Policy (1930) Committee, 29 March 1930; see also Skidelsky, *Mosley*, pp. 195–6.

148 PRO, Cabinet Papers, CAB 24/CP 145, Lansbury Memorandum on CP134, 6 May 1930.

149 LPA, PLP Minutes, 8 March 1930.

150 Ibid., 18 March 1930.

151 LPA, CC Minutes, 26 March 1930.

152 LPA, PLP Minutes, 30 April 1930.

153 BLPES, Passfield Papers, B. Webb's Diary, 31 May 1930, noted that Lindsay had said that MacDonald was 'very angry with Mosley'. PRO, MacDonald Papers, Diary, PRO 30/69/1753/1, 19 May 1930 bears this out.

154 BLPES, Dalton Papers, Diary, 21 May 1930.

155 Ibid.

156 Ibid.

157 Skidelsky, *Mosley*, p. 213, has claimed that it was Strachey who urged Mosley to go to a division. Even if this was the case, the final responsibility for the error lay with Mosley himself; see Newman, *John Strachey*, p. 31.

158 The Conservatives had done likewise on 19 May, and had only lost the vote by 224 to 209, with a number of the ILP voting with them; *HC Debs.*, Vol. 239, 19 May 1930, cols 55–172.

159 *HC Debs.*, Vol. 239, cols 1348–72.

160 Skidelsky, *Mosley*, p. 216.

161 N. Mosley, *The Rules of the Game: Sir Oswald and Lady Cynthia Mosley, 1896–1933* (London, 1982), p. 148.

162 *HC Debs.*, Vol. 239, cols 1387–94.

163 Ibid., cols 1404–7.

164 Ibid., cols 1414–19. The final vote on the Tory Censure motion was 241 to 270 in the government's favour.

165 BLPES, Passfield Papers, B. Webb's Diary, 29 May 1930.

166 BLPES, Dalton Papers, Diary, 20 November 1930.

167 This included young Conservatives like Bob Boothby and Harold Macmillan; a number of disillusioned Liberals; the press barons Beaverbrook and Rothermere, who had recently come close to toppling Baldwin; and even Lloyd George and Winston Churchill.

168 See Mosley, *Rules of the Game*, pp. 149–53, and Skidelsky, *Mosley*, pp. 224–8.

169 BLPES, Dalton Papers, Diary, 29 July 1930.

170 Ibid., 10 November 1930.

171 On 25 November the latter was able to persuade Mosley to withdraw a motion on the economic situation and promised to consult MacDonald on the issues concerned. See LPA, NEC Minutes, 25 November 1930.

172 *HC Debs.*, Vol. 244, Debate on the Address, 21 October 1930, cols 67–80.

173 Skidelsky, *Mosley*, pp. 238–9.

174 Quoted in Skidelsky, *Mosley*, p. 241.

175 BLPES, Dalton Papers, Diary, 5 December 1930.

176 *HC Debs.*, Vol. 248, 12 February 1931, cols 685–91.

177 Mosley, *Rules of the Game*, p. 170.

178 BLPES, Passfield Papers, B. Webb's Diary, 1 March 1931.

179 BLPES, Dalton Papers, Diary, 18 July 1929.

180 Trevelyan at the time of the government's formation was clearly enjoying his close proximity to MacDonald; see Robinson Library, University of Newcastle (hereafter RL), Trevelyan Papers, CPT.EX.123, Trevelyan (hereafter CPT) to his wife, M. K. Trevelyan (hereafter MKT), e.g. 5 June 1929, after his appointment to the Board of Education.

181 Ibid., CPT to MKT, 27 June 1929.

182 RL, Trevelyan Papers, CPT.EX.124(1), CPT to MKT, 24 February 1930.

183 LPA, CC Minutes, 11 February 1930.

184 RL, Trevelyan Papers, CPT.EX.124(1), CPT to MKT, 24 February 1930.

185 LPA, CC Minutes, 4 March 1930.

186 RL, Trevelyan Papers, CPT.EX.124(1), CPT to MKT, 18 March 1930.

187 *HC Debs.*, Vol. 239, 22 May 1930, col. 587.

188 On 6 May Scott Lindsay forwarded a petition from the PLP calling for the early passage of the Bill; LPA, CC Minutes, H. Scott Lindsay to MacDonald, 6 May 1930.

189 A. J. A. Morris, *C. P. Trevelyan, 1870–1958: Portrait of a Radical* (Belfast, 1977), p. 179.

190 *HC Debs,*, Vol. 239, 28 May 1930, cols 1522–3.

191 Ibid., cols 1524–5.

192 Ibid., cols 1542–6.
193 Ibid., cols 1569–91.
194 Ibid., cols 1591–2.
195 Ibid., 30 May 1930, cols 1701–6.
196 Ibid., cols 1722–3 and 1726–8.
197 RL, Trevelyan Papers, CPT.EX.124(1), CPT to MKT, 19 and 25 June 1930.
198 Ibid., see CPT. EX.124(2), CPT to MKT, 15 September 1930.
199 Ibid., CPT to MKT, 23 October 1930.
200 *HC Debs.*, Vol. 244, 6 November 1930, col. 1089.
201 Ibid., cols 1130–43.
202 RL, Trevelyan Papers, CPT.EX.124(2), CPT to MKT, 30 November 1930.
203 BLPES, Dalton Papers, Diary, 21 January 1931. Dalton had been close to Trevelyan in the 1920s, which makes the remark all the more significant.
204 Bodleian Library, Oxford, Sankey Papers, Diary, MSS. Eng. Hist., 15 February 1931.
205 RL, Trevelyan Papers, CPT. 142, draft letter of resignation, 19 January 1931.
206 Morris, *C. P. Trevelyan*, pp. 183–4.
207 PRO, MacDonald Papers, Diary, PRO 30/69/1753/1, 3 March 1931.
208 RL, Trevelyan papers, CPT. 142.
209 BNL, *The Tablet*, 3 January 1931, and Bodleian Library, Amulree Papers (W. W. MacKenzie), MSS. Eng. C.2363, Oldfield to Amulree, 21 January 1931.
210 PRO, MacDonald Papers, PRO 30/69/1176, Bromley to MacDonald, 27 January 1931.
211 RL, Trevelyan Papers, CPT. 142, Bromley to CPT, 3 March 1931.
212 PRO, MacDonald Papers, PRO 30/69/1176, MacDonald to Shepherd, 17 April 1931.
213 BLPES, Dalton Papers, Diary, 22 January 1931.
214 *HC Debs.*, Vol. 256, 6 March 1930, cols 968–77.
215 *HC Debs.*, Vol. 239, 19 May 1930, Debate on Lord Privy Seal's Supply Estimates, cols 111–18.
216 *HC Debs.*, Vol. 244, 29 October 1930, cols 109–19.
217 R. E. Dowse, *Left in the Centre: The Independent Labour Party, 1893–1940* (London, 1966), pp. 156–8.
218 Ibid., p. 159.
219 G. D. H. Cole, *A History of the Labour Party from 1914* (London, 1948), pp. 246–7.
220 Dowse, *Left in the Centre*, pp. 160–1.
221 As a result of the growing problem of back-bench disloyalty, the most extreme manifestation of which was when John Beckett, the MP for Peckham, removed the mace on 22 July 1930, a Joint Committee of the CC and the NEC on Party Discipline was established, which issued its report in April 1931. This report called for greater loyalty and recommended a Joint Standing Committee on Party Discipline, with the power to recommend withdrawal of the Party Whip; House of Lords Record Office, Viscount Stansgate Papers, ST/94.
222 Cole, *History of the Labour Party*, pp. 228–9.
223 W. Knox, *James Maxton* (Manchester, 1987), pp. 100–1.
224 G. Walker, *Thomas Johnston* (Manchester, 1988), pp. 93–5, and the *Glasgow Forward*, Editorial, 10 August 1929.
225 *HC Debs.*, Vol. 247, 6 February 1931, cols 2269–337.
226 BLPES, Dalton Papers, Diary, 29 December 1930.

227 Dame L. Manning, *A Life for Education: An Autobiography* (London, 1970), p. 87.
228 NC, Cripps Papers, MSS 689, Ponsonby to Cripps, 19 January 1931.
229 PRO, MacDonald Papers, PRO 30/69/1176, MacDonald to Shepherd, 17 April 1931, and reply 20 April.
230 BLPES, Passfield Papers, B. Webb's Diary, 9 September 1930.
231 A. Thorpe, 'Arthur Henderson and the British Political Crisis of 1931', *Historical Journal* 31: 1 (1988), 117–39.
232 PRO, MacDonald Papers, PRO 30/69/1176, Rosbotham to MacDonald, 24 January 1931. Note that Rosbotham was to stand for National Labour in October 1931.
233 Ibid., Hicks to MacDonald, 27 June 1931.
234 Snowden, *Autobiography*, pp. 853–6.
235 *HC Debs.*, Vol. 237, 16 April 1930, col. 2960.
236 *HC Debs.*, Vol. 239, 20 May 1930, cols 332–4.
237 Ibid., cols 285–96.
238 Snowden, *Autobiography*, pp. 874–5.
239 Ibid., pp. 868–73.
240 See Bodleian Library, Sankey Papers, Diary, 29 October 1930, and PRO, MacDonald Diary, PRO 30/69/1753/1, 30 October 1930, where he wrote, 'Mr Chancellor gets more impossible ... immovable in mind like a Buddha'.
241 BLPES, Dalton Papers, Diary, 10 November 1930.
242 Snowden, *Autobiography*, pp. 890–2.
243 Ibid., p. 893.
244 *HC Debs.*, Vol. 248, 11 February 1931, cols 447–9.
245 Snowden, *Autobiography*, p. 896.
246 *HC Debs.*, Vol. 248, 11 February 1931, cols 479–80.
247 Ibid., cols 493–8.
248 Ibid., cols 506–13.
249 *HC Debs.*, Vol. 248, 12 February 1931, cols 631–741.
250 Snowden, *Autobiography*, pp. 897–8.
251 LPA, PLP Minutes, 17 February 1931.
252 Ibid.
253 PRO, MacDonald Papers, Diary, PRO 30/69/1753/1, 4 March 1931.
254 Ibid., 9 March 1931.
255 Ibid., 11 March 1931.
256 BLPES, Passfield Papers, B. Webb's Diary, 18 June 1931. He told MacDonald on 13 April that he did not wish to reveal budget details in advance because he was afraid of leakages to the press! PRO, MacDonald Papers, PRO 30/69/1176, Snowden to MacDonald, 13 April 1931.
257 Snowden, *Autobiography*, pp. 905–9.
258 See BLPES, Dalton Papers, Diary, 15 June 1931.
259 PRO, MacDonald Papers, PRO 30/69/1176, MacDonald to Snowden, 12 June 1931.
260 *HC Debs.*, Vol. 231, 28 April 1931, col. 1409.
261 Ibid., col. 1406.
262 Ibid., cols 1516–25.
263 *HC Debs.*, Vol. 245, 1 December 1930, cols 1833–1908.
264 *HC Debs.*, Vol. 246, 9 December 1930, cols 277–9.
265 *HC Debs.*, Vol. 248, 18 February 1931, col. 1325.

266 Ibid., 19 February 1931, col. 1573.
267 See BLPES, Passfield Papers, B. Webb's Diary, 4 February 1931, and Dalton Papers, Diary, 5 February 1931.
268 See BLPES, Dalton Papers, Diary, 5 February 1931.
269 Ibid., 10 June 1931.
270 *HC Debs.*, Vol. 254, 22 June 1931, cols 73–4.
271 Ibid., col. 114.
272 Ibid., cols 125–50.
273 BLPES, Dalton Papers, Diary, 16–17 July 1931.
274 *HC Debs.*, Vol. 255, 17 July 1931, col. 1308.
275 NC, Cripps Papers, MSS 496, speech at Birmingham, 18 July 1931, and Bodleian Library, Oxford, Denman Papers, Box 5, article on 'The Week in Parliament', n.d., July 1931.

5

Socialist intellectuals

The Webbs

Secretary for the Colonies and the Dominions

Sidney Webb reluctantly accepted the peerage offered to him by MacDonald after the election and went to the Lords as Secretary of State for the Colonies and the Dominions with a seat in the Cabinet.[1] Beatrice was not pleased to lose him to Westminster and upset the constitutionally sensitive MacDonald by refusing to accept the title of Lady.[2] As in 1924, Sidney was to demonstrate that his abilities did not include the attributes needed to be a successful minister. Although he enjoyed much of the work, he found the position very tiring, often with unfortunate results.[3] Unfortunately for Webb, he was to be confronted by a series of complex issues, and, although able to construct plans of action which were fair-minded, he often failed to confront political realities. He was also too self-effacing to push his points home in Cabinet or in the House.

The first major controversy concerned Webb's proposals for Kenya. In attempting to tread a fine line between not offending the white settlers and their supporters in Britain, whilst improving the position of the indigenous population, he succeeded not only in upsetting this former group but also those on the left of his own party who felt he had not gone far enough.[4] His poor handling of this situation, together with the problems surrounding India and Egypt, resulted in the responsibilities of the Dominions being handed over to Thomas in July 1930. Beatrice was angered by this demotion, not least because she had little regard for the 'disreputable' Thomas, but Sidney was ready to accept it since he found the Colonial Office 'more than sufficient for his energies'.[5]

179

It was the issue of Palestine, however, that caused Webb the greatest degree of discomfort. As has been noted in Chapter 3, he provoked the extreme
hostility of the Jewish community with his White Paper. Webb proposed that
investment was needed to resettle and educate landless Arabs, that the piecemeal buying of land by Jewish settlers should be discouraged and that further
immigration should be limited to 20,000 Jewish families. Although a fair and
balanced policy, and a brave attempt not to be pressurised into a pro-Zionist
policy by powerful Jewish interest groups, Webb was utterly unprepared in
October 1930 for the outrage his paper would provoke. He did not bear sole
responsibility for this error. The Cabinet had endorsed the White Paper and
MacDonald only came out against it once he was aware of the extent of Jewish
hostility, even going as far as to imply that he had never seen the paper.[6]
Nevertheless, by November 1930, Webb's position was becoming untenable.
MacDonald handed over responsibility for Palestine to a Cabinet committee
chaired by Henderson, and it was Henderson who conducted negotiations
with Chaim Weizmann, President of the World Zionist Organisation, who refused to meet either Webb or the Colonial Office.[7] Webb's humiliation was
completed by MacDonald's repudiation of the White Paper in a letter to
Weizmann in February 1931.[8]

Webb felt he had been poorly treated. In February 1931 he suggested
that: 'Some Ministers would have resigned rather than stand what I have had
to stand since last October.' He decided against this option because of his
loyalty to the government; his resignation 'would have aggravated the Government's troubles'.[9] As early as December 1930 Beatrice recorded that
Sidney would have liked 'to retire' but had not done so both because there had
to be two Secretaries of State in the Lords and because it would be seen as a
Jewish victory over Palestine.[10] By May 1931, however, Webb had finally
decided that he could not carry on much longer and wrote to MacDonald
asking to be allowed to retire by the following October, suggesting Ponsonby
as his successor. He informed MacDonald that he was beginning to feel his age
and that he could not 'continue without risk of breakdown'.[11] In the event,
however, he was still to undertake the most traumatic responsibilities of his
ministerial career, those of August 1931.

Reaction to the government

The Webbs had been enthused by the election result and wished to make a
valuable contribution to the government. Beatrice, for her part, felt a duty to
invite over 200 MPs and assorted interesting individuals to lunch over the
next two years. Soon, however, the Webbs experienced a growing discontent-
ment and uneasiness. Neither enjoyed a good relationship with MacDonald.
Beatrice, whilst she acknowledged his hold on the movement, had always
doubted MacDonald's leadership. In a memorable assessment in December

1929, she suggested that MacDonald was 'the greatest political *artist* (as distinguished from orator or statesman) in British political history'.[12] In particular, she feared that MacDonald's fondness for aristocratic socialising and a corresponding detachment from the Labour movement was becoming more marked by this date.

Although they both respected Henderson, the Webbs doubted the abilities of the rest of the Cabinet. Beatrice feared Snowden had lost his utopian zeal and had become 'the upholder of the banker, the landed aristocrat and the Crown',[13] Thomas she saw as totally ill-equipped to deal with unemployment, and she was generally perturbed about the lack of youthful dynamism in the Cabinet. By February 1931 both Webbs were convinced that the government had 'no policy' and had 'completely lost its bearings' and that the Labour front bench had lost the desire for real change. Such was the extent of Sidney's discontent with the sense of drift that he felt by early 1931 that it would be best for the Labour movement if the government was defeated.[14]

This growing sense of dissatisfaction provoked a questioning of the whole 'inevitability of gradualness' strategy, particularly from Beatrice. Increasingly she began to fear that the parliamentary system was breaking down and was incapable of implementing Labour's reforms. On 30 July 1930 she gave a radio talk, later turned into a *Political Quarterly* article and a Fabian pamphlet entitled *A New Reform Bill*, in which she stressed the urgent need for radical parliamentary reform in order to avoid either a fascist or a communist dictatorship. Beatrice felt the parliamentary system was outmoded, largely because of the tremendous growth in government responsibilities. The state had now taken on board extensive social services and sought to regulate private enterprise and unemployment. The result was a constant stream of new legislation and the annual raising of over £800 million of revenue. Abroad, the government participated extensively in the activities of the League of Nations and was faced with the complex problems of a vast empire. In consequence, ministers were so immersed in the affairs of their own department that Cabinet co-ordination was undermined. Equally, ministers could no longer master all of the details of their area of responsibility, resulting in reliance upon the judgement of permanent officials. Meanwhile, the majority of MPs were not involved in any constructive activity. The only answer to this congestion was devolution; Beatrice proposed that a new National Assembly should be created, with 350 members, each elected for a two-year period. This new Parliament would have its own independent revenue and would administer health, education, labour, agriculture and fisheries, transport, mines, electricity and the BBC. Business would be dealt with by committees involving all members. The Commons would remain the sovereign body and would deal with constitutional legislation, foreign affairs and defence.[15]

The Webbian answer, then, to the problems of Britain in 1931 was parliamentary reform. The implication was that the policies of the Labour Party were the right ones, it was only the system that needed changing. The Webbs said nothing about how the government could deal with the most urgent problem of the time, economic collapse. This suggests a bankruptcy in Webbian ideas by this juncture; faced by an economic problem of enormous magnitude, they were able only to reiterate plans for parliamentary reform that were ten years old. Despite their criticisms of the government's unemployment policies, neither of the Webbs had any new ideas to offer. Essentially, the extent of the depression was a tremendous shock to them. Products of the Victorian age, they had long believed that the application of reasoned, scientific investigation would be able to solve capitalism's central problem, that of distribution, and that socialism could then be built from a prosperous capitalism. Confronted by a capitalist machine that appeared to be breaking down, they had no answers. There had been no 'inevitability of gradualness' and this left the creators of this philosophy as ideologically rudderless as the government which had attempted to implement it.

Neither of the Webbs had any real grasp of the new economic ideas of Keynes and admitted that their understanding of the reasons for the August 1931 financial crisis was limited. On 22 August 1931 Beatrice recorded that:

> Sidney observes, sadly, that he would have resented being excluded from the consultations of the inner Cabinet about the financial position if it were not that he feels that he knows no more than other people about the real situation of the British people in the world welter, and he has no clear idea of the way out.[16]

Both stuck strongly to free trade and in the final Cabinet discussions Sidney, fully endorsing the need for a balanced budget, could see no alternative to the cut in unemployment benefit.[17] The failure of the government, coupled with the nature of its demise, dealt a fatal blow to the Webbs' belief in the inexorable logic of Fabianism and they were forced to look elsewhere for a means to create the well-ordered civilisation of the future for which they strove.

R. H. Tawney

In the absence of any extensive private papers, it is difficult to detail Tawney's activities during the government, and his attitudes towards it. In view of his ready agreement to aid MacDonald in the campaign, there can be no doubt that Tawney was hopeful for Labour's chances and pleased by the electoral success. Yet, surprisingly, he seems to have had few direct contacts with the government and devoted most of his time to academia. MacDonald offered him some position of responsibility in May 1930, most likely a peerage, but he politely refused.[18] He did take part in the EAC for a brief period but was not involved in any other committees. He wrote little on politics during the course of the government. The explanation for this lack of activity centres around two key factors, which may well have been interlinked. First, he took the opportunity in July 1930 to make an academic study of China, a country whose civilisation had long fascinated him, and from there visited the USSR, only returning to Britain in June 1931. As such he was out of the country for eleven of the twenty-six months that Labour was in office. Secondly, although disillusioned greatly by the government's lack of success, he had few suggestions to amend the situation. Perhaps it is not too unrealistic to propose, therefore, that Tawney's research trip represented a convenient opportunity to distance himself both physically and ideologically from this struggling government.

The only area in which Tawney played a prominent role was predictably that of education. Having formulated the party's policy, Tawney was understandably anxious to see at least part of his vision enacted by the government. Not only did he assign education a central role in the creation of socialism but, both as President of the Workers' Educational Association (WEA) from 1928, and through his teaching activities at the LSE, Tawney had extensive practical experience of the limitations of the current educational system. He seems to have enjoyed good personal relations with Trevelyan, and was most likely involved on some level in the initial negotiations over the Education Bill in late 1929 and early 1930. It is evident from a number of articles that he was irritated by the failure to introduce educational reform. In an article for the *New Statesman* in February 1930, Tawney complained that:

> [government] procedure in carrying out its educational promises has hitherto been marked ... by a curious ineptitude. It made one grave blunder in omitting to announce its intention of raising the school leaving age till compelled to do so by pressure from its supporters. It will make another, and graver, if it delays till next session the passage of legislation.[19]

Tawney warned that if the Bill did not become law before July, it would be difficult to secure the extra teachers needed, would play into the hands of both the Lords and those local authorities who were against the proposals, and would hamper those authorities that had made preparations for the changes. In a censorious tone, he predicted that: 'the Government, which has not made a brilliant success of its unemployment policy, cannot afford to risk the postponement of a measure which is desired by all persons of goodwill irrespective of party ...'.[20]

Tawney wrote a similar article for the *Schoolmaster and Woman Teacher's Chronicle* in March 1930, and Webb recorded in her diary entry for 24 July that he was 'in revolt' at the dropping of the Bill.[21] It has often been suggested that Tawney had saintly qualities.[22] Yet it is also apparent that he could become prickly over issues about which he felt passionate, and it is feasible that he was one of the intellectuals whom MacDonald claimed were pushing for the election of Henderson as leader in July 1930.[23] Tawney, then, was deeply dissatisfied with the government's failure to implement its avowed policies in the domestic sphere, particularly on education, and he no doubt resented the administration's incompetence not only because it was doing so little to further the socialist cause but also because it reflected badly upon a programme he personally had done much to create.

Tawney's only other direct connection with the government was his brief involvement with the EAC, which he also seems to have found a frustrating experience. Tawney, despite being an 'economic historian', never had any great personal understanding of pure economics; yet it would be wrong to infer that he did not recognise the importance of serious consideration of the available economic alternatives. He was concerned that such issues as the viability of the gold standard should be explored fully and along with Cole, Bevin and Citrine he felt that the EAC was unable to play the advisory role assigned to it because of the presence of government ministers.[24] Tawney, however, had few ideas to offer. The extent of the economic problems facing Britain by mid-1930 must have come as a great shock to him and his ethical socialism offered no guidelines as to what a Labour government should do faced by a capitalist system in crisis. In a real sense, the government's crisis was a personal ideological crisis for Tawney. In this context, it is easy to see how a trip to China appealed to a Labour intellectual who had little advice left to offer the party he had helped to put into power.[25]

In a letter from Russia to Trevelyan in May 1931, Tawney expressed regret both at the failure of the educational reforms and over Trevelyan's resignation, suggesting that Trevelyan had 'done more than any other public man since the war to fight for the educational issues which really matter'. Yet Tawney said little about the government and it is possible to detect a sense of relief in his detachment; his statement that he had 'seen little English news' was not written with any sense of sorrow. Certainly, he was not in any hurry to return from a country which could lay claim, however dubiously, to be a socialist state. When he did finally return in June 1931, Tawney may have wished he had stayed away a little while longer.

Harold Laski

Any consideration of Laski's role in the government must first take into account that he was notorious for inflating his own influence. He certainly made up a number of fictitious conversations with ministers. Beatrice Webb noted that: 'The intimate talks he reports with "Mac" (so he addresses him) about appointments and policy are, I think, "imaginary conversations"; there was a curious hesitation as to whether they were at Downing Street or Chequers.'[26] Laski claimed in June and July 1929 that he had watched the formation of the Cabinet 'from close at hand', that he had written a number of memoranda for different ministers, and had long discussions with MacDonald on Anglo-French and Anglo-American relations.[27] He also claimed that MacDonald had asked him to go with the delegation to the USA, but he had refused, primarily because he wished 'to avoid anything which suggested an official connection with the Government'.[28] All of these statements may have been exaggerated, but are not wholly unbelievable in view of Laski's close involvement in MacDonald's election campaign and his recognised knowledge of American affairs. Laski was undoubtedly involved heavily in the work of the government during its first year and a half, and for a time seems to have been MacDonald's favoured intellectual adviser.[29]

Laski's first major undertaking followed his appointment by his close friend, Lord Sankey, to a committee set up to investigate administrative law in England under Earl Donoughmore. The committee's brief was to assess whether the increase in legislation delegated to civil servants was undermining the sovereignty of Parliament and the supremacy of the law. Laski was excited by the appointment and was prepared to postpone his plans to teach at Yale Law School in the spring of 1930 in order to participate.[30] He worked hard on the committee and largely accepted its report of 1932, which concluded that such delegation was inevitable and that as long as adequate safeguards were taken there was no constitutional infringement.[31]

Laski's involvement in the issue of Palestine was more significant than most commentators have realised and was important in turning him against the government. Far from being a mere theoretical adviser upon the issue, Laski was used by the government as a trouble-shooter with the powerful American Zionist lobby. Laski was not himself a Zionist, believing that integration rather than a Jewish National Home was the more desirable means of dealing with the problem of persecution, but many of his influential American friends were, and as such he was immensely useful to MacDonald. This was first evident during the Prime Minister's visit to Washington in October 1929, when Laski arranged for MacDonald to meet Louis Denbitz Brandeis, a Zionist member of the US Supreme Court, to discuss the Palestinian troubles that had flared up in August.

In October 1930 Laski, together with Weizmann, urged MacDonald to delay publication of Webb's White Paper to allow time for Felix Frankfurter, Laski's distinguished lawyer friend, and Felix Warburg, an American Jewish banker, to come to Britain to persuade Webb to change his mind. Laski was angered by the government's poor handling of the situation and by Webb's refusal to reconsider. The incident demonstrated to Laski that his Jewishness was more significant in defining his identity than he previously wished to concede. Although still not a Zionist, he told Frankfurter that: 'as a Jew I resented a policy which surrendered Jewish interests, in spite of a pledged word, to the authors of an unjustifiable massacre'.[32] Despite pleas from MacDonald and Henderson that he should attempt to mollify the government's American critics, Laski refused to do their bidding and instead campaigned against the White Paper, writing an anonymous article in *Week-End Review* on 25 October 1930 which condemned the personnel of the government as 'incompetent and vain'.[33]

Laski was authorised by Brandeis to be one of the representatives of American Zionism on Henderson's Cabinet committee and played a prominent role in negotiations. Brandeis wanted the government to issue a new pro-Zionist White Paper, but Laski persuaded him that a published government letter, also to be read in Parliament, was sufficient repudiation of the Webbian policy.[34] Beatrice Webb recorded on 22 January 1931 that Laski was 'bubbling over with delight at his own importance'.[35] Yet the experience was to undermine Laski's belief that secular rationalism would inevitably supersede religion and nationalism, and the government's poor handling of the situation led him to question the capabilities of the Labour Cabinet.

Laski was also involved in the formulation of government policy on Africa and India. At the end of December 1929, MacDonald asked him to produce a critical analysis of Webb's proposed constitution for East Africa. Although opposed to the White Supremacists, Laski accepted that benevolent white rule was justified, but, despite his claims, his policy was not implemented by the government.[36] Sankey also used him to work upon a policy for Kenya and the rest of Africa, and in the spring of 1930 asked him to help to plan the first Indian Round Table Conference. Laski was considered to be an expert upon federal constitutions and was known to have contacts with Indian activists in Britain, most notably Krishna Menon, whom he had taught at the LSE, and who was the head of the London-based Indian League. Laski found the task to be extremely complex, writing frustratedly in 1930 that India 'was a ghastly problem of which the real essence is that we can't govern it and it really is not fit to govern itself',[37] and of his fear that 'India [would] become the Ireland of the next generation'.[38] None the less, he prepared a detailed memorandum upon constitutional history and gave a successful talk upon the history of federalism to the delegates at the conference of November 1930. Sankey was grateful for Laski's input and he was invited to participate in the second conference in the autumn of 1931 after the fall of the government.

Ideological repercussions

It is generally suggested that the increasing failure of the administration pushed Laski steadily leftwards and facilitated the more radical stance he would adopt after the 1931 crisis.[39] Such an interpretation is, however, misleading, for it fails to recognise the extent of Laski's early commitment to the government and his continuing endorsement of its strategy until the end of 1930. Laski greatly enjoyed the work he was commissioned to do for the government and relished his closeness to the corridors of power. Despite the government's increasing problems, until mid-1930 his spirits remained high and he had few criticisms of the administration's general direction or its personnel. Arguably, his newly found influence upon the centre stage of British political life blunted Laski's usual critical edge. His closeness to the government made it difficult for him to be openly critical of it once his doubts crystallised after June 1930, and it was not until his departure for America in February 1931, to teach at Yale Law School, that Laski began to question systematically the government's whole strategy.

Laski published three books during 1930–31. His *Danger of Obedience and Other Essays* brought together a number of his American essays upon the decline of liberty around the world; *Liberty and the Modern State* (1930) concentrated upon the USA and the USSR; and *An Introduction to Politics* (1931) was essentially a populist précis of *Grammar*. All of these works were largely theoretical and paid little attention to contemporary politics. Laski's journalistic writings throughout 1930 were sparse by his own standards, and contained few criticisms of the government. His weekly 'Pen Portraits' for the relaunched *Daily Herald* included a highly favourable character assessment of the Prime Minister in April 1930. Readers were informed that the Labour leader possessed 'extraordinary qualities', had 'the magnetic art of leadership' and that his tendency to be aloof was explained by his 'profound sense of compassion for the pain of the world'.[40] The writing of articles which amounted to little more than crude propaganda made it difficult for Laski to disassociate himself from the government later on, and arguably meant that, when he finally did so, he felt a psychological need to do so in dramatic fashion. In private, Laski was increasingly critical of the Prime Minister from mid-1930, fearing in particular the repercussions of MacDonald's vanity and of his inability to accept criticism: 'unless you can convey your criticism in the form of eulogy, it is likely to do your cause more harm than good'.[41] Yet until he left for America Laski showed no signs of distancing himself from MacDonald, and was still visibly savouring the proximity to him.[42]

Laski's long-standing theoretical doubts with gradualism publicly resurfaced from mid-1930. Significantly, it was in an article for an American journal that he first expressed them; once again he used his American journalism for his own cathartic ends. In a seven-page piece entitled 'Aristocracy Still Ruling in England', Laski demonstrated that the economic power of the country and the key positions in the civil service and the judiciary remained in the hands of the upper and middle classes. The conclusions he drew were threefold. First, he feared Labour had become a party of social reform rather than a truly socialist party, citing the government's slum clearance programme as an example of 'controlled individualism' as opposed to socialism, and Snowden's 1930 budget as 'a wholly admirable application of the complete canon of Gladstonian finance'. Secondly, he suggested that the British governing class exercised so much power that an immense sacrifice on their behalf would be necessary if Labour's ends were to be achieved. Finally, he feared that in the current political and economic situation there was little scope for concessions and that the parliamentary system could break down if there was a real attack upon the rights of private property.[43] Laski's implication here, and in a controversial speech given to the Royal Institute of International Affairs in December 1930, was that unless reforms were introduced more vigorously, the working classes might turn to communism.[44]

An article for the newly created *Political Quarterly* in the July–September edition also warned of the apocalyptic consequences if swift reform was not introduced. Laski suggested that the masses in the West were more aware of social inequalities and more impatient to see them overturned than ever before. Even in Britain, with its long 'tradition of compromise', there were still 'grave reasons for fear':

> To conserve the gains of political evolution in the last century, we have to satisfy a population more critical, and more explicit about its criticism than ever before, that the foundations of our society inherently secure its happiness, its comfort, and its self-respect. The peaceful transformation of society depends upon our ability to produce that conviction.[45]

What Laski proposed to achieve this end was fundamental reform of the parliamentary system in order that the demands of the masses could be satisfied with speed. Yet, despite the urgent tone in this analysis, in contrast to his post-1931 position Laski still believed that peaceful and constitutional change could be implemented as long as the political structure was overhauled. Although he now desired a more courageous and radical Labour administration, Laski still wanted it to be an essentially gradualist one.

In the same manner as Tawney's trip to China, Laski's crossing to the USA provided him with the opportunity to distance himself both physically and intellectually from a government with which he had been closely associated, but with which he was increasingly uncertain. The immediate effect of his ocean voyage was to objectify his perception of the government and to make him more critical of it. On 22 March 1931 he told his wife that: 'it is difficult when people ask you what legislation this government has passed to have to confess that it has done nothing at all'.[46] Three days later he confided: 'The truth is, and one sees it much more clearly at this distance, the party ought to get into opposition again to make moral adjustments.'[47] Devoid of much information upon the British political situation, Laski gradually withdrew from his own close involvement with the government and assumed once more the role of the independent critic. By 12 April he saw government defeat as the only means 'to preserve the party's morale'.[48] Laski also felt Snowden was not the dynamic force he had once been; on 14 May he described the Chancellor of the Exchequer as 'an incubus to the party',[49] and he began to feel that Henderson should take over as party leader.[50]

Yet, even as late as June 1931, he was loath to give up completely on the government. On 15 June he was the guest of honour at a *New Republic* dinner in New York, where he gave a speech praising the government for improving the position for the unemployed, raising taxes on the rich and thereby laying the ground for 'a bloodless social revolution' in Britain.[51] Perhaps the rationale behind this speech was as much to convince Laski himself as to win over his sceptical listeners. He was no doubt aware that any acknowledgement that gradualism was bankrupt would force him to reconsider his entire political ideology. In retrospect, therefore, one can legitimately pinpoint this speech as the final cry of Laski's dying gradualist faith.

Laski had never had much to say about economics and, like the Webbs and Tawney, had never considered economic factors to be central to his socialist philosophy. Indeed, his sole contribution to the economic debate was to pour cold water upon MacDonald's decision to set up the Economic Advisory Council, which he believed, with some justification, to be 'administratively unworkable'.[52] In the summer of 1931 Laski was on holiday on the Continent and the events of August took him very much by surprise.[53] Fearful of the situation awaiting him and in some uncertainty over the implications of developments, he was, not surprisingly, in no great hurry to return to Britain.[54] Such, then, was Laski's distant experience of the events that would alter fundamentally both his political philosophy and his whole world-view.

G. D. H. Cole

It soon became apparent to G. D. H. Cole that the government was not prepared to push ahead even with the programme it had promoted in its election manifesto. At first, he was ready to give the administration the benefit of the doubt. As early as 13 July, Cole was disappointed with Thomas, but expressed the hope that, although he had 'announced no new scheme' for dealing with unemployment, this was because he was only putting forward 'an instalment of a more comprehensive scheme'.[55] Cole took the same rationalising approach to Greenwood's announcements on the government's housing plans, suggesting that the restoration of a local authority subsidy was to be commended as a first step in the right direction.[56]

189

By October 1929, however, Cole was becoming openly critical. His chief concern remained unemployment policy, and he used every avenue open to him to attempt to push the government into a more innovative approach. In a vast array of articles in a multitude of publications, Cole reiterated the arguments of *The Next Ten Years* in synopsis, emphasising the need to provide work, the importance of improving the home market and the benefits of a national labour corps.[57] He also published *Gold, Credit and Unemployment: Four Essays for Laymen* in April 1930, which concentrated upon the beneficial effects of a more 'managed currency.' Further, Cole used his participation in a number of committees and commissions to press his ideas upon the government at closer quarters. On 18 February 1930 he was called to give evidence to a Ministry of Health Committee on Vagrancy, in the course of which he presented a strong case for the national labour corps.[58] He also gave evidence to the Holman Gregory Commission in March 1931, presenting a memorandum of over seventy pages calling for the government to maintain benefit rates, put the scheme on a more sound financial footing by funding it directly from taxation, extend the scheme to those workers currently excluded and concentrate on providing work rather than maintenance.[59] Finally, he was a member of the EAC, where he emphasised the centrality of unemployment policy to economic recovery wherever the limited terms of reference would allow and was appointed Chairman of a sub-committee to examine unemployment benefit.[60] Throughout these various activities, Cole's essential message remained the same: the unemployment situation constituted 'a national emergency of the first order' and a Labour government would be judged first and foremost on its ability to tackle the problem.[61] As the number of unemployed increased dramatically, Cole's sense of urgency grew ever more marked.

Cole's growing frustration with unemployment policy was paralleled in other areas. The Vice-President of the WEA expected the government to act quickly on the issue of raising the school leaving age.[62] Cole believed that this was an important reform not only to improve the level of education but also because of its positive effects for industry in reducing the number of school-leavers, and he was frustrated by the government's failure to manoeuvre a Bill through the Commons. He took a keen interest in mining legislation, and urged the government to intervene early on to solve the disagreement over hours and wages.[63] He was again to be disappointed by the temerity of the government's final proposals in December 1929, in particular by the absence of proposals for compulsory amalgamation.[64]

By as early as the end of 1929 Cole was disappointed with what he saw as the government's weakness on all areas of domestic policy. Whilst he appreciated the difficulties, Cole feared the government's minority position was being used as a fig-leaf to hide its shortcomings and 'as the excuse for a policy which will fail because it lacks courage, and does not go far enough to be effective'.[65]

By mid-1930 Cole's respect for MacDonald's style of leadership, never high, had clearly diminished; although he did not indulge in public criticism, he believed MacDonald had waited too long to remove Thomas and was frustrated by the refusal to create a new ministry to deal specifically with unemployment.[66] It was only now that Cole decided to submit to pressure from the Webbs and from Henderson, to allow his name to go forward as a prospective parliamentary candidate. Henderson had tried to get him adopted for the safe Brightside seat in Sheffield, and, on MacDonald's advice, Cole had already turned down the unpromising seat of Worcester in December 1929.[67] Henderson believed Cole's abilities could be better utilised inside the Commons but Cole was never instinctively attracted to the parliamentary world and only accepted the nomination to the King's Norton seat in Birmingham in May 1930 because he believed it would offer him the best opportunity to influence a party strategy he so desperately wished to see changed. In December 1929 Cole had been hopeful that MacDonald would assign him a position of great influence in the EAC; by May 1930 he doubted the potential of that body and his own capacity to effect any real change from within it. It is possible that he was closer to Mosley than he was later ready to admit. In July 1930 he wrote that Mosley's programme was 'broadly on the right lines' and it was at least a coincidence that he accepted a nomination for a seat in Birmingham, whose Borough Labour Party, as illustrated in Chapter 3, had almost become a Mosley fiefdom.[68] As it was, he did not stand in the 1931 election as a result of his diagnosis as a diabetic in 1931. Like Laski, Cole's eclecticism was important to him and he would have disliked the restrictions parliamentary life would have placed upon his other activities. Cole saw himself first and foremost as an intellectual and the role he most coveted in the Labour movement was one which would give him at least as much, and probably more, influence than that of the MP, and would place no restraints on his teaching, his writing or his intellectual freedom: that of the party's *éminence grise*.

The NFRB and SSIP

Ironically, it was the failure of the government which would give Cole his greatest opportunity to fulfil this role. Convinced by mid-1930 that the administration had grounded itself in a 'stagnant swamp', the Coles decided to create a 'New Fabian Group'.[69] This would 'rally the young men, among whom there is some excellent stuff ... and get some decent Socialist literature instead of ILP or Mosley amateur clap-trap'.[70] Cole had been deeply aware of what he saw as a growing generation gap in the Labour movement from the mid-1920s and felt that many Labour slogans were increasingly stale and meaningless to the ears of a young audience.[71] Cole came to see himself as the necessary mediator between the young and the old and hoped to create a new and vigorous 'ginger group' which would update Labour's ideas to meet the demands of the new decade.[72] It was to this end that the Coles initiated a series of weekend meetings in early 1931 to ascertain 'whether or not there were others around who felt as we did'.[73] These initial meetings were attended by a number of individuals who were, or were to become, important figures, including Attlee, Cripps, Lansbury, Lord Ponsonby, Ellen Wilkinson, Philip Noel-Baker, the young Hugh Gaitskell, Colin Clark and Evan Durbin, as well as the trade unionists Bevin and Arthur Pugh. It was decided that two bodies should be set up: the New Fabian Research Bureau (NFRB), to research all areas of long-term socialist policy, and the Society for Socialist Inquiry and Propaganda (SSIP), to diffuse the results of these investigations and promote discussion of them within the wider Labour movement.

Both bodies received the enthusiastic endorsement of the Webbs, who recognised that the Fabian Society was not the intellectual force it had once been, and the blessings of Henderson, who gave a dinner at the Commons to selected guests on 2 March 1931 to discuss the new organisations.[74] Henderson's attitude was not shared by other party leaders, whose under-standable fears were inflamed by numerous rumours that the NFRB was in-tending to form close links with the New Party.[75] Despite Cole's reassurance that the NFRB had no intentions of becoming a focus for an anti-government campaign,[76] MacDonald was annoyed that he was not consulted at the outset and seems to have been a prime mover in the decision of the NEC on 23 June 1931 to send a delegation to 'ascertain the intention' of Cole's new groups.[77] Cole's intention was always to remain firmly within the party and his criti-cism remained that of 'the loyal grouser'. Whilst he hoped, however, that the two bodies could help to rescue the government from its malaise, Cole believed that their primary function was to reshape the long-term strategy of the movement. By the summer of 1931 the NFRB had already set up three wide-ranging inquiries, to study all aspects of economics, international affairs and the political system.

The SSIP and NFRB launched into a feverish programme of meetings, discussions and 'kite-flying' with the various executives of the Labour move-ment. A regular 'forum' was created in London with lectures on all aspects of political and economic policy and these meetings stimulated considerable interest from socialists eager to discuss new ideas against the background of a Labour government fast running out of them. Special educational meetings were arranged for students, women and young union officials, and arrange-ments were made for a two-week summer school. Paradoxically, the Coles had not felt so invigorated since the days of the Labour Research Department in 1918; although the government appeared to be stumbling towards an un-known destiny in 1931 the two organisations moved stridently forward, con-fident in the validity of their long-term aims.[78] So great was Cole's enthusiasm that it could not be dented even by serious illness, which was diagnosed as diabetes in June, and which was to cause him considerable disability for the rest of his life.[79]

The involvement of so many key figures gave the two bodies an important air of both respectability and intellectual weight. Crucial to their prospects was not only the involvement of members of the government, but the significant contributions of Bevin and Pugh, who became, respectively, Chairman and Vice-Chairman of the SSIP in March 1931 and who between them represented over half a million workers. Cole was impressed by Bevin's raw intellect and practical mind and the two men quickly established a good working relationship. Cole recognised that if the two bodies were to avoid becoming mere talking shops or another ILP, which by 1931 seemed to Cole to offer little in the way of feasible alternatives, it was important they should develop strong roots in all sections of the movement. The election of Attlee as Chairman of the NFRB in June 1931 ensured the bureau would receive considerable publicity within the PLP.

Economics and economic crisis

The strong emphasis which both the SSIP and NFRB placed upon economic policy represented an extension of Cole's growing realisation from 1929 that Labour's economic understanding was woefully inadequate. He believed that if Labour was to achieve a peaceful transition to socialism it was essential it should have a coherent strategy for dealing with a capitalist system which, following the logic of socialist analysis, would be subject to continual crises. Unlike the majority of the movement, including his fellow socialist intellectuals, Cole believed it futile to argue that the economic problems were inherent in capitalism and that a minority Labour government could do nothing until it was possible to implement socialism. As a natural progression from the ideas of *The Next Ten Years*, Cole began to question still further the central concepts of classical economics; in particular, the need for balanced budgets, the role of the gold standard and the continuing utility of free trade. As Wright argues, Skidelsky's suggestion that none of the Labour intellectuals showed any interest in unorthodox economics during the government is totally indefensible in the case of Cole.[80] Even in *The Next Ten Years* Cole had implied a belief in a multiplier effect, through his discussion of the economic benefits that would accrue to a government prepared to undertake an extensive programme of expenditure. He was a strong advocate of the need for the EAC and hoped it would be given a wide scope to explore new avenues of economic thought.[81] From as early as April 1930, Cole was calling for a more 'managed currency' and proposed that the gold standard should remain only for international exchange and no longer as the basis of the internal currency.[82]

Although he worked closely with Keynes on the EAC's sub-committee on economic outlook, however, Cole did not endorse a revenue tariff.[83] Cole wished to move away from the slogans of free trade versus protection and attempted to find a middle way. He favoured what he called 'non-tariff protection' – import boards to regulate goods coming into the country – and a limited extension of co-operation with the Empire to import foodstuffs that Britain was unable to produce at home.[84] However, he continued to prioritise the need to secure economic recovery through an extension of the home market. He believed the causes of capitalism's growing economic crisis were twofold: first, the lack of planned production, and secondly, the inefficiency of the world banking and financial system. Consequently, the solutions he proposed concentrated upon remedying these two weaknesses. First, he emphasised the need for international co-operation to prevent the downward spiral of world prices. Secondly, he continued to argue the need for rationalisation and the state planning of industry. Finally, Cole advocated a more efficiently managed money supply, ideally through the socialisation of banking, in order to meet the needs of industry for credit.[85]

Cole took a great interest in the proceedings of the Macmillan Inquiry and welcomed the report published in July 1931 as 'a great advance on any previous document dealing with banking policy', despite the fact that it was a compromise between conflicting viewpoints. He was in complete agreement with the addendum signed by Keynes and Bevin, which advocated a policy of economic expansion promoted by the state.[86] Cole immediately rejected the recommendations of the May Report, not only on the grounds that it was the working classes who would have to bear the brunt of the sacrifices but also because he believed the proposed £96 million cuts would do little to improve Britain's economic situation.[87]

Conclusion

For all the Labour intellectuals, observing the limitations of the government had been both a depressing and a frustrating experience. They had been hopeful that MacDonald's administration would make some progress towards the creation of a socialist society in Britain, but recognised by at least mid-1930 that the government would not achieve even this limited objective. These five intellectual figures had all been involved, to varying degrees, in the government's activities. Beatrice Webb was the most detached of all of them, and perhaps as such was critical of the government's strategy from an early date. Her husband, however, was the intellectual most visibly connected with the government's failure, both through his membership of the Cabinet and as the principal figure in the definition of the 'inevitability of gradualness' philosophy. Laski and Tawney were also involved at close hand in policy formulations. Laski was a government adviser on Palestine and the Empire and for a time appears to have been both Sankey's and MacDonald's favoured intellectual adviser. Tawney had been responsible for drafting *Labour and the Nation* in 1928 and for writing a number of MacDonald's key election speeches and had been the chief architect of Labour's education policy. Concerned that they might have placed themselves into too close an association with a government not succeeding in its tasks, both used the opportunities provided by academic trips overseas in 1930 and 1931 to distance themselves from it.

The effect of the failure of the government was to lead all of these figures, at least privately, to question the validity of both the party's and their own socialist ideologies long before the 1931 crisis, and to question whether socialism could be achieved by parliamentary means alone. Ironically, by 1931, at a time when the government was desperately in need of new ideas, these Labour intellectuals, both for their own reasons and because the Labour leadership had pushed them away, provided little or no input into government policy-making. The most apparent weakness in the government's strategy had been its deficiency in financial understanding. The Webbs, Tawney and Laski all had little to say on this fundamental issue. Cole, on the other hand, had recognised from an early date the need for greater Labour economic knowledge. Of all these intellectuals, then, it was Cole who had maintained most successfully the role of the semi-independent socialist critic, who had the most coherent alternative strategy to offer, and who, through the creation of the SSIP and NFRB, was best placed to take advantage of the demise of the government to attempt to convert the party to his own line of thinking.

NOTES

1 British Library of Political and Economic Science (hereafter BLPES), Passfield Papers, B. Webb's Diary, 4 June 1929.
2 Ibid., 6 June and 20 June 1929. Beatrice felt that by so doing she would help to undermine the 'too much regard for rank and social status in the British Labour Movement'.
3 On one memorable occasion, MacDonald was annoyed to discover that Webb was not in the Colonial Office, where he expected him to be, but at home resting; Public Record Office (hereafter PRO), MacDonald Papers, Diary, PRO 30/69/1753/1, 25 August 1929.
4 BLPES, Passfield Papers, B. Webb's Diary, 15 November 1929.
5 Ibid., 9 July 1930.
6 Ibid., 14 December 1930.
7 BLPES, Dalton Papers, Diary, 12 November 1930.
8 L. Radice, *Beatrice and Sidney Webb* (London, 1984), p. 282.
9 Bodleian Library, Oxford, Amulree Papers, Ms. Eng. C.2363, Webb to Amulree, 10 February 1931.
10 BLPES, Passfield Papers, B. Webb's Diary, 14 December 1930.
11 Ibid., 31 May 1931, and BLPES, Passfield Papers, IV, undated letter to MacDonald, late May 1931.
12 BLPES, Passfield Papers, Diary, 21 December 1929.

13 Ibid., 18 August 1931.

14 Ibid., 4 February 1931.

15 'A Reform Bill for 1932', *Political Quarterly* 3 (1932), 4.

16 BLPES, Passfield Papers, B. Webb's Diary, 22 August 1931.

17 Ibid.

18 PRO, MacDonald Papers, PRO 30/69/1174, Tawney to MacDonald, 12 May 1930.

19 'The Government and the School Age', *New Statesman*, 22 February 1930, pp. 627–8.

20 Ibid.

21 BLPES, Passfield Papers, B. Webb's Diary, 24 July 1930.

22 Even B. Webb once suggested that Tawney was 'A scholar, a saint and a social reformer ... loved and respected by all who know him'; BLPES, Passfield Papers, Diary, 8 December 1935. This image has persisted in the eyes of his subsequent admirers.

23 PRO, MacDonald Papers, PRO 30/69/1753/1, Diary, 22 July 1930.

24 S. Howson and D. Winch, *The Economic Advisory Council, 1930–1939: A Study in Economic Advice during Depression and Recovery* (Cambridge, 1979), pp. 34–9.

25 PRO, MacDonald Papers, PRO 30/69/676, Tawney to MacDonald, 23 July 1930, suggests the decision to go to China had only just been reached, even if it was a notion which he had been entertaining for some time.

26 BLPES, Passfield Papers, B. Webb's Diary, 22 January 1931.

27 Laski to Holmes, 11 June and 22 July 1929, in M. D. Howe (ed.), *Holmes–Laski Letters* (London, 1953).

28 Laski to Holmes, 2 August 1929, in Howe (ed.), *Holmes–Laski Letters*.

29 As both M. Newman, *Harold Laski: A Political Biography* (Basingstoke, 1993) and I. Kramnick and B. Sheerman, *Harold Laski: A Life on the Left* (London, 1993) illustrate, many of the claims Laski made had far more truth in them than was generally credited by his contemporaries.

30 Laski to Holmes, 3 November 1929, in Howe (ed.), *Holmes–Laski Letters*.

31 Kramnick and Sheerman, *Harold Laski*, pp. 271–3.

32 Laski to Frankfurter, 26 October 1930, cited in Kramnick and Sheerman, *Harold Laski*, p. 278.

33 Cited in Kramnick and Sheerman, *Harold Laski*, pp. 278–9.

34 Ibid., pp. 274–81.

35 BLPES, Passfield Papers, B. Webb's Diary, 22 January 1931.

36 Laski to Holmes, 12 April 1930, in Howe (ed.), *Holmes–Laski Letters*.

37 Laski to Holmes, 15 June 1930, in Howe (ed.), *Holmes–Laski Letters*.

38 Laski to Holmes, 28 June 1930, in Howe (ed.), *Holmes–Laski Letters*.

39 Newman, *Harold Laski*, pp. 133–51, and Kramnick and Sheerman, *Harold Laski*, pp. 300–1.

40 BNL, 'Ramsay MacDonald – The Dreamer who Triumphed', *Daily Herald*, 25 April 1930.

41 Laski to Holmes, 1 November 1930, in Howe (ed.), *Holmes–Laski Letters*.

42 For example, see Laski to Holmes, 27 December 1930 and 25 January 1931, in Howe (ed.), *Holmes–Laski Letters*.

43 Newman, *Harold Laski*, pp. 134–6.

44 Ibid., p. 136.

45 Laski, 'The Prospects of Constitutional Government', *Political Quarterly* 1 (1930), 314.

46 Brynmor Jones Library, University of Hull, Laski Papers, DLA/33, Laski to Frida, 22 March 1931.
47 Ibid., 25 March 1931.
48 Ibid., 12 April 1931.
49 Ibid., 14 May 1931.
50 Ibid., 11 June 1931.
51 Kramnick and Sheerman, *Harold Laski*, p. 295.
52 Laski to Holmes, 23 December 1929, in Howe (ed.), *Holmes–Laski Letters*.
53 Kramnick and Sheerman, *Harold Laski*, p. 295, give the misleading impression that Laski was in England when the crisis broke.
54 Laski to Holmes, from Antwerp, 26 August 1931, in Howe (ed.), *Holmes–Laski Letters*.
55 'Thomas's Plans', *New Statesman* 33 (1929), 428.
56 'The Government's Housing Policy', *New Statesman* 33 (1929), 461.
57 For an indication of the form the articles took see 'Work or Doles', *New Statesman* 33 (1929), 768; British Newspaper Library (hereafter BNL), 'The Cure for Unemployment', *Everyman*, 10 October 1929; and Nuffield College (hereafter NC), Oxford, Cole Papers, GDHC/A1/43, *King's Norton Labour News*, October 1930.
58 NC, Cole Papers, GDHC/F5/2, 'Evidence of G. D. H. Cole to Committee on Vagrancy, Ministry of Health', 18 February 1930.
59 NC, Cole Papers, GDHC/F5/3, 'Memorandum of Evidence Submitted to the Royal Commission on Unemployment Insurance', March 1931.
60 Howson and Winch, *The Economic Advisory Council*, p. 42.
61 'How I Would Relieve Unemployment', *Everyman*, 3 July 1930.
62 'The School Age', *New Statesman* 33 (1929), 490; NC, Cole Papers, GDHC/A1/24, 'Do the Working Classes Want the Bill?', *Schoolmaster and Woman Teachers' Chronicle*, 13 March 1930.
63 'The Government and the Mines', *New Statesman* 34 (1929–30), 78, and 'Miners' Wages', 34 (1929–30), 217.
64 'The Coal Bill', *New Statesman* 34 (1929–30), 356.
65 'The Old Year and the New', *New Statesman* 34 (1929–30), 409.
66 Howson and Winch, *The Economic Advisory Council*, p. 39, and 'The Ghost That Walks', *New Statesman* 34 (1929–30), 829.
67 M. Cole, *The Life of G. D. H. Cole* (London, 1971), p. 168; PRO, MacDonald Papers, PRO 30/69/672, correspondence Cole and MacDonald, 10 to 27 December 1929.
68 NC, Cole Papers, GDHC/A1/43, *King's Norton Labour News*, July 1930. Cole, *G. D. H. Cole*, sheds little light upon the reasons for Cole's change of mind; PRO, MacDonald Papers, PRO 30/69/672, Cole to MacDonald, 4 December 1929, suggests he was reluctant to give up his position at Oxford and felt he had insufficient income to become an MP. Cole wished to have nothing to do with Mosley once he started campaigning against Labour from December 1930. BLPES, Passfield Papers, II/4, Cole to B. Webb, 9 December 1930, reveals he refused to sign Mosley's Manifesto which he saw as a 'conspiracy against the government'.
69 Cole, *G. D. H. Cole*, p. 175.
70 BLPES, Passfield Papers, II/4, Cole to B. Webb, 9 December 1930.
71 NC, Cole Papers, GDH/A1/43, hand-written article, undated, *c.*1928.
72 'The New World and its Challenge', *Everyman*, 2 January 1930, and 'How

Things Have Changed', *Everyman*, 9 January 1930.

73 Cole, *G. D. H. Cole*, p. 175.

74 NC, Fabian Society Papers, J9/1, fo. 15B, Webb to Cole, 17 February 1931.

75 NC, Fabian Society Papers, J6/4, newspaper cuttings, *World Press News*, 5 March 1931, and *The Times*, 15 June 1931; Cole, *G. D. H. Cole*, pp. 177–8.

76 PRO, MacDonald Papers, PRO 30/69/1175, Cole to MacDonald, 9 December 1930.

77 PRO, MacDonald Papers, PRO 30/69/1176, MacDonald to Captain E. N. Bennett, MP, 8 August 1931; LPA, NEC Minutes, 23 June 1931.

78 Cole, *G. D. H. Cole*, pp. 174–82, and BLPES, Passfield Papers, II/4, Cole to B. Webb, 9 December 1930.

79 Such was the severity of his illness that there seemed a genuine possibility he would not recover, yet he refused to allow it to affect his work. Margaret Cole paints a vivid picture of her husband in his hospital bed surrounded by charts and diagrams, feverishly working away at *British Trade and Industry* (London, 1932); Cole, *G. D. H. Cole*, p. 186.

80 A. W. Wright's criticism of R. Skidelsky, *Politicians and the Slump: The Labour Government of 1929–1931* (London, 1967) in *G. D. H. Cole and Socialist Democracy* (Oxford, 1979), pp. 185–6.

81 'The Economic Council', *New Statesman* 34 (1929–30), 560.

82 G. D. H. Cole, *Gold, Credit and Employment* (London, 1930). This suggestion does appear economically flawed; at this juncture Cole was not prepared to accept the logical conclusion of his argument, that Britain should abandon gold altogether.

83 See Howson and Winch, *The Economic Advisory Council*, pp. 34–5.

84 Ibid., 25 July 1930, p. 1.

85 NC, Cole Papers, GDHC/A1/12, 'Gold and the World Trade Crisis', *New World*, June 1931, pp. 1–2, and Notes for Lectures on the Economic Situation, GDHC/E1/5, May–June 1931, pp. 53–5.

86 'Money, Wages and Expansion', *New Statesman and Nation* 2 (1931), 69; see also BNL, *Daily Herald*, 15, 17 and 20 July 1931, Cole's assessment of the Macmillan Report, pp. 8, 6 and 6 respectively.

87 'Britain's Economic Future', *New Statesman and Nation* 2 (1931), 216.

6

The 1931 crisis and aftermath

The crisis

The history of the August 1931 crisis and the fall of the second Labour government is generally written with almost sole reference to decisions at Westminster and, in particular, within the Cabinet.[1] The rapid onset of the crisis following the publication of the May Report at the end of July 1931 resulted in a flight from the pound and the recall of a bewildered Cabinet to London. The call of the opposition leaders and the bankers for a cut in unemployment benefit in order to restore international confidence in sterling led to the final split of the Cabinet on 23 August and the termination of the government. The next day, however, Labour leaders learned with amazement that MacDonald had consented to the King's appeal that he should head a 'National Government'. To a considerable extent, these events were ones of 'high politics'. Yet it would be wholly misleading to assume that, since it was seldom involved directly in the key decision-making processes, the wider Labour movement played no part in the events of August 1931. In contrast, a closer examination reveals that the movement played a central role in shaping the crisis and its outcome.

In the first place, the views of the wider movement were central to the final Cabinet split. Although humanitarian notions of a duty to defend the unemployed played a part in the decision of those nine members of the Cabinet who voted against the benefit cut, of more significance was their awareness that the wider movement would have found it an exceedingly bitter pill to swallow. The whole Cabinet had, after all, been prepared to accept, albeit reluctantly, a £56 million package of cuts, containing a number of measures highly unpalatable to Labour's whole philosophy. These included a reduction in transitional benefit and in the period of entitlement to that benefit, together with cuts in education and in public servants pay.[2] Whilst it was possible that the wider movement, with a great deal of effort, could have been convinced of the need for these measures,[3] this was not the case with unemployment benefit. Equally, awareness of the perceptions of the movement played an important role in determining the actions of MacDonald. Although increasingly detached from the movement by August 1931, and in many ways contemptuous of it, MacDonald was aware on the eve of the government's fall that if the Labour Cabinet ignored the movement's likely opposition to the cuts then it risked a seismic split in the party. He was convinced nevertheless that he had a duty to the nation to push through the cuts in order to restore financial stability. As such, as the only means of avoiding a split in the Labour movement and carrying out his perceived national duty, MacDonald was to embrace the concept of a National Government.

In the longer term, the 1931 crisis was shaped by the multiple tensions which had developed between the wider movement and the government over the previous two years. If the wider movement was to be convinced of the necessity for unpalatable measures in the face of a perceived national crisis, it was vital that relations should be harmonious. As has been illustrated at length, however, relations between the second Labour government and the wider movement were anything but harmonious. The greatest cause for concern for the government, of course, was the disgruntled TUC. In large part a problem of the government's own creation, the breakdown in relations with the trade unions would now play a pivotal role in its collapse.

The TUC's reaction to the proposed cuts in unemployment benefit contained in the Majority Report of the May Committee was totally predictable, given its earlier hostility to the Holman Gregory Commission. The majority of unions might have been prepared to accept 'equality of sacrifice' but this was not an option with which they were presented. Rather, it was those at the bottom level who were to be hardest hit. For the unions, the implication for wage levels was unacceptable. The initial conviction of the Labour leadership that it could win over the trade unions was a reflection of the detachment of the political from the industrial wing of the movement by July 1931. The unions believed the long-term unemployed were the state's responsibility and that the cost of benefit should be borne by general taxation. Moreover, they felt that the government was being fed partisan advice by the banking community to bring about a cut in social services. The ASW spoke for all unions when it suggested that: 'If there is to be economy it should be at the expense of those who live handsomely on rent, interest and profit derived from the toil of those who labour.'[4] All union leaders urged the TUC to withstand the attack on working-class living standards engendered in the report and many wrote to the TUC to urge it not to compromise.[5]

Many trade unionists doubted that a real crisis existed at all. In the view of the TUC Research Department, 'the present "crisis" [was] psychological rather than economic'. Further, it was felt, with some justification, that Britain had withstood the Depression better than many other leading countries and that there were options available which the government was not considering, largely as a result of pressure from the City.[6] Yet, only by August 1931 had the TUC begun to formulate anything approaching a coherent alternative to the proposed cuts and even then many of the details had yet to be worked out. Significantly, this policy was largely drawn up as a reaction to the government's proposals and it was not until a joint meeting with the NEC and the government on 20 August that the GC received an exact idea as to what the government's proposals were. Nevertheless, even before the publication of the May Report in 1931, the unions attempted to create a climate of opinion in which it would be impossible for the proposed cuts to be implemented.[7] On 29 July the TUC-controlled *Daily Herald* wrote that the report 'was so extreme as to make it very unlikely that any government could implement the main proposals'. On 1 August the front page declared that: 'Generally, the view was held that most of the committee's recommendations were dead almost before they were born.' On 19 August it reported that the Cabinet had before it proposals for a temporary suspension of the sinking fund, a conversion of the war loan, an increase in unemployment insurance contributions, a 10 per cent revenue tariff and a super-tax on fixed-interest-bearing securities. However, a study of the Cabinet Minutes for 19 and 20 August makes it clear that cuts in national expenditure received far greater Cabinet attention than any of these issues.[8] Finally, on 20 August, in a front-page headline, the *Herald* declared there would be no reduction in unemployment benefit.[9] The result of these distortions was not only to add to the already strong union opposition to cuts, but also to influence greatly the attitude of local Labour parties, for whom the *Daily Herald* was the most important source of information on the crisis.

A joint meeting of the GC and the NEC on 20 August produced the exact opposite result to the one intended. Arranged by Henderson in the interests of maintaining the unity of the movement and softening-up the TUC,[10] the meeting served only to highlight the extent of the deterioration in relations and to harden TUC opposition. Henderson himself said nothing during the meeting and clearly felt himself to be in an awkward position, with his loyalties divided between the government and the union movement from which he had risen.[11] Snowden and MacDonald both attended with extreme reluctance. Snowden 'had never recognised the right of the TUC Committee to be consulted on matters of cabinet policy'[12] and yet found himself attempting to win TUC support for the proposed Cabinet cuts. It is clear from MacDonald's diary that, in line with his growing disrespect for the movement in general, the Prime Minister's dislike for the TUC had become more pronounced throughout 1931, and by August had reached a level of absolute contempt. Angered by the fact that the TUC seemed to be deliberately making the government's task more difficult, MacDonald felt that the balancing of the budget had nothing to do with the GC. He had never felt that the TUC had any intrinsic right to be consulted even on industrial policy and he certainly did not believe that it would be anything other than a hindrance in a time of national crisis.[13]

As had been the case throughout the previous two years, the GC was angered as least as much by the manner in which it was treated as it was by the content of government policy. MacDonald's rhetorical speech on the gravity of the crisis was scarcely calculated to restore union faith. The GC was greatly frustrated by the lack of detail since it felt that it was being told no more than could be read in any newspaper. Citrine in particular was infuriated by this apparent lack of trust from a Labour leadership more than ready to discuss intricate financial details with the opposition leaders. A visibly irritated Snowden was forced to rise and attempt to clarify the situation. The Chancellor's speech left the GC with little doubt as to the extent of the proposed cuts, but unfortunately led them to believe that there would definitely be no cut in unemployment benefit.[14] After a number of questions, the meeting broke up in an atmosphere of some bitterness and the GC retired to discuss its reaction to the government proposals, which were later presented to a Cabinet sub-committee on the evening of 20 August. Rejecting all proposals for cuts, Citrine told MacDonald that the unions 'could not assent to a proposal which would make it impossible for them to keep up the level of wages any longer'.[15]

As an alternative to the cuts, the GC put forward proposals for taxes on fixed-interest-bearing securities, a suspension of the sinking fund and a conversion of the war debt. As to the revenue tariff, the GC 'had come to the conclusion that this was a matter of policy that could only be determined by Congress'.[16] The meeting soon reached a point of deadlock as a result of the complete absence of any common ground. MacDonald and Snowden felt that the TUC had failed to grasp the gravity of the crisis, MacDonald telling the GC that not a single one of their proposals had 'touched the problem that faced the Government',[17] whilst the trade unionists remained convinced that the situation was not 'quite so desperate as was alleged'.[18] The TUC's opposition proved to be the crucial factor in the final Cabinet split. Not only was MacDonald motivated by his strong belief that the state of national emergency was such that cuts were the only option, but also by a determination to resist the TUC. In his diary, MacDonald described the GC's stand as 'practically a declaration of war' and outlined his difference of opinion and lack of respect for both the TUC and the people whom it represented. 'The TUC undoubtedly voice the feelings of the mass of the workers', he wrote, but 'their minds are rigid and think of superficial appearances and so grasping at the shadow lose the bone.' On 22 August he voiced his determination not to allow the TUC to 'dictate' to the government: 'If we yield now to the TUC we shall never again be able to call our bodies or souls or intelligence our own.' MacDonald, however, failed to recognise the extent of union power in the movement and its effective ability to veto decisions with which it disagreed passionately.[19] Henderson realised this reality only too well. Initially prepared to countenance a cut in benefit, 'Henderson began to change his position' as soon as he was aware of the full extent of TUC opposition.[20] Whilst he still attempted to find a suitable compromise after 20 August, Henderson's top priority, in contrast to MacDonald, remained what it had always been: the unity of the movement, even if that meant the fall of the government.

Like MacDonald, Sidney Webb was hardened in his commitment to cuts as a result of the TUC, whom he referred to as 'pigs'.[21] Although three union-sponsored ministers voted for the cut (Bondfield, Thomas and Shaw), the impact of the GC's opposition had been sufficient to bring the government down. This was a consequence of its actions for which the TUC was prepared to accept responsibility. By August 1931, the unions had given up on a government to which, only two years previously, they had been prepared to offer their complete support. They recognised that the government was likely to fall in the near future regardless of their actions, and were concerned not to compromise their own principles any longer. Already thinking of the post-crisis period, the TUC was beginning to set the conditions for the future reunification of the movement, which meant not only opposition to the cuts, but also the acceptance by the party of general TUC control of policy. It is, however, difficult to substantiate the suggestion that the TUC had 'dictated' to the government in the August crisis in the strict sense of that word. The government had, after all, asked for the GC's opinion on the cuts.

The aftermath

The wider movement played a more significant role in defining the actions of the Labour Party in the aftermath of the crisis than is generally recognised. As had been the case during the crisis itself, there was a two-way process of cause and effect between the wider movement and the party at the centre. Ironically, despite the breaking away of National Labour, the short-term effect of the crisis would be to bring much of the movement together, thus demonstrating the truism that Labour was never more united than when it believed it was defending itself against a common enemy.

The 1931 crisis brought to a head a number of fundamental issues for the movement and for its ideology. To what extent did the capitalist establishment still hold extensive extra-parliamentary powers? Was a Labour government in power enough to change society, and had Labour's previous belief in state neutrality proved to be naive? Did Labour have a duty to place 'country' before party, and, if so, on what occasions? What should Labour's economic policy be, deflation and 'sound finance', under-consumptionist theories, or Keynesian counter-cyclical ideas? Should socialism replace capitalism gradually, or should capitalism be overthrown with speed? Finally, within the party, who was to hold ultimate power, the Labour leadership or the wider Labour movement, and what should the role of the leadership be? To some extent, the party was ready to address these issues, but it was able also, because of the nature of the government's demise, to resort to the easier option of convenient scapegoat and conspiracy theories.

The period of late August to October 1931 can best be viewed as a struggle for control within the Labour movement.[22] For much of the party, the initial reaction to the formation of the National Government was one of tremendous shock and bewilderment, to be followed swiftly by a desire for a set of arguments sufficiently coherent for them both to be able to explain the crisis and to oppose on firm foundations the formation of the new government. For the ex-Cabinet ministers, the situation was a highly uncomfortable one. Having endorsed most of the cuts which the National Government intended to implement, it was difficult for them to provide the rousing opposition needed to maintain the unity of the movement. Essentially, there were only two sections of the movement with the potential to provide such a lead. The first was the party's 'left' or radical wing, which interpreted the crisis in 'pure socialist' terms by suggesting that it was manufactured by financial interests to institute cuts, and proposed that the National Government was the inevitable outcome of two years of compromise by the Labour government. The second was the TUC, which had not only played a prominent role in the government's demise, but also had an apparently coherent alternative economic policy. Stepping into the vacuum created by the crisis, it was the TUC, rather than the 'left', which was initially to provide the firm lead needed to prevent further splintering of the movement.

Trade unions

The objectives of the GC in the wake of the crisis were twofold. Organisationally, it wished to see greater union input into the executive bodies of the Labour Party, both in order that the TUC could secure greater control of policy, and also so that a future Labour government would have no option but to consult the unions on legislation. In policy terms, the GC had both long-term and short-term objectives. In the short term, it wanted the party to adopt a position of firm opposition to the cuts and to support the TUC's own remedies for the country's financial problems. In the long term, it wished to commit the party to union policies on industry and nationalisation and to the quasi-corporatist role for trade unions which the GC had been formulating since the late 1920s.

The reactions of nearly all unions to the formation of the National Government concurred with those of the GC. They too feared that the cut in unemployment benefit would be the beginning of a general wage-cutting policy.[23] The only two unions that professed any sympathy for MacDonald were the cotton workers and the Railway Clerks' Association. The *Cotton Factory Times* declared on 28 August that 'nobody [would] question' the 'sterling purpose, high courage and patriotism' of MacDonald, Snowden and Thomas, and the *Railway Service Journal* declared in October that the ex-Labour leaders had 'acted bravely and sincerely; if wrongly'.[24] The majority of trade unionists agreed with the GC that they had been betrayed by the Labour leadership and rallied behind the opposition to the government provided by the two leading figures in the TUC, Bevin and Citrine.[25]

At a very heated joint meeting of the NEC, GC and the CC on 26 August, the GC pushed for the party to come out firmly against the National Government, and, after a great deal of bitterness had been expressed, it was agreed unanimously that it should do so.[26] The meeting appointed a committee to draw up a manifesto for the following day, whose composition was dominated by the GC's economic committee of ten. On 27 August the joint meeting approved this manifesto, which condemned the new government as no more than a smokescreen for financial interests to reduce social expenditure, denied that the crisis was as serious as the government suggested and put forward the TUC's alternative economic package for dealing with the budget deficit.[27]

This high degree of TUC supervision had lessened by the time of the October election as the Labour leadership began to reassert its authority. Aware that Labour would be defeated, and concerned not to damage further Labour's electoral prospects by provoking greater disunity, the GC decided to bide its time before attempting to secure a permanent redistribution of power.[28] Following the election defeat, the GC acted swiftly. At a joint meeting with the NEC on 10 November Citrine stated that MacDonald, Snowden and Thomas must never return to the party and proposed that the gulf that had developed between the TUC and the second Labour government should never be allowed to repeat itself. Since it had been the unions which had created the Labour Party in the first place, Citrine argued, the TUC was entitled to be involved fully in the party's policy formulation.[29] The means which the GC chose to increase its executive powers was the very committee which had functioned so ineffectively during the lifetime of the Labour government, the National Joint Council. On 27 January 1932 the PLP endorsed a memorandum drawn up by the GC which proposed that the NJC should meet once a month and secure the greatest possible degree of co-ordination between the GC, the NEC and the PLP Executive.[30] Unlike the last time such a proposal was tabled by the TUC, the Labour leadership was not in a sufficiently strong position to ignore it and the NJC (renamed the National Council of Labour in 1934) became the avenue through which union supervision of Labour decision-making was ensured for the next decade. By using the 1931 crisis and the election defeat to their own advantage, Bevin and Citrine had at least partially converted their vision for the future role of trade unionism into reality. Union power over policy had been increased, but it would take a crisis of a very different sort, in 1939, to enable them to fulfil their corporatist ambitions.

The Parliamentary Labour Party

The immediate reaction of the PLP to the formation of the National Government was one of astonishment. With the end of a very disappointing parliamentary session, many had looked forward to a long and welcome break from politics. Although the CC had been consulted on 20 August,[31] the majority of MPs were away from Westminster when the crisis broke. Some were forced to return from holiday and to attempt to come rapidly to terms with what had happened.[32] As has been noted, the financial understanding of the bulk of the PLP was limited and many no doubt felt the same way as Arthur Ponsonby, who confessed on 27 August that the crisis 'remain[s] rather inexplicable to most of us'.[33]

The extent of latent support amongst back-benchers for MacDonald, Snowden and Thomas is difficult to gauge. It was certainly far more widespread in the initial aftermath of the crisis than many Labourites later claimed. Whilst nearly all Labour MPs reacted instinctively against the proposed cuts, the claim that the situation constituted a grave national emergency would have played on the consciences of many, and few would not have thought very hard about abandoning three figures who had done so much to establish Labour as a party of government. The majority had accepted the reasoning of MacDonald and Snowden that the budget had to be balanced, and it would seem likely that if MacDonald had made a more concerted appeal to the PLP, rather than the detached and ambivalent attempts he did make, up to as many as half of the parliamentary party might have pledged him their support.[34] Dalton's total disregard for MacDonald following the Prime Minister's meeting with the junior ministers on 24 August was certainly not universal,[35] and Morrison, Shaw, Bondfield and Wedgwood Benn all thought hard before deciding not to support the National Government.[36] As it was, opposition to MacDonald hardened in stages: first, following the acceptance of the TUC line on 28 August; secondly, after the reopening of Parliament on 8 September; and, finally, once it was known that he intended to fight an election. Ultimately, despite the initial sympathies and press speculation, only twelve MPs (of whom only five were back-benchers) went with MacDonald and

National Labour was never to be a serious organisational rival to the Labour Party.[37]

The PLP accepted the TUC's programme of 27 August for a number of reasons. Although Henderson and the leadership on 24 August had expressed their intention to make no statement at all on the National Government until Parliament reconvened,[38] they feared that if no coherent lead was given then sections of the PLP might come out in favour of MacDonald. Despite their reservations, and the awareness that they were laying themselves open to accusations of hypocrisy, the ex-ministers recognised that a stance of total opposition to the cuts and to the government offered the best means of reuniting the party. The TUC was making very threatening noises and Henderson was well aware that the party could not risk a serious split with its industrial wing. Not only could it ill afford to lose union support politically, but also, with the strong possibility of an election on the horizon, it was in desperate need of union money. For the bulk of the PLP, the TUC programme provided both a common enemy and a means of justifying their opposition to the cuts and to the new government. In so doing it served to bring together what had become a bitter and divided party; Leah Manning later noted that the PLP became 'more united than [it] had been for many months'.[39] Having endured a long period of impotence during the troubled days of the Labour government, the PLP found itself with what it saw as a black and white issue on which to fight and the defensive instincts of Labourism could now be invoked. At this stage many believed the National Government would not hold together for very long, and shared Dalton's belief that the PLP would be able to give the administration a 'hell of a time'.[40]

Divisions, however, could not be resolved simply by the adoption of a common programme. The chief problem was that the party leadership, and particularly Henderson, was out of step with the general mood. Henderson had accepted the leadership only with great reluctance and was not in agreement with either the tone or the policies of the 27 August manifesto. His overriding concern was to hold the movement together, but he wished also to moderate Labour's opposition and to leave the door open for MacDonald's return. He did not conclude from the crisis that any fundamental readjustment was needed to Labour's gradualist philosophy and he believed that everything in *Labour and the Nation* was still valid.[41] He accepted that the budget needed to be balanced and felt it was Labour's national duty to support the government in this objective. Yet the bulk of the PLP, including a number of ex-ministers, had been radicalised by the crisis. Morrison declared that 'Labour must come to the Left – the real socialist Left',[42] and even Clynes was prepared to consider the use of the Emergency Powers Act by a future Labour government to overcome opposition.[43] Lord Sankey, after attending the meeting of the PLP on 28 August, concluded that the party had 'gone mad' because it 'talk[ed] about the class war'.[44]

The gulf between Henderson and the bulk of the party became apparent immediately after the re-opening of Parliament on 8 September. His initial speech demonstrated that he was highly uncomfortable in opposing the government, that he held only minor criticisms of its policies and that he wished to restrain Labour opposition to it.[45] Matters became worse when, during the course of the initial debates on the government's programme, it became apparent to Labour back-benchers just how far all members of the previous Cabinet had gone in accepting the need for cuts. In a devastating attack on the ex-Cabinet members on 8 September, the now 'Independent' W. J. Brown suggested that the difference between the government's policy and the proposals accepted by the late Cabinet was minimal:

> The difference is that one will go ten-tenths of the way, and the other will go nine-tenths of the way ... The only difference is that those men carry the logic of their position to its conclusion, and that these men retreat ... behind the hope of electoral success.[46]

Brown's claims were substantiated on 10 September when Thomas revealed, to much consternation on the Labour benches, that the whole Cabinet had accepted provisionally a £56 million package of cuts.[47] Back-bench dissatisfaction with Henderson's conciliatory line came to a head when he failed to exploit the Gold Standard Bill on 21 September, in which a government formed to save the gold standard was forced to abandon it. Rejecting Henderson's advice that they should abstain, 112 Labour MPs opposed the Bill's second reading. Rumours had begun to abound that it was Henderson's intention to enter the government and he was subjected to a sustained attack at a PLP meeting on 22 September,[48] with the result that he came close to resigning at a meeting of the PLP Executive on the same afternoon.[49]

Contrary to what one might expect, however, the demise of the Labour government and the radicalisation of the PLP did not ease relations between the ILP and the party. The Maxtonites disliked the appointment of Henderson and refused to accept that those who had opposed the cut in unemployment benefit were heroic figures. Instead they believed that the whole Cabinet had been responsible for the crisis, and that all notions of gradualism had been shown to be bankrupt. Maxton believed that the whole capitalist system was on the point of breakdown and that the country was 'rapidly approaching a revolutionary situation'.[50] Outside of Labour, he believed, the ILP would be better placed to channel the perceived desire of the working classes for a more radical socialist party. It was this logic that was to lead to the disaffiliation of the ILP in July 1932, and its rapid decline as an influential force on the left thereafter.[51] The irony was that, whilst many in the PLP and the movement had moved closer to the position the Maxtonites had advocated before the fall of the government, the Maxtonites themselves moved even further 'left' and therefore did not exploit what could have been a highly favourable situation for them.

Despite the high level of internal tension, many MPs still believed the party could perform well in the October election.[52] Relations with the unions had improved and the October Labour Conference, despite many deep divisions over policy, had seen the movement in fighting mood.[53] Certainly no one predicted the enormity of the defeat, which reduced Labour to only forty-six MPs, resulted in the loss of the bulk of its former leaders and left the party unable to offer any effective parliamentary opposition.[54] The defeat completed the removal of the leaders of the parliamentary party of the 1920s. Bondfield, Clynes, Adamson, Johnston, Trevelyan, Wedgwood Benn, Graham, Passfield and Parmoor were never again to be the powerful figures that they had once been, and Henderson, out of Parliament, became no more than a nominal leader thereafter.[55] Many of the 287 MPs elected in 1929 were never to return to Parliament, although a minority were able to fight their way back later in the decade or in 1945. The change in the background of the parliamentary leadership was profound; whereas all of the 'Big Five' had been of humble working-class origin, those prominent in the party of the 1930s and 1940s tended to be middle- or even upper-class.[56] Although lessons would be learned from the years 1929–31, in particular the need for more harmonious leadership/PLP relations, not until 1945 would this wisdom be used by a future Labour government. The PLP for over a decade would be forced to endure even greater impotence than it had experienced during the second Labour government, and would have to wait until the post-Second World War period to exert any real influence on the policies adopted by the government of the day.

Local parties

The formation of the National Government created a 'bewildering situation' for local Labour parties.[57] Most parties tended to reduce their activities over the summer period and had therefore to arrange hasty emergency meetings. The initial reaction in most instances was one of shock, followed by a desire for information. To begin with, the only source of news available was the press and, in particular, the *Daily Herald*. Those parties with MPs were impatient to receive an account of the crisis from their national representative. Such requests, however, placed those MPs in a very difficult position, since they themselves were uncertain initially of what had happened and what the party's reaction to it should be. In consequence, those MPs who addressed their local parties in late August tended to be unsure of anything other than their instinctive opposition to cuts and their belief that Henderson should be supported.[58] Few were keen to discuss what the attitude of the party should be to MacDonald, Snowden and Thomas. Those MPs who spoke to their local parties in September tended to be less ambivalent and more outspoken in their condemnation of the National Government and its leaders.[59]

The reaction of the vast majority of local parties was one of instinctive opposition to expenditure cuts. Most passed resolutions within the first two weeks of the government's formation which condemned its creation and supported the stand of the ex-Cabinet ministers and the TUC. It can be proposed tentatively that those local parties who were union-dominated were the quickest to endorse the TUC's opposition, for example South Shields and Wansbeck.[60] Yet, as with the PLP, the latent support which existed initially for MacDonald was more substantial than admitted subsequently and has been underestimated even in recent historical studies of the 1931 crisis.[61] MacDonald believed he would attract considerable support from local parties,[62] and he had good reason for this belief. The degree to which he had been a figure of hero worship should not be forgotten; this had extended even to some local organisations naming their buildings after him.[63] Such a cult of personality could not be wiped out overnight. A number of local parties were visibly reluctant to condemn MacDonald, Snowden and Thomas, and were clearly saddened to lose them,[64] and others were slow to abandon parliamentary candidates who had pledged support for the National Government.[65] The example of Thomas and Derby DLP is the best demonstration of the proposition that if more MPs had supported the National Government then significant sections of Labour's local organisations would have gone with them.[66] Had Snowden made a strong personal appeal to Colne Valley DLP and MacDonald to Seaham Harbour, they too would have created similar splits in their local parties.[67]

The local dimension to the need of the national party to adopt a firm line in the wake of the crisis should not be underestimated. For the divisional parties themselves, many of whom were in serious financial difficulty and suffering from falling memberships, the prime concern was to hold their organisations together. They had little time to think deeply about the issues involved, and the TUC line of opposition to the government and to all cuts provided them, as well as the PLP, with the most obvious means of retaining party unity. To view the National Government as the enemy of organised Labour was the ideal means of invoking the defensive spirit of the movement and of papering over the internal cracks. Pervading all local party minutes is a definite desire to retain the facade that everything was business as usual. It was by holding on to their rituals and by identifying a common enemy that the local parties were able to steer their way through the crisis.[68]

Nevertheless, there was a widespread radicalisation of local parties in the aftermath of the crisis. A number passed resolutions calling for bolder socialist commitments,[69] although it is fair to say that the more established and the more union-dominated parties tended to be less radical, for example

Wansbeck, than the newer organisations, like Chichester.[70] In a sense, the latter could afford to be more radical since they had less to lose in terms of established organisation and support. The almost universal nature of this radicalisation was evident at the 1931 conference, where resolutions calling for 'socialism', nationalisation of coal, disarmament and public ownership of banking and credit were all passed with little or no local party opposition.[71] A number of local organisations expressed their dissatisfaction with Labour's lacklustre performances in the Commons in September and urged the leadership to adopt a more combative approach.[72]

By the time of the preparations for the election, many parties were in severe difficulties, through lack of money, problems of finding a suitable candidate and apathy or confusion amongst activists.[73] Yet, despite these problems, many party workers remained optimistic and were totally unprepared for the crushing defeat that followed. Some were unable to comprehend what had happened. Doncaster DLP was perhaps the most extreme case, since the Labour candidate had not even had an opponent until two weeks before the election.[74] After having secured the breakthrough of 1929, many local parties had believed that Labour would never again lose these seats. The repercussions of the result were felt in many constituencies for the next decade and beyond. Many parties did not come even close to regaining their 1929 positions of strength in both national and municipal terms until 1945. This was the case in Birmingham, York, Salford and Peterborough, to name only a few. Others, like Stockport, had to wait even longer. Some local organisations, generally those with sizeable memberships and those in heavily industrial areas, were able to recover more quickly, for example Woolwich, Sheffield and Colne Valley. What was remarkable was that, as a result of the continuing commitment of a hardened band of activists, the majority of local organisations were able to ride out the storm and to embark on the long task of rebuilding.

The effect of the crisis and election defeat upon the position of local parties within the national movement was to reduce further their already limited power. As a result of financial problems, the decline in individual membership, and the withdrawal of many wealthy patrons, the divisional parties were forced to rely to an even greater degree on union money. The defection of the ILP increased further this union hold on local organisations, and the greater dominance of the unions at national conference resulted in considerable frustration within some local parties. In 1933 a movement was launched which called for a national 'Association of Constituency Labour Parties' to increase collective local party influence, and in 1937 the local parties achieved a major success when it was agreed that their number of nominees to the NEC should be increased from five to seven and that they alone would elect them.[75]

As with the rest of the movement, for the local parties the 1931 crisis represented a sharp break between the Labour Party of the 1920s and the one that emerged in the 1930s. The 1920s had witnessed a rapid growth in party organisation and a sizeable increase in membership which was never to be repeated. The almost overnight success in many constituencies was now to be replaced by a long, hard struggle for seats at both a municipal and national level. It might be said that 'an age of innocence' had passed. The consequence was a local organisation more ready to question its local and national leadership and less idealistic in its world-view. The 1930s was to be a barren period for most local parties and they would not come close to reaping the rewards for their continuing endeavours until the landslide of 1945.

Intellectuals

The demise of the second Labour government had a profound effect on the political thought of Labour's intellectuals, leading them all to question the assumptions on which the party's and their own ideologies had been founded. The Webbs concluded that the political philosophy of gradualism had been largely discredited. Whilst they continued to believe that Labour was the best vehicle for socialism, and Sidney wrote what was to become the classic Labour conspiracy theory of the formation of the National Government,[76] their previous belief that socialism could be implemented through piecemeal parliamentary methods was very badly shaken and, in desperation, they looked overseas for a new creed in which they might place their faith. Fearful that parliamentary government was breaking down all over Europe, they became convinced that the USSR offered the only hope for the preservation of European civilisation. Brushing aside the brutality of the Soviet regime, they came to see Soviet Communism as the living model of the well-ordered socialist system in which they had long believed.[77] Their contribution to the re-examination of Labour's socialism in the aftermath of 1931 was therefore minimal; rather than confront the fundamental questions that the failure of the government had raised, the Webbs sought a replacement ideological faith.

The failure of the government created a crisis of equal magnitude in the thought of R. H. Tawney. Unlike Sidney Webb, Tawney did not resort to conspiracy theories, and actively sought to debunk them. In a powerful article written in early 1932, 'The Choice Before the Labour Party',[78] Tawney proposed instead that Labour was 'the author ... of its government's own misfortunes',[79] and that the administration's failure had been due to flaws in both its ideology and its strategy throughout the 1920s. He suggested that Labour's programmes had offered too many things to too many people and that the leadership had been guilty of both a lack of courage and a lack of conviction when in office. Since Tawney had himself been heavily involved in Labour's policy formulation of the 1920s, this was a brave attempt at critical self-examination. Yet, despite his penetrating critique, he was once more better at pointing out what was wrong than at proposing an alternative. He drew on his long-standing belief that Labour needed a quasi-religious 'creed' or 'a common end' to suggest that the party should become a band of hardened socialists, even if this alienated many of its previous supporters.

Significantly, the 1931 crisis had a radicalising short-term effect even on Tawney, the man often held to be the founding father of British social democracy. In concluding the article, he proposed that a majority Labour government should not hesitate to pass an Emergency Powers Act if this was needed to overcome hostile capitalist opposition. In the long term, however, Tawney was uncomfortable in the more militant mood of the 1930s, and, holding on to his ethical socialist beliefs, he largely withdrew from politics.[80] The failure of the second Labour government therefore brought with it the eclipse of Tawney's ethical socialism for over a decade.

For Harold Laski, the 1931 crisis was the catalyst for his swing to the left, both in ideological and in factional terms. His explanation of the crisis drew on his long-standing intellectual doubts that socialism could ever be implemented in a constitutional fashion. In an article in late 1931, he interpreted the crisis as a deliberate plot on the behalf of financial interests and concluded that 'finance capital' would always subvert the parliamentary process when it felt itself under threat, with the implication that socialism could be achieved only through revolutionary means.[81] Although he condemned MacDonald, Laski saw the events of August not in terms of personalities but in terms of a crisis in the British constitutional system. In February 1932 his pamphlet 'The Crisis and the Constitution: 1931 and After' argued that not only financial interests but also the Crown had acted unconstitutionally, and he urged Labour to recognise the need to introduce emergency powers immediately it was returned to office and to confront socialism's opponents head-on.[82] Whilst he was heavily involved in the 1931 election and wrote the party manifesto, Laski feared that Britain's parliamentary system was on the verge of collapse.[83] The dichotomy in Laski's thought from the late 1920s, between his deep-seated faith in liberal democracy and his intellectual assessment that socialism might be conceivable only after a period of revolutionary upheaval, now came to the forefront. The result was that throughout the 1930s, and, indeed, for the rest of his life, Laski attempted in his writings to reconcile Marxist socialism and libertarianism, to find a middle way between the political systems of the USSR and the USA. Throughout the 1930s, he was involved at the very heart of Labour politics (from 1937 on the NEC) and the intellectual tug-of-war in which he engaged was deeply reflective of the dilemma which the whole Labour left experienced in that decade.[84]

The events of August were less traumatic an experience for G. D. H. Cole than they were for most of the movement. He believed that the policy vacuum that had been created by the crisis presented Labour with the perfect opportunity to reject the flawed policy of 'MacDonaldism' and to 'stand, as it ha[d] never in effect stood before, for socialism as an immediate political objective'.[85] He rejected notions of leadership betrayal and of 'bankers' ramps', and argued that the crisis was a direct result of gradualism's inability to deal with a capitalist system in crisis. The only logical conclusion within the restraints of that philosophy in August 1931 had been for MacDonald and Snowden to argue that Labour had to submit to capitalist demands in the short term in order to resume its strategy of concessions when stability was restored. Although the bulk of the movement had instinctively resisted this line, they had no coherent alternative socialist analysis to put in its place.[86] It was Cole's intention after the October election defeat to provide the movement with such a strategy. Unlike Laski, Cole did not believe that revolution was a serious possibility,[87] but proposed instead a policy of what he called 'sensible extremism'.[88] He reiterated the need for a future Labour government to prioritise the control of finance in order that it could manage the economy.[89] As it had done for all the other Labour intellectuals, the experience of the crisis severely strained Cole's democratic commitment, for he also accepted the need for the next Labour government to introduce emergency legislation if need be.[90]

The 1931 crisis and the election defeat created initially a very favourable climate for the activities of the SSIP and NFRB. They not only attracted a number of new figures of importance to their ranks,[91] but also formed close ties with the new Labour leader in the House, George Lansbury. Yet, whilst Cole succeeded in convincing the parliamentary leadership of the validity of his programme, and witnessed some notable successes at the 1932 party conference,[92] he was blocked by the more moderate NEC and TUC. Nevertheless, whilst the SSIP was transformed into the Socialist League in 1932, and, against Cole's wishes, adopted an increasingly confrontational strategy, the NFRB was invited to co-operate with the NEC policy committee in November 1933 and thereafter made a number of important contributions to Labour programmes, particularly in the field of economics.[93] Of all of the Labour intellectuals, therefore, it was Cole who provided the most significant ideological contribution to the party's policy reassessment in the wake of the 1931 crisis. His emphasis on the need for detailed plans of action was of great importance in the emergence of the well-researched policy documents produced in the next decade, which were to form the basis of the legislative programme of the Attlee governments. Equally, his contribution to Labour's economic understanding was crucial. He was of major importance in adapting the fruits of Keynes's unorthodox work to socialist ends and also in fostering the ideas of corporatism within the movement.

The initial result of the 1931 crisis was to create a situation which was more favourable to the contributions of Labour's intellectuals. It was recognised both by the leadership and by the wider party that greater emphasis should be placed on ideas, and the leadership of Lansbury and then Attlee was more welcoming to the intellectuals than that of MacDonald had been. New emphasis was placed upon the need for more detailed policy statements and Labour's intellectuals, including a number of younger figures like Hugh Gaitskell, Douglas Jay and Evan Durbin, were involved in their creation. Both Laski and Cole to some extent thrived in the more radical atmosphere after 1931 and were both engaged with the movement's radical wing in trying to keep the movement left throughout the 1930s and the 1940s. The Webbs and Tawney were more marginal figures in the 1930s, but their equally distinctive contributions to Labour's ideology thereafter should not be underestimated. The nationalisation strategy of the 1945 government owed much to Webbian collectivist notions and the welfare measures pursued in the same period drew at least some of their inspiration from Tawney. In terms of their collective position within the Labour movement, however, little had changed. Whilst they benefited from the amendments to the local party representation on the NEC in 1937, of which Laski made the greatest use, intellectuals in the party essentially remained dependent on the patronage of the Labour leadership. When the party came into office in 1945, the desire of the parliamentary leadership to limit policy discussions was to be strikingly similar to the attitude of the leaders of the party in the late 1920s.

NOTES

1 It is not my intention here to enter into a detailed account of the 1931 crisis; these events are well covered in A. Thorpe, *The British General Election of 1931* (Oxford, 1991) and in P. Williamson, *National Crisis and National Government: British Politics, the Economy and Empire, 1926–1932* (Cambridge, 1992).

2 Thorpe, *General Election 1931*, pp. 68–71.

3 Henderson, for example, following a meeting with the CC on 20 August, believed that the PLP could be talked around to the majority of the cuts; Public Record Office (hereafter PRO), Cabinet Conclusions, CAB 23/67/42(31), 20 August 1931.

4 Modern Records Centre, University of Warwick (hereafter MRC), MSS 78/ASW/4/1/11, ASW Journal, Address, September 1931 (written in August).

5 MRC, TUC, MSS 292/420/5, 'Financial Crisis 1931, Correspondence with Trade Unions'.

6 MRC, TUC, MSS 292/420/2, Research Document on 'The Financial Situation', pp. 2–7.

7 R. Skidelsky, *Politicians and the Slump: The Labour Government of 1929–1931* (London, 1967), pp. 368–70.

8 PRO, Cabinet Conclusions, CAB 23/67/41(31) and /42(31), 19 and 20 August.

9 British Newspaper Library, Colindale (hereafter BNL), *Daily Herald*, 29 July to 20 August.

10 MRC, TUC, MSS 292/420/2, 'Committee on National Expenditure', 13 August 1931.

11 British Library of Political and Economic Science (hereafter BLPES), Dalton

Papers, Diary, 20 August 1931.

12 P. Snowden, *An Autobiography, Vol. 2: 1919–1934* (London, 1934), p. 940.

13 PRO, MacDonald Papers, Diary, 26 November 1930, is most revealing: 'Now TUC officials ... assume that with [a] Labour Government they must be consulted in and approve of every industrial policy. They are not going to have their way!'

14 Harvester Press, Microfilm, GC Minutes, Joint Meeting, 20 August 1931, p. 85f, 'They have not made any proposals for a reduction with regard to benefit'.

15 Harvester Press, Microfilm, GC Minutes, 21 August 1931, p. 85a.

16 Ibid., p. 85b. In contrast to the claims of A. Bullock and F. Williams that Bevin was the GC figure most committed to the tariff, it was Milne-Bailey who had first come up with the suggestion and he and Citrine were more outspoken in favour of the policy than Bevin, who urged caution; see BLPES, Citrine Papers, I/7/4, note on William's book on Bevin for review, p. 2. Congress was due to meet on 7 September, so it was not the GC's intention to put the discussion off for long. When Congress did finally meet, however, the tariff issue was not addressed.

17 Harvester Press, Microfilm, GC Minutes, 21 August 1931, p. 85c.

18 Ibid.

19 P. Williamson's suggestion in *National Crisis and National Government*, p. 316, that MacDonald on 21 August was determined to 'save sterling, the Labour government and the Labour Party' is misleading. MacDonald's top priority was to save the British currency by balancing the budget, and the welfare of the Labour Party ran a poor second to this. From the pages of his diary, it is clear by August that MacDonald had little respect for his colleagues and was exasperated by their inability to agree. Equally he was tired of the wrangles of the party political system. It was only in this context that he was prepared to accept the invitation of the King to head a National Government. His subsequent deep concern over what the party thought of him was not foremost in his mind at the time he made the decision.

20 Bodleian Library, Oxford, Sankey Papers, MSS Eng. Hist. e.285, Diary, 21 August 1931. Sankey had been on holiday with Henderson when the crisis broke. His suggestion, however, that Henderson was after the leadership was wide of the mark; see A. Thorpe, 'Arthur Henderson and the British Political Crisis of 1931', *Historical Journal* 31: 1 (1988), 117–39.

21 BLPES, Passfield Papers, B. Webb's Diary, 22 August 1931.

22 Thorpe, *General Election 1931*, p. 127.

23 MRC, TUC, MSS 292/420/5, correspondence on the crisis. For MFGB, see SWCA, A1, Minutes, Executive Committee, 27 August 1931. For NUGMW, SWML Journal, September 1931, Editorial. For NUR and its attitude to Thomas, see P. S. Bagwell, *The Railwaymen* (London, 1963), pp. 352–533. For TGWU, MRC, MSS 126/T&G/4/2/8, *The Record*, Editorial, and 'Message from Bevin', September 1931. For NASOHSPD, MRC, MSS 78/NASOHSPD/4/1/11, Journal, October 1931. For ASLEF, MRC, MSS 127/NU/5/2/94, *Locomotive*, October 1931.

24 BNL, *Cotton Factory Times*, Editorial, 28 August 1931, and *Railway Service Journal*, October 1931.

25 Bevin was more radicalised than Citrine, who, whilst he wished to impose the TUC's economic policy on the party, was concerned that Labour should not

move too far to the left. Bevin was greatly angered with MacDonald and became more militant in his socialism. The experience, however, greatly reinforced the belief of both men that in the final instance the workers could only truly rely on trade unionism.

26 See Labour Party Archive, National Museum of Labour History, Manchester (hereafter LPA), NEC Minutes, 26 August 1931, and BLPES, Dalton Papers, Diary, 26 August 1931. Dalton recorded that the GC was 'very irritating and full of suspicion', and it would seem likely that the TUC went as far as to threaten to sever its ties with the party unless it was given its own way.

27 This was in large part a reiteration of the GC's programme of the 20 August, with the significant additional proposal for the mobilisation of foreign investments, which probably came from Pethick-Lawrence. For a report on this joint meeting, see BLPES, Dalton Papers, Diary, 27 August 1931.

28 See Thorpe, *British General Election of 1931*, pp. 141–4.

29 LPA, NEC Minutes, Joint Meeting of the NEC and GC, 10 November 1931.

30 LPA, PLP Minutes, 27 January 1932.

31 LPA, PLP Minutes, 28 August 1931.

32 For example, Stockport TCLP, E.P. Microfilm (1980), Reel 2, 27 August 1931; A. E. Townend, MP, had been on holiday and told his party that he had no more knowledge of the crisis than they did.

33 Bodleian Library, Oxford, Ponsonby Papers, MS Eng. Hist. C672, draft letter to MacDonald, 27 August 1931.

34 D. Kirkwood believed had MacDonald attended the PLP meeting on 28 August he could have swung the PLP around to his line; quoted in R. T. McKenzie, *British Political Parties: The Distribution of Power Within the Conservative and Labour Parties* (London, 2nd edn, 1963), p. 384. MacDonald's attitude is difficult to determine. It would seem likely that he hoped as many as a third of the PLP would come with him of their own accord. He did not canvass seriously for their support through a combination of contempt for the party and because he did not wish to face up to the consequences of his actions for the Labour movement. He also undoubtedly displayed signs of a martyr complex. For a full discussion of his reasoning, see D. Marquand, *Ramsay MacDonald* (London, 1977), pp. 641–9.

35 See BLPES, Dalton Papers, Diary, 24 August 1931.

36 See Thorpe, *British General Election of 1931*, p. 130, and Williamson, *National Crisis*, p. 372. For potential support for MacDonald, see Bodleian Library, Oxford, Papers of R. D. Denman, uncatalogued, Box 5.

37 See PRO, MacDonald Papers for letters expressing sympathy. PRO 30/69/1314, Bondfield to MacDonald, 24 August; Cripps to MacDonald, 28 August, said he admired 'immensely the courage and conviction' of MacDonald; Parmoor to MacDonald, n.d., late August/early September. PRO 30/69/1315, J. Lawson, MP, told MacDonald he would always have his 'undying affection'; W. Leach, 31 August, accepted MacDonald had acted from high motives; as did G. MacDonald, 29 August; J. Milner and Pethick-Lawrence, 26 August; Ponsonby, 28 August; Tillett, 31 August; Wedgwood Benn, 30 August; and Ben Turner, 29 August.

38 BLPES, Passfield Papers, B. Webb's Diary, 24 August 1931.

39 L. Manning, *A Life for Education: An Autobiography* (London, 1970), p. 98.

40 BLPES, Dalton Papers, Diary, 27 August 1931. The joint manifesto was approved by the PLP on 28 August with only seven dissentients; LPA, PLP

Minutes, 28 August 1931.

41 Churchill College, Cambridge, Noel-Baker Papers, 2/3, Henderson's interview with *News Chronicle*, 2 October 1931.

42 *The Times*, 8 September 1931.

43 *House of Commons Debates* (hereafter, *HC Debs.*), Vol. 256, 11 September 1931, col. 436.

44 Bodleian Library, Oxford, Sankey's Diary, Ms Eng. Hist. e.285, 28 August 1931.

45 *HC Debs.*, Vol. 256, 8 September 1931, cols 25–40.

46 Ibid., 8 September 1931, col. 102.

47 Ibid., 10 September 1931, cols 483–7.

48 LPA, PLP Minutes, 22 September 1931.

49 See Thorpe, *General Election 1931*, pp. 146–7, and Williamson, *National Crisis*, pp. 429–30.

50 *HC Debs.*, Vol. 256, 8 September 1931, cols 50–5.

51 For Maxton's outlook, see W. Knox, *James Maxton* (Manchester, 1987), pp. 96–104. For the Maxtonite interpretation of the crisis, see BLPES, ILP Papers, 5, various pamphlets and leaflets, 1931.

52 Churchill College, Cambridge, Noel-Baker Papers, 3/62, Dalton to Noel-Baker, 4 September 1931, and E. Thurtle, *Times Winged Chariot: Memoirs and Comments* (London, 1945), p. 114.

53 Labour Party, *Annual Report 1931* (London, 1931).

54 Williamson, *National Crisis*, p. 456, and Thorpe, *General Election 1931*, pp. 179–80.

55 Williamson, *National Crisis*, p. 456.

56 D. E. McHenry, *The Labour Party in Transition, 1931–1938* (London, 1938), p. 144.

57 Cambridgeshire Record Office, Cambridgeshire TCDLP, 416/0.20, Annual Report of the Executive, 1931–32, p. 3.

58 Stockport TCLP, E.P. Microfilm (1980), Reel 2, A. E. Townend, MP, Full Delegate Meeting, 27 August 1931; Dyfed Archives, Carmarthen, Llanelli TLC, D/Pol/1/2, Dr J. H. Williams, MP, GM, 29 August 1931.

59 Working Class Movement Library, *Nelson Gazette*, report of Greenwood's speeches, 1 and 8 September 1931, and J. Walker, MP, and Newport DLP, SWCA, A5 General Council, 4 September 1931.

60 South Shields LPTC, E.P. Microfilm (1979), Reel 2, EC, 25 August 1931, and Northumberland Record Office, Wansbeck DLP, 527/A/2, Special EC, 5 September 1931.

61 Thorpe, *General Election 1931*, p. 88, suggests that 'it is clear that the wider Labour movement would not have accepted the economies even if the general council had'.

62 Marquand, *MacDonald*, pp. 654–5.

63 Gloucester TCLP, E.P. Microfilm, (1980), Reel 2.

64 Stockport TCLP, E.P. Microfilm (1980), Reel 2, Special Meeting, 4 September 1931.

65 Gloucester DLP, E.P. Microfilm (1980), General Council, 9 September 1931; Cambridgeshire Record Office, Cambridgeshire TCLP, 416/0.4, Special EC, 26 September 1931.

66 The Secretary of the party and a number of prominent local figures went with Thomas; Derby Local Studies Library, Derby DLP, DL 116, EC, 26 August to 3 October 1931, and GC, 6 September to 12 October 1931.

67 For MacDonald and Seaham, see Marquand, *MacDonald*, pp. 651–3.
68 See York Record Office, York Labour Party, ACC 196/4, delegate meeting, 9 September 1931, for the clearest articulation of this need. This meeting instructed the MP to oppose the National Government 'as only by such drastic methods and policy can the Labour Party hope to retain the confidence of the workers'.
69 Durham County Archives, Darlington DLP, D/X 922/3, GC, 30 September 1931; Greenwich Local History Library, Greenwich DLP, EC, 10 September 1931; SWCA, Newport DLP, 12 October 1931, when J. Walker announced that he would fight for 'socialism'.
70 West Sussex Record Office, Chichester DLP, LA/1CH/1/1/1, 11 October 1931, called for a future Labour government to pursue a policy of 'revolutionary legislation'.
71 Labour Party, *Annual Report 1931*, pp. 162–87.
72 West Yorkshire Archive Service, Sheepscar, Leeds City Labour Party, 4/7, GC, 16 September 1931.
73 Thorpe, *General Election 1931*, pp. 151, 181–2.
74 Doncaster Archives Department, A. D. Buchan, 'The Doncaster DLP, 1918–1939' (Lancashire Polytechnic, BA dissertation, 1988), p. 12.
75 McHenry, *The Labour Party in Transition*, pp. 86–8. See also B. Pimlott, *Labour and the Left in the 1930s* (London, 1977), pp. 111–40.
76 S. Webb, 'What Happened in 1931: A Record', *Political Quarterly* 3 (1932), 1–17.
77 *Soviet Communism: A New Civilisation?* (London, 1935), which followed a visit to the USSR in 1932. Significantly, when it was reissued in 1937, the question mark was dropped. For the Webbs' conversion to Soviet Communism, see L. Radice, *Beatrice and Sidney Webb* (London, 1984), pp. 291–309.
78 R. H. Tawney, 'The Choice Before the Labour Party', *Political Quarterly* 3 (1932), 323–45.
79 Ibid., p. 326.
80 He did draft the 1934 policy document, *For Socialism and Peace*, and participated to a limited extent in the SSIP and NFRB.
81 H. J. Laski, 'Some Implications of the Crisis', *Political Quarterly* 2 (1931), 466–9.
82 'The Crisis and the Constitution: 1931 and After', analysed in I. Kramnick and B. Sheerman, *Harold Laski: A Life on the Left* (London, 1993), pp. 298–300, and M. Newman, *Harold Laski: A Political Biography* (Basingstoke, 1993), pp. 144–6.
83 H. Laski, *Democracy in Crisis* (London, 1933). Laski was heavily involved in the activities of the SSIP and NFRB from late 1931 and later the Socialist League, and was nominated for one of the two Derby seats by head office, but not chosen by the Derby party, presumably for financial reasons; Derby Local Studies Library, Derby DLP, DL 116, Minutes of Special GC, 12 October 1931.
84 For a more detailed discussion, see Kramnick and Sheerman, *Harold Laski*, pp. 297–311, and Newman, *Harold Laski*, pp. 142–51.
85 'A socialist view', *The Economist*, 17 October 1931.
86 G. D. H. Cole, *The Intelligent Man's Guide Through World Chaos* (London, 1932), pp. 611–12.
87 'Some Essentials of Socialist Propaganda: A Tract for the Times', Fabian Tract no. 238 (London, 1932), pp. 4–5.

88 Ibid. p. 17.
89 Cole, *The Intelligent Man's Guide*, pp. 612–16.
90 Nuffield College, Oxford, Cole Papers, GDHC/D4/5, Memorandum, *c*.1932.
91 This included Tawney and Laski, Susan Lawrence, Tom Johnston, Arthur Greenwood, Emanuel Shinwell, C. T. Cramp (General Secretary of the NUR) and Ebby Edwards (the new President of the MFGB).
92 See Labour Party, *Annual Report 1932* (London, 1932). The most significant of these victories for the left was the resolution committing a future Labour government to the immediate nationalisation of the joint-stock banks.
93 For a more detailed discussion of Cole's significance in the post-1931 period, see N. Riddell, '"The Age of Cole"? G. D. H. Cole and the British Labour Movement, 1929–1933', *Historical Journal* 38: 4 (1995), 933–57.

Conclusion

Within the Labour movement of May 1929 expectations for the second Labour government had been almost universally high. The trade unions were generally united in the belief that the government would implement reforms to improve the lives of the working classes and lay the foundations for a better society. Local Labour parties were even more optimistic, believing that 'the inevitability of gradualness' had been proved correct and that the government would begin the forward march towards socialism. The PLP, particularly those MPs elected for the first time, was equally enthusiastic about the government's prospects. Finally, the party's intellectuals, although holding some reservations, believed that the government, despite the constraints imposed upon it by its minority position, would introduce significant change. From this perspective, then, the prospects in May 1929 looked bright, both in terms of the likelihood of the movement benefiting from the existence of the government and in terms of harmonious relations between movement and government. As has been shown, however, a closer examination reveals that there were substantial problems and tensions within the Labour movement of the late 1920s and also significant differences of aspiration. In consequence, the scope for tension when Labour took office, both between the different components of the movement and, most significantly, between movement and government, was considerable.

Labour's leading intellectuals, whose theoretical role was to provide the movement with the ideas, strategies and the policies needed to begin the transition to a socialist society, were under-utilised. Reliant largely upon the patronage of the Labour leadership, they found it difficult to gain its confidence, and to overcome the instinctive anti-intellectualism that pervaded much of the movement. This did not bode well for a government that would find itself desperately in need of new ideas. For the PLP, different interpretations continued to exist as to what its function should be and, in particular, the extent to which it should be free from outside control. The Labour leadership believed the PLP should be an autonomous entity, whereas others, including the party's radical wing, felt the PLP must be accountable to the movement outside. Such was the speed with which the PLP had grown in the 1920s that it was inevitable there would be considerable problems of party management under the next Labour government. Most potentially problematic was the Maxtonite ILP, whose outlook was already wholly at odds with that of the leadership. This was not a comforting reality for a government in a minority which placed a high premium on party unity.

Local parties in 1929, despite their expansion since 1918, continued to fail to live up to the ideals of the national leadership. Despite the repeated attempts to encourage standardisation, they continued to display a tremendous diversity in organisation. Attempts to create a broader membership base had produced disappointing results; local parties continued to be dominated overwhelmingly by affiliated members, which in most cases meant trade unionists. Equally, despite the significant contribution of the women's sections, Labour failed to utilise its potential level of female support and local parties were largely male-dominated. Although the union base offered considerable benefits, not least financially, it was a cause of resentment amongst many individual party members and was detrimental to the creation of a mass party with extensive roots outside the union movement. The resistance of unions to the pooling of funds meant that local parties in non-unionised areas, where it was most imperative that Labour should make a breakthrough, remained under-funded. One consequence was that, due to the pressure for expansion in the 1920s, many parties resorted to reliance on wealthy individuals, sometimes regardless of their unsuitability in political terms. Potential for religious tension also remained pronounced. By the end of the 1920s, then, local Labour parties were over-stretched and often brittle, not least financially, and not well-equipped to deal with a significant downturn in Labour's national fortunes.

Most potentially problematic for the second Labour government were the trade unions. The Labour leadership and the leading trade unionists held very differing notions of the nature of relations between a Labour government and the movement's industrial wing. Whilst it wished to retain its independence in the industrial sphere, the TUC expected that a Labour government would consult it on all areas of industrial policy and prioritise those reforms which it most cherished. This was in line with the developing corporatist ambitions of the leading figures on the General Council, articulated most powerfully by Bevin and Citrine, which envisaged a future in which the trade unions would be accepted by the state as a key interest group and brought regularly into national decision-making processes. Bevin and Citrine also already held the belief that the aspirations of trade unionism would best be served by a Labour Party under the general control of the TUC. This was totally at odds with the views of the Labour leadership, which was often uncomfortable with the union link and even doubted the right of the TUC to be consulted on industrial policy. In light of these opposing views, it was essential that there should be a high level of co-ordination between the political and industrial wings. Yet, as a result of the breakdown of joint departments in the mid-1920s, and the reluctance of the Labour leadership, with the exception of Henderson, to acknowledge this need, a serious deterioration in relations between the second Labour government and the TUC was highly probable from the moment Labour took office.

Predictably, the disappointments of the second MacDonald government exacerbated many of these long-standing tensions and difficulties and brought a number of them to a head. Despite their varying degrees of involvement, for all Labour intellectuals, the government was a serious disappointment. All were led to question the party's ideology, not least the 'inevitability of gradualness' and the extent to which socialism could be achieved by parliamentary avenues. Equally significantly, all became progressively less involved in government policy-making and thus, just at the point when it was most in need of new ideas, the party leadership had nowhere to turn, having done little to court these figures.

The PLP was damaged badly by the experiences of two years of limited achievement. The many new and enthusiastic Labour MPs of 1929 had become frustrated with the limitations of the parliamentary system and with their own impotence, particularly on the issue of unemployment. A diverse group, they failed to gain a strong collective identity and internal tensions grew, particularly as a result of the increasingly confrontational strategy of the Maxtonite ILP. Relations between the PLP and the government were poor from the beginning, as a result of both the failure of the consultative machinery to function effectively and, with the exception of Henderson, the lack of interest on behalf of the Labour leadership. Confidence in the leadership diminished, whilst suspicion of the government's intentions increased. Despite their growing frustration, however, and their occasional tendency not to vote with the government, the bulk of the party would not be attracted sufficiently to the few alternative strategies on offer, notably from Mosley and the Maxtonites, and descended instead into a state of inertia and bitterness. Yet, at the same time, concerns increased that the PLP was not being faithful to the wider movement, with the consequence that many Labour MPs would be open to the argument in August 1931 that the attitudes of the movement should be given at least equal weight to those of the parliamentary leadership.

For local parties, the difficulties created by the deficiencies of the Labour government were manifold. The Maxtonite ILP created serious tensions in many areas, the failed Education Bill led to an increase in religious sectarianism, and the activities of Mosley had serious consequences for those parties with Mosleyite MPs. More damagingly still, as a result both of the Depression and the disillusionment felt with government policies, from 1930 local parties experienced a general trend of declining support and finance, despite the attempts of the national party to paint it otherwise. By 1931 the dangers of the over-optimism of 1929 were becoming increasingly apparent and many parties were involved in what was essentially a struggle for survival.

Trade unions had derived far less benefit from the government than they had anticipated and were greatly disappointed by the failure to pass legislation, in particular the repeal of the Trade Disputes Act, the ratification of the Washington Hours Convention and the reform of the coal mines. Their disillusionment was exacerbated greatly by the disrespectful manner in which they felt the government had treated them. The government had repeatedly ignored TUC procedures for the appointment of trade unionists to committees, had showed little concern for joint committees and, most damagingly, had been unprepared to accept a need for regular consultation. In consequence, the justifications the government gave for the failure to implement reforms, often highly convincing ones, did not receive the credence that they merited from the GC. By 1931, relations were growing ever more distant, and distrust and bitterness increased on both sides. This breakdown in relations inevitably found expression in the area where the differences between government and union priorities was most pronounced: unemployment policy. As such, the battle lines of August 1931 were already being drawn long before the collapse of the government.

The movement influenced the government and played a significant role in the direction taken by it. Although generally unable to influence directly the decisions of the Labour Cabinet, the wider movement was usually able to define the parameters of government policy. The parliamentary leadership was acutely aware that it would have great difficulty in implementing any policy with which the movement was not in agreement, and that the TUC in particular would soon make this disapproval known to the government. There were a number of examples during the two-year period when the leadership was forced to go ahead with legislation, despite its own reservations, because it was aware that pressure for it in the movement was pronounced: most notably the Coal Bill, educational reform, the repeal of the Trades Disputes Act and the initial commitment to the ILO to ratify the Washington Hours Convention. Equally, it was rare for the leadership to proceed with policies it knew would provoke strong opposition. The appointment of Lord Hunsdon and the Anomalies Act were the most notable exceptions, both of which resulted in bitter confrontations between government and the wider movement. The realistic options available to the government to attempt to deal with the country's economic problems from 1930 were limited indeed, due not only to opposition from the City, the Treasury and the opposition parties, but also to the awareness that there was little it could do which would not upset some section of the Labour movement. Tariffs, increased trade with the Empire, reduced expenditure on armaments, cuts in social expenditure, wage reductions, and, above all, changes to the system of unemployment insurance were all guaranteed to cause consternation.

The wider movement also played a pivotal role in the events of August 1931. Despite their basic agreement with the conclusions of the Holman Gregory Report, MacDonald and Snowden were forced to refrain from implementing them principally because of trade union opposition, and the Chancellor devised a strategy whereby he hoped that the May Committee would overcome the movement's opposition for him. In the financial crisis which followed the publication of the May Report, it was awareness of the movement's opposition to any cut in unemployment benefit, voiced in no uncertain terms by the TUC, which was central to the final Cabinet split. Henderson and those who voted against the cut believed that the unity of the movement must be paramount. MacDonald and Snowden were all the more determined in the face of TUC opposition to push the cuts through in 'the national interest', but resolved that only by stepping outside of the parameters imposed by the Labour movement would this be politically possible. This pattern of events was shaped, then, not only by banking interests, the money markets, the Treasury, the opposition parties, the Labour Cabinet and the King: the Labour movement must also be added to this equation.

The events of the years 1929–31 suggest that the wider Labour movement exercised more power in the Labour Party of this period than has generally been acknowledged and that the commonly accepted thesis of R. T. McKenzie, that the parliamentary leadership was largely autonomous when Labour was in office, is misleading.[1] MacDonald did have considerable freedom of manoeuvre over the appointment of the Cabinet and the legislative timetable, but, as has been suggested, in terms of policy he was far more constrained than McKenzie suggests.[2] Furthermore, the events of August 1931 would suggest that ultimate power in the Labour Party of this period lay with the trade union movement, even when Labour was in office. Although unable to control directly the policy of the government, the TUC demonstrated it had sufficient power of veto to limit severely the leadership's freedom of manoeuvre. One of the grave weaknesses of MacDonald's party, demonstrated all too well when Labour was in office, was that the majority of its leaders tried to ignore this

reality. Determined to appear 'respectable' and not the puppets of trade unionism, MacDonald and Snowden were particularly culpable in this tendency.
The federal structure of the movement, and the continuing power of the unions in decision-making, was seen by many voters as detrimental to Labour's
capacity to be an effective party of government. Yet, rather than face the
reality of the movement's structure, and attempt either to change it, or to
accept it and manage it in the best way possible (by stressing the value of
unionism and ensuring that the government went through the motions of
regular consultation), MacDonald and most of his Cabinet attempted to pre-
tend that the PLP was an independent entity which owed no loyalty to sectional allegiances. Henderson was alone amongst the 'Big Five' in recognising
the problems of this approach, and his realisation in the midst of the 1931
crisis that the Cabinet must heed the opposition of the TUC was significant in
preventing a more seismic splintering of the movement than the one which
finally occurred. The great irony of the role of union power is that, whilst the
TUC was instrumental in the government's collapse and placed considerable
restraints on the party in the 1920s and particularly in the 1930s, it was
Labour's union base which ensured that the party held together in the aftermath of the 1931 crisis.

In light of the many tensions and inefficiencies outlined, it must be concluded
that the role of the leadership in the late 1920s was a vital one, both in its
contribution to the party's electoral advance and in holding the movement
together. Despite the uneasiness of their personal relations, the 'Big Five' of
MacDonald, Henderson, Snowden, Thomas and Clynes were all significant.
Clynes and Thomas were both important for their union credentials, with the
dependable, hard-working Clynes appealing to a different aspect of working-
class culture than the more flamboyant and reckless General Secretary of the
NUR.[3] Snowden represented traditional ILP values of sound finance and evangelical socialism. More important, however, were the colossal contributions of
Henderson and MacDonald. Henderson's party management skills were central to the effective co-ordination of the movement and his incapacity to fulfil
this role during the second Labour government had all too obvious detrimental results, not least for relations with the trade unions. The reliance of the
party machine upon one individual to such a degree was scarcely desirable for
a mass party of government.

The role of Labour's first real party leader was more significant still.
Ramsay MacDonald, 'the focus of the mute hopes of a whole class',[4] arguably
had a greater hold on the Labour movement than any leader before or since.[5]
The cult of personality that surrounded him and his ability to articulate the
aspirations of working-class audiences were central to Labour's rise. Despite
some reservations, not least amongst trade union leaders, the bulk of the

movement concurred with Henderson that MacDonald was by far the best man for the job in the late 1920s.[6] Yet, as with the very different role filled by Henderson, there was a major downside to such a dependence on one individual. Hero-worship resulted in the movement all too often evading recognition of its own limitations and the necessary task of considering the practicalities of policy. By turning socialism almost into a faith, MacDonald's evolutionary ideology convinced many that it was enough simply *to believe* for Labour's future to be guaranteed.

The assumptions of many Labour historians that the Labour leadership in the 1920s was not reflective of the militancy of the rank-and-file is not sustainable.[7] There were sections of the movement who wanted a more radical policy, most notably the Maxtonite ILP and those with communist sympathies, but the bulk of the movement endorsed MacDonald's gradualist ethical socialism in the 1920s. Whilst there was an almost universal wave of radicalisation in the wake of the 1931 crisis, despite their undoubted frustrations and disappointments, many of the party's supporters continued to believe in MacDonald right up to the time of the government's fall. The Labour movement did not consist solely of radical, free-thinking socialists as later generations of Labour historians would have us believe; for each of these there was a deferential, often conservative, working man or woman who wished to be led. This was what MacDonald picked up on so well in the 1920s and that is why his defection was far more devastating an experience for much of the movement than the majority were later prepared to confess.[8]

Ideological weaknesses played a central role in the failure of the government. Its ethical socialism, derived from Tawney and MacDonald's own concepts of 'organic' socialism, and flabby notions of 'the inevitability of gradualness', provided little guidance on the crucial question of how the transformation from capitalism to socialism would be achieved, not least at a time of economic depression. Essentially, Labour was committed to fair-weather socialism, for it had no notion of how to proceed with a capitalist system in crisis. Above all, as Cole in particular recognised only too well, Labour was very weak on its financial and economic understanding.

During the course of the government, coherent socialist alternatives came chiefly from three avenues, all requiring a strategy fundamentally different from the one to which the government was committed. The first, and the earliest, came from the Maxtonite ILP, whose under-consumptionist ideas had definite transitional implications. For the Maxtonites, the difficulties of the capitalist system were seen as an opportunity to argue the logic of the case for socialism, and Labour was urged to stand or fall by its socialist programme. This was a logical position to adopt, particularly the implication that as soon as Labour was involved in attempting to solve capitalism's problems, the party would be tainted and compromised by it. As the government's problems increased, there was growing sympathy for the Maxtonite position in the movement. Yet the often confused message the Maxtonites transmitted, together with their confrontational strategy, undermined their potential support. Most significantly, they were at odds with many of the power brokers in the movement, particularly the Labour leadership and the trade unions.

The two other alternatives advocated tinkering with capitalism to make it more economically efficient before the move to socialism. The first came from the Mosleyites, with their arguments for a combination of quasi-Keynesianism and protectionism. These were powerful ideas, and attracted considerable interest in 1930 across the Labour movement. Yet Mosley too failed to maximise his potential support, not least as a result of his impatience and inflated personal ambition. Leaving this aside, however, together with the debate over the feasibility of his economic diagnosis, perhaps the key point is that powerful opposition to Mosley's ideas came not only from the Treasury and the financial interests so often cited, but also from within the Labour movement. The Labour leadership, much of the PLP, many local party members and the majority of trade unionists were all instinctively opposed to Mosley's radical proposals. The final alternative came from Cole's NFRB and SSIP. These brought together a significant number of intellectuals, MPs and even leading trade unionists looking for a bolder policy, and seemed capable for a time of offering a radical strategy in a form more acceptable to the movement than that offered by Mosley or the Maxtonites. This arrived too late to influence the government, however, and was symbolic of the extent to which the leadership had distanced itself from socialist thinkers by that date.

It is apparent, then, that the politically realistic ideological options on offer from 1930 were decidedly limited. Undoubtedly, the unwillingness of the Labour leadership to adopt new strategies was central to the unadventurous path pursued and to the policy of drift, but it is misleading, as Skidelsky has done with Snowden,[9] to explain the government's conservatism largely in the context of the party leadership. These figures must be understood as representative of the movement which they led. The government's cautiousness was linked to its precarious minority position and to the major obstacles from outside the movement to the adoption of radical alternatives. More significantly, however, the government was trapped ideologically by the strategy pursued since 1918. In the first place, the continuing importance of Labourism raised a formidable barrier to the adoption of radical alternatives. An instinctively defensive and conservative philosophy, Labourism was suspicious not only of radical ideas but also of the notion of working with proponents of new ideas from outside of the movement.[10] Secondly, the determination of Labour's leadership in the 1920s to demonstrate that Labour accepted the conventions of the parliamentary system and was capable of governing responsibly made it exceedingly unlikely, and perhaps an impossibility, that this same leadership, in a minority government faced by an economic depression of grave proportions, would fly in the face of orthodox opinion and turn to untested radical alternatives.

The second Labour government was equally a victim of its vague policy formulations and poor long-term strategy. Labour's 1929 programme promised far too much to far too many: in Tawney's evocative metaphor, it was 'a glittering forest of Christmas trees, with presents for everyone'.[11] Even if Labour had come to power with a majority, it would still have been able to achieve only a fraction of what was proposed. Labour failed to plan the details of its proposals whilst in opposition, and in office relied on numerous committees of inquiry, which took a long time to report and invariably concluded that Labour's policies were not workable. Labour's industrial policy was little worked out; nationalisation was generally held to be the panacea for all industry's ills and, unable to implement socialisation from its minority status, the government relied heavily on the notion of rationalisation, a policy ill-suited to a time of depression. When in government, Labour did not plan ahead in any systematic way, in terms of avoiding conflicts where possible and predicting likely obstacles in its path. Partly, of course, this was due to the nature of the government's precarious existence, but a more sophisticated notion of how long the government wished to remain in office and what exactly it intended to achieve, rather than cling on as long as possible, would have been a more advisable strategy. All too often the government's handling of its parliamentary position and of its own supporters amounted to little more than 'crisis management'.

The conclusion which must be drawn is that the Labour movement of the late 1920s was not equipped to provide effective government, least of all in the context of the serious difficulties facing Britain from 1929. The collapse of MacDonald's second administration represented the failure not only of the government but also of 'a decade of Labour politics'.[12] Whilst external factors, particularly the onset of the world depression and the government's minority status, were important in its demise, as were the deficiencies of the party leadership, the administration's failure was due in large measure to the shortcomings of the party's structure, its policies, its strategy and its ideology. Arguably, the nature of Labour's electoral progress in the 1920s was too swift for the party's own good. Success at the ballot box did not encourage critical self-examination.[13] Whilst political, economic and social circumstances continued to change, and an expanding Labour movement brought with it a growing diversity of membership and aspiration, Labour in 1929 essentially remained wedded to a set of decisions taken in the very different surroundings of 1918.

Critical re-examination, exhibited briefly in the wake of the collapse of the first MacDonald government, only became extensive during the course of the second Labour government and, in particular, in the wake of the events of August 1931. A number of the faults and deficiencies outlined were resolved, or at least improved upon. The TUC used the opportunity provided by the crisis to tighten its means of direct influence upon Labour's policy formulation and through the NJC was able to ensure that co-ordination between the industrial and political wings of the party was greatly improved. Although this was far from the only reason, this development was significant in the generally harmonious relations between the unions and the Attlee govern-ments. These governments would also enjoy far better relations with their parliamentary parties than the MacDonald governments. Again, there were a number of reasons for this, but a contributory factor was the lessons Attlee and a number of his Cabinet colleagues had learnt from the failings of the CC between 1929 and 1931. Local parties would be less trusting of prospective parliamentary candidates and more questioning of their national leadership, and the second Labour government perhaps played some role in their push for greater input on the NEC. Whilst still dependent upon the patronage of the leadership, intellectuals would enjoy greater input into policy-making in the 1930s, particularly in the immediate aftermath of 1931.

The anomalous position of the ILP in the movement would finally be brought to an end in 1932 when the decision was taken to disaffiliate from Labour. Attitudes to the role of the party leadership also underwent a radical transformation as a result of 1929–31. In the 1930s, the movement exhibited a determination not to allow its leaders to accumulate the power enjoyed by MacDonald. In 1935, in Clement Attlee, the party would pick a leader who could not have been less like the ex-Labour leader. Equally, the pivotal organi-sational role of Henderson in the party of the 1920s would not be repeated in the party of the 1930s. Finally, in terms of ideas and strategies, important lessons would be learnt. Policy documents in the 1930s would display a more effective prioritisation, a much improved propensity to work out the details of policy and to plan ahead and, perhaps most significantly, they would demon-strate a vastly superior understanding of economics.

Portrayed in this light, then, the second Labour government could be seen as a beneficial learning experience en route to a greater political maturity. Such a view is, however, dangerously Whiggish; it is incorrect to view the government as an unfortunate, but temporary, setback on 'the road to 1945'. From the perspective of October 1931, matters look rather different. As the events of 1929–31 had demonstrated, there was nothing inevitable about Labour's continued progress or any guarantee that Labour would one day enjoy a parliamentary majority. The short-term consequences of the collapse of the government were disastrous for the movement and the longer-term re-examination produced changes for the worse as well as those for the better. First, the movement's fear of 'MacDonaldism' produced an exaggerated fear of powerful leaders. Attlee, the antithesis of MacDonald, for all the attributes he displayed after 1939, was a decidedly uninspiring leader of the opposition before the Second World War. Secondly, whilst the greater co-ordination of the political and industrial wings was desirable, in the 1930s the TUC was often to exert too great a hold on the Labour Party. Thirdly, there was much disagreement in the movement over the meaning of 1931, and the 1930s was far from being a decade of ideological consensus. Differences in approach between the party's 'right', 'centre' and 'left', now in the shape of the Socialist League, were as heated and divisive as ever they had been in the MacDonald party, arguably more so. Debate in itself was no bad thing; continued factional infighting, however, did not improve the party's electoral fortunes. Fourthly, in ideological terms, Labour after 1931 became committed to an even greater extent to statist socialism, and decentralised notions such as guild socialism and syndicalism, with their emphasis upon the creation of socialism from the grass roots, were no longer advocated as serious alternatives. Although there were a number of reasons for this, the nature of the second Labour government's demise played a significant part. Finally, too much comfort was sought in scapegoat and conspiracy theories. Many Labourites would continue to believe that it was the treachery of MacDonald, Snowden and Thomas which had brought about the government's ruination, and this notion, in alliance with the myth that the first Labour government had been 'destroyed by a Red Letter' and 'the second by a Bankers' Order',[14] was all too convenient a means for many in the party to fail to confront the serious issues which the failure of the government had raised.

The failure of the second Labour government was an enormous blow to the political left in Britain. Equally, it was symbolic of the defeat of democratic socialism across Europe in the next decade. With the defeat of the second Labour government, international socialism had lost its 'Battle of the Marne'.[15] For the Labour Party the price was nearly a decade of frustrating opposition. As has been suggested, however, for all of its attempts to look for others to blame, in truth the Labour movement was itself chiefly responsible for this series of events.

NOTES

1 McKenzie's thesis is very much a product of the political environment of the post-1945 period, when two-party politics and a large PLP were the norm. British politics of the 1920s were more fluid than this.

2 R. T. McKenzie, *British Political Parties: The Distribution of Power Within the Conservative and Labour Parties* (London, 2nd edn, 1963), pp. 412–567.

3 For the appeal of Thomas, see A. Thorpe, 'J. H. Thomas and the Rise of Labour in Derby, 1880–1945', *Midland History* 40 (1990), 111–28.

4 E. Wertheimer, *Portrait of the Labour Party* (London, 1929), pp. 176–7.
5 Writing in 1998, a case could certainly be made that MacDonald has a challenger for this title in the shape of the current Labour Prime Minister.
6 British Library of Political and Economic Science (hereafter BLPES), Passfield Papers, B. Webb's Diary, 2 December 1929; Henderson told the Webbs that MacDonald was 'absolutely irreplaceable'.
7 For example, M. Foot, *Aneurin Bevan: A Biography, Vol. 1: 1897–1945* (London, 1962) and R. Miliband, *Parliamentary Socialism: A Study in the Politics of Labour* (London, 1961).
8 H. M. Drucker, *Doctrine and Ethos in the Labour Party*, (London, 1979) underlines the importance of comprehending Labour's 'ethos' as well as its doctrine.
9 R. Skidelsky, *Politicians and the Slump: The Labour Government of 1929–1931* (London, 2nd edn, 1994), pp. 68–70, 287–9.
10 D. Marquand, *The Progressive Dilemma* (London, 1991).
11 R. H. Tawney, 'The Choice Before the Labour Party', *Political Quarterly* 3 (1932), 329.
12 Ibid., p. 326.
13 Ibid., p. 327.
14 BLPES, Dalton Papers, Diary, 28 August 1931.
15 Wertheimer, *Portrait of the Labour Party*, pp. 211–12.

APPENDIX 1

The Labour Cabinet and Junior Ministers

	Minister	Date of appointment	Junior ministers	Date of appointment
IN THE CABINET				
Prime Minister	J. R. MacDonald	5.6.29		
Lord President	Lord Parmoor	7.6.29		
Lord Chancellor	Lord Sankey	7.6.29		
Lord Privy Seal	J. H. Thomas	7.6.29		
	V. Hartshorn	5.6.30		
	T. Johnston	24.3.31		
Chancellor of the Exchequer	P. Snowden	7.6.29	F. Pethick-Lawrence	11.6.29
			T. Kennedy	14.6.29
			Junior Lords of the Treasury	
			C. Edwards	11.6.29
			W. Whitely	27.6.29
			W. Paling	27.6.29
			J. Parkinson	11.6.29
			A. Barnes	11.6.29
			E. Thurtle	23.10.30
			H. Charleton	13.3.31
Foreign Secretary	A. Henderson	7.6.29	H. Dalton	11.6.29
Home Secretary	J. R. Clynes	7.6.29	A. Short	11.6.29
First Lord of the Admiralty	A. V. Alexander	7.6.29	C. Ammon	11.6.29
			G. Hall	11.6.29
Minister for Agriculture and Fisheries	N. Buxton	7.6.29	C. Addison	11.6.29
	C. Addison	5.6.30	Earl De La Warr	5.6.30
Minister for Air	Lord Thomson	7.6.29	F. Montague	11.6.29
	Lord Amulree	14.10.30		
Secretary of State for Colonies	Lord Passfield	7.6.29	W. Lunn	11.6.29
			D. Shiels	1.12.29

233

	Minister	Date of appointment	Junior ministers	Date of appointment
Secretary of State for Dominions	Lord Passfield J. H. Thomas	7.6.29 5.6.30	M. Jones	11.6.29
President of the Board of Education	Sir C. Trevelyan H. Lees-Smith	7.6.29 2.3.31		
Minister of Health *Secretary of State for India*	A. Greenwood W. Wedgwood Benn	7.6.29 7.6.29	S. Lawrence D. Shiels Earl Russell Lord Snell	11.6.29 11.6.29 1.12.29 13.3.31
Minister of Labour	M. Bondfield	7.6.29	J. Lawson	11.6.29
Secretary of State for Scotland	W. Adamson	7.6.29	T. Johnston J. Westwood	7.6.29 25.3.31
President of the Board of Trade	W. Graham	7.6.29	W. Smith *Overseas Trade Dept* G. Gillett *Mines Dept* B. Turner E. Shinwell	11.6.29 7.7.29 11.6.29 5.6.30
Minister of Transport	H. Morrison	19.3.31	Earl Russell Lord Ponsonby J. Parkinson	11.6.29 1.12.29 1.3.31
Minister of War	T. Shaw	7.6.29	Earl De La Warr Lord Marley E. Shinwell W. Sanders	11.6.29 5.6.30 11.6.29 5.6.30
First Commissioner of Works	G. Lansbury	7.6.29		

NOT IN THE CABINET

Chancellor of the Duchy of Lancaster	Sir O. Mosley C. Attlee Lord Ponsonby	7.6.29 23.5.30 13.3.31		
Paymaster-General	Lord Arnold	7.6.29		
Minister of Pensions	F. Roberts	7.6.29	(post vacant)	
Postmaster-General	H. Lees-Smith C. Attlee	7.6.29 2.3.31	S. Viant	7.7.29
Minister of Transport	H. Morrison (in Cabinet March 1931)	7.6.29	See above	

Appendix 1

	Minister	Date of appointment	Junior ministers	Date of appointment
LAW OFFICERS				
Attorney-General	Sir W. Jowitt	7.6.29		
Solicitor-General	Sir J. Melville	7.6.29		
	Sir S. Cripps	22.10.30		
Lord Advocate	C. Aitchison	17.6.29		
Solicitor-General for Scotland	J. Watson	17.6.29		

Source: R. Skidelsky, *Politicians and the Slump: The Labour Government of 1929–1931* (London, 1967), Appendix I.

APPENDIX 2

Trade union sponsored Members of Parliament, 1929

Name of trade union	Number of MPs	Government members[a]
Miners' Federation of Great Britain	41	W. ADAMSON W. Lunn J. J. Lawson G. H. Hall J. A. Parkinson C. Edwards
Railwaymen, National Union of	8	J. H. THOMAS
Railway Clerks' Association	7	
Transport and General Workers' Union	7	
Workers' Union	6	
Woodworkers, Amalgamated Society of	6	
General and Municipal Workers, National Union of	6	J. R. CLYNES M. BONDFIELD
Iron and Steel Trades Confederation	4	
United Textile Factory Workers' Association	4	T. SHAW
Distributive and Allied Workers, National Union of	4	
Engineering Union, Amalgamated	3	
Boilermakers' and Iron and Steel Shipbuilders' Society	2	A. Short
London Society of Compositors	2	
Boot and Shoe Operatives, National Union of	2	W. R. Smith
Scottish Mine Workers' Association	1	
Locomotive Engineers and Firemen, Associated Society of	1	
Foundry Workers, National Union of	1	A. HENDERSON
Patternmakers' Association, United	1	
Vehicle Builders, National Union of	1	
Chain Makers' and Strikers' Association	1	
Printers and Assistants, National Society of Operative	1	
Typographical Association	1	F. O. Roberts
Textile Workers, National Union of	1	B. Turner

Name of trade union	Number of MPs	Government members[a]
Dyers, Bleachers, Finishers and Kindred Trades, Amalgamated Society of	1	
Pottery Workers, National Society of	1	
Shop Assistants, Warehousemen and Clerks, National Amalgamated Union of	1	
Prudential Staff Union	1	

Note: [a] CAPITAL letters signify member of the Cabinet.

Source: Taken in part from Modern Records Centre, Warwick University, TUC Papers, MSS 292/750.1/10, Research Document, 'Representation of Trade Unions in Parliament'.

APPENDIX 3

Unemployment figures, 1930 and 1931

Date	Unemployed[a]	% Change from previous month	Number in work[b]	% Unemployed
1930				
January	1,491,519		10,076,000	12.9
February	1,539,265	+3.1	10,029,000	13.3
March	1,638,799	+6.1	9,993,000	14.1
April	1,698,386	+3.6	9,922,000	14.6
May	1,770,051	+4.0	9,857,000	15.2
June	1,815,342	+2.5	9,861,000	15.5
July	1,972,730	+8.0	9,746,000	16.8
August	2,039,702	+3.3	9,734,000	17.3
September	2,109,658	+3.3	9,691,000	17.9
October	2,237,501	+5.7	9,593,000	18.9
November	2,286,460	+2.1	9,576,000	19.3
December	2,408,371	+5.1	9,487,000	20.2
1931				
January	2,592,650	+7.2	9,227,000	21.9
February	2,617,658	+1.0	9,338,000	21.9
March	2,580,118	−1.5	9,395,000	21.5
April	2,520,113	−2.4	9,494,000	21.0
May	2,506,937	−0.5	9,528,000	20.8
June	2,627,386	+5.6	9,438,000	21.8
July	2,713,350	+3.2	9,345,000	22.5
August	2,733,782	+0.7	9,377,000	22.6
September	2,811,615	+2.8	9,338,000	23.1
October	2,726,092	−3.1	9,448,000	22.4
November	2,615,115	−4.2	9,552,000	21.5
December	2,509,921	−4.2	9,605,000	20.7

Notes: [a] On employment exchange registers.
  [b] Estimated number of insured persons.

Source: PRO, MacDonald Papers, PRO 30/69/580, Ministry of Labour document.

APPENDIX 4

Individual local Labour Party membership affiliated to the national party, 1929–1931

County	Local party	1929	1930[a]	% Change 1929–30	1931	% Change 1930–31
Bedfordshire	Bedford	180	410	+128	266	−35
	Mid-Bedford	100	465	+365	450	−3
	Luton	81	240	+196	240	0
Berkshire	Reading	2500	2654	+6	2800	+6
	Abingdon	300	350	+17	243	−31
	Newbury	310	240	−23	240	0
	Windsor		240		240	0
Buckinghamshire	Aylesbury	677	726	+7	740	+2
	Buckingham	974	2500	+157	1000	−60
	Wycombe	344	315	−8	341	+8
Cambridgeshire	Cambridge	780	570	−27	677	+19
	Cambridgeshire	1091	1400	+28	1559	+11
Cheshire	Birkenhead	375				
	Birkenhead, E.		240			
	Birkenhead, W.		240			
	Stockport	840	240	−71	939	+291
	Wallasey	235	300	+28	240	−20
	Altrincham	525	372	−29	254	+32
	Chester	480	582	+21	586	+1
	Crewe	894	840	−6	307	−63
	Eddisbury	180	240	+33	240	0
	Knutsford and Macclesfield	360	280	−22	545	+95
	Northwich	750	775	+3	351	−55
	Stalybridge and Hyde	653	1406	+115	1156	−18
	Wirral	169	828	+390	563	−32
Cornwall	Bodmin	240	420	+75	371	−12
	Camborne		240		240	0
	Northern	314	400	+27	240	−40
	Penryn and Falmouth	1081	1518	+40	907	−40
	St Ives	425	380	+11		
Cumberland	Carlisle	1000	2480	+148	2873	+16
	Northern		240		240	0
	Penrith and Cockermouth	180	240	+33	240	0
	Whitehaven	100	240	+140	240	0
	Workington	432	684	+58	622	−9

County	Local party	1929	1930[a]	% Change 1929–30	1931	% Change 1930–31
Derbyshire	Derby	2018	1620	−20	1260	−22
	Belper	528	549	+4	401	−27
	Chesterfield	322	293	−9	246	−16
	Clay Cross	180	488	+171	293	−40
	High Peak	180	673	+274	551	−18
	Ilkeston	331	500	+51	395	−21
	North Eastern	140	391	+179	289	−26
	Southern	600	992	+65	1118	+13
	Western	180	240	+33	240	0
Devon	Exeter	630	250	−60	540	+116
	Plymouth, Drake	1000	645	−36	613	−5
	Plymouth, Devonport	960	1870	+95	1823	−3
	Plymouth, Sutton	180	510	+183	753	+48
	Barnstaple	180	460	+156	268	−42
	Honiton	180	276	+53	240	−13
	South Molton	180	675	+275	518	−23
	Tavistock	180	281	+56	266	−5
	Tiverton	246	365	+48	240	−34
	Torquay	815	900	+10	640	−29
	Totnes	241	505	+110	400	−21
Dorset	Eastern	420	339	−19	373	+11
	Northern	180	240	+33	240	0
	Southern	150	350	+133	260	−26
	Western	288	240	−17	240	0
Durham	Darlington	1500	1480	−1	1000	−48
	Gateshead	360	240	−33	300	+25
	Hartlepool	150	240	+60	240	0
	South Shields	123	240	+95	240	0
	Stockton	360	593	+65	1091	+84
	Sunderland	360	480	+33	480	0
	Barnard Castle	600	500	−17	600	+20
	Bishop Auckland	510	240	−53	424	+77
	Blaydon	700	660	−6	400	−39
	Chester-le–Street	1000	1000	0	700	−30
	Consett	360	455	+26	445	−2
	Durham	250	307	+23	458	+49
	Houghton-le-Spring	700	800	+14	758	−5
	Jarrow	372	264	−29	300	+14
	Seaham	180	340	+89	416	+22
	Sedgefield	260	719	+177	548	−31
	Spennymoor	600	500	−17	600	+20
Essex	East Ham, N.	1359	2086	+53	2106	+1
	East Ham, S.	750	1622	+116	1485	−9
	Ilford	1700	1930	+14	2264	+17
	Leyton E.	257	630	+145	608	−4
	Leyton W.	910	762	−16	717	−6
	Southend	52	240	+362	240	0
	Walthamstow, E.	373	634	+70	569	−10
	Walthamstow, W.	450	725	+61	790	+9

County	Local party	1929	1930[a]	% Change 1929–30	1931	% Change 1930–31
	West Ham, Plaistow	180	240	+33	240	0
	West Ham, Silverton	180	240	+33	240	0
	West Ham, Stratford		240		240	0
	West Ham, Upton	180	240	+33	240	0
	Chelmsford	541	900	+66	663	−26
	Colchester	1069	1128	+6	826	−27
	Epping	356	510	+43	455	−11
	Harwich		322		418	+30
	Maldon	1464	1134	−23	763	−33
	Romford	1742	3400	+95	3620	+6
	Saffron Walden	500	524	+5	450	−14
	South Eastern		817		979	+20
Gloucestershire	Bristol		300			
	Bristol, Central	500	560	+12	527	−6
	Bristol, E.	900	2368	+163	2494	+5
	Bristol, N.	600	722	+20	635	−12
	Bristol, S.	1020	800	−22	1700	+113
	Bristol, W.	617	678	+10	525	−23
	Cheltenham	180	240	+33	240	0
	Gloucester	210	540	+157	475	−12
	Cirencester	180	240	+33	240	0
	Forest of Dean	260	400	+54	400	0
	Stroud	252	489	+94	629	+29
	Thornbury	500	1261	+152	747	−41
Hampshire	Bournemouth	420	450	+7	283	−37
	Portsmouth	180				
	Portsmouth, Central	534	675	+26	2055	
	Portsmouth, N.	498	776	+56		
	Portsmouth, S.	287	514	+179		
	Southampton	1468	2172	+48	1842	−15
	Aldershot	420	500	+19	350	−30
	Basingstoke	180	257	+43	256	−1
	Fareham	300	240	−20	240	0
	New Forest	180	339	+88	345	+2
	Petersfield	138	280	+103	250	−11
	Winchester	80	410	+413	430	+5
Hereford	Hereford	180				
	Leominster				240	
Hertfordshire	Hemel Hempstead	280	469	+68	370	−21
	Hertford	300	442	+47	400	−10
	Hitchin	385	600	+56	638	+6
	St Albans	1335	1100	−18	1500	+36
	Watford	1550	1095	−29	1391	+27
Huntingdonshire	Huntingdon	180	266	+48	324	+22
Isles	Isle of Ely	540	643	+19	485	−25
	Isle of Wight	483	778	+61	661	−15
Kent	Bromley	724	291	−60	743	+155
	Hythe	166	240	+45	250	+4
	Rochester, Chatham	180	240	+33	344	+43

County	Local party	1929	1930[a]	% Change 1929–30	1931	% Change 1930–31
	Rochester, Gillingham	360	500	+39	600	+20
	Ashford	117	240	+105	340	+42
	Canterbury	179	430	+140	336	−22
	Chislehurst	180	240	+33	240	0
	Dartford	1620	1903	+17	1775	−7
	Dover		661		767	+16
	Faversham	2036	2380	+17	1923	−19
	Gravesend	504	522	+4	468	−10
	Isle of Thanet	240	329	+37	289	−12
	Maidstone	351	263	−25	240	−9
	Sevenoaks	180	240	+33	240	0
	Tonbridge	428	547	+28	495	−10
Lancashire	Accrington	1000	1165		1083	−7
	Ashton-under-Lyne	405	240	−41	342	+43
	Barrow-in-Furness	500	322	−35	341	+6
	Blackburn	892	800	−10	500	−38
	Blackpool	356	410	+15	423	+3
	Bolton	1200	750	−38	480	−36
	Bootle	324	305	−6	450	+48
	Burnley	900	1280	+42	1000	−22
	Bury	240	240	0	240	0
	Eccles	521	862	+65	700	−19
	Leigh	180	240	+33	250	+4
	Liverpool, East Toxteth	180	412	+129	240	−42
	Liverpool, Edge Hill	252	350	+39	296	−15
	Liverpool, Everton		240		240	0
	Liverpool, Exchange		240		240	0
	Liverpool, Fairfield	273	635	+133	515	−19
	Liverpool, Kirkdale	224	240	+7	240	0
	Liverpool, Scotland	180	420	+133	320	−24
	Liverpool, Walton	180	989	+449	600	−39
	Liverpool, Wavertree	240	490	+104	574	+17
	Liverpool, West Derby		450		362	−20
	Liverpool, West Toxteth	180	880	+389	360	−59
	Manchester, Ardwick	360	557	+55	424	−24
	Manchester, Blackley	300	541	+80	482	−11
	Manchester, Clayton	500	564	+13	386	−32
	Manchester, Exchange		240		240	0
	Manchester, Gorton	780	985	+26	855	−13
	Manchester, Hulme	300	496	+65	500	+1
	Manchester, Moss Side	180	652	+262	328	−50
	Manchester, Platting	360	1070	+197	906	−15
	Manchester, Rusholme	180	329	+83	271	−18
	Manchester, Withington		788		512	−35
	Nelson and Colne	960	1000	+4	1000	0
	Oldham	2280	3500	+54	2160	−38
	Preston	1032	1000	−3	1400	+40
	Rochdale	375	241	−36	559	+132
	Rossendale	1035	1000	−3	625	−38

County	Local party	1929	1930[a]	% Change 1929–30	1931	% Change 1930–31
	St Helens	360	240	−33	240	0
	Salford, N.	2250	2200	−2		
	Salford, S.	600	800	+33	240	−70
	Salford, W.	1200			400	
	Southport	180	240	+33	240	0
	Warrington	308	350	+14	411	+17
	Wigan	256	250	−2	250	0
	Chorley	160	240	+50	240	0
	Clitheroe	660	1380	+109	1056	−23
	Darwen	240	300	+25	470	+57
	Farnworth	600	240	−60	281	+17
	Fylde	468	600	+28	400	−33
	Heywood and Radcliffe	571	734	+29	624	−15
	Ince	600	640	+7	640	0
	Lancaster	480	1212	+153	942	−22
	Lonsdale	180	579	+222	387	−33
	Middleton and Prestwich	180	376	+109	468	+24
	Mossley				240	0
	Newton	230	240	+4	319	+33
	Ormskirk	172	644	+274	519	−19
	Royton	223	280	+26	350	+25
	Stretford	270	918	+240	886	−3
	Waterloo	180	240	+33	240	0
	Westhoughton	233	240	+3	240	0
	Widnes	180	410	+128	240	−41
Leicestershire	Leicester Borough		1000	+13	1220	+22
	Leicester, E.	247				
	Leicester, S.	247				
	Leicester, W.	247				
	Bosworth	923	1000	+8	735	−27
	Harborough	300	683	+128	555	−19
	Loughborough	180	507	+182	423	−17
	Melton	180	240	+33	240	0
Lincoln and Rutland	Grimsby	252	560	+122	350	−38
	Lincoln	596	240	−60	569	+137
	Holland	750	572	−24	363	−37
	Kesteven, Grantham	310	260	−16	250	−4
	Kesteven, Rutland	180	322	+79	317	−2
	Lindsey, Brigg	264	422	+60	300	−29
	Lindsey, Gainsborough	180	240	+33	240	0
	Lindsey, Horncastle	132	274	+108	240	−12
	Lindsey, Louth	261	252	−3	293	+16
London	Battersea, N.	180	523	+191	607	+16
	Battersea, S.	180	675	+275	525	−22
	Bermondsey, W	1800	1441	−20	1517	+5
	Bermondsey, Rotherhithe	1250	967	−23	1125	+16
	Bethnal Green, N.E.	300	300	0	499	+66

County	Local party	1929	1930[a]	% Change 1929–30	1931	% Change 1930–31
	Bethnal Green, S.W.	180	240	+33	240	0
	Camberwell, N.	1000	360	−64	890	+147
	Camberwell, N.W.	180	240	+33	240	0
	Camberwell, Dulwich		295	0	265	−10
	Camberwell, Peckham	900	638	−29	240	−166
	Chelsea	64	240	+275	240	0
	Deptford	1720	2600	+51	2800	+8
	Finsbury	240	240	0	240	0
	Fulham, E.	500	690	+38	632	−8
	Fulham, W.	750	1069	+43	1112	+4
	Greenwich	2435	2704	+11	2821	+4
	Hackney, Central	490	318	−35	359	+13
	Hackney, N.	495	480	−3	470	−2
	Hackney, S.	500	1086	+117	1009	−7
	Hammersmith, N.	180	444	+147	438	−1
	Hammersmith, S.	362	240	−34	275	+15
	Hampstead	300	400	+33	240	−40
	Holborn	90	240	+167	240	0
	Islington, E.	180	240	+33	343	+43
	Islington, N.	400	500	+25	500	0
	Islington, S.	165	240	+45	240	0
	Islington, W.	180	240	+33	240	0
	Kensington, N.	653	554	−15	610	+10
	Kensington, S.	93	240	+158	240	0
	Lambeth, Brixton	288	300	+4	311	+4
	Lambeth, Kennington		350		274	−22
	Lambeth, N.	224	400	+79	300	−25
	Lambeth, Norwood	386	400	+4	400	0
	Lewisham, E.	2500	2874	+15	2580	−10
	Lewisham, W.	989	1031	+4	944	−8
	Paddington, N.	596	812	+15	820	+1
	Paddington, S.	82	240	+193	285	+19
	Poplar, Bow and Bromley	1200	1688	+41	1412	−16
	Poplar, South	1612	3000	+86	2500	−17
	St Marylebone	101	240	+138	240	0
	St Pancras, N.	405	546	+35	573	+5
	St Pancras, S.E.	600	600	0		
	St. Pancras, S.W.	120	300	+150	240	−20
	Shoreditch	175	863	+393	870	+1
	Southwark, Central	452	240	−47	240	0
	Southwark, N.	300	576	+92	570	−1
	Southwark, S.E.	713	240	−66	300	+25
	Stepney, Limehouse	596	1100	+85	975	−11
	Stepney, Mile End	600	1634	+172	1083	−34
	Stepney, Whitechapel	180	1739	+866	1361	−22
	Stoke Newington	339	536	+58	454	−15
	Wandsworth, Balham and Tooting	510	554	+9	704	+27

County	Local party	1929	1930[a]	% Change 1929–30	1931	% Change 1930–31
	Wandsworth, Central	400	500	+25	406	−19
	Wandsworth, Clapham	244	371	+52	260	−30
	Wandsworth, Putney and South Shields	356	240	−33	607	+153
	Wandsworth, Streatham	216	331	+53	282	−15
	Westminster, St Georges		240			
	Westminster, Abbey		240		240	0
	Woolwich	4355	4424	+2	3955	−11
Middlesex	Ealing	288	479	+66	421	−12
	Edmonton	1040	1416	+36	1051	−26
	Hornsey	274	409	+49	378	−8
	Tottenham, N.	1000	2000	+100	1800	−10
	Tottenham, S.	500	728	+46	616	−15
	Willesden, E.	180	318	+77	321	+1
	Willesden, W.	910	1100	+21	950	−14
	Acton	250	578	+131	443	−14
	Brentford and Chiswick	310	492	+59	420	−15
	Enfield	1465	1848	+26	1493	−19
	Finchley	257	300	+17	270	−10
	Harrow	1260	1423	+13	1238	−13
	Hendon	1038	1320	+27	1334	+1
	Spelthorne	1040	832	−20	803	−4
	Twickenham	943	1146	+22	442	−61
	Uxbridge	300	708	+136	948	+34
	Wood Green	840	1000	+19	655	−35
Norfolk	Great Yarmouth	180	240	+33	240	0
	Norwich	1818	1040	−43	1500	+44
	Eastern	240	300	+25	240	−20
	King's Lynn	600	400	−33	1200	+200
	Northern	1065	240	−77	553	+130
	Southern	180	594	+230	581	−2
	South-West	180	240	+33	380	+58
Northampton	Northampton	1200	1500	+25	240	−84
	Daventry	360	240	−33	240	0
	Kettering	180	410	+128	240	−41
	Peterborough	840	640	−76	1378	+115
	Welling-borough	1200	1366	+14	1589	+16
Northumber-land	Morpeth	178	592	+233	469	−21
	Newcastle, Central		240		240	0
	Newcastle, E.	180	240	+33	340	+42
	Newcastle, N.	127	240	+89	240	0
	Newcastle, W.	237	240	+1	568	+137
	Tynemouth	216	240	+11	240	0
	Wallsend	527	1023	+94	831	−19
	Berwick	180	388	+116	240	−38
	Hexham	180	240	+33	240	0
	Wansbeck	834	1130	+36	767	−32

County	Local party	1929	1930[a]	% Change 1929–30	1931	% Change 1930–31
Nottinghamshire	Nottingham, Central	360	538	+49	610	+13
	Nottingham, E.	180	308	+71	257	−17
	Nottingham, S.	929	850	−9	636	−25
	Nottingham, W.		590		504	−15
	Bassetlaw	180	682	+279	556	−18
	Broxtowe	372	800	+115	400	−50
	Mansfield	300	358	+19	351	−2
	Newark		240		240	0
	Rushcliffe	240	539	+125	331	−39
Oxfordshire	Oxford	441	500	+13	300	−40
	Banbury	193	259	+34	240	−7
	Henley	390	377	−3	356	−6
Salop	Ludlow	150	240	+60	240	0
	Oswestry	180	285	+58	420	+47
	Shrewsbury	180	390	+117	240	−39
	The Wrekin	360	584	+62	430	−26
Somerset	Bath	266	240	−10	240	0
	Bridgwater	180	370	+106	286	−23
	Frome	480	1352	+182	600	−56
	Taunton	480	643	+34	508	−21
	Wells	450	477	+6	339	−29
	Weston	118	287	+143	240	−16
	Yeovil	180	723	+302	492	−32
Staffordshire	Newcastle-under-Lyme	180	240	+33	240	0
	Smethwick	240	240	0	240	0
	Stoke, Burslem		240		240	0
	Stoke, Henley	180	240	+33	240	0
	Stoke	360	321	−11	321	0
	Walsall	180	340	+89	360	+6
	Wednesbury	180	508	+182	461	−9
	West Bromwich	180	240	+33	358	+49
	Bilston	660	240	−64	750	+213
	Wolverhampton, E.	180	240	+33	240	0
	Wolverhampton, W.	300	650	+117	400	−38
	Burton	180	531	+195	240	−55
	Cannock	400	500	+25	360	−28
	Kingswinford	378	340	−10	713	+110
	Leek	167	321	+92	390	+21
	Lichfield	180	240	+33	240	0
	Stafford	420	605	+44	548	−9
	Stone	180	240	+33	240	0
Suffolk	Ipswich	231	428	+85	507	+18
	Suffolk East, Eye	180	498	+177	317	−36
	Suffolk East, Lowestoft	405	1080	+167	1018	−6
	Suffolk East, Woodbridge	162	528	+226	419	−21
	Suffolk West, Bury	150	240	+60	240	0
	Suffolk West, Sudbury	200	408	+104	560	+37

County	Local party	1929	1930[a]	% Change 1929–30	1931	% Change 1930–31
Surrey	Croydon, N.	318	534	+68	829	+55
	Croydon, S.	317	466	+47	801	+72
	Kingston	450	533	+18	504	−5
	Richmond	100	240	+140	240	0
	Wimbledon	900	960	+7	1085	+13
	Chertsey		180		40	−78
	Eastern	271	296	+9	345	+17
	Epsom	621	548	−18	447	−18
	Farnham	355	410	+15	270	−34
	Guildford	360	340	−6	500	+47
	Mitcham	1038	983	−5	879	−11
	Reigate	697	1112	+60	1009	−9
Sussex, East	Brighton	200	414	+107	480	+16
	Hastings LP	500	308	−38	429	+39
	Hastings TLC	186				
	Eastbourne	110	240	+118	240	0
	East Grinstead	180	817	+354	796	−3
	Lewes	629	539	−14	637	+18
	Rye		240		240	0
Sussex, West	Chichester	325	416	+28	381	−8
	Horsham and Worthing	321	648	+102	406	−37
Warwickshire	Birmingham, Aston	396	400	+1	371	−7
	Birmingham, Deritend	180	360	+100	280	−22
	Birmingham, Duddeston	168	240	+43	240	0
	Birmingham, Edgbaston	180	710	+294	490	−31
	Birmingham, Erdington	180	782	+334	507	−35
	Birmingham, Handsworth	322	491	+52	475	−3
	Birmingham, King's Norton	630	1002	+59	936	−7
	Birmingham, Ladywood	350	493	+41	322	−35
	Birmingham, Moseley	180	755	+319	667	−12
	Birmingham, Sparkbrook	283	382	+35	251	−34
	Birmingham, W.	420	600	+43	624	+4
	Birmingham, Yardley	600	610	+2	440	−28
	Coventry	600	480	−20	556	+12
	Nuneaton	180	1150	+539	970	−17
	Rugby	360	240	−33	240	0
	Tamworth	360	335	−7	320	−4
	Warwick and Leamington	148	240	+62	240	0

County	Local party	1929	1930[a]	% Change 1929–30	1931	% Change 1930–31
Westmorland	Westmorland	120	240	+100	365	+52
Wiltshire	Chippenham	241	588	+144	519	−12
	Devizes	180	240	+33	240	0
	Salisbury	240	615	+156	512	−17
	Swindon	1900	1947	+2	1918	−1
	Westbury	987	1180	+20	844	−28
Worcestershire	Dudley		240		880	+267
	Worcester	180	240	+33	240	0
	Bewdley	180	240	+33	240	0
	Evesham	180	240	+33	240	0
	Kidderminster	180	240	+33	240	0
	Stourbridge	930	1010	+9	1079	+7
Yorkshire	Barnsley	180	240	+33	240	0
	Batley, Morley and Ossett	545	240	−56	240	0
	Morley TC	100				
	Bradford		240		240	0
	Bradford, C.	180	240	+33	240	0
	Bradford, E.	180	240	+33	240	0
	Bradford, N.	180	240	+33	240	0
	Bradford, S.					
	Dewsbury	374	240	−36	240	0
	Halifax	180	688	+282	600	−13
	Huddersfield	180	590	+228	810	+37
	Kingston-upon-Hull, Central	120	240	+100	240	0
	Kingston-upon-Hull, E.	180	340	+89	240	−29
	Kingston-upon-Hull, N.W.	169	240	+42	240	0
	Kingston-upon-Hull, S.W.	180	240	+33	240	0
	Leeds, Central	316	284	−10	308	+8
	Leeds, N.	300	460	+53	620	+35
	Leeds, N.E.	200	240	+20	609	+154
	Leeds, S.	780	786	+1	651	−17
	Leeds, S.E.	295	428	+45	435	+2
	Leeds, W.	180	240	+33	273	+14
	Middlesbrough, E.	300	351	+17	340	−3
	Middlesbrough, W.	180	400	+122	500	+25
	Rotherham	450	300	−33	240	−20
	Sheffield, Attercliffe	480	394	−18	334	−15
	Sheffield, Brightside	180	688	+282	722	+5
	Sheffield, Central	240	612	+155	570	−7
	Sheffield, Ecclesall	150	240	+60	240	0
	Sheffield, Hallam	180	240	+33	240	0
	Sheffield, Hillsborough		240		240	0
	Sheffield, Park	345	545	+58	514	−6
	Wakefield	360	240	−33	360	+50

County	Local party	1929	1930[a]	% Change 1929–30	1931	% Change 1930–31
	York	500	2023	+305	1742	−14
	East Riding, Buckrose					
	East Riding, Holderness	170	240	+41	240	0
	East Riding, Howdenshire	109	240	+120		
	North Riding, Cleveland	550	240	−44	529	+120
	North Riding, Richmond	180	240	+33	240	0
	North Riding, Scarborough and Whitby	208	340	+63	262	−23
	North Riding, Thirsk and Malton				120	
	West Riding, Barkston Ash	420	607	+45	709	+12
	West Riding, Colne Valley	414	300	−28	240	−20
	West Riding, Doncaster	512	820	+60	612	−25
	West Riding, Don Valley	360	551	+53	482	−13
	West Riding, Elland	480	670	+40	540	−19
	West Riding, Hemsworth	95	529	+457	701	+33
	West Riding, Keighley	280	320	+14	320	0
	West Riding, Normanton	80	240	+200	240	0
	West Riding, Penistone	376	466	+24	434	−7
	West Riding, Pontefract	360	507	+41	378	−25
	West Riding, Pudsey and Otley	330	607	+84	510	−16
	West Riding, Ripon	180	315	+75	240	−24
	West Riding, Rother Valley	550	400	−27	600	+50
	West Riding, Rothwell	25	320	+1180	480	+50
	West Riding, Shipley	320	576	+80	455	−21
	West Riding, Skipton	1200	1324	+10	1017	−23
	West Riding, Sowerby	570	698	+22	762	+9
	West Riding, Spen Valley	900	806	−10	586	−27
	West Riding, Wentworth	360	369	+3	240	−35

County	Local party	1929	1930[a]	% Change 1929–30	1931	% Change 1930–31
WALES						
Anglesey	Anglesey	180	423	+135	270	+36
Brecon and Radnor	Brecon and Radnor	240	1000	+317	485	−52
Cardigan	Cardigan	159	240	+51	240	0
Carmarthen	Carmarthen		240		240	0
	Llanelly	180	240	+33	320	+33
Carnavon	Carnarvon Borough	168	329	+96	240	−27
	Carnarvon	600	720	+20	640	−11
Denbigh	Denbigh	150	240	+60	240	0
	Wrexham	360	1022	+184	683	−33
Flint	Flint	360	670	+86	828	+24
Glamorgan	Cardiff, Central	624	376	−40	400	+6
	Cardiff, E.	550	442	−20	487	+10
	Cardiff, S.	522	260	−50	339	+30
	Merthyr Tydfil				240	0
	Merthyr Tydfil, Aberdare	252	282	+12	240	−15
	Merthyr Tydfil	60	240	+300		
	Rhondda, E.	360	240	−33	240	0
	Rhondda, W.	360	240	−33	240	0
	Swansea	180	627	+148	647	+3
	Aberavon	360	620	+72	519	−16
	Caerphilly	199	769	+286	1008	+31
	Gower	180	449	+149	600	+34
	Llandaff and Barry	360	1198	+233	244	+4
	Neath	180	269	+49	240	−11
	Ogmore	180	530	+194	464	−12
	Pontypridd	180	315	+75	286	−9
Merioneth	Merioneth	250	910	+264	331	−64
Monmouth	Newport	1605	2206	+37	1793	−19
	Abertillery	180	240	+33	240	0
	Bedwellty	250	280	+12	500	+108
	Ebbw Vale	180	240	+33	240	0
	Monmouth	300	550	+83	533	−3
	Pontypool	315	751	+138	281	−63
Montgomery	Montgomery	158	240	+52	348	+45
Pembroke	Pembroke	180	477	+165	408	−14
SCOTLAND						
Aberdeen and Kincardine	Aberdeen	222	480	+116	1670	+248
	Aberdeen and Kincardine, Central	180	250	+39	240	−4
	Aberdeen and Kincardine, E.	148	240	+62	240	0
	Aberdeen and Kincardine, W.					
Argyll	Argyll					

County	Local party	1929	1930[a]	% Change 1929–30	1931	% Change 1930–31
Ayr and Bute	Ayr Burghs	180	240	+33	240	0
	Bute and North Ayr	180	240	+33	240	0
	Kilmarnock	180	240	+33	240	0
	South Ayrshire		240		240	0
Banff	Banff	178	240	+35	240	0
Berwick	Berwick and Haddington	180	240	+33	240	0
Caithness and Sutherland	Caithness and Sutherland					
Dumbarton	Dumbarton and Clydebank	180	240	+33	240	0
	Dumbarton	120	251	+109	330	+31
Dumfries	Dumfries	100	240	+140	240	0
Fife	Dumfermline	180	240	+33	240	0
	Kirkcaldy	180	340	+89	300	−12
	Eastern	180	240	+33	240	0
	Western	180	382	+112	256	−33
Forfar	Dundee	205	480	+134	480	0
	Montrose	180	240	+33	240	0
	Forfar	185	240	+30	240	0
Galloway	Galloway		240		240	0
Inverness	Inverness	180	240	+33	296	+23
	Ross and Cromarty		240			
	Western Isles					
Lanark	Glasgow, Bridgeton		240			
	Glasgow, Camlachie	106	240	+126	372	+55
	Glasgow, Cathcart	155	240	+55	320	+33
	Glasgow, Central		240		240	0
	Glasgow, Gorbals	180	240	+33	240	0
	Glasgow, Govan		240			0
	Glasgow, Hillhead	45	240	+433	240	0
	Glasgow, Kelvingrove				240	0
	Glasgow, Maryhill	180	240	+33	240	0
	Glasgow, Partick	56	240	+329	240	0
	Glasgow, Pollok	46	240	+422	240	0
	Glasgow, St Rollox					
	Glasgow, Shettleston	35	240	+586	240	0
	Glasgow, Springburn	59			240	
	Glasgow, Tradeston		240		240	0
	Bothwell	180	240	+33	240	0
	Coatbridge	237	314	+32	290	−8
	Hamilton	240	240	0	240	0
	Lanark	180	240	+33	240	0
	Motherwell	180	240	+33	240	0
	Northern	160	240	+50	240	0
	Rutherglen	134	240	+79	240	0
Linlithgow	Linlithgow	180	272	+51	240	−12
Midlothian and Peebles	Edinburgh, Central	80	240	+200	240	0
	Edinburgh, E.	120	346	+188	350	+1

County	Local party	1929	1930[a]	% Change 1929–30	1931	% Change 1930–31
	Edinburgh, N.	180	240	+33	416	+73
	Edinburgh, S.	140	240	+71	240	0
	Edinburgh, W.	535	402	−25	485	+21
	Leith	170	240	+41	240	0
	Northern	180	646	+259	674	+4
	Peebles and Southern	170	335	+97	393	+17
Moray and Nairn	Moray and Nairn	360	375	+4	488	+30
Orkney and Zetland	Orkney and Zetland					0
Perth and Kinross	Perth	180	240	+33	240	0
	Kinross	40			40	0
Renfrew	Greenock	180	240	+33	240	0
	Paisley	180	240	+33	240	0
	Eastern	180	240	+33	240	0
	Western	180	453	+152	372	−18
Roxburgh and Selkirk	Roxburgh	180	905	+403	412	−54
Stirling and Clackmannan	Stirling and Falkirk	180	255	+42	240	−6
	Clackmannan and East Stirling	180	240	+33	240	0
	Clackmannan and West Stirling		240		312	+30

UNIVERSITY SEATS

		1929	1930	% Change	1931	% Change
Cambridge		150	155	+3	240	+55
London		180	240	+33	240	0
Scotland		180	240	+33	240	0

CALCULATED TOTAL MEMBERSHIP		227,917	319,715		298,214	
FIGURE GIVEN IN ANNUAL REPORTS		227,897	277,211		297,003	

Note: [a] Minimum affiliated membership increased from 180 members to 240 at the 1929 Party Conference.

Source: Labour Party Annual Reports, 1929 to 1932.

BIBLIOGRAPHY

MANUSCRIPT COLLECTIONS

Public records

Public Record Office, Kew
Cabinet: CAB 23 (Cabinet Conclusions, 1929–31); CAB 24 (Memoranda, 1929–31)
Board of Education: ED 31; ED 24; ED 136
Prime Minister's Office: PREM 1

Private papers

C. Addison Papers (Bodleian Library, Oxford)
A. V. Alexander Papers (Churchill College, Cambridge)
Baron C. Ammon Papers (Brynmor Jones Library, University of Hull)
Lord Amulree Papers (Bodleian Library, Oxford)
C. R. Attlee Papers (Churchill College, Cambridge)
E. Bevin Papers (Churchill College, Cambridge and Modern Records Centre, University of Warwick)
Cardinal Bourne Papers (Westminster Diocesan Archives, Kensington)
D. Chater Papers (Brynmor Jones Library, University of Hull)
Lord Citrine Papers (British Library of Political and Economic Science)
G. D. H. Cole and M. Cole Papers (Nuffield College, Oxford)
Sir S. Cripps (Nuffield College, Oxford)
H. Dalton Papers (British Library of Political and Economic Science)
S. O. Davies Papers (South Wales Coalfield Archive, University College, Swansea)
R. D. Denman Papers (Bodleian Library, Oxford)
D. Graham Pole Papers (Borthwick Institute of Historical Research, York)
A. Greenwood Papers (Bodleian Library, Oxford)
G. H. Hall Papers (Nuffield College, Oxford)
Sir M. Hankey Papers (Churchill College, Cambridge)
Dr S. Hastings Papers (Brynmor Jones Library, University of Hull)
A. Henderson Papers (Labour Party Library, National Museum of Labour History, Manchester)
Cardinal Hinsley Papers (Westminster Diocesan Archives, Kensington)
Sir W. Jowitt Papers (Brynmor Jones Library, University of Hull)
G. Lansbury Papers (British Library of Political and Economic Science)
H. Laski Papers (Brynmor Jones Library, University of Hull and British Library of Political and Economic Science)
Dr H. B. Lees Smith (Brynmor Jones Library, University of Hull)
J. Henry Lloyd Papers (Brynmor Jones Library, University of Hull)
D. Lloyd George Papers (House of Lords Record Office)
R. MacDonald Papers (Public Record Office, Kew)
Sir F. Messer Papers (Brynmor Jones Library, University of Hull)
J. S. Middleton Papers (Labour Party Library, National Museum of Labour History, Manchester and Ruskin College, Oxford)
H. Morrison Papers (Nuffield College, Oxford)

Bibliography

P. Noel-Baker Papers (Churchill College, Cambridge)
R. Page Arnot Papers (Brynmor Jones Library, University of Hull)
Passfield Papers [Lord Passfield and Beatrice Webb] (British Library of Political and Economic Science)
F. W. Pethick Lawrence Papers (Trinity College, Cambridge)
Dr M. Phillips Papers (Labour Party Library, National Museum of Labour History, Manchester)
Lord Ponsonby Papers (Bodleian Library, Oxford)
Lord Sankey Papers (Bodleian Library, Oxford)
E. Shinwell Papers (British Library of Political and Economic Science)
R. Smith Papers (Bodleian Library, Oxford)
Rev. R. W. Sorensen Papers (House of Lords Record Office)
Viscount Stansgate Papers [William Wedgwood Benn] (House of Lords Record Office)
Sir A. Steel-Maitland Papers (Scottish Record Office, Edinburgh)
R. H. Tawney Papers (British Library of Political and Economic Science)
J. H. Thomas Papers (Kent Archives Office, Maidstone)
Sir C. Trevelyan Papers (Robinson Library, University of Newcastle)
W. Whiteley Papers (Borthwick Institute of Historical Research, York)
E. Wilkinson Papers (Labour Party Library, National Museum of Labour History, Manchester)

Labour Party records

National

Independent Labour Party Minutes, Pamphlets and Leaflets (British Library of Political and Economic Science)
Labour Party National Executive Committee Minutes and Subject Files (Labour Party Library, National Museum of Labour History, Manchester)
Labour Party Pamphlets and Leaflets (Labour Party Library, National Museum of Labour History, Manchester)
Labour Party: General Correspondence and Political Records (Microfilm, British Library of Political and Economic Science)
Parliamentary Labour Party Executive Minutes (Labour Party Library, National Museum of Labour History, Manchester)
Parliamentary Labour Party Minutes (Labour Party Library, National Museum of Labour History, Manchester)

Borough

Birmingham BLP (Microfilm, Reference Library, Birmingham)
Bristol BLP (City Record Office, Bristol)
Chichester City Labour Party (West Sussex Record Office, Chichester)
Doncaster BLP (Archives Department, Doncaster)
Glasgow BLP (Microfilm, Reference Library, Birmingham)
Leeds City Labour Party (West Yorkshire Archive Service, Leeds)
Nelson and Colne BLP (Working-Class Movement Library, Salford)
Salford City Labour Party (Working-Class Movement Library, Salford)
Sheffield City Labour Party (Sheffield City Archives, Sheffield)
Woolwich Labour Party (Microfilm, Reference Library, Birmingham)

Divisional

Barnard Castle DLP (Durham County Record Office, Durham)
Batley and Morley DLP (West Yorkshire Archive Service, Bradford)
Bristol East DLP (City Record Office, Bristol)

Broxtowe DLP (Nottinghamshire Record Office, Nottingham)
Cambridge TCLP (Cambridgeshire Record Office, Cambridge)
Cambridgeshire TCLP (Cambridgeshire Record Office, Cambridge)
Canterbury DLP (Kent Archives Office, Maidstone)
Chichester DLP (West Sussex Record Office, Chichester)
Colne Valley DLP (Microfilm, Reference Library, Birmingham)
Darlington DLP (Durham County Record Office, Durham)
Derby DLP (Local Studies Library, Derby)
Derbyshire West DLP (Derbyshire Record Office, Matlock)
Doncaster DLP (Archives Department, Doncaster)
Durham DLP (Durham County Record Office, Durham)
East Anglia ILP (British Library of Political and Economic Science)
Glasgow ILP Federation (Microfilm, Reference Library, Birmingham)
Gloucester TCLP (Microfilm, Reference Library, Birmingham)
Greenwich DLP (Local History Library, Greenwich)
Hamilton DLP (Microfilm, Reference Library, Birmingham)
Houghton-le-Spring DLP (Durham County Record Office, Durham)
Jarrow DLP (Durham County Record Office, Durham)
Lambeth North DLP (British Library of Political and Economic Science)
Leeds Central DLP (West Yorkshire Archive Service, Leeds)
Merton and Morden Labour Party (British Library of Political and Economic Science)
Mid-Sussex DLP (West Sussex Record Office, Chichester)
Newark DLP (Nottinghamshire Record Office, Nottingham)
Newport DLP (South Wales Coalfield Archive, University College, Swansea)
Nottingham Co-operative and Labour Party (Nottinghamshire Records Office, Nottingham)
Nottingham South DLP (Nottinghamshire Records Office, Nottingham)
Paddington South DLP (British Library of Political and Economic Science)
Penistone and Holmfirth Labour Party (Microfilm, Birmingham Reference Library)
Peterborough DLP (Microfilm, Reference Library, Birmingham)
Pontypridd TCLP (Microfilm, Reference Library, Birmingham)
Roxburgh and Selkirk DLP (National Library of Scotland, Edinburgh)
Sheffield TCLP (Microfilm, Reference Library, Birmingham)
Sheffield Brightside DLP (Sheffield City Archives, Sheffield)
South Shields TCLP (Microfilm, Reference Library, Birmingham)
Sowerby DLP (West Yorkshire Archive Service, Calderdale, Halifax)
Stockport TCLP (Microfilm, Reference Library, Birmingham)
Wansbeck DLP (Northumberland Record Office, Newcastle)
Wolverhampton West Labour Party (Microfilm, Reference Library, Birmingham)
Worcester Labour Party (Hereford and Worcester Record Office, Worcester)
Wrexham TCLP (Microfilm, Reference Library, Birmingham)
York DLP (York Archives Office)

Trade union records

TUC

Trades Union Congress General Council Minutes (Modern Records Centre, University of Warwick)
Trades Union Congress Pamphlets and Leaflets 1887–1930 (Microfilm, British Library of Political and Economic Science)
Trades Union Congress Papers (Modern Records Centre, University of Warwick)

Bibliography

Individual unions

Amalgamated Engineering Union (Modern Records Centre, University of Warwick)
Amalgamated Society of Locomotive Engineers and Firemen (Modern Records Centre, University of Warwick)
Amalgamated Society of Woodworkers (Modern Records Centre, University of Warwick)
Amalgamated Union of Building Trade Workers (Modern Records Centre, University of Warwick)
British Iron and Steel and Kindred Trades Association (Modern Records Centre, University of Warwick)
Miners' Federation of Great Britain (South Wales Coalfield Archive, University College, Swansea)
National Amalgamated Society of Operative House and Ship Painters and Decorators (Modern Records Centre, University of Warwick)
National Union of Foundry Workers (Modern Records Centre, University of Warwick)
National Union of General and Municipal Workers (South Wales Miners' Library, Swansea)
Railway Clerks' Association (Modern Records Centre, University of Warwick)
South Wales Miners' Federation (South Wales Coalfield Archive, University College, Swansea)
Transport and General Workers' Union (Modern Records Centre, University of Warwick)

Trades councils

Birmingham Trades Council (Microfilm, Reference Library, Birmingham)
Edinburgh Trades Council (Microfilm, Reference Library, Birmingham)
Leeds Trades Council (West Yorkshire Archive Centre, Leeds)
Llanelli Trades Council (Dyfed Archives Office, Carmarthen)

PRINTED SOURCES

Government publications

Report of the Committee on Finance and Industry, Cmd. 3897 (1930–31)
Hansard, Parliamentary Debates: Official Report, 5th Series, Vols 229–59

Yearbooks (1929–33)

Labour Party, *Annual Report*
Labour Yearbook
Trades Union Congress, *Annual Congress Report*

Newspapers and periodicals

National daily:
Daily Herald
Daily Worker
Manchester Guardian
The Times

Local:
Birmingham Town Crier
Glasgow Forward

Bibliography

Leeds Weekly Citizen
London Catholic Herald
Manchester Guardian
Nelson Gazette
Preston Catholic Times
South Coast Catholic Herald

Trade union journals:
Cotton Factory Times
The Locomotive
The Miner
Monthly Journal of the National Amalgamated Society of Operative House and Ship Painters and Decorators
Monthly Journal (Amalgamated Society of Woodworkers)
Monthly Journal (National Union of General and Municipal Workers)
Railway Service Journal (Railway Clerks' Association)
The Record (Journal of Transport and General Workers' Union)

Other:
Christian World and Independent
Encounter
Everyman
Fabian News
Labour Monthly
Labour Organiser
Methodist Times
New Dawn
New Leader
New Statesman
New Statesman and Nation
Political Quarterly
The Tablet
The Universe

Works by socialist intellectuals

Books

Cole, G. D. H., *World of Labour* (London, 1913).
Cole, G. D. H., *Organised Labour: An Introduction to Trade Unionism* (London, 1924).
Cole, G. D. H., *The Next Ten Years in British Social and Economic Policy* (London, 1929).
Cole, G. D. H., *Gold, Credit and Employment* (London, 1930).
Cole, G. D. H., *The Economic System: An Elementary Outline* (London, 1931).
Cole, G. D. H., *British Trade and Industry, Past and Future* (London, 1932).
Cole, G. D. H., *Economic Tracts for the Times* (London, 1932).
Cole, G. D. H., *The Intelligent Man's Guide Through World Chaos* (London, 1932).
Cole, G. D. H., *A Short History of the British Working-Class Movement* (London, 1932).
Cole, G. D. H. (ed.), *What Everybody Wants to Know About Money* (London, 1933).
Cole, G. D. H., *A History of the Labour Party from 1914* (London, 1948).
Laski, H., *Studies in the Problem of Sovereignty* (New Haven, 1917).
Laski, H., *Authority in the Modern State* (New Haven, 1919).
Laski, H., *A Grammar of Politics* (London, 1925).
Laski, H., *Communism* (London, 1927).

Bibliography

Laski, H., *The Dangers of Disobedience and Other Essays* (New York, 1930).
Laski, H., *The Foundations of Sovereignty and Other Essays* (London, 1931).
Laski, H., *Democracy in Crisis* (London, 1933).
Tawney, R. H., *The Acquisitive Society* (London, 1921).
Tawney, R. H., *Education: The Socialist Policy* (London, 1924).
Tawney, R. H., *The British Labour Movement* (New Haven, 1925).
Tawney, R. H., *Religion and the Rise of Capitalism* (London, 1926).
Tawney, R. H., *Equality* (London, 1931).
Tawney, R. H., *The Attack and Other Papers* (London, 1953).
Webb, S., and Webb, B., *A Constitution for the Socialist Commonwealth of Great Britain* (London, 1920).
Webb, S., and Webb, B., *Industrial Democracy* (London, 1897).
Webb, S., and Webb, B., *Soviet Communism: A New Civilisation?* (London, 1935).

Articles

Cole, G. D. H., 'Education and Industry', *New Statesman* 31 (1928), 381.
Cole, G. D. H., 'Policy of Labour', *New Statesman* 31 (1928), 444.
Cole, G. D. H., 'Concerning Nationalisation', *New Statesman* 31 (1928), 473.
Cole, G. D. H., 'Safeguarding and Protection', *New Statesman* 31 (1928), 556.
Cole, G. D. H., 'Trade Unions and the Mond Report', *New Statesman* 31 (1928), 629.
Cole, G. D. H., 'Trade Unionism and the Future', *New Statesman* 31 (1928), 688.
Cole, G. D. H., 'Trade unionism and Politics', *New Statesman* 31 (1928), 721.
Cole, G. D. H., 'The Labour Party and the Nation', *New Statesman* 32 (1928–29), 4.
Cole, G. D. H., 'Debates on Unemployment', *New Statesman* 32 (1928–29), 181.
Cole, G. D. H., 'Labour and Safeguarding', *New Statesman* 32 (1928–29), 280.
Cole, G. D. H., 'Finding Work', *New Statesman* 32 (1928–29), 376.
Cole, G. D. H., '1928 and 1929', *New Statesman* 32 (1928–29), 400.
Cole, G. D. H., 'Work Can Be Found', *New Statesman* 32 (1928–29), 433.
Cole, G. D. H., 'Can We Conquer Unemployment?', *New Statesman* 32 (1928–29), 752.
Cole, G. D. H., 'The Two Problems of Unemployment', *New Statesman* 32 (1928–29), 784.
Cole, G. D. H., 'More About the Prevention of Unemployment', *New Statesman* 33 (1929), 5.
Cole, G. D. H., 'Trade Unionism and the Labour Party', *New Statesman* 33 (1929), 74.
Cole, G. D. H., 'The Coal Problem Reconsidered', *New Statesman* 33 (1929), 110.
Cole, G. D. H., 'Houses', *New Statesman* 33 (1929), 140.
Cole, G. D. H., 'We Can't Conquer Unemployment', *New Statesman* 33 (1929), 175.
Cole, G. D. H., 'Road and Rail', *New Statesman* 33 (1929), 205.
Cole, G. D. H., 'The Limits of Democracy', *New Statesman* 33 (1929), 232.
Cole, G. D. H., 'Second Thoughts on the Election', *New Statesman* 33 (1929), 261.
Cole, G. D. H., 'Mr. Thomas's Task', *New Statesman* 33 (1929), 297.
Cole, G. D. H., 'The Miners Take the Field', *New Statesman* 33 (1929), 328.
Cole, G. D. H., 'The Temper of Trade Unionism', *New Statesman* 33 (1929), 362.
Cole, G. D. H., 'The Case for Repealing the Trades Disputes Act 1927', *New Statesman* 33 (1929), 397.
Cole, G. D. H., 'Thomas's Plans', *New Statesman* 33 (1929), 428.
Cole, G. D. H., 'The Government's Housing Policy', *New Statesman* 33 (1929), 461.
Cole, G. D. H., 'The School Age', *New Statesman* 33 (1929), 490.
Cole, G. D. H., 'Arbitration and After', *New Statesman* 33 (1929), 617.
Cole, G. D. H., 'Rationalisation and the Public', *New Statesman* 33 (1929), 673.
Cole, G. D. H., 'Parliament and the Coal Trade', *New Statesman* 33 (1929), 702.
Cole, G. D. H., 'What Does Raising the School Age Mean?', *New Statesman* 33 (1929), 733.
Cole, G. D. H., 'Work or Doles?', *New Statesman* 33 (1929), 768.
Cole, G. D. H., 'The Problem of the Bank Rate', *New Statesman* 34 (1929–30), 4.
Cole, G. D. H., 'Second Thoughts on the Bank Rate', *New Statesman* 34 (1929–30), 45.
Cole, G. D. H., 'The Government and the Mines', *New Statesman* 34 (1929–30), 78.

Cole, G. D. H., 'Mr. Thomas and the Unemployed', *New Statesman* 34 (1929–30), 149.

Cole, G. D. H., 'Rationalisation', *New Statesman* 34 (1929–30), 151.

Cole, G. D. H., 'Waste and Profiteering', *New Statesman* 34 (1929–30), 181.

Cole, G. D. H., 'Miners' Wages', *New Statesman* 34 (1929–30), 217.

Cole, G. D. H., 'Miss Bondfield's Bill', *New Statesman* 34 (1929–30), 256.

Cole, G. D. H., 'The First Six Months', *New Statesman* 34 (1929–30), 289.

Cole, G. D. H., 'The Marketing Scheme', *New Statesman* 34 (1929–30), 320.

Cole, G. D. H., 'The Coal Bill', *New Statesman* 34 (1929–30), 356.

Cole, G. D. H., 'Cheaper Money, Rationalisation and Employment', *New Statesman* 34 (1929–30), 384.

Cole, G. D. H., 'The Old Year and the New', *New Statesman* 34 (1929–30), 409.

Cole, G. D. H., 'The Banks and Industry', *New Statesman* 34 (1929–30), 494.

Cole, G. D. H., 'The Economic Council', *New Statesman* 34 (1929–30), 560.

Cole, G. D. H., 'Mr. Thomas and his Colleagues', *New Statesman* 34 (1929–30), 593.

Cole, G. D. H., 'Second Edition', *New Statesman* 34 (1929–30), 657.

Cole, G. D. H., 'The Problem of the Joint Stock Banks', *New Statesman* 34 (1929–30), 696.

Cole, G. D. H., 'The Ghost That Walks', *New Statesman* 34 (1929–30), 729.

Cole, G. D. H., 'Problem of Greater London', *New Statesman* 34 (1929–30), 797.

Cole, G. D. H., 'War on the Slums', *New Statesman* 34 (1929–30), 829.

Cole, G. D. H., 'Fewer and Better', *New Statesman and Nation* 2 (1931), 36.

Cole, G. D. H., 'Money, Wages and Expansion', *New Statesman and Nation* 2 (1931), 69.

Cole, G. D. H., 'Britain's Economic Future', *New Statesman and Nation* 2 (1931), 216.

Cole, G. D. H., 'Was it a Bankers' Conspiracy?', *New Statesman and Nation* 2 (1931), 245.

Cole, G. D. H., 'The Policy of the Trade Unions', *New Statesman and Nation* 2 (1931), 273.

Cole, G. D. H., 'What Going Off the Gold Standard Means', *New Statesman and Nation* 2 (1931), 365.

Cole, G. D. H., 'Why and How We Must Socialise the Banks', *New Statesman and Nation* 2 (1931), 397.

Cole, G. D. H., 'The Danger of Inflation', *New Statesman and Nation* 2 (1931), 505.

Cole, G. D. H., 'Gold and the Crisis, *New Statesman and Nation* 2 (1931), 520.

Cole, G. D. H., 'The Old Labour Party and the New', *New Statesman and Nation* 2 (1931), 601.

Cole, G. D. H., 'Tariffs By Order', *New Statesman and Nation* 2 (1931), 632.

Cole, G. D. H., 'The Essentials of Socialisation', *Political Quarterly* 2 (1931), 394–410.

Cole, G. D. H., 'Some Essentials of Socialist Propaganda: A Tract for the Times', Fabian Tract no. 238 (London, 1932).

Cole, G. D. H., 'Chants of Progress', *Political Quarterly* 6 (1935), 530–40.

Laski, H., 'The Prospects of Constitutional Government', *Political Quarterly* 1 (1930), 307–25.

Laski, H., 'The Future of the Civil Service', *New Statesman and Nation* 2 (1931), 134–5.

Laski, H., 'Some Implications of the Crisis', *Political Quarterly* 2 (1931), 466–9.

Laski, H., 'The Underlying Assumptions of the National Government', *Political Quarterly* 5 (1934), 18–29.

Tawney, R. H., 'The Government and the School Age', *New Statesman* 34 (1929–30), 627–8.

Tawney, R. H., 'The Necessity for Early Legislation', *Schoolmaster and Woman Teachers' Chronicle*, 13 March 1930.

Tawney, R. H., 'The Choice Before the Labour Party', *Political Quarterly* 3 (1932), 323–45.

Tawney, R. H., 'The Choice Before the Labour Movement: Mr. Tawney's Answer', *Political Quarterly* 3 (1932), 521–4.

Tawney, R. H., 'Labour Honours', *New Statesman and Nation* 22 June 1935, 478.

Webb, B., 'A Reform Bill for 1932', *Political Quarterly* 2 (1931), 1–22.

Webb, S., 'What Happened in 1931: A Record', *Political Quarterly* 3 (1932), 1–17.

Biographies, memoirs and diaries

Bellamy, J., and Saville, J. (eds), *Dictionary of Labour Biography*, 8 vols (London, 1972–87).

Blaxland, G., *J. H. Thomas: A Life for Unity* (London, 1964).

Bondfield, M. G., *A Life's Work* (London, n.d., 1948).

Brittain, V., *Pethick-Lawrence: A Portrait* (London, 1963).

Brockway, A. F., *Inside The Left: Thirty Years of Platform, Press, Prison and Parliament* (London, 1942).

Brockway, A. F., *Socialism Over Sixty Years: The Life of Jowett of Bradford, 1864–1944* (London, 1946).

Brown, W. J., *So Far ...* (London, 1943).

Bullock, A., *The Life and Times of Ernest Bevin, Vol. 1: Trade Union Leader, 1881– 1944* (London, 1960).

Campbell, J., *Nye Bevan and the Mirage of British Socialism* (London, 1987).

Carpenter, L. P., *G. D. H. Cole: An Intellectual Biography* (London, 1973).

Citrine, Lord, *Men and Work: An Autobiography* (London, 1964).

Clynes, J. R., *Memoirs*, 2 vols (London, 1937–8).

Cole, M., *Growing Up Into Revolution* (London, 1948).

Cole, M., *The Webbs and Their Work* (London, 1949).

Cole, M., *Beatrice Webb's Diaries, 1912–24* (London, 1952).

Cole, M., *Beatrice Webb's Diaries, 1924–32* (London, 1956).

Cole, M., *The Life of G. D. H. Cole* (London, 1971).

Cooke, C., *The Life of Richard Stafford Cripps* (London, 1957).

Cross, C., *Philip Snowden* (London, 1966).

Dalton, H., *Call Back Yesterday: Memoirs, 1887–1931* (London, 1953).

Davies, P., *A. J. Cook* (Manchester, 1987).

Donoughue, B., and Jones, G. W., *Herbert Morrison: Portrait of a Politician* (London, 1973).

Eastwood, G., *Harold Laski* (London, 1977).

Edwards, H. T., *Hewn for the Rock* (Cardiff, 1967).

Estorick, E., *Stafford Cripps: A Biography* (London, 1949).

Evans, T., *Ernest Bevin* (London, 1946).

Foot, M., *Aneurin Bevan: A Biography, Vol. 1: 1897–1945* (London, 1962).

Gallacher, W., *Revolt on the Clyde: An Autobiography* (London, 2nd edn, 1949).

Graham, T. N., *Willie Graham: The Life of the Rt. Hon. William Graham* (London, n.d., 1948).

Hamilton, M. A., *Arthur Henderson: A Biography* (London, 1938).

Hamilton, M. A., *Remembering My Good Friends* (London, 1944).

Harris, K., *Conversations* (London, 1967).

Harris, K., *Attlee* (London, 1982).

Hastings, P., *The Autobiography of Sir Patrick Hastings* (Melbourne, 1948).

Howe, M. D. (ed.), *Holmes–Laski Letters*, 2 vols (Cambridge, 1953).

Jenkins, E. A., *From Foundry to Foreign Office: The Romantic Life Story of the Rt. Hon. Arthur Henderson, MP* (London, 1933).

Johnston, T., *Memories* (London, 1952).

Jones, T., *A Diary With Letters, 1931–1950* (Oxford, 1954).

Kenworthy, J. M., *Sailors, Statesmen and Others: An Autobiography* (London, 1933).

Kirkwood, D., *My Life of Revolt* (London, 1935).

Knox, W., *James Maxton* (Manchester, 1987).

Knox, W. (ed.), *Scottish Labour Leaders, 1918–1939: A Biographical Dictionary* (Edinburgh, 1984).

Kramnick, I., and Sheerman, B., *Harold Laski: A Life on the Left* (London, 1993).

Lansbury, G., *Looking Backwards – and Forwards* (London, 1935).

Laybourn, K., and James, D. (eds), *Philip Snowden: The First Labour Chancellor of the Exchequer* (Bradford, 1987).

Lee, J., *This Great Journey* (New York, 1942).

Leventhal, F., *Arthur Henderson* (Manchester, 1989).

McAllister, G., *James Maxton: Portrait of a Rebel* (London, 1935).

MacDonald, M., *People and Power: Random Reminiscences* (London, 1969).

Bibliography

MacKenzie, N. (ed.), *The Letters of Sidney and Beatrice Webb, Vol. 3: Pilgrimage, 1912–1947* (Cambridge, 1978).

MacKenzie, N., and J. (eds), *The Diary of Beatrice Webb, Vol. 4: The Wheel of Life, 1924–1943* (London, 1985).

McNair, J., *James Maxton, The Beloved Rebel* (London, 1950).

McShane, H., and Smith, J., *Harry McShane: No Mean Fighter* (London, 1978).

Manning, L., *A Life For Education: An Autobiography* (London, 1970).

Marquand, D., *Ramsay MacDonald* (London, 1977).

Martin, K., *Harold Laski* (London, 1953).

Middlemas, K. (ed.), *Tom Jones. Whitehall Diary, Vol. 2: 1926–1930* (London, 1969).

Morgan, A., *James Ramsay MacDonald* (Manchester, 1987).

Morgan, K., and Morgan, J., *Portrait of a Progressive: The Political Career of Christopher, Viscount Addison* (Oxford, 1980).

Morgan, K. O., *Labour People: Hardie to Kinnock* (Oxford, 2nd edn, 1992).

Morris, A. J. A., *C. P. Trevelyan, 1870–1958: Portrait of a Radical* (Belfast, 1977).

Morrison, H., *An Autobiography: By Lord Morrison of Lambeth* (London, 1960).

Morrison, H., *Government and Parliament: A Survey from the Inside* (London, 3rd edn, 1964).

Mosley, N., *Rules of the Game: Sir Oswald and Lady Cynthia Mosley, 1896–1933* (London, 1982).

Mosley, O., *My Life* (London, 1968).

Newman, M., *John Strachey* (Manchester, 1989).

Newman, M., *Harold Laski: A Political Biography* (Basingstoke, 1993).

Oldmeadow, E., *Francis Cardinal Bourne*, 2 vols (London, 1940 and 1944).

Parmoor, Lord, *A Retrospect: Looking Back Over a Life of More Than Eighty Years* (London, 1936).

Pethick-Lawrence, F. W., *Fate Has Been Kind* (London, 1943).

Phillpott, H. R. S., *J. H. Thomas: Impressions of a Remarkable Career* (London, 1932).

Pimlott, B., *Hugh Dalton* (London, 1985).

Pimlott, B. (ed.), *The Political Diary of Hugh Dalton, 1918–1940, 1945–1960* (London, 1986).

Postgate, R., *The Life of George Lansbury* (London, 1951).

Pritt, D. N., *The Autobiography of D. N. Pritt, Part One: From Right to Left* (London, 1965).

Radice, E. A., and Radice, G. H., *Will Thorne, Constructive Militant: A Study in New Unionism and New Politics* (London, 1974).

Radice, L., *Beatrice and Sidney Webb* (London, 1984)

Roskill, S., *Hankey, Man of Secrets, Vol. 2: 1919–1931* (London, 1972).

Sexton, J., *Sir James Sexton, Agitator: The Life of the Dockers' MP* (London, 1936).

Shinwell, E., *Conflict Without Malice* (London, 1955).

Shinwell, E., *I've Lived Through it All* (London, 1973).

Simmons, C. J., *Soap-Box Evangelist* (Chichester, 1972).

Skidelsky, R., *Oswald Mosley* (London, 1975).

Snowden, P., *An Autobiography, Vol. 2: 1919–1934* (London, 1934).

Stenton, M., and Lees, J. (eds), *Who's Who of British Members of Parliament: A Biographical Dictionary of the House of Commons*, 4 vols (Hassocks, 1977–81).

Tawney, R. H., *The Webbs in Perspective* (London, 1953).

Terrill, R., *R. H. Tawney and His Times: Socialism as Fellowship* (Cambridge, 1973).

Thomas, H., *John Strachey* (London, 1973).

Thomas, J. H., *My Story* (London, 1937).

Thurtle, E., *Time's Winged Chariot: Memoirs and Comments* (London, 1945).

Tiltman, H. H., *James Ramsay MacDonald: Labour's Man of Destiny* (London, 1929).

Vansittart, Lord, *The Mist Procession: An Autobiography* (London, 1958).

Vernon, B., *Ellen Wilkinson, 1891–1947* (London, 1982).

Walker, G., *Thomas Johnston* (Manchester, 1988).

Webb, B., *Our Apprenticeship* (London, 1926).

Webb, B., *Our Partnership* (London, 1948).

Wedgwood, C. V., *The Last of the Radicals: Josiah Wedgwood, MP* (London, 1951).

Weir, L. M., *The Tragedy of Ramsay MacDonald* (London, n.d., 1938).

Williams, F., *Ernest Bevin: Portrait of a Great Englishman* (London, 1952).

261

Williams, J. R., Titmuss, R. M., and Fisher, F. J., *Tawney: A Portrait by Several Hands* (London, 1960).

Williams, P. M., *Hugh Gaitskell: A Political Biography* (London, 1979).

Wood, I., *John Wheatley* (Manchester, 1990).

Wright, A., *G. D. H. Cole and Socialist Democracy* (Oxford, 1979).

Wright, A., *R. H. Tawney* (Manchester, 1987).

Wrigley, C., *Arthur Henderson* (Cardiff, 1990).

Other published books

Aldcroft, D. H., *The British Economy, Vol. 1: The Years of Turmoil, 1920–1951* (Brighton, 1986).

Allen, V. L., *Trade Unions and the Government* (London, 1960).

Bagwell, P. S., *The Railwaymen* (London, 1963).

Baker, B., *Labour in London: A Study in Municipal Achievement* (London, n.d., 1937).

Ball, S., *Baldwin and the Conservative Party: The Crisis of 1929–1931* (New Haven, 1988).

Barker, R., *Education and Politics, 1900–1951: A Study of the Labour Party* (London, 1992).

Bassett, R., *Nineteen Thirty One: Political Crisis* (London, 1958).

Bealey, F. W. (ed.), *The Social and Political Thought of the British Labour Party* (London, 1970).

Bealey, F., Blondel, J., and McCann, W. P., *Constituency Politics: A Study of Newcastle-under-Lyme* (London, 1965).

Beck, G. A., *The English Catholics, 1850–1950* (London, 1950).

Belchem, J. (ed.), *Popular Politics, Riot and Labour: Essays in Liverpool History, 1790–1940* (Liverpool, 1992).

Bevan, A., *In Place of Fear* (London, 1952).

Birch, A. H., *The Labour Party: Small-Town Politics: A Study of Political Life in Glossop* (Oxford, 1959).

Blaazer, D., *The Popular Front and the Progressive Tradition: Socialists, Liberals and the Quest for Unity, 1884–1939* (Cambridge, 1992).

Boston, S., *Women Workers and the Trade Union Movement* (London, 1980).

Brand, C. F., *The British Labour Party* (Stanford, 2nd edn, 1974).

Brown, H. P., *The Origins of Trade Union Power* (Oxford, 1983).

Buchanan, T., *The Spanish Civil War and the British Labour Movement* (Cambridge, 1992).

Butler, D., and Butler, G., *British Political Facts, 1900–1985* (London, 6th edn, 1986).

Callaghan, J., *Socialism in Britain since 1884* (Oxford, 1990).

Carlton, D., *MacDonald versus Henderson: The Foreign Policy of the Second Labour Government* (London, 1970).

Clarke, P., *The Keynesian Revolution in the Making, 1924–1936* (Oxford, 1988).

Clegg, H. A., *General Union: A Study of the National Union of General and Municipal Workers* (Oxford, 1954).

Clegg, H. A., *A History of British Trade Unions since 1889, Vol. 2: 1911–1933* (Oxford, 1985).

Clinton, A., *The Trade Union Rank and File: Trades Councils in Britain, 1900–1940* (Manchester, 1977).

Clinton, A., *Post Office Workers: Trade Unions and Social History* (London, 1984).

Coates, D., *The Labour Party and the Struggle for Socialism* (London, 1975).

Cole, M., *Makers of the Labour Movement* (London, 1948).

Cole, M., *The Story of Fabian Socialism* (London, 1961).

Connelly, T. J., *The Woodworkers, 1860–1960* (London, 1960).

Cook, C. (ed.), *Sources in British Political History, 1900–1951*, 6 vols (London, 1975–85).

Cook, C., and Stevenson, J. (eds), *The Longman Handbook of Modern British History, 1714–1987* (London, 1988).

Cook, C., and Taylor, I., *The Labour Party* (Harlow, 1980).

Craig, F. W. S., *British Parliamentary Election Results, 1918–1949* (London, 1969).

Davison, J., *Northumberland Miners, 1919–1939* (Newcastle, 1973).

Bibliography

Deane, H. A., *The Political Ideas of Harold J. Laski* (New York, 1955).

Dennis, N., and Halsey, R. H., *English Ethical Socialism: Thomas More to R. H. Tawney* (Oxford, 1988).

Dougan, D., *The Shipwrights: The History of the Shipconstructors' and Shipwrights' Association, 1882–1963* (Newcastle, 1975).

Dowse, R. E., *Left in the Centre: The Independent Labour Party, 1893–1940* (London, 1966).

Doyle, P., 'The Catholic Federation, 1906–29', in W. J. Sheils and D. Wood (eds), *Voluntary Religion* (London, 1986).

Drucker, H. M., *Doctrine and Ethos in the Labour Party* (London, 1979).

Durbin, E., *New Jerusalems: The Labour Party and the Economics of Democratic Socialism* (London, 1985).

Edwards, N., *History of the South Wales Miners' Federation, Vol. 1* (London, 1938).

Fielding, S., *Class and Ethnicity: Irish Catholics in England, 1880–1939* (Buckingham, 1992).

Foote, G., *The Labour Party's Political Thought: A History* (London, 1985).

Francis, H., and Smith, D., *The Fed: A History of the South Wales Miners in the Twentieth Century* (London, 1980).

Fraser, D. (ed.), *A History of the National Union of Boot and Shoe Operatives, 1874–1957* (Oxford, 1958).

Gallacher, T., *Glasgow: The Uneasy Peace* (Manchester, 1987).

Garside, W. R., *The Durham Miners, 1910–1960* (London, 1971).

Graves, P. M., *Labour Women: Women in Working-Class Politics, 1918–1939* (Cambridge, 1994).

Greenleaf, W. H., *The British Political Tradition, Vol. 2: The Ideological Heritage* (London, 1983).

Griffen, A. R., *The Miners of Nottinghamshire, 1914–1944: A History of the Nottinghamshire Miners' Unions* (London, 1962).

Groves, R., *Sharpen the Sickle: The History of the Farmworkers' Union* (London, 1949).

Hamilton, M. A., *The Labour Party Today* (London, n.d., 1938).

Hastings, A., *A History of English Christianity, 1920–1990* (London, 3rd edn, 1991).

Hazlehurst, C., and Woodland, C., *A Guide to the Papers of British Cabinet Ministers, 1900–1964* (Cambridge, 1974).

Higgenbottam, S., *Amalgamated Society of Woodworkers: Our Society's History* (Manchester, 1939).

Hilton, W. S., *Foes to Tyranny: A History of the Amalgamated Union of Building Trade Workers* (London, 1963).

Hinton, J., *Labour and Socialism* (Brighton, 1983).

Hinton, J., *Protests and Visions: Peace Politics in 20th Century Britain* (London, 1989).

Hirst, P. Q. (ed.), *The Pluralist Theory of the State: Selected Writings of G. D. H. Cole, J. N. Figgis and H. J. Laski* (London, 1989).

Howell, D., *British Social Democracy: A Study in Development and Decay* (London, 1976).

Howell-Thomas, D., *Socialism in West Sussex: A History of Chichester Labour Party* (Chichester, 1983).

Howson, S., and Winch, D., *The Economic Advisory Council, 1930–1939: A Study in Economic Advice during Depression and Recovery* (Cambridge, 1979).

Hutt, A., *A Post-War History of the British Working Class* (London, 1937).

Hutt, A., *British Trade Unionism: A Short History* (London, 6th edn, 1975).

Jefferys, J. B., *The Story of the Engineers, 1800–1945* (London, 1945).

Jowitt, J. A., and McIvor, A. J. (eds), *Employers and Labour in the English Textile Industries, 1850–1939* (London, 1988).

Koss, S., *Nonconformity in Modern British Politics* (London, 1975).

Koss, S., *The Rise and Fall of the Political Press in Britain, Vol. 2: The Twentieth Century* (London, 1984).

Lewis, D. S, *Illusions of Grandeur: Mosley, Fascism and British Society, 1931–1981* (Manchester, 1987).

Lloyd, J., *Light and Liberty: The History of the Electrical Telecommunication and Plumbing Union* (London, 1990).

Lovell, J., *British Trade Unions, 1875–1933* (London, 1977).

Lowe, R., *Adjusting to Democracy: The Role of the Ministry of Labour in British Politics, 1916–1939* (Oxford, 1986).

Lyman, R. W., *The First Labour Government* (London, 1957).

MacDonald, J. R., *Socialism and Society* (London, 1905).

MacDonald, J. R., *Socialism; Critical and Constructive* (London, 1921).

McHenry, D. E., *The Labour Party in Transition, 1931–1938* (London, 1938).

MacIntyre, A., *Against the Self-Images of the Age: Essays on Ideology and Philosophy* (London, 1971).

McKenzie, R. T., *British Political Parties: The Distribution of Power Within the Conservative and Labour Parties* (London, 1955; 2nd edn, 1963).

McKibbin, R. I., *The Evolution of the Labour Party, 1910–1924* (Oxford, 1974).

McKibbin, R. I., *The Ideologies of Class: Social Relations in Britain, 1880–1950* (Oxford, 1990).

McKillop, N., *The Lighted Flame: A History of the Association of Locomotive Engineers and Firemen* (London, 1950).

McKinlay, A., and Morris, R. J. (eds), *The ILP on Clydeside, 1893–1932* (Manchester, 1991).

McLean, I., *The Legend of Red Clydeside* (Edinburgh, 1980).

Marquand, D., *The Progressive Dilemma* (London, 1991).

Marriott, J., *The Culture of Labourism: The East End Between the Wars* (Edinburgh, 1991).

Martin, R. M., *TUC: Growth of a Pressure Group, 1868 to 1976* (Oxford, 1980).

Michels, R., *Political Parties: A Sociological Study of the Oligarchical Tendencies of Modern Democracy* (London, 1915).

Middlemas, K., *The Clydesiders: A Left Wing Struggle for Parliamentary Power* (London, 1965).

Middlemas, K., *Politics in Industrial Society: The Experience of the British System since 1911* (London, 1979).

Miliband, R., *Parliamentary Socialism: A Study in the Politics of Labour* (London, 1961; 2nd edn, 1972).

Minkin, L., *The Labour Party Conference: A Study in the Politics of Intra-Party Democracy* (London, 1978).

Minkin, L., *The Contentious Alliance: Trade Unions and the Labour Party* (Edinburgh, 1991).

Misner, P., *Social Catholicism in Europe: From the Onset of Industrialisation to the First World War* (London, 1991).

Moloney, T., *Westminster, Whitehall and the Vatican: The Role of Cardinal Hinsley, 1935–1943* (Tunbridge Wells, 1985).

Moran, J., *NATSOPA: Seventy Five Years* (Oxford, 1964).

Morris, W., *News From Nowhere* (Harmondsworth, 1986).

Mortimer, J. E., *A History of the Association of Engineering and Shipbuilding Draughtsmen* (London, 1960).

Mortimer, J. E., *History of the Boilermakers' Society, Vol. 2: 1906–1939* (London, 1982).

Mowat, C. L., *Britain Between the Wars, 1918–1940* (London, 1955).

Norman, E. R., *Church and Society in England, 1770–1970: A Historical Survey* (Oxford, 1976).

Page Arnot, R., *A History of the Scottish Miners* (London, 1955).

Page Arnot, R., *The Miners in Crisis and War: A History of the Miners' Federation of Great Britain* (London, 1961).

Panitch, L., *Ideology and Integration: The Case of the British Labour Party* (London, 1972).

Parker, B., *Ramsay MacDonald's Political Writings* (London, 1972).

Pelling, H., *A Short History of the Labour Party* (London, 1961; 5th edn, 1976; 8th edn, 1985).

Pelling, H., *A History of British Trade Unionism* (Harmondsworth, 4th edn, 1987).

Pimlott, B., *Labour and the Left in the 1930s* (Cambridge, 1977).

Pimlott, B., and Cook, C. (eds), *Trade Unions in British Politics* (London, 1982).

Pollard, S., *The Development of the British Economy, 1914–1950* (London, 4th edn, 1962).

Pollard, S. (ed.), *The Gold Standard and Employment Policy Policies Between the Wars* (London, 1970).

Pugh, Sir A., *Men of Steel* (London, 1951).

Roskill, S., *Naval Policy Between the Wars, Vol. 2: The Period of Reluctant Rearmament, 1930–1939* (London, 1976).

Savage, M., *The Dynamics of Working-Class Politics: The Labour Movement in Preston, 1880–1940* (Cambridge, 1987).

Scanlon, J., *Decline and Fall of the Labour Party* (London, n.d., 1932).

Skidelsky, R., *Politicians and the Slump: The Labour Government of 1929–1931* (London, 1967; 2nd edn, 1994).

Soldon, N. C., *Women in British Trade Unions, 1874–1976* (Dublin, 1978).

Soloway, R. A., *Birth Control and the Population Question in England, 1877–1930* (Chapel Hill, 1982).

Stevenson, J., *British Society, 1914–45* (Harmondsworth, 1984).

Stevenson, J., and Cook, C., *The Slump: Society and Politics during the Depression* (London, 1977).

Tanner, D., *Political Change and the Labour Party, 1900–1918* (Cambridge, 1990).

Taylor, A. J. P., *English History, 1914–1945* (Oxford, 1965; Harmondsworth, 3rd edn, 1975).

Thorpe, A., *The British General Election of 1931* (Oxford, 1991).

Thorpe, A., *Britain in the 1930s* (Oxford, 1992).

Thorpe, A., *A History of the British Labour Party* (Basingtoke, 1997).

Thorpe, A. (ed.), *The Failure of Political Extremism in Inter-war Britain* (Exeter, 1989).

Tracey, H. (ed.), *The Book of the Labour Party: Its History, its Growth, its Policy and Leaders*, 3 vols (New York, 1925).

Turner, J. E., *Labour's Doorstep Politics in London* (London, 1978).

Waller, P. J., *Democracy and Sectarianism: A Political and Social History of Liverpool, 1868–1939* (Liverpool, 1981).

Waller, P. J. (ed.), *Politics and Social Change in Modern Britain* (Brighton, 1987).

Waller, R. J., *The Dukeries Transformed: The Social and Political Development of a Twentieth Century Coalfield* (London, 1983).

Walton, J. K., *Lancashire: A Social History, 1558–1939* (Manchester, 1987).

Wertheimer, E., *Portrait of the Labour Party* (London, 1929; 2nd edn, 1930).

Williams, A. J., *Labour and Russia: The Attitude of the Labour Party to the USSR, 1924–1934* (Manchester, 1989).

Williams, F., *Fifty Years' March: The Rise of the Labour Party* (London, 1949).

Williams, J. E., *The Derbyshire Miners: A Study in Industrial and Social History* (London, 1962).

Williamson, P., *National Crisis and National Government: British Politics, the Economy and Empire, 1926–1932* (Cambridge, 1992).

Winter, J. M. (ed.), *The Working Class in Modern British History: Essays in Honour of Henry Pelling* (Cambridge, 1983).

Winter, J. M., and Joslin, D. M., *R. H. Tawney's Commonplace Book* (London, 1972).

Wright, A., *Socialisms: Theories and Practices* (London, 1986).

Wright, A. (ed.), *British Socialism* (London, 1983).

Wyncoll, P., *The Nottingham Labour Movement, 1880–1939* (London, 1985).

Zylstra, B., *From Pluralism to Collectivism: The Development of Harold Laski's Political Thought* (Assem, 1968).

Articles

Barker, R., 'Political Myth: Ramsay MacDonald and the Labour Party', *History* 61: 1 (1976), 46–56.

Beloff, M., 'The Age of Laski', *Fortnightly* 1002 (1950), 378–84.

Carpenter, L. P., 'Corporatism in Britain, 1930–45', *Journal of Contemporary History* 11: 1 (1976), 3–25.

Catterall, P., 'Morality and Politics: The Free Churches and the Labour Party Between the Wars', *Historical Journal* 36: 3 (1993), 667–85.

Dare, R., 'Instinct and Organisation: Intellectuals and British Labour after 1931', *Historical Journal* 26: 3 (1983), 677–97.

Doyle, P. J., 'Religion, Politics and the Catholic Working Class', *New Blackfriars* 54 (1973),

218–25.

Eatwell, R., and Wright, A., 'Labour and the Lessons of 1931', *History* 63 (1978), 38–53.

Greenleaf, W. H., 'Laski and British Socialism', *History of Political Thought* 2: 3 (1981), 573–91.

Horner, A., 'Citrine and the TUC', *Labour Monthly* 47: 2 (1965), 88–90.

MacDonald, G. W., and Gospel, H. F., 'The Mond–Turner Talks, 1927–37', *Historical Journal* 16 (1973), 807–29.

McKibbin, R. I., 'Arthur Henderson as Labour Leader', *International Review of Social History* 23: 1 (1978), 79–101.

McKibbin, R. I., 'The Economic Policy of the Second Labour Government, 1929–31', *Past and Present* 68 (1975), 95–123.

Malament, B. C., 'Philip Snowden and the Cabinet Deliberations of August 1931', *Bulletin of the Society for the Study of Labour History* 41 (1980), 31–3.

Marwick, A., 'The ILP in the 1920s', *Institute of Historical Research Bulletin* 35 (1962), 62–74.

Miliband, R., 'Harold Laski: An Exemplary Public Intellectual', *New Left Review* 200 (July–August 1993), 175–81

Page Arnot, R., 'A Memoir of G.D.H. Cole', *Labour Monthly* (February 1959), 66–70.

Peretz, M., 'Laski Redivivus', *Journal of Contemporary History* 1: 2 (1966), 87–101.

Pollard, S., 'Trade Union Reactions to the Economic Crisis', *Journal of Contemporary History* 4: 4 (1969), 101–15.

Riddell, N., '"The Age of Cole"? G. D. H. Cole and the British Labour Movement, 1929–1933', *Historical Journal* 38: 4 (1995), 933–57.

Riddell, N., 'The Catholic Church and the British Labour Party, 1918–1931', *Twentieth Century British History* 8: 2 (1997), 165–93.

Stapleton, J., 'Localism Versus Centralism in the Webb's Political Thought', *History of Political Thought* 12: 1 (1991), 147–65.

Thorpe, A., 'Arthur Henderson and the British Political Crisis of 1931', *Historical Journal* 31: 1 (1988), 117–39.

Thorpe, A., 'J. H. Thomas and the Rise of Labour in Derby, 1880–1945,' *Midland History* 40 (1990), 111–28.

Thorpe, A., '"I am in the Cabinet": J. H. Thomas's Decision to join the National Government in 1931', *Historical Research* 64 (1991), 389–402.

Thorpe, A., 'The Industrial Meaning of "Gradualism": The Labour Party and Industry, 1918–31', *Journal of British Studies* 35: 1 (1996), 84–113.

Williamson, P., 'A "Bankers' Ramp"? Financiers, and the British Political Crisis of 1931', *English Historical Review* 99: 4 (1984), 770–806.

Williamson, P., 'The Labour Party and the House of Lords, 1918–1931', *Parliamentary History* 10: 2 (1991), 317–41.

Winter, J. M., 'R. H. Tawney's Early Political Thought', *Past and Present* 47 (1970), 71–96.

Wright, A. W., 'Guild Socialism Revisited', *Journal of Contemporary History* 9 (1974), 165–80.

Theses

Catterall, P., 'The Free Churches and the Labour Party in England and Wales, 1918–39' (Ph.D., London University, 1989).

Riddell, N., 'The Second Labour Government, 1929–31, and the Wider Labour Movement' (Ph.D., Exeter University, 1995).

Thorpe, A., 'The British General Election of 1931' (Ph.D., Sheffield University, 1988).

INDEX

Index

and religion 22–3, 34–5, 107–14, 159
and 'respectability' 1, 2, 13, 21, 137, 148–50, 226, 228–9
rise of 1–2
and socialist intellectuals 28–31, 87
and trade unions 9–15, 16, 21, 29, 30, 56, 204–7, 209, 223, 225–6, 230, 231
and unemployment 14, 36, 45, 155–6
women's sections 16, 17–18, 24, 102, 108, 115
youth sections 16
Labour Research Department 29–30, 41, 192
Lancashire Cotton Corporation 69–70
land nationalisation 85, 105
land tax 85, 166
Lang, Archbishop Cosmo 112–13
Lang, Reverend Gordon 141, 142
Lansbury, George 2, 152, 153–4, 158, 159, 192, 214, 215
Laski, Harold
in the 1930s 215
and Africa 186
Authority in the Modern State (1919) 37
Communism (1927) 39
and communism 39, 188
and constitutional reform 38
contribution to Labour movement 31, 37
and corporatism 38
Danger of Obedience and Other Essays (1930) 186
and economics 38, 189
and the Fabian Society 38
general election (1929) 39
general election (1931) 213
and the General Strike 39
gradualism 39–40, 186–9, 213
Grammar of Politics 38, 187
and guild socialism 37
and Henderson 189
and India 186
and the Industrial Court 37
An Introduction to Politics (1931) 187
and Jewishness 185–6
and Kenya 186
and Labour government (1929–31) 184–9, 195
and liberalism 37–8, 213
Liberty and the Modern State (1930) 187
and MacDonald 38–40, 184–5, 187, 189, 195, 213
and Marxism 39, 213
and Mond–Turner talks 39
and nationalisation 38
and Palestine 185–6, 195
and parliamentary reform 188
as Party Chairman (1945) 37
and pluralism 37–9
and political crisis (1931) 187, 189, 213, 215
popularity amongst party members 37
and role of intellectuals 28–9, 39–40
and Snowden 39, 188, 189
socialist ideology 37–40, 186–9, 195, 213
and the Soviet Union 187
and the state 37–9
story-telling of 184–5
Studies in the Problems of Sovereignty (1917) 37

and syndicalism 37
and Tawney 38
and Thomas, J. H. 39
and USA 185, 187, 188–9
and the Webbs 38
and workers' education 37
Lateran Pacts, the (1929) 110
Lawrence, Susan 102, 143, 145, 146
League of Nations 2, 181
Leeds Weekly Citizen 117, 122
Lee, Jennie 24, 141, 143, 144
Lewis, T. 141
Liberal Party
and electoral reform 137–8
and Labour government (1929–31) 54, 62, 68, 105, 137–9, 151, 165, 166, 169, 199, 225
and proposed government cuts (1931) 2, 165
and the Trade Disputes Act 71–5
and unemployment 36, 43–5, 80, 137, 156
Liberal 'Industrial Inquiry' (1928) 43–5
Lloyd George, David 45, 68, 137–9, 160
Local Government (Scotland) Act (1929) 140
local Labour parties *see also* Labour parties, Borough; Labour parties, Divisional
activists 17, 211
affiliation fees 100–1
agents 20, 121–2
and agriculture 19, 105
Association of Constituency Labour Parties 211
benefactors 21–22, 104, 211, 222
'Bid for Power Fund' (1929) 23
birth control 22, 107–8
coal-mining 105, 211
and Co-operative movement 19
and *Daily Herald* 114, 201
development of (1920s) 15–17
disarmament 107, 211
disillusionment (1929–31) 124–5, 224
diversity in organisation 16–17, 18–20, 222
education 22, 106–7, 125, 224
finances 15–17, 18, 20–2, 106, 120–4, 210, 211, 222, 224
general election (1929) 23–4, 100
general election (1931) 121–2, 211–12
and Holman Gregory Commission 124
housing 107
and Independent Labour Party (ILP) 19, 116–17, 125, 211, 224
and Labour government (1929–31) 6–7, 24, 100–25, 221, 224
and Labour Party constitution (1918) 15–16
legislation (1929–31) 100, 104–7
local elections 15, 17, 18, 19, 100, 106, 112, 115, 116–17, 120–2, 125, 211–12
and MacDonald 210
May Report 124
membership 15–18, 23, 100–1, 106, 120–4, 210, 211–12, 222, 224
and Mosley 117–20, 125, 224, 228
MPs 19, 23–4, 26, 102–4, 105, 209–10, 230
and National Government 209–11
and national party 18–19, 100–2, 211–12, 230
and national speakers 20, 23
nepotism within 17

271